LENINGRAD

Shaping a Soviet City

Lane Studies in Regional Government

A Publication of the Franklin K. Lane Memorial Fund, Institute of Governmental Studies, University of California, Berkeley

The Franklin K. Lane Memorial Fund takes its name from Franklin Knight Lane (1864–1921), a distinguished Californian who was successively New York correspondent for the San Francisco *Chronicle*, city and county attorney of San Francisco, member and later chairman of the United States Interstate Commerce Commission, and secretary of the interior in the cabinet of President Woodrow Wilson.

The general purposes of the endowment are to promote "better understanding of the nature and working of the American system of democratic government, particularly in its political, economic, and social aspects," and the "study and development of the most suitable methods for its improvement in the light of experience."

New York: The Politics of Urban Regional Development, by Michael N. Danielson and Jameson W. Doig

Governing the London Region: Reorganization and Planning in the 1960s, by Donald L. Foley

Governing Metropolitan Toronto: A Social and Policy Analysis, by Albert Rose

Governing Greater Stockholm: Policy Development and Urban Change in Stockholm, by Thomas J. Anton

Metropolitan Winnipeg: Politics and Reform of Local Government, by Meyer Brownstone and T. J. Plunkett

Governing Metropolitan Indianapolis: The Politics of Unigov, by C. James Owen and York Willbern

Governing the Island of Montreal: Language Differences and Metropolitan Politics, by Andrew Sancton

Leningrad: Shaping a Soviet City, by Blair A. Ruble

LENINGRAD

Shaping a Soviet City

Blair A. Ruble

Published for the Institute of Governmental Studies
and the Institute of International Studies
University of California, Berkeley

UNIVERSITY OF CALIFORNIA PRESS
BERKELEY   LOS ANGELES   OXFORD

University of California Press
Berkeley and Los Angeles, California
University of California Press, Ltd.
Oxford, England
© 1990 by
The Regents of the University of California
Printed in the United States of America
1   2   3   4   5   6   7   8   9

Library of Congress Cataloging-in-Publication Data

Ruble, Blair A., 1949–
    Leningrad : shaping a Soviet city / Blair A. Ruble.
        p.   cm.
    Bibliography: p.
    Includes index.
    ISBN 0–520–06534–4 (alk. paper)
    1. City planning—Russian S.F.S.R.—Leningrad—History—20th
century.   2. Leningrad (R.S.F.S.R.)—History—1917–   I. Title.
HT169.S642L467   1989
307.7′64′094745—dc19   89–4716

*So this two-hundred-and-seventy-six-year-old city
has two names, maiden and alias, and by and large
its inhabitants tend to use neither. When it comes to
their mail or identity papers, they certainly write
"Leningrad," but in a normal conversation they
would rather call it simply "Peter." This choice of
name has very little to do with their politics; the
point is that both "Leningrad" and "Petersburg" are
a bit cumbersome phonetically, and anyway, people
are inclined to nickname their habitats—it's a
further degree of domestication. "Lenin" certainly
won't do, if only because this was the last name of
the man (and an alias at that); whereas "Peter"
seems to be the most natural choice. For one thing,
the city has already been called that for two
centuries. Also, the presence of Peter I's spirit is still
much more palpable here than the flavor of the new
epoch. On top of that, since the real name of the
Emperor in Russian is Pyotr, "Peter" suggests a
certain foreignness and sounds congenial—for there
is something distinctly foreign and alienating in the
atmosphere of the city: its European-looking
buildings, perhaps its location itself, in the delta of
that northern river which flows into the hostile open
sea. In other words, on the edge of so familiar a
world.*

—Joseph Brodsky, 1979

Contents

Illustrations

Figures

Maps

Charts

Tables

Foreword

Objectives of the Lane Books

The Lane series of books—of which this Leningrad volume is the eighth and most recent—is sponsored by the Institute of Governmental Studies and the Institute of International Studies, and examines similarities and differences in metropolitan policy-making in various nations and cultures. Of principal concern is how policies affect the metropolis, including its social needs, economy, land use, physical structure, and natural and man-made environment. Emphasis is on the ways in which political and administrative processes and institutions adapt to changes in the urban condition and respond to national and international influences. What organizational structures and policies govern major metropolitan regions? What new or modified organizations and policies are being urged? By whom, and to what purpose? Under what conditions can life in the metropolis become more satisfying and productive, or less dreary and economically marginal? How can educational, cultural, and intellectual objectives best be promoted?

Increasingly, the opportunities and constraints in national systems of intergovernmental relations influence the way metropolitan regions are governed. Government leaders and civic leaders are often in contest: defenders of established philosophies versus proponents of new approaches to local and regional governance. Similarly, there are debates over which public-private relationships are appropriate and workable. The content and intensity of such ideological conflicts vary over space and time and between cultural and political systems.

Policy-makers are responding to the sheer increases in the size of metropolitan regions by attempting to contain and limit growth, direct it into certain portions of the metropolis, or divert it into the hinterland. In the effort to ameliorate the deleterious effects of growth and congestion, some urban policies include urgently needed improvements in the infrastructure. Other policies are an attempt to maximize benefits and control adverse effects of large population agglomerations by emphasizing large-scale facilities, concentrations of cultural institutions, enhanced communications and transport capabilities, and so forth.

The Lane books examine these matters in order to contribute to a better understanding of (1) what people and their leaders want to do with their metropolitan regions, (2) how they try to accomplish their aims, and (3) what results have been achieved. The focus is on the ways decision-makers—local and national—deal with major problems and try to increase each region's problem-solving capacity. The books concentrate on the readily comparable "slices" of national polities: the metropolitan regions.

A Good Time for Comparative Urban Studies

The substance and methodology of Ruble's book on Leningrad should be of great interest to students of urban affairs. His inclusion of valuable collateral information should help new researchers outside formal Sovietology become familiar with the terrain and gain a better grasp of research opportunities. For example, Ruble's appendices contain a wealth of information and useful background, including a description of the structure of the Soviet municipal system; and his documentation is extensive. All this should help Western urbanists with little or no previous experience in Soviet studies make a good start. Furthermore, by providing baseline examples of the workings of Leningrad's and the USSR's planning and economic development, Ruble helps set benchmarks for future comparative studies that should be useful in identifying and evaluating change. We sincerely hope that this book will encourage and stimulate other researchers in urban studies to explore this new territory. As Sovietologist Jerry Hough observed (in a private communication), studies of the Soviet Union are very weak in the field of urbanism and urban studies.

In any event, this seems a good time to expand urban research on the Soviet Union. The future holds promise as a time of accelerated change in the USSR, thanks to *perestroika* (restructuring), *glasnost'* (openness), and Mikhail Gorbachev's whole program of basic reform. If the promise is borne out—if, for instance, there are shifts toward more "democratic" and market-oriented political and economic arrangements—there could be wonderful opportunities for both Western and Eastern researchers in urban studies as well as in other fields. The increased openness and access to information, plus somewhat greater candor in private and public discussion in the Soviet Union, could greatly facilitate the quest of social science and policy researchers for the essential data and evidence required for in-depth studies. Changes in outlook and vision could also offer marvelous opportunities to follow events and trace phenomena—perhaps over many years—in some fascinating and potentially significant experiments in socioeconomic-political "engineering" and reform.

Comparisons and Contrasts:
Market vs. Nonmarket Economies

The similarities and differences between East and West offer a multitude of options for comparative studies both of market versus nonmarket economies and strategies and of the ways that political-governmental power is organized and functions in various Eastern and Western polities. What Lindblom characterizes as the privileged position of business and businesspersons in market economies, and the "close but uneasy relation between private enterprise and democracy,"[1] will afford many comparisons and contrasts with the privileged position of party figures, the apparatchiki, and others in the USSR, with their roles in the party, in government, and in enterprises and institutions.

Parallels and contrasts can be sought in the play of personal and institutional motivations in the two systems. What makes key actors "tick"? What characterizes the things that people strive for? Why do they seek those things in preference to others, and how do their choices influence the larger systems? How do the information-discussion-propaganda mechanisms of the two systems compare and contrast in their roles of organizing the metropolis, shaping opinion, influencing behavior (including consumer behavior), and otherwise affecting the lives of the inhabitants?

In a market economy with private property, personal monetary gain and related perquisites are powerful motivators, but so is the quest for esteem, recognition, deference, sense of achievement, and other psychic rewards. How do these factors operate in the two systems, and how do they correlate with patterns of recruitment and career development? What are the parallels and contrasts in a society and economy like the USSR's, with little private property and an entirely different system of rewards and coercions? One could go on at length enumerating the multitude of factors that could be studied.

For example, Ruble notes how analysts of urban affairs in the United States have dealt with such matters as "labor supply, industry mix, capital construction, tax rates, personal income, and consumption rates," in analyses that assume the operation of a free-market economy, where communities "compete for resources much as private corporations do." He then observes,

> What makes the Leningrad-based studies in this volume unusual is that they illustrate the importance of the economy to urban health in nonmarket industrial economies. The frenzied promotional activities of American city governments and chambers of commerce, and the preoccupation with property taxes that so

dominate the U.S. urban scene, do not at first seem to have a parallel in a Soviet system where land has no conventional monetary value and where local management is dominated by centralized bureaucracies. Yet our examination of Leningrad has discovered bureaucratic and political behavior analogous to that based on tax codes and real estate booms. In the USSR, the lack of market mechanisms may prevent complex policy questions from being reduced to market-oriented terms, but their absence does not prevent policy questions from arising in the first place.

Political and Governmental Variables

Future students of comparative local-metropolitan area governance not only will need to consider the strictly market/nonmarket variables, but also must try to determine the way political and governmental power is organized and distributed among various polities and to understand how this state of affairs influences developments in urban areas, in various Western contexts as well as in the USSR. For example, in Western nations there is a range or spectrum in the composition, "strength," and constitutional power of the local-state-national governments, and in the way the respective partners in nonunitary systems exercise power to influence metropolitan-area developments.

But formal governmental boundaries may count for a good deal less in the Soviet system than in most Western contexts, owing in part to the pervasive role of the Communist Party in providing linkages between successive tiers of both party and government. Another factor may be the "freewheeling" behavior of some of the Soviet enterprises, and particularly of the interenterprise associations, to which local boundaries may mean relatively little. Such institutions not only may be less encumbered by the barriers that governmental boundaries often represent in a Western context, but also may be more able, in a centrally planned society, to do things without regard for some of the constitutional and pluralistic interest-group impediments that can influence outcomes in Western systems.

On the other hand, the very complexity of the Soviet system and the ability of bureaucrats at many levels to foot-drag or otherwise "torque" the system may in their own right represent a whole realm of impediments and related influences. These forces and influences may be played out in quite interesting ways as the struggle to implement and modify the Gorbachev reforms proceeds. We must also remember that in political, economic, and social systems operating as differently as those of the United States, the United Kingdom, France, and other Western countries, there are similar slippages of information (including orders) both up and down the hierarchies and throughout the interorganizational complex that allow foot-dragging, misreading, and even noncompliance.

Perspective on the Leningrad Experience

In evaluating Ruble's book it is important to consider some of the restrictions under which he worked, such as the limited amount of social and economic data or of reliable social indicators available to him. He simply did not have access to the wealth and variety of information that one expects when studying Western systems. Perhaps, under glasnost, future researchers will have easier access to more data.

Also, Ruble's study is a study of *Leningrad*, an atypical Soviet city that differs in important ways from other large Soviet cities. Readers need to be aware of this special character, and cautious when generalizing from the Leningrad experience. Nevertheless, despite being atypical (and in some ways even because of it), Leningrad and its experiments can have a much broader significance. Thus, when noting Leningrad's unique role, Ruble also attempts to place it in context:

> Leningrad's region-oriented centralized managerial structures (i.e., managerial authority is concentrated in middle-level institutions rather than either in the ministries in Moscow or in individual enterprises) stand in opposition to more market-oriented reform packages that have emerged as dominant under Mikhail Gorbachev. Leningrad nurtured organizational forms that were intended to be activist in that they required leadership by a new set of institutions on the periphery but, at the same time, were profoundly conservative in that they preserved a centralized bureaucratic ethos. When Romanov's bid for national power was crushed in 1985 by the Gorbachev juggernaut, such centralizing reform packages fell by the wayside. Nonetheless, the Leningrad experience of the 1960s and 1970s continues to offer an important alternative economic vision to that of either Brezhnev's ministry-oriented approach or Gorbachev's focus on quasi-market enterprise reform.

Ever since World War II, Leningrad has engaged in a strong effort at reconstruction and socioeconomic development. It has educated a new workforce, used social science research for policy innovation and implementation, and emphasized technologically intensive industry to counter the region's intrinsic natural and locational disadvantages. Crucial to Leningrad's effort has been its experiments with the integration of science and technology, aimed at improving the use of science in the interest of technological and economic development.

Since these are also crucial issues for the entire Soviet Union, the

Leningrad experience should be viewed in the light of nationwide efforts in science and technology. These are also big issues for other countries, including the United States, Japan, the European nations, and the developing countries, all of which seek to benefit from the better functioning of science and scientific research and more effective use of science to feed technological advances and improve productivity and economic standing.

In still other ways the Leningrad experience parallels those elsewhere. The growth of Silicon Valley in the San Francisco Bay Area is a classic example of the use of local intellectual and professional communities as a resource to spark science and high-technology-based economic growth and development. Leningrad has been working in a similar direction, using its intellectuals as both a positive economic force and a political resource. The professional and research communities have done staff work for the politicians, writing position papers and helping them set their agendas. For future students of comparative urban studies and of technology and public policy, some fascinating analogies and contrasts should come to light in examining the roles of professionals and intellectuals in various Western and non-Western systems.

As important as Ruble's book is in its own right, its greatest value may be in serving as a benchmark to measure the effects—in one huge metropolitan region—of the rise and stabilization or decline of glasnost and perestroika. And we should not foreclose the possibility that the Leningrad industrial-scientific-technological linkages now constitute such powerful political ties that they may be able to act as brakes on perestroika, if not roadblocks. Undoubtedly there will be many accommodations to local as well as national elites, and perhaps to previously unheard-of popular demands.

The significance of Ruble's work as a baseline analysis is demonstrated by rapidly moving changes in Soviet politics. In March 1989, voters in the USSR's first real elections in 70 years rejected party establishment figures in many parts of the nation. Particularly striking were the Leningrad results. The region's party boss, Iurii Solov'ev, had his name crossed off by some 55 percent of the voters, and several other key figures also lost. Solov'ev then lost his party post in July 1989, when Mikhail Gorbachev traveled to Leningrad to witness the appointment of Boris Gidaspov to replace Solov'ev.

While we are obviously still too close to these events to have any clear understanding of their implications for the longer-term future, the defeat of the Leningrad political machine in the election for delegates to the Congress of People's Deputies marks the likely end of a conservative chapter in Leningrad history that began with the emergence of Frol Kozlov after the Leningrad Affair of the 1940s. This postwar era was dominated by the economic and institutional interests that Ruble has documented in his study. He demonstrated the sources of stability and power of the conservative coalition, but he also pointed to initial signs of decline and the rise of incipient protest, especially in his discussion of preservation and environmental issues surrounding the 1986 general plan. Few, however, seemed to anticipate the strength of the response registered in the March elections. Whatever happens next, Ruble's book will serve as a valuable guide, helping Westerners compare the future with the past 40 years in Leningrad's political life.

Stanley Scott and Victor Jones
Editors, Lane Studies in Regional Government
Berkeley, California, April 1989

Acknowledgments

This book examines many of the physical, economic, and social forces that have shaped the contemporary face of the Soviet Union's second—and Europe's sixth—largest metropolitan center. Those political scientists interested in learning about the structure and function of Soviet municipal institutions prior to the Gorbachev-inspired wholesale reorganization of governmental institutions launched in 1988 will be better served by such works as David Cattell's *Leningrad: A Case Study of Soviet Urban Government* and Everett Jacobs' *Soviet Local Politics and Government*, while those readers intent upon knowing more about local political participation in the Soviet Union should consult Jeffrey Hahn's *Soviet Grassroots: Citizen Participation in Local Soviet Government*.[1] *Leningradovedy* expecting to read about the blood purges of the 1930's and 1940's or the brutishly ham-handed cultural policies of the (Grigorii) Romanov era similarly will be disappointed. They should refer to such works as Werner Hahn's *Postwar Soviet Politics* or then KGB chief Aleksandr Shelepin's address to the Twenty-Second Party Congress in 1961 for discussion of the earlier period; as well as various essays in Joseph Brodsky's *Less than One* for a scent of the cultural atmospherics of the 1960's and 1970's.[2] Such themes as these are not totally absent from the study to follow, but they appear only insofar as they illuminate our central concern, namely, how is it that today's Leningrad looks and feels the way it does.

Readers who still wish to read further might like to know something about how this book has come about. Originally, this volume was to have been based primarily upon field research in the Soviet Union. For a variety of reasons, this has not been the case. Professional and personal obligations have conspired to make it difficult for me to travel to the Soviet Union for extended visits. More of a problem by far, however, were the responses of various Soviet academic institutions to the project.

I was accepted by the International Research and Exchanges Board (IREX) to participate during the fall of 1982 in the American Council of Learned Societies/USSR Academy of Sciences exchange program supported by funds provided by the National Endowment for the Humanities and the U.S. Information Agency. The USSR academy did not immediately respond to my nomination for a four-month stay, and probably never would have were it not for the strong support I received from IREX, a debt I would like to acknowledge here. In the end, the academy accepted me for a one-month visit to the Institute of Socio-economic Problems in Leningrad during February–March 1984. This trip proved to be the most difficult of any research trip I have made to the Soviet Union. I immediately came to understand that some Soviet officials were unwilling to accept the notion that an American would wish to study contemporary Leningrad for any purpose other than espionage.

I left Leningrad in March 1984 with a verbal invitation to return to the institute upon the completion of a draft manuscript. Taking my hosts at their word, I reapplied for participation on the exchange and was accepted by the American side. All went well until 48 hours before my scheduled departure in January 1986, when IREX received word that "Leningrad" was not prepared to receive me. After frantic last-minute arrangements, IREX and the academy agreed that I could spend one month in Moscow at the academy's Institute of Scientific Information in the Social Sciences (INION). Aware of the superb facilities at INION, which is one of the world's premier social scientific libraries, I agreed to go.

As it turned out, my visit to Moscow in 1986 could not have been more different from that to Leningrad two years previously. The INION collections contained all the published materials I needed to complete my research. In the end, by not being permitted access to Leningrad, I lost only the opportunity to experience the city yet again and to conduct a few final interviews. All in all, I consider my 1986 research trip to have been among the most valuable research experiences of my career.

Once I was able to move beyond my dealings with various officials (especially in Leningrad), individual Soviet scholars responded generously to my queries. The study that follows has been enriched by numerous formal and informal discussions with social scientists in Moscow and Leningrad. In particular, I found those scholars assigned to supervise my visits—Marat Nikolaevich Mezhevich of Leningrad's Institute of Socioeconomic Problems and Leonid Konstantinovich Shkarenkov of Moscow's INION—to be experienced professionals. I would like to take this opportunity to express my gratitude for their assistance.

As this book goes to press, Mikhail Gorbachev's *perestroika* (restructuring) and *glasnost'* (openness) campaigns are in full swing. Perestroika will probably lead to a fundamental reorganization of the various administrative arrangements described in this volume. Certainly, full implementation of the resolutions of the June 1988 Nineteenth Communist Party Conference and the constitutional amendments ratified in 1988 by the USSR Supreme Soviet concerning local government would transform many of the relationships central to this study.[3] Such reorganization is a response to the various difficulties confronting the Leningrad politicians populating the pages of this particular study. The proposed changes in municipal governance neither negate the profound role of economic forces in shaping Soviet cities nor challenge the critical brokerage function we attribute to regional officials.

Concerning glasnost, I can only hope that the new openness in Soviet society nurtures a realization that Western scholars may choose to study Soviet society for reasons of pure intellectual interest. I would be tremendously pleased if the next Western scholar who endeavors to study contemporary Leningrad is able to go beyond my own work as the result of having ready access to the sort of empirical data that would be used to study a major urban center outside of the Soviet Union.

Realizing that my study could not be based primarily upon field research, I began to reorient my research strategy around those materials available in the West. Happily, an immense amount of knowledge concerning contemporary Leningrad exists outside of the Soviet Union, though it can be gleaned only with considerable effort. Consequently, I came to rely heavily on the tolerance and support, both direct and indirect, of my various employers, the Kennan Institute for Advanced Russian Studies of the Woodrow Wilson International Center for Scholars, the National Council for Soviet and East European Research, and the Social Science Research Council. This revised strategy also meant far too many lost weeknights and weekends. My wife, Sally, endured my work on this study with far more patience than could ever have been reasonably expected.

I have benefited a great deal from the comments and critiques of too many colleagues to list here. A dozen or so (Harley Balzer, Theodore Bestor, Edward Bubis, Barbara Chotiner, Timothy Colton, Murray Feshbach, Abbott Gleason, Paul Goble, Jeffrey Hahn, Werner Hahn, Peter Hauslohner, Jerry Hough, Edith Klein, Mary McAuley, and S. Frederick Starr) deserve special thanks for having offered excessive amounts of time to hear me out, offering useful suggestions and, at times, harsh critiques. I can hardly repay my intellectual debt to them; I at least would like to thank them publicly for their encouragement. Jack Kollmann generously offered his assistance in gathering illustrative material, with most of the photographs to follow—and all of the best—being taken by him. William Craft Brumfield has provided the photograph for the jacket with an equal measure of goodwill. Similarly, I acknowledge with gratitude the work of Kristin Antelman, Regina Smyth, and Sandra Barrow, who spent many more hours than they ever imagined possible converting various drafts and revisions to an acceptable machine-readable state. Jeanne Sugiyama and Jane-Ellen Long brought an impressive and constructive professionalism to their work on my manuscript.

From the beginning I have conceived of this volume as fitting into the Franklin K. Lane Series of Studies in Regional Government. I have gained an enormous respect for Victor Jones and Stanley Scott, the editors of the series. I would like to express my appreciation to them and to the series sponsors, the University of California's Institute of Governmental Studies and its Institute of International Studies, for working with me over the past several years.

I should note at this point that I have used the Library of Congress standard literary transliteration scheme for the Russian language throughout the volume, except in reference to a few very well known places and people (e.g., Moscow, Kharkov, Nikolai Podgorny).

I have sought to approach the available data on Leningrad, both official and unofficial, in as dispassionate a manner as possible. I hope that the resulting study is an honest assessment of the city's political, social, and economic management over the past three to four decades. I would now like to step back from my role as an "objective" social scientist and offer a purely personal observation.

This work focuses on a number of social, economic, and political forces that are evident in Leningrad's recent development. It necessarily fails, however, to communicate a sense of the city's overwhelming pathos. The sadness that pervades Leningrad is in part a consequence of its fall from preeminence to provincial status during the first half of the century. Hulking edifices stretch out along one canal embankment after another, a poignant reminder that today's provincial city inhabits the carcass of a long-tarnished imperial capital. Nor can one ever forget the unfathomable human suffering associated with the city throughout its history, from the serfs whom Peter the Great conscripted to turn a frozen swamp into his stately court, through the swarming hordes of underpaid and overworked laborers in late imperial Petersburg, to the starving and beleaguered victims of the Finno-German blockade in World War II. Nature also conspires with a climate so severe that it permanently impresses humans with the indelible awareness that this is in no way their native habitat. Even the city's faded northern light seems to transmute solid matter into subdued shadows.

Leningrad is no ordinary city, as attested far more eloquently than my words by those of generations of Leningraders past and present, resident and expatriate, who share their native city's sad dignity. I undertook this study for a very select handful of such "Petersburgers," and it is with them in mind that I invite the reader to consider the material that follows.

Blair A. Ruble
New York City
December 1988

Introduction

*A nation has no individuality. No single phrase can
fairly sum up the characteristics of a people. But a
town is like one face picked out of a crowd. . . . In
all [its] slow development a character that is individual and inseparable is gradually formed. . . . It is
to be found first in the geographical laws of permanent or slowly changed surroundings, and secondly,
in the outward aspect of the dwellings built by man.*
        —Theodore Andrea Cook, 1899

Shaping the face of a great city is a complex task. Order within a
metropolitan region results from the accumulation of layer upon layer
of social, economic, cultural, and political sediment. For the vast majority of the inhabitants, much of what takes place in a city seems
spontaneous. To the extent that conscious rationality determines a city's
fate, it appears as a sum of the rationalities of its constituent parts.
Otherwise, the ecology of a city emerges from a multitude of processes—
small and large; local, regional, and national; micro- and macrolevel—
controlled in theory, at least, by the market and/or autocrat looming
mysteriously out of the sight of most residents.[1]

Decades, even centuries, of intellectual, financial, and political
effort have been expended in the attempt to come to terms with the
urban experience. Over the years, the veil concealing the motivational
forces underlying urban growth and development has been turned up
at the corner. Throughout much of this century, cities around the world
have sought to gain control of their urban destinies through concerted
government action intended to mold their economic, social, cultural,
and architectural futures. Nowhere has this process of state interven-
tionism gone further than in the Soviet Union, where socialist revo-
lutionaries wrested ownership of all land away from landlords, granting
the centralized state full command over physical and, eventually, economic planning.

In contrast, American observers of urban life find it difficult to
conceptualize urban development in the absence of the market. So
much of what we say, write, and think about our cities is dominated
by an obsession with the most overt manifestations of the market: land

values, the fees of real estate agents, taxes of various kinds, utility rates, consumption levels, media markets, and the like. Americans intuitively defer to the logic of the market, understanding how its relentless energy imposes order on the chaos of metropolitan development. By examining such market-oriented factors, commentators predict with confidence such monumental events as the cloning of Manhattan in Hoboken, Weehawken, and Secaucus, or the construction of more commercial and residential "space" in the sleepy northern Virginia hamlet of Tyson's Corner than is found in the central business districts of many world capitals. The market is no mystery to American students of and participants in urban affairs. Nor, for that matter, are the various mechanisms (legal and otherwise) available to local politicians, planners, and real estate developers who wish to produce a given set of environmental and spatial outcomes in one metropolitan region or another. What remains largely shrouded from view, however, are the strategies used by local politicians, planners, and managers in a highly centralized and bureaucratized nonmarket political economy like that of the Soviet Union, as they attempt to shape and reshape their neighborhoods, cities, and metropolitan regions.

Nonmarket Metropolitan Strategies

The central purpose of this volume will be to explore some of the ways in which local and regional political, economic, and cultural leaders in a major Soviet metropolis, Leningrad, determine the physical and socioeconomic contours of their city and region. The study attempts to establish the importance within Leningrad of those economic variables deemed so crucial to sound development in the American milieu: maintenance and expansion of local productive capacity and labor supplies, enhanced access to resources of all kinds, and the like. It sets forth various bureaucratic and political strategies for obtaining economic objectives, searching for behavior patterns that differentiate market and nonmarket experiences. To what extent, for example, do competing national, regional, and local policy vistas determine planning strategies? The boundaries for autonomous action by local Soviet* politicians, planners, and managers emerge as we inquire into the nature and process of planning this major metropolitan region.

It is significant that, in searching out these varied patterns, three hitherto ignored features of the Soviet urban experience reveal them-

---

*"Soviet" (with an upper case "S") will be used throughout this work to refer to phenomena that are national in character and may be thought of as being "of the USSR"; "soviet" (with a lowercase "s") will be used to refer to the various local, regional, republic, and national legislative bodies of the USSR and their constituent parts.

selves. First, this study demonstrates that Leningrad's leaders play a dual role in urban governance in that they become political and bureaucratic brokers between the center and the periphery.[2] They serve this broker function as much as they merely impose central authority on the local scene or represent their distinctly local interests before central institutions. The resulting vision of regional and municipal leaders as being activist and vigorous intermediaries, between and among central and local institutions, stands at odds with more passive images deduced from the Soviet Union's centrally controlled political and economic systems.[3] This brokerage function may be seen both in the relationship between institutions physically located at the political center and those on the periphery and in the relationship among local institutions and representatives of central interests physically located on the periphery. While local municipal institutions such as the soviets (or councils)[4] are responsible for the balanced development of a given jurisdiction, industrial enterprises and other institutions directly subordinate to the ministries in Moscow are evaluated according to their fulfillment of central goals and objectives. This unending tension between economic center and territorial unit dominates strategies intended to guide socioeconomic and physical development in Leningrad, as well as more generally in other Soviet cities and their regions.

Second, this volume posits a regional policy innovation cycle that stands in stark contrast to existing notions of how the Soviet system operates. Indeed, the mere existence of such a cycle may surprise some readers. The cycle will be set forth in greater detail throughout the study. It is important to recognize, however, that it is precisely at the regional level that Soviet politicians and administrators struggle to bring local empirical reality into conformity with central policy pronouncements. The gap between reality and pronouncement produces small-scale creative responses that will have an impact on both central practice and central policy. In this manner, local officials attempt to recast central policy initiatives to reflect local conditions better and, in so doing, to influence future central policies.

Third, this book shows how city planning efforts in Leningrad have become ever more regional in scope. Prerevolutionary physical planning schemes, dating back to the initial ill-fated 1717 city design of Alexandre-Jean-Baptiste Le Blond through to Ivan Fomin's "New Petersburg" projections nearly two centuries later, sought to mold construction efforts essentially within the city and its immediate surroundings. The grandiose Soviet-era plans of the 1930s were similarly city-focused, even as they projected the abandonment of the nineteenth-century city center in favor of an expansive new socialist city to the south. By the 1960s, however, local planning efforts extended beyond physical concerns to encompass economic and, eventually, social variables. Simultaneously, the planning region grew beyond the juridical bounds of the city soviet (hereafter referred to as the "city of Leningrad" or, more simply, the "city"), an area nearly the size of the city of Chicago, to incorporate the entire metropolitan area (hereafter referred to as the "Leningrad metropolitan area" or, more simply, the "Leningrad area"), an area approximately the size of the city of Houston. Finally, in large part as a consequence of the growing influence of Western systems approaches on Soviet urban and geographical thought, the 1986 general plan—which serves as the termination point for this particular study—incorporated within its scope the entire Leningrad region, or oblast (*oblast'*, hereafter usually referred to as the "Leningrad region" or, more simply, the "region"), a unit only slightly smaller than the state of Indiana (see Maps 1–2).

An Urban Future

While exploring these dimensions of urban management, we must remember that Leningrad long predates the coming to power of the Bolsheviks. Municipal and regional officials in Leningrad, as well as in many other Soviet cities founded prior to 1917, must struggle to match local reality with central decrees within a quite distinct pre-revolutionary environment. This necessary blending of pre- and post-revolutionary inheritances was initially complicated by the Bolsheviks' own ill-defined sense when they seized power that existing urban conditions must somehow be changed.[5] In February 1918, the new Soviet government nationalized land and, eight months later, abolished private property in cities.[6] These policies elevated the state to the status of single agent for all large-scale construction and planning—a condition that perhaps more than any other single factor explains the arid, monotonous, and even oppressive character of much Soviet urban development ever since.

During the 1920s, politicians, planners, and architects engaged in extensive theoretical debates on nearly every urban planning, management, and architectural issue.[7] Throughout most of the decade, the search for new forms of socialist urban settlement was often obscured by factional disputes, which engaged competing groups whose origins lay in prewar Europe and Russia. In essence, these debates narrowed to a disagreement between theorists such as Leonid Sabsovich, who demanded the urbanization of rural areas into nodal points, and their counterparts such as Nikolai Miliutin and Ivan Leonidov, who proposed the dispersal of cities along continuous linear communities adjacent to transportation and power corridors.[8] The second group offered what Sabsovich decried as "automobile socialism." They envisioned services and employment dispersed along efficient road systems linked by fast, flexible, and individually operated transportation.[9] While such a "Cali-

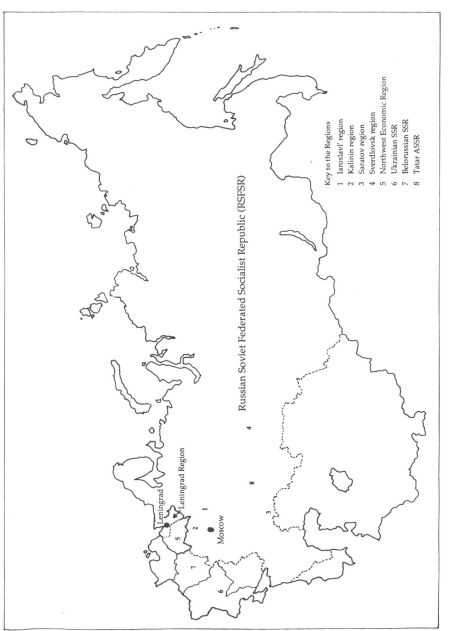

Map 1. The Russian Soviet Federated Socialist Republic (RSFSR) in the Union of Soviet Socialist Republics (USSR), showing the Leningrad region (oblast) and the major sources of postwar population migration to Leningrad.

Russian Soviet Federated Socialist Republic (RSFSR)

Leningrad

Leningrad Region

Moscow

Key to the Regions

1 Iaroslavl' region
2 Kalinin region
3 Saratov region
4 Sverdlovsk region
5 Northwest Economic Region
6 Ukrainian SSR
7 Belorussian SSR
8 Tatar ASSR

central planners in Moscow, for whom no specification was too small to receive their undivided attention. Despite remarkable zealotry on the part of Stalin's planners, however, even they could not be everywhere at once. Hence, responsibility was delegated primarily to economic ministries organized along the production principle (i.e., each ministry was responsible for a limited number of interrelated economic sectors).

Such a chain of command established primary operating rules for a city's economic leaders, flowing downward from the national state planning agency, Gosplan,[14] through the industrial ministries to the individual enterprise, and eventually to the shop floor. At each regional level within the administrative hierarchy, however, ministerial officials were also attached to the primary regional governing body—the soviet—and were to act in accordance with the needs of the locality. This complex supervisory system created bureaucratic contradictions and tensions that have remained unresolved and continue to dominate Soviet municipal administration to this day.[15] Over time, it created an environment that required city and regional officials to serve as brokers and intermediaries between local and national interests.

State administration in the Soviet Union is based on a dual system of organizational subordination—a situation that prompted Mikhail Gorbachev's 1988 proposals for a reorganization of local administration. Local government agencies—the soviets—are responsible for the activities of their own constituent agencies and for the activities of institutions and organizations located within their territorial jurisdictions but not directly subordinate to them.[16]

As may be seen by examining the solid lines in Chart 1, "all-union" ministries are directly subordinate to the USSR Council of Ministers, while "union-republic" ministries are subordinate to republican councils, which, in turn, are subordinate to the USSR Council of Ministers. In other words, all-union ministries—which tend to be in heavy industry, such as the Ministry of Machine-Building—have no republic-level counterpart, operating as a single centralized unit for the country as a whole. Union-republic ministries such as the Ministry of Finance, on the other hand, are responsible for coordinating the work of ministries of the same name and similar purpose operating within each of the Soviet Union's fifteen republics. To complete this overview of the Council of Ministers, we should note that, in addition to ministries responsible for management of a single economic sector, several state committees retain responsibilities that cut across a number of economic branches and issue decrees that govern activities of more than one ministry. The USSR State Committee on Construction, Gosstroi, is one such institution that will appear from time to time in this volume.

Major enterprises are directly subordinate to either union-republic or all-union ministries. Less important enterprises, however, remain subordinate to regional or city soviets and to their administrative de-

Chart 1. *Territorial/ministerial supervision of enterprises.*

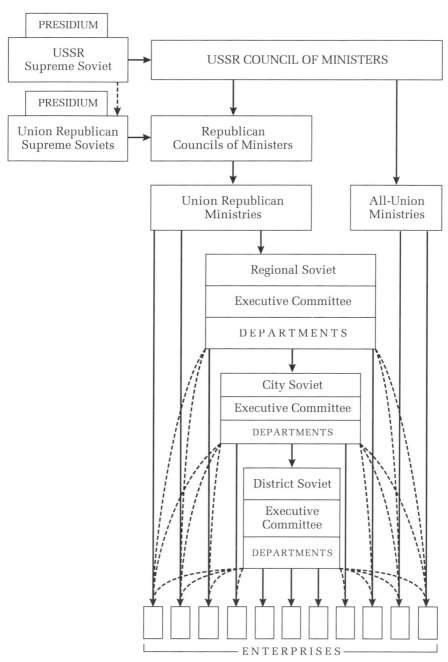

PRESIDIUM

USSR
Supreme Soviet

PRESIDIUM

Union Republican
Supreme Soviets

USSR COUNCIL OF MINISTERS

Republican
Councils of Ministers

Union Republican
Ministries

All-Union
Ministries

Regional Soviet

Executive Committee

DEPARTMENTS

City Soviet

Executive Committee

DEPARTMENTS

District Soviet

Executive
Committee

DEPARTMENTS

ENTERPRISES

↓ Direct supervisory authority

↓ General review authority

partments and agencies. Moreover, the regional and city soviets retain indirect responsibility and general review authority for the activities of all enterprises within their respective geographic areas (see dotted lines in Chart 1). Consequently, any plant in the Soviet Union serves two masters: its own national ministry and the local city soviet. While the ministry retains responsibility for guaranteeing adherence to planning norms established in Moscow, the local soviet seeks to coordinate the activities of all economic institutions within its territory, to ensure the optimally balanced development of its jurisdiction.[17] In this way, the soviet theoretically serves as the "master of the city" (*khoziain goroda*), a status confirmed by constitutional, legislative, and administrative statutes.[18]

As already noted, factory managers are in reality rewarded and promoted by the ministries and not by the local governments, so that the ministries frequently hold the upper hand in various interactions among ministries, factories, and municipalities. Moreover, the linking of territorial and sectorial planning dramatically expands the economic functions of Soviet local administration beyond previously known limits. Municipal administrators become industrial managers, with a considerable portion of the local bureaucratic effort being directed toward economic functions that in the West are reserved for the private production sector.[19]

Strict hierarchy was also a major feature of Stalinist economic planning. Individual enterprises as well as entire sectors gained priority, or in less fortunate instances were relegated to subordinate status by central planners in Moscow. Each economic unit was assigned a priority ranking, access to valuable resources being determined by this relative primacy. Similarly, cities, towns, and municipalities across the Soviet Union were identified as serving national, republic, regional, or merely local interests.[20] Once locked into this hierarchy, a given city could flourish or fail accordingly. During a 1984 interview, for example, Leningrad urbanist Marat Mezhevich argued that his city's designation as one of national status with an individual listing in the USSR state budget guaranteed adequate capital for future economic growth and development.[21] Moreover, just a year earlier, the Politburo had generally extended the rights and responsibilities of local Leningrad and Moscow officials.[22] By contrast, leaders of other cities without such status must negotiate for resources with competing jurisdictions without the benefit of supporting central policy statements.

The establishment of a highly centralized planning system, followed by the evolution of a system of territorial administration in which local soviets assumed responsibility for the overall balanced development of their jurisdiction, has created a primary tension within the Soviet Union's system of municipal administration—a tension between economic sector and territorial unit, between ministry and municipality.[23] This continuous strain runs throughout the efforts of Leningraders to shape the face of their city, discussed in later chapters. It constitutes a particularly fateful legacy of the introduction of centralized planning by Joseph Stalin in 1928.

Expanding Municipal Responsibilities

This institutionalization of centralized economic planning under Stalin proved to be of critical importance for both Soviet municipal administration and center-periphery relations. Municipal obligations multiplied to encompass previously unrecognized industrial responsibilities, as every economic unit from factory shops to urban districts to industrial ministries was locked into the same strictly hierarchical, centralized system. Soviet city elites soon found themselves responsible for entire areas of industrial planning and management hitherto left to the marketplace.

The launching of the first Five-Year Plan in 1928 doomed all but the most ephemeral private enterprise in Soviet Russia. Throughout the 1920s, Lenin's "New Economic Policy" (NEP, 1921–1928) had tolerated and at times encouraged small-to-medium-scale entrepreneurship, especially in agriculture and commerce. Stalin's forced collectivization, however, abolished all private agriculture (except for small family-cultivated plots), replacing small- and medium-scale private farms with behemoth state and collective farms. The era was dominated by Stalin's drive against private farmers and his accompanying rapid industrialization program. These policies were joined by a less momentous but no less disruptive drive against commerce in cities.

At the end of the First Five-Year Plan, the Soviet state had seized control of nearly all urban commercial activities and the vast majority of housing, as well as almost the entire range of entertainment facilities. Much of the daily administrative responsibilities in each of these areas fell to municipalities or, more precisely, to local soviets.[24] Local governments became grocers, haberdashers, and candlestick makers. By the early 1980s, for example, the 37 administrations of the Leningrad city soviet included separate administrations for housing, health, culture, local industries, trade, consumer services, hotels, public dining, film production, TV and radio broadcasting, publishing and the book trade, individual tailoring services, cottage (*dacha*) services, and distribution and storage of potatoes and other vegetables.[25] These were in addition to those administrations controlling such traditional municipal functions as education, water and sewerage services, highway and bridge maintenance, parks, transportation, and trams and trolleybuses. Many of these administrations did not limit their activities to supervision, as they might have in the West, but maintained production capacity as well. Indeed, ever since the launching of the First Five-Year Plan in 1928, there has scarcely been a human activity beyond the bounds of municipal administration. Every basic human need—from food to shelter to clothing—has fallen essentially under the operational control of one or another municipal agency.[26]

Even if we set aside the issues of efficiency and rationality, we must note the expansion of municipal administration beyond any limits known under the NEP or anywhere else, although we must concede that such tendencies were already evident during the Civil War period (1917–1921) and, although to a far lesser degree, even before. This explosion of administrative and operational capacity had a profound and all-encompassing influence on Soviet (and, later, socialist) municipal governance. Its impact was hardly reduced during the 1951–1986 period under examination in this volume, although the 1986 Law on Individual Labor Activities, which took effect in May 1987, may come to represent the beginning of a departure from the previous pattern in the delivery of consumer goods and services.[27] That law legalized the establishment of cooperative stores and services that minister to the interests of society and have been registered with local district administrators. We might note that initial experimentation with private-run services began as early as March 1987 within Leningrad's taxi industry.[28]

Overall, then, the state socialist character of the Soviet political economy had enormous consequences for urban governance. The responsibility for planning every aspect of city life, managing major industrial operations, and performing a score of secondary and tertiary social, economic, and cultural functions previously relegated to non-municipal institutions was thrust upon Soviet municipal administrators.

The Place of the Party

Local institutions in the Soviet Union are also subject to a dual system of political subordination: that within the state system of ministries and soviets, and that within a parallel network of party agencies.[29] This system of subordination and supervision is represented in Chart 2: the solid lines show the flow of direct administrative authority within the state bureaucracy; the dotted lines highlight the flow of party review over state institutions at various administrative levels. The broadly political and ideological obligations established by the party for state bodies are imposed on soviet municipal leaders and institutions and have few if any counterparts in the West.

The Communist Party constitutes a network designed to coordinate the establishment of policy that is to be implemented by the state.

Chart 2. *System of party/state dual subordination.*

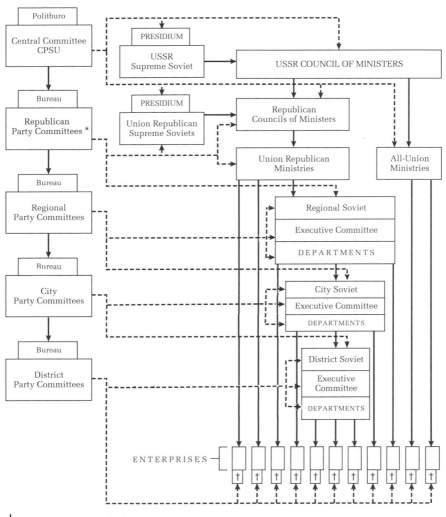

↓ Direct supervisory authority

↓ General review authority

* There is no republican party organization for the Russian Republic. The party's
  oversight function in that republic is exercised by the CPSU Central Committee.

† Primary Communist Party Committees.

The state bureaucracy, in turn, is intended to coordinate policy implementation. The end result is a bureaucratic structure that at first glance appears needlessly complex but can actually function as a rather streamlined and wholly integrated system. Anatomically, government and party organizations at any given level of this total administrative matrix are equivalent; in daily practice, the Communist Party dominates the entire system.

At the local level, municipal party institutions (the dotted lines in Chart 2) assume responsibility for general supervision and coordination of all economic, social, political, and cultural activities within their jurisdiction. Unlike the local soviets, which have an administrative role, local party committees supervise the commanding policy heights of management, leaving the soviets to wrestle with details.

Party supervision of local state institutions takes three primary forms. The first is the least formal: party members within state institutions are required to adhere to principles of party discipline by working to implement party policies. Whenever there are more than three party members within a given institution, those members are to form a party group that monitors the implementation of party pronouncements.[30] During the early 1980s, for example, there were over 21,000 such party groups throughout the Leningrad region.[31] In this manner state institutions become inexorably tied to their party equivalent through an invisible net of crosscutting membership ties.

The second mode of party supervision is the most formal and visible. State bodies officially cooperate with their party equivalent, and both sets of institutions prepare fully integrated plans of action.[32] Equivalent party and state institutions frequently have interlocking and overlapping executive councils. Moreover, as is illustrated in Chart 2, they have parallel organizational structures, with party committees exercising superior authority over partner state bodies (see once again the dotted lines in the chart). In Leningrad, for example, the regional party committee elects a bureau parallel to the regional soviet executive committee and operates sixteen departments parallel to the regional soviet executive committee's thirty-nine departments and administrations.[33] The Leningrad city party committee, for its part, similarly elects a bureau with a dozen members and operates twelve departments, while the city soviet's executive committee has established some forty-one departments and administrations.[34] The smaller number of party departments reflects their more general policy and supervisory mission, while the larger number of soviet departments and administrations illustrates a penchant among state agencies for more circumscribed bureaucratic vigilance.

The third form of party supervision, which is neither formal nor particularly visible, has become the subject of intense scrutiny by Western political scientists. We speak here of the integrated system of personnel appointment known as the Communist Party's *nomenklatura*, whereby higher-ranking party and state institutions are responsible for the personnel placement of cadres in subordinate organizations. This pattern is repeated throughout the state and party hierarchies up to careers that fall within the domain of the most senior *nomenklatura* agency of all, the Central Committee of the Communist Party.[35]

Shaping Leningrad

Thus far, we have discussed conflicts between ministries and municipalities. We have noted the place of the soviet in urban life, the institution most responsible for linking a city's administrative structure to national and republic bureaucratic institutions (the Soviet Union's fifteen union republics form the core units of the Soviet federal system).[36] We have also reviewed the role of the only municipal institution capable of providing a broad policy framework, the party committee. Taken together, these institutions and the rules of their operation provide the institutional world and establish the strictly defined limits within which local officials in Leningrad and elsewhere in the Soviet Union must function. To appreciate how they succeed or fail in achieving various physical and socioeconomic objectives, or even in coming to terms with the process by which such objectives are established in the first place, this study will explore the ways in which central and local elites have sought to mold Leningrad during the period 1951–1986.

Leningrad offers a useful case with which to begin an examination of the strategies by which local officials within the centralized non-market Soviet political economy set out to shape a city. With a population of some 5 million people, Leningrad's metropolitan region is the second largest in the Soviet Union and the sixth largest in Europe, being surpassed only by London, Rhein-Ruhr, Paris, Moscow, and Milan.[37] Despite efforts to inhibit further growth, the population continues to expand as nearly a million new residents have moved to or been born in the city during approximately the past 15 years.[38] Moreover, Leningrad is the Soviet Union's second most important industrial center, with an economic profile encompassing precisely those sectors that either dominate the Soviet economy at present (machine construction, shipbuilding, and other heavy industries) or are likely to be vital to that system's future success (radio technology, electronic-instrument making, and the biochemical and chemical industries).[39] These are industries that have benefited disproportionately from the historic Stalinist emphasis on development of "Group A" (generally heavy) industry, an emphasis that continued well into the Brezhnev era.[40]

Leningrad has an extensive scientific establishment. Scientific institutions and related service industries represent the second largest employer in the city, behind industry. The city's 300-odd scientific research establishments and forty-one institutions of higher learning employ almost one-fifth of the Leningrad workforce, and the city is second only to Moscow in the number of scientific workers employed.[41] The city's powerful industrial base and enormous scientific community interact. The close ties between these sectors are apparent in a growing emphasis on applied rather than basic research. Their increasingly close coordination has put the city of Leningrad ahead of all other Soviet industrial centers in various measures of technological innovation. It has also contributed to the city's primary role in the Soviet defense program at all levels, ranging from R&D and defense production to training facilities and military bases.

Leningrad has an additional resource that few other Soviet cities can draw on: a tremendous symbolic presence, rooted in its unique history. The city has long been identified with major forces shaping post-Petrine Russian history: Westernization, industrialization, and revolution. To these powerful forces was later added the truly heroic defense of the city during World War II. The existence of these powerful historic images, aided by the preservation of the physical environment identified with them, constitutes a symbolic resource as important as the industrial and scientific resources we have described.

We should also observe that Leningrad political leaders have greater political power than do many of their counterparts in other Soviet cities outside of Moscow. The city so dominates its regional unit, the oblast, that regional officials serve as the primary overseers for the city itself. For example, the most powerful political figure in Leningrad is the regional, as opposed to the city, Communist Party first secretary. Rather than diminishing the city's political standing, however, this situation enhances its status, as the future careers and reputations of influential regional officials depend more than normally on the success of the city itself. The local Leningrad party organization has experienced unusually long-standing cadre stability throughout the period of this study, thereby engendering a sense of cohesion and knowledge of local traditions that has historically been absent from many other regions of the Soviet Union. Indeed, the regional party organization has emerged as the primary integrative institution within the oblast, a territory that, as already noted, is only slightly smaller than Indiana. Beyond increasing the political visibility and influence of city officials, the dominance of regional party institutions helped make possible the continued expansion of physical, economic, and social planning strategies until the 1986 Leningrad general plan set for itself the task of shaping the face, not just of the city and its metropolitan area, but of the entire Leningrad region as well. This latter development will be a major element of the study to follow.

Each of these distinctive features of the Leningrad scene makes the city and its surrounding metropolitan area a particularly appropriate starting point for an attempt to explore and explain many of the ways in which Soviet urban officials seek to shape the face of their communities. All these features accentuate the various ways in which the political periphery seeks to maximize its operational space vis-à-vis the political center. The city's long-standing economic prominence and reputation for architectural excellence provide benchmarks against which current urban planning performance in both its physical and its socioeconomic dimensions may be evaluated. The size and importance of the regional economy lend a visibility to local management and planning that is not found in less significant urban centers. The city's extensive network of scientific and educational institutions provides critical expertise for local decision-making largely independent of central dominance. The political power and prestige of Leningrad municipal and Communist Party leaders and institutions offer a considerable power base. Moreover, we should expect Leningrad politicians, planners, and managers to be concerned with the fate of their city, to have resources on which to draw for local initiatives, to be well disposed to political and economic activism, and yet, unlike Moscow, to be firmly attached to the political periphery rather than to the center. An examination of Leningrad's physical and socioeconomic planning experience should help illuminate Soviet practice more generally. In short, the study of Leningrad can serve as a beginning for more general investigations of the means by which local urban officials in the Soviet Union function.

Four Policy Studies

To explore the Leningrad experience, the remainder of this volume is organized around four interrelated policy studies: (1) physical planning innovation, (2) integrated scientific-production "associations," (3) vocational education, and (4) enterprise and urban socioeconomic planning. These studies cover the period from the promulgation of the region's section of the Fifth Five-Year Plan (1951–1955), the first economic plan that was dominated by a science-oriented development strategy, to the enactment of the most recent general development plan for the city, metropolitan area, and region in 1986.

Our studies begin with *physical planning*. Over the course of these years, urban planners and architects, acting in concert with municipal leaders, have altered architectural and land use practices through a series of pragmatic solutions to pressing design problems. These solutions—including the introduction of social variables into city planning, concern over historical preservation standards, and regional as opposed to merely citywide planning approaches—came to the fore in the period between the 1966 and 1986 Leningrad general plans. Many of these changes have subsequently been adopted as national planning norms. Their emergence will be examined in Part 1.

Leningrad Communist Party officials have also supported efforts to integrate entire production cycles under a single managerial unit, through the creation of *integrated associations* combining several factories, research centers, and scientific facilities engaged in related activities. Ever since the Fifth Five-Year Plan (1951–1955), Leningrad managers have led attempts to enhance industrial innovation through the institutional integration of research-development-production cycles. While many Western observers had become skeptical of the effectiveness of various Soviet innovation programs, they nonetheless acknowledged Leningrad's success at implementing the new managerial arrangements, particularly during the 1960s and 1970s. Our examination of these innovation efforts will open Part 2, devoted to the socioeconomic environment. We will review Leningrad's shift to a technology-driven city economic plan in 1951 and continue through to the incorporation into the 1986 Leningrad general plan of measures to motivate regional economic performance through technological innovation.

Leningrad's educational and industrial planners and factory administrative personnel sought the resurrection of prewar networks of enterprise *vocational educational facilities*, with the result that nearly a majority of Leningrad school-age children now attend some form of vocational education center. These activities gained prominence during the educational reform debate in 1958, and the emphasis on vocational education continued to be reflected a quarter-century later in the April 1984 national educational reforms adopted by the USSR Supreme Soviet. In a related move, local Leningrad plant managers, economic planners, and sociologists cooperated during the 1960s to foster the integration of social and economic factors into single all-encompassing *socioeconomic plans* for enterprises, urban districts, and eventually the city as a whole. By the mid-seventies, factories and towns across the Soviet Union were required to establish similar plans, based on models created by Leningrad social scientists, and the national Five-Year Plan had also incorporated social and economic development. As these third and fourth policy initiatives both confront the city's, area's, and region's chronic labor shortages, and as they have both been incorporated into the 1986 Leningrad general plan, they will be discussed at the close of Part 2.

Individually and in concert, these local efforts suggest ways in which Soviet, or at least Leningrad, urban elites have been able to adjust central policies and constraints so as to foster new opportunities for themselves and their communities within the context of a centrally planned political-economic system. Leningrad municipal leaders have pursued economic development policies that enhance their community's economic position and political power. They have done so by combining economic and political resources and by manipulating existing vertical and horizontal administrative relationships. These governing traditions and relationships emerge from the city's distinctive physical environment, the historical dimensions of which form the central focus of our first chapter.

I

The Physical Environment

1

The Petersburg Tradition

On one side, the sea;
on the other, sorrow;
on the third, moss;
on the fourth, Oh!
—Balakiriev, Court Jester
  of Peter the Great,
  early eighteenth century

A Tsar's Vision

St. Petersburg was founded by Peter I the Great in 1703 on the marshy frontier of two competing empires (those of Peter's Russia and the Sweden of Charles XII).[1] The Neva River delta's strategic importance in the imperial competition dictated its fortification despite the area's insalubrious climate and the absence of a commercial base (see Map 3).[2] Millennia before Peter proclaimed the Neva delta to be the site of his imperial capital, the region's 101 islands, 66 rivers, and 100 lakes and ponds lay under 1,000 meters of ice.[3] As the glaciers receded, a flat marshland remained, covered with scant vegetation and subject to frequent flooding.[4] In such an area, the construction even of a village, let alone a world-class metropolis, demanded the kind of perseverance and obstinacy that could be assured only by unrestrained greed for gain or by the iron-willed determination of an autocrat. In either case, the resulting settlement could never emerge as a "natural" extension of its environment. Peter's city—or any other community imposed upon this bleak landscape—would have to be an artifact of human willpower.

The city is situated on the 40-odd islands in the Neva River delta at the eastern end of the Gulf of Finland, surrounded by 50 rivers, streams, channels, and canals. The Neva's main streams divide the city into three general sectors: the right bank to the north and east, the left bank to the south and west, and the marshy islands in between. Nearly all the city's nineteenth-century core is under water once the river rises to four meters above flood stage.

As the present-day city approaches the end of its third century,

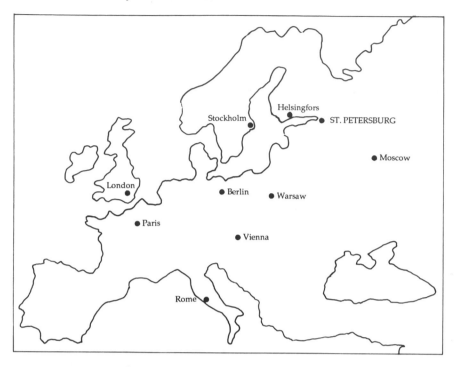

Map 3. *St. Petersburg in relation to other European capitals.*

the continuing influence of Peter's original autocratic vision remains
undeniable. Efforts to regulate contemporary Leningrad's urban environment must still deal with the imperial capital that Peter and his
successors built along the Neva's now granite-lined embankments (see
Figures 1 and 2). Before Peter's arrival, the delta's fate seemed to depend
primarily on the fortunes of kings and princes hundreds of miles removed. Only some eight years later, in 1711, Peter proclaimed this
precarious fortress-settlement as the site of his imperial court. He immediately commanded Russian noblemen and diplomatic emissaries
to take up residence in his new capital, while importing conscripted
serf labor and foreign artisans to reproduce Amsterdam on the Gulf of
Finland. By the time Peter died in 1725, 40,000 souls had come to dwell
in his new town (See Table 1 and Map 4).

For nearly 200 years following Peter's death, architects and planners consciously laid out the city as a symbol of the Romanov dynasty
and its majesty, suitably encasing in stone the ostentation of Peter and
his successors.[5] As a result of this imperial vision, Leningrad remains
today anything but a typical Soviet city. The product of human planning
and resolution, the city is living evidence of both the best and the worst
of nearly three centuries of urban planning. As a "planned city" its
successes and failures are shared with cities as diverse as Washington,

Figure 1. *View of the banks of the Neva River from the Palace embankment.*

New Delhi, and Canberra, but not with Moscow, Tbilisi, and Kazan'. Moreover, as the former capital of an empire, it has been demoted to become a still-important but nonetheless provincial center. This experience it shares with Vienna, Istanbul, Rio de Janeiro, and Karachi, but not with Dnepropetrovsk, Novosibirsk, Sverdlovsk, and Vladivostok. Finally, as we have noted, the city's imperial architectural and planning legacies provide contemporary city planners and architects with a unified urban vision. The city's historic reliance on sweeping urban vistas and grand harmonious spaces filled with dynamic plastic facades continues to influence present-day efforts to regulate the urban environment.[6] To understand its role, we must return to Peter's original vision for his new capital city.

The Romanov Imperial Legacy

Peter conceived a well-ordered and regular brick town, similar to the Dutch cities he had seen during his famous excursion through Western Europe. He hoped that his little Dutch town would contrast sharply with the chaos of traditional Russian cities such as his native capital of Moscow.[7] His efforts focused initially on Vasil'evskii Island, where Peter, his governor Prince Menshikov, and his architect, Frenchman Jean-Baptiste Alexandre Le Blond, decided to locate the town's center

Figure 2. The painting, executed in 1824, depicts the difficulties posed by the frequent floods of the Neva River for the city of Leningrad.

Table 1. *Leningrad Population, 1725–1987*

	St. Petersburg, Petrograd, Leningrad (City)	Metropolitan Leningrad[a]
1725	40,000[b]	
1750	95,000[b]	
1825	420,000[b]	
1850	487,000[b]	
1854	525,000[c]	
1856	475,000[c]	
1865	539,122[c]	
1869	667,207[c]	
1897	1,265,000[d]	
1910	1,906,000[d]	
1917	2,300,000[d]	2,500,000[e]
1920	720,000[d]	
1923	1,071,000[d]	
1926	1,619,000[f]	
1929	1,775,000[d]	
1939	3,119,000[f]	3,421,000[f]
1942	1,100,000[g]	
1943	639,000[g]	
1945	1,240,000[h]	
1959	3,003,000[f]	3,367,000[f]
1970	3,550,000[f]	4,027,000[f]
1979	4,073,000[f]	4,588,000[f]
1983	4,255,000[i]	4,779,000[i]
1987	4,393,000[j]	4,948,000[j]

[a]In the Soviet period, includes suburban jurisdictions subordinated to the Leningrad city soviet.

[b]James H. Bater, *St. Petersburg: Industrialization and Change* (Montreal: McGill-Queen's University Press, 1976), 67–69.

[c]Ibid., 158–165.

[d]*Malaia sovetskaia entsiklopediia* (Moscow: Sovetskaia entsiklopediia, 1930), 4:572.

[e]TsSU SSSR, *Narodnoe khoziaistvo SSSR, 1922–1972 gg.* (Moscow: Statistika, 1972), 19.

[f]*Narodnoe khoziaistvo Leningrada i Leningradskoi oblasti v desiatoi piatiletke: Statisticheskii sbornik* (Leningrad: Lenizdat, 1981), 23–24.

[g]Leon Goure, *The Siege of Leningrad: August, 1941–January, 1944* (New York: McGraw-Hill Book Co., 1964), 239.

[h]"Iz letopisi sobytii," *Leningradskaia panorama*, 1982, no. 6:7.

[i]Kh. Kh. Karimov, *Leningrad v tsifrakh i faktakh* (Leningrad: Lenizdat, 1984), 15–16.

[j]TsSU SSSR, *Narodnoe khoziaistvo SSSR za 70 let* (Moscow: Finansy i statistika, 1987), 397.

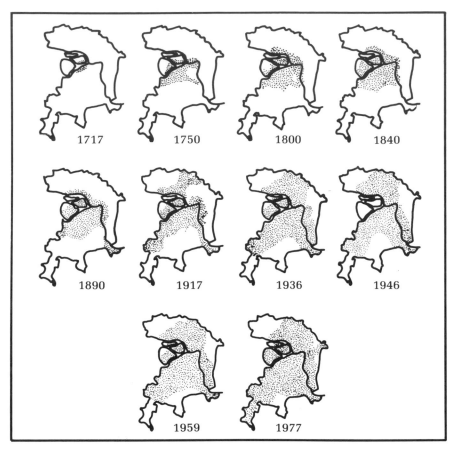

Map 4. *Settled areas of the city of Leningrad, 1717–1977.*

(see Figure 3).[8] Le Blond's 1717 plan, the first of many citywide planning efforts, called for an overtly geometric configuration on Vasil'evskii
Island, reminiscent of Amsterdam, with streets and canals intersecting
at right angles, thereby dividing the city into strictly organized functional zones. These early plans were doomed to failure, however, by
strains on the state budget caused by Peter's constant warring, together
with the hazards of travel from the mainland across treacherous currents and the constant threat of severe flooding.[9]

Peter's city never truly conformed to the Dutch building practices
of the day. Town planning concepts in Holland had begun to develop
during the Middle Ages, and by the seventeenth and eighteenth centuries the Dutch were acknowledged leaders in the field.[10] For the
Dutch, the concept of "town" had a very precise meaning. It always
contained a market, was surrounded by a wall, and had been granted
a charter. In short, the Dutch town remained a mercantile invention

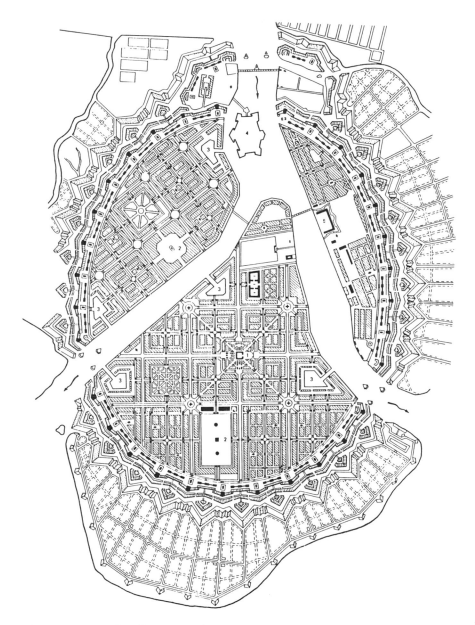

Figure 3. *Le Blond's 1717 plan.*

developed over the years to meet the needs of multiple users. In contrast, St. Petersburg had only one prime user—the tsar, the Romanov autocrat—who wanted the capital to embody dynastic grandeur.

Peter visited Amsterdam a half-century after the Dutch had gained their independence from Spain in 1648. There he saw a boomtown that had developed according to one of the most comprehensive and ambitious town plans in all of Europe—the Amsterdam plan of 1607. By the time of Peter's visit, the plan, characterized by strict building codes and functional zoning, had created an orderly and compact city. Peter was also undoubtedly aware of the Copenhagen city plan, drafted by Dutch architects and implemented between 1588 and 1648.[11] Thus we should hardly be surprised that he would have desired to copy the bourgeois Dutch. Had he succeeded in the face of the Russian autocratic tradition, however, it would have been a miracle. True, the Saint-Iler plan of St. Petersburg developed in 1764–1773 at Catherine II's behest portrays in almost photographic detail networks of facades conforming to a uniform street line as in Dutch practice. In this sense, Dutch influence remained evident in the city's physical development well into the eighteenth century. Yet, just behind these formal facades vast open spaces and eclectic courtyards betray their essentially Russian origins.[12]

Following the reigns of Peter and later his widow, Catherine I (1725–1727), St. Petersburg embarked upon a stormy half-century that witnessed the capital's return to Moscow under Peter's grandson Peter II (1727–1730); its restoration to Petersburg by Peter's niece, Anna (1730–1740); and its embellishment during a brilliant explosion of Russian rococo under Peter I's daughter, Elizabeth (1741–1762) (see Chart 3).[13] The period proved critical for the city's development. The distinctive triradial street system centering on the Admiralty spire emerged during Anna's rule (see Map 5), while Elizabeth launched an impressive network of imperial parks and satellite palaces and towns. More importantly, the city's role as capital was secured as its population grew to 90,000 by the middle of the eighteenth century. By the time Elizabeth's niece by marriage, Catherine II, the Great (1762–1796), seized power in a palace coup, the city had developed a distinctive urban culture. Although this culture remained essentially Russian, it had become permeated with European ideas.[14]

In the reigns of Catherine II and her grandsons Alexander I (1801–1825) and Nicholas I (1825–1855), St. Petersburg grew into a great European capital. The city's center emerged as one of the world's leading ensembles of neoclassical architecture,[15] and the population more than quadrupled as migrants began to arrive from the countryside. Urban growth abated only slightly, after a mid-century cholera epidemic.

Catherine II and her progeny saw themselves as rulers of a major European power, and to express their new pretensions, they turned to

Chart 3. *The Romanov dynasty.*

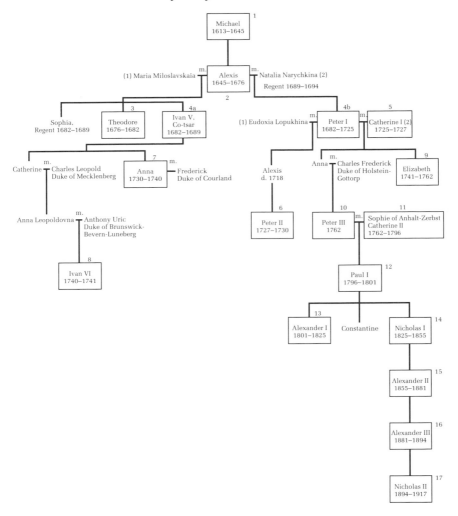

a neoclassicism then popular in France. The result was nearly a century of neoclassical construction as extensive as any similar project elsewhere in the world (see Figures 4 and 5). What is known today as Leningrad—and what Soviet architects of the 1930s sought to reproduce on an even grander scale—is the neoclassical city of Catherine the Great and her grandsons. It is the model against which all subsequent planning and design efforts for the city have been and continue to be judged.

The Catherinian achievement paved the way for the apex of Russian neoclassical architecture and urban design under Alexander I.[16] During Catherine's rule, as comprehensive planning efforts were under-

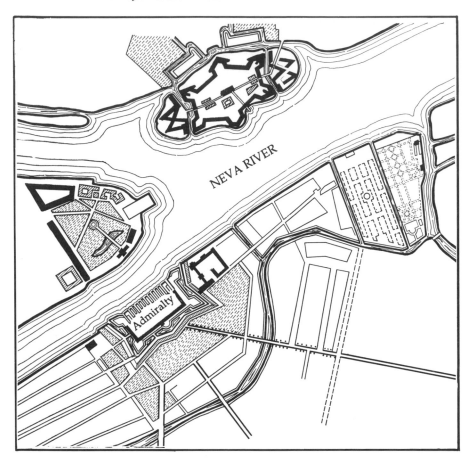

Map 5. *St. Petersburg at the end of the reign of Elizabeth. Outline highlights the triradial street system focusing on the Admiralty spire.*

taken, new spatial concepts for the architectural organization of the city had come to the fore. Town builders spared no effort to make their capital more magnificent and beautiful. Moreover, they believed that nothing served their purpose better than to fill the city's central core with significant buildings and regular squares (see Figure 6). Each building retained its individuality, while also being integrated into the entire urban ensemble. Large-scale building efforts were not always practical, so that only a limited number of monumental structures could be built. Consequently, for maximum effect vigorous buildings were to be placed at critical junctions, with secondary spaces left for later generations to deal with.

The immediate task of finishing Catherine's classical masterpiece

Figure 4. *The Senate/Synod building—an example of neoclassical architecture.*

Figure 5. *The Senate/Synod building overlooking Senate Square.*

Figure 6. *The Admiralty from Palace Square.*

fell to her son Paul I (1796–1801) and her grandsons Alexander I and
Nicholas I. Under the autocracy, the selection of a chief architect and
a general superintendent of government buildings remained the pre-
rogative of the sovereign. It was thus inevitable that the monarch's
fancies would influence the course of architectural history. During
Paul's brief reign, which ended with his assassination in a palace closet,
St. Petersburg assumed a somber military air appropriate for its dour
autocrat's temperament. Under Alexander I, by contrast, the autocrat's
good taste and clear understanding of what his grandmother had accomplished led to the pinnacle of imperial Russian neoclassicism. Alexander particularly wanted his capital to be the most harmonious and
beautiful in Europe, and acted to ensure that it would become so. The
near-realization of his goal has left an indelible mark on Leningrad to
this day.[17] The construction of several central squares surrounding the
Admiralty district and the beautification of Nevskii Prospekt mark the
culmination of planning efforts of the Alexandrian epoch (see Map 6).
A century and a half later, these achievements still influence the work
of Leningrad city planners and architects (see Figures 7 and 8).

   The completion of the city's central squares containing nearly 100
acres of open space, together with the establishment of Nevskii Prospekt
as the city's central axis (see Figure 9), created an urban system that
Soviet architects sought at first to surpass, but more recently to preserve.[18] Under Alexander I and Nicholas I, St. Petersburg was transformed into a grand spatial composition of seemingly unbroken chains

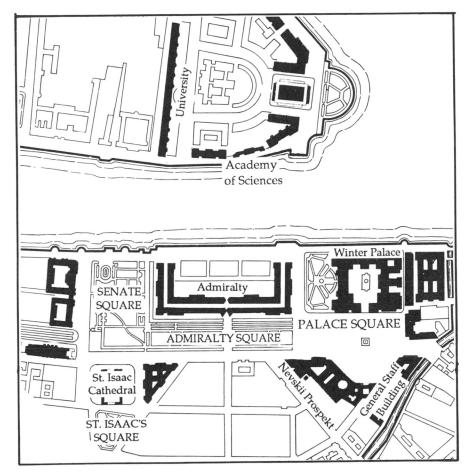

Map 6. *St. Petersburg's central squares.*

of related ensembles. Present-day Leningrad architects have come to regard this "Petersburg tradition" as demanding a large expanse of unbroken facade. This legacy is now venerated, although during its own century it proved to be rather short-lived, as social forces unleashed by the industrial revolution swept away the order and predictability of the capital of Alexander I and Nicholas I.

Cradle to Revolution

The omnipresent order that the city had at the beginning of the nineteenth century faded under the press of industrialization. By the beginning of the twentieth century, St. Petersburg had become the most expensive and least healthful capital in all of Europe.[19] With a high

Figure 7. *Painting of Nevskii Prospekt.*

Figure 8. *Painting of corner near the Winter Palace.*

Figure 9. *Photo of Nevskii Prospekt at the turn of the century.*

mortality rate even by urban Russian standards, the capital experienced fierce outbreaks of infectious diseases attributable in part to geography and climate and in part to municipal ineptitude. In addition, the city suffered from chronic epidemics of venereal disease, a high incidence of drunkenness, a soaring crime rate, abysmal housing conditions, and high levels of illiteracy.[20] St. Petersburg apartments housed twice as many people as apartments in the already overcrowded European capitals Berlin, Vienna, and Paris.[21]

Between 1870 and 1914, a million and a half new residents moved to the city; of these, a million came after 1890 and 350,000 arrived in the boom years of 1908 to 1913.[22] By 1914, when it was renamed Petrograd, the Russian capital was Europe's fifth largest city, surpassed only by London, Paris, Vienna, and Berlin. Its population and employment were dominated by businessmen and workers. Many of the latter, however, had arrived fresh off the farm, as the city experienced its first major wave of migration from the countryside. The pressures of industrialization soon coincided with a rapidly escalating population, overwhelming municipal administrators. Housing and zoning codes were largely ignored, municipal services were far outstripped by demand, and the city's severe climatic conditions made a bad situation worse.[23]

The causes of the municipal administration's near-total collapse in the final quarter of the nineteenth century were cultural, structural, and financial. Russian society remained essentially preurban in outlook.[24] Prince and peasant alike regarded their residence in the capital as only transitory. For the nobility, St. Petersburg was the place to go for the winter social season. For the peasant, it was a place to earn money for the family back home. By harvest time many workers simply returned to the fields.[25] This generally low level of commitment to the city, combined with an autocratic administrative system, forced municipal officials to become more closely tied to the needs of the monarch than to those of the ostensibly passive populace. The city's largely underdeveloped municipal institutions retained essentially a static view of their role in a rapidly changing society.

One major reason for the municipality's apparent inaction remained financial. The city's operating budget was modest by European and even by Russian standards. City funds were derived largely from profits generated by such municipal concessions as the tram system, the water system, the gasworks, and a municipal slaughterhouse.[26] Under constant inflationary pressure, the city government eventually was forced to seek additional funds from the bond markets of London and Paris. The charges for servicing the municipal debt, while small by the practice of the period, nonetheless tripled between 1901 and 1910, reaching 2.9 million rubles annually.[27] In the end, the underdeveloped and underfinanced municipal structure was totally incapable of coping with the changes brought about by the industrial revolution.

Many in the city deplored the transformation of their capital from the relative order during the reign of Nicholas I to the growing chaos during that of Nicholas II. As industrialization swept across the Russian empire, antithetical nationalist and internationalist currents were felt throughout the capital's intellectual and cultural elites. In architecture, the nationalist movement shared broad concerns with the emergence throughout Europe of a romantic interest in the past.[28] As in Western Europe, this process of discovery took place in reverse chronological order, leading to an extensive eclecticism in design, which in St. Petersburg clashed with the city's predominantly classical spirit. Prime examples of this genre can be seen in the more "Russian" Moscow. In Petersburg, the Church of the Savior on the Blood, erected on the site of Alexander II's assassination, is the best local example of this drive

Figure 10. *Church of the Savior of the Blood.*

to re-create a mythical national Russian architectural form (see Figure 10).[29]

Against this national romantic revival were posed the overtly internationalist predilections of those associated with the journal *Mir iskusstva*, which appeared from 1898 until 1904, as well as its successors *Starye gody* (1907–1916), *Zolotoe runo* (1906–1909), and *Appolon* (1909–1917). These journals represented the major Russian components of the international symbolist movement of the 1890s and early 1900s. Such groups were concentrated in the more Western-oriented capital, and were primarily attracted to the city's past, with the neoclassicism of Catherine II and Alexander I holding particular fascination for them. This movement's image was reflected in the works of the brothers Benois (Leontii and Alexander) as well as in Ivan Fomin's massive proposal for a "New Petersburg" project on Golodai (later Decembrist) Island, a design every bit as classical in style and grand in execution as the original city (see Figure 11).[30]

These prerevolutionary reactions to the disintegration of the urban fabric caused by industrialization constitute the final imperial legacy for later generations of planners and architects in the Soviet period.

Figure 11. *Example of the "New Petersburg" project.*

Their architectural strategies—which dismissed private property, demanded large-scale state intervention, and produced a style characterized by grandeur and unity—offered an urban vision that awaited an
audience.[31] That audience was found by the end of the 1920s, as a new
Stalinist cult of the state began to emerge, one that was receptive to
fundamental characteristics of the Petrine-Catherinian-Alexandrine tradition of St. Petersburg as translated by the *Mir iskusstva* movement
of the 1890s and early 1900s.

In the interim, the Bolshevik seizure of power on November 7
(October 24, Old Style), 1917 had unleashed a bloody civil war. By
March 1918, Lenin was forced to transfer his government to the protective sanctuary of Moscow's Kremlin. With the seat of government
removed to rival Moscow and with food supplies disrupted by fighting
in the countryside, Petrograd residents fled their city. The gentry and
merchant classes largely sought refuge abroad, while workers in many
instances returned to their native villages or joined the Red Army. The
city's population plummeted from a prewar high of 2,300,000 to a civil
war low of only 720,000.

Once the new government had consolidated power and launched
its New Economic Policy (NEP), designed to encourage small busi-
nesses, Petrograd—renamed Leningrad after Lenin's death in 1924—
began to regain population. Still, with urban unemployment rates continuing high and trade flourishing in the countryside throughout the
1920s, its population remained well below pre-World War I levels. The
launching of Stalin's collectivization and industrialization drive in
1928 unleashed yet another torrent of peasants fleeing the countryside.
Every Soviet city expanded at unprecedented rates. The influx into
Leningrad increased the local population by over 1.3 million between
1929 and the prewar census of 1939, which tallied a record population

of 3,119,000, with an additional 300,000 residing in the surrounding urban areas. This population increase combined with a revival of interest in grandiose neoclassicism to produce a distinctively Stalinist Leningrad.

Stalin's Soviet Legacy

The collapse of the Romanov dynasty touched off a vigorous anti-urban revolt among many intellectuals, particularly in the small community of professional urbanists and architects. At least among professional circles, this revulsion against the urban environment was centered in Moscow, where living conditions were every bit as pestilential as in Petrograd,[32] but where the city's physical unruliness offered none of the psychic relief provided by the lingering orderly aesthetic impact of the still-visible Alexandrine physical plant in Petrograd. In Petrograd, revulsion against the city's abysmal living conditions took a slightly different turn.[33]

As in Moscow, local Petrograd officials moved immediately to clean up particularly noxious neighborhoods.[34] Nevertheless, the local architectural community's image of the city remained essentially the original Romanov vision as transmitted through the prism of the "New Urbanism" of the city's turn-of-the-century artistic intelligentsia. The continued nurturing of this tradition by Leningrad architects throughout the 1920s psychologically prepared that community for Lazar Kaganovich's 1931 declaration that the Soviet Union's industrial future would be urban by definition.[35]

Immediately after Kaganovich's 1931 address, central elites instructed the city governments and Communist Party organizations in Moscow and Leningrad to prepare comprehensive physical development plans for their cities. In 1935 the Central Committee of the All-Union Communist Party (Bolshevik) and the USSR Council of People's Commissars joined with Moscow municipal institutions to promulgate a comprehensive plan for the reconstruction of Moscow.[36] The following year the same central institutions joined with the Leningrad city soviet to enact an equally far-reaching general development plan for the old imperial northern capital.[37]

According to the 1936 Leningrad general plan drawn up under the direction of Lev Il'in and Vladimir Vitman, the city would abandon its historic center focused on the Admiralty and Neva for a new and grander city center along an expansive boulevard (International [now Moskovskii] Prospekt) running directly south from the Peace Square for some ten kilometers (see Map 7).[38] This new city center, which together with the buildings of the 1920s has recently become a hub of historic preservation efforts,[39] was unified through a common focus on

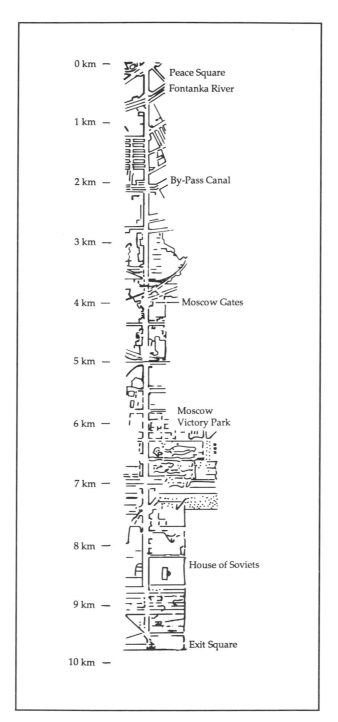

0 km — Peace Square
Fontanka River

1 km —

2 km — By-Pass Canal

3 km —

4 km — Moscow Gates

5 km —

6 km — Moscow
Victory Park

7 km —

8 km —

House of Soviets

9 km —

Exit Square

10 km —

Map 7. *International/Moscow Prospekt project.*

Figure 12. *House of Soviets building.*

a gargantuan House of Soviets building placed strategically along the new thoroughfare.[40] That whole complex, when constructed, covered a total of 13 acres, nine of which were deemed to be usable building space.[41] Heavy and neoclassical, this ponderous building overwhelmed the as-yet vacant surrounding territory. The House of Soviets, and the 1936 general plan that produced it, captured not only the ethos of Stalinist statism but also that of the "New Petersburg" movement of three decades earlier (see Figure 12). This project represented the logical culmination of an imperial Petersburg tradition that sought to symbolize the pomposity of state authority in stone. Its neoclassical inspiration similarly testifies that the arrogant assertion of human order over nature, visible in the classicism of the Renaissance, continued to inspire imperial Russian and Soviet architects centuries later.

In his memoirs, Nikolai Baranov attests to the direct influence of Renaissance design principles and philosophy on his generation of Leningrad architects as they set to work during the Stalinist period.[42] Baranov, who was the city's chief architect from 1938 until 1950 and was one of the most influential Soviet city planners of his era,[43] reports that Lev Il'in, his predecessor as chief architect from 1925 until 1938, served as a primary mentor to the city's numerous young architects throughout the twenties and thirties (Il'in was later killed during a German bombardment of the city in December 1942).[44] Il'in, it turns out, collected eighteenth- and nineteenth-century furniture, paintings, carpets, china, and crystal.[45] He also compiled a 5,000-volume library of rare architectural works focusing primarily on the period of the Italian Renaissance, including works by Palladio, Alberti, and Piranesi.[46]

Il'in's chosen visual environment was that of Renaissance classicism and Russian neoclassicism. Through his thoughtful supervision of their work, he transmitted his aesthetic preferences to a generation of apprentice architects. Similarly, his own designs for Leningrad, as well as for Baku, where he also served as chief architect throughout most of the 1930s, displayed an intense interest in neoclassical principles.[47] Confronted with the strong neoclassical tradition of Leningrad and of its professional architectural elite, the new-found statism of the Stalinist regime saw in Peter's former capital a ready outlet for its pretensions.

Soon, however, Leningrad city administrators came to view the initial 1936 general plan as impractical. In 1938, a team of architects under Baranov and Aleksandr Naumov revised the original plan, seeking a more effective use of the available land.[48] As part of this revision, the new city center project was scaled down from 99 acres to 28. Baranov later observed that this reduction brought the planned ensemble into scale with such urban vistas as the Mall in Washington, D.C., and the Champs-Elysées in Paris.[49] The new plan also noted that "serious inconveniences" would result from an immediate abandonment of the historic city center. Nevertheless, the primary thrust of new construction was still concentrated in the same four districts first designed in 1936: Avtovo, Shchemilovka, Malaia Okhta, and the International Prospekt Project (see Map 8).[50] From 1936 until 1941 more than 800,000 square meters of housing space, 213 schools, and 200 preschool facilities were built in the city, mainly in these four areas.[51]

Three overarching considerations explain the plan's preoccupation with moving the city's population southward. First, the new center was designed to overwhelm the historic city core, thereby destroying the political symbolism of the prerevolutionary architectural ensemble by erecting an even grander "socialist" statist environment nearby. Second, by moving the city to higher ground, the planners sought to reduce a tragic pattern of flooding. Third, once the decision was made to abandon the historic city center, movement to the south became inevitable. With the Finnish border only 22 miles to the north, national security interests demanded urban development in the opposite direction. The short but bloody Winter War with the Finns in 1939–1940 demonstrated the military wisdom of such a plan, as Leningrad was quickly transformed into a garrison city. Of the 200,000 Soviet casualties suffered in that war, by far the largest percentage were among Leningraders.[52] This loss was, of course, soon overshadowed by the virtual annihilation that occurred during World War II's blockade.

On the night of June 21–22, 1941, Hitler's *Wehrmacht* rolled across the Soviet Union's western frontier, and within a few weeks the

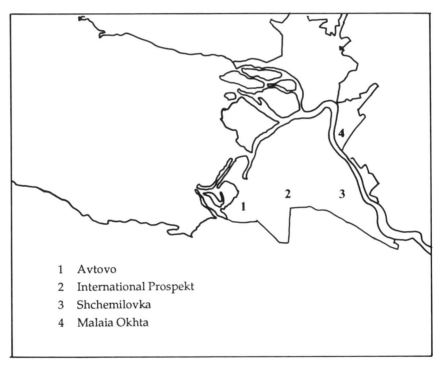

1   Avtovo
2   International Prospekt
3   Shchemilovka
4   Malaia Okhta

Map 8. *Major construction projects during the 1930s.*

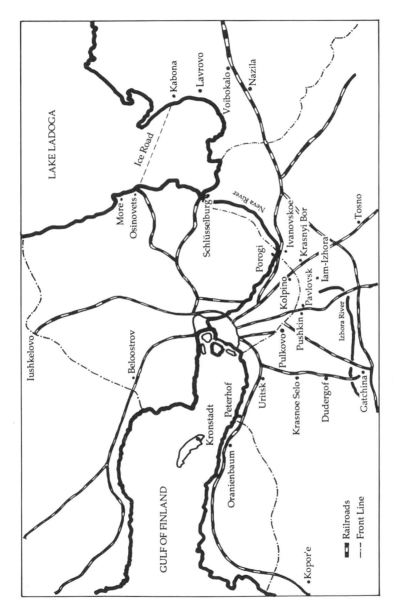

Map 9. The front line on September 25, 1941.

Figure 13. *Photo of effects of the blockade.*

country's second largest city was under a siege that was to last two and a half years (see Map 9 and Figure 13).[53] The fate of over 40 percent of the city's prewar population is unknown and cannot be reconstructed from official Soviet statistics.[54] What is known is that, by early 1942, Leningrad's population had been cut by two thirds through war-related casualties, starvation (as many as 30,000 civilians died on each of the worst February days), and evacuation (over a half-million civilians successfully left the city on the 237-mile "Road of Life" across the ice of Lake Ladoga and through surrounding forests to the nearest railhead).[55] To put these figures into comparative perspective, the number of Leningraders who perished during the blockade approximately equals the total number of U.S. armed forces personnel who died in all wars from the American Revolution through the war in Vietnam.[56] By the end of the blockade's second winter, Leningrad had shrunk to only 639,000 residents—less than the city's population at the height of the Civil War—and its industrial base was operating at only 10 percent of its prewar capacity when measured by the value of industrial production.[57]

2

The Postwar City, 1945–1966

St. Petersburg, Petrograd had gone for ever. This was
Leningrad. It had inherited many things from the
other two, but it had its own substance, its own personality. . . . One no more felt like calling Leningrad
"St. Petersburg" or "Petrograd" than one felt like
calling Stalingrad "Tsaritsyn."
                                    —Alexander Werth, 1944

Reconstruction

After March 1943, the city's fortunes began to improve, and the
Finno-German blockade was lifted in January 1944. Later in 1944, when
the city was fully liberated, the State Defense Committee in Moscow
announced a plan for rebuilding Leningrad.[1] Recognizing that the population had fought and died for their "Peter," as residents affectionately
called the city, the framers of the 1943–1947 reconstruction plan aban-
doned the previous effort to shift the city core southward and reasserted
the primacy of Leningrad's historic center. For example, October 30
Prospekt once again officially became Nevskii Prospekt (while International Prospekt was also renamed, in honor of Stalin).[2] In 1945–1946
more than 700 million rubles were invested in the city's reconstruction,
with 1.6 million square meters of housing erected in the traditional city
center, as well as low-rise structures in the Primorskii Prospekt, Avtovo,
Bol'shaia and Malaia Okhta, Shchemilovka, and Prospekt Stachek districts (see Map 10).[3] Gas heat was introduced on a large scale for the
first time, and water and sewage systems were upgraded.[4] Two large
victory parks were opened on Stalinskii Prospekt (the 250-acre Moscow
Victory Park) and on Krestovskii Island (the 470-acre Maritime Victory
Park).[5] The 1950 dedication of the 100,000-seat Kirov Stadium on that
island marked the culmination of Leningrad's reconstruction period
(see Figure 14).[6]

The placement of the massive Kirov Stadium along the Gulf of
Finland reflected a new set of spatial priorities enunciated for the first
time in a new 1947 general plan developed by a team of architects led

by Nikolai Baranov. The 1947 plan carried forward the city's development beyond the original postwar reconstruction period. Its overall conception for future development in Leningrad had several components that would dominate local city planning efforts for decades. In it, for example, Baranov set forth his pet notion that Leningrad should, at long last, become the true maritime city Peter I had initially envisioned.[7] He would later claim that the original idea for the city's "face to the sea" dated from the work of eighteenth-century architect Adreian Zakharov.[8] The 1947 general plan also anticipated new transportation facilities, with a major airport south of the city near the eventual site of today's Pulkovo airport.[9]

Despite these very real achievements, however, the final document—as with all Soviet general city plans of the period—largely ignored major social and economic trends then shaping the city's destiny. These forces rendered Chief Architect Baranov's plans fanciful and obsolete almost as soon as they left his drawing board. To fully appreciate how this was the case, it is necessary to review the entire postwar period down to the 1980s—a period of sweeping social and economic change in Leningrad.

Social Change

To begin with, a major social and demographic transformation was afoot. By September 1945, Leningrad's wartime population had doubled with the arrival of rural in-migrants (coming from such regions as Iaroslavl', Kalinin, Saratov, and Sverdlovsk oblasts) and demobilized soldiers (see Map 1).[10] In other words, a large number, perhaps even a majority, of the city's residents had not lived in the city before the outbreak of hostilities, had only limited personal or familial ties to the city, and, as a rule, had fewer work skills at the beginning of this migratory process than did the city's prior inhabitants.[11] It would take another decade and a half before prewar population levels would be achieved, but, by as early as 1945, Leningrad was becoming primarily a city of migrants. Such disproportionate reliance on migration as a source for new population magnified the demographic chasm created by the horrific civilian losses of the blockade.[12] Among the most visible manifestations of this intense social change have been the "feminization" and aging of the city's inhabitants throughout the postwar period.[13]

Fortunately for local economic and civil leaders, Leningrad continued to attract significant numbers of migrants well into the 1980s, with net annual increases through the 1960s and 1970s running mostly in the 20,000 to 40,000 range, so that the city's population has continued

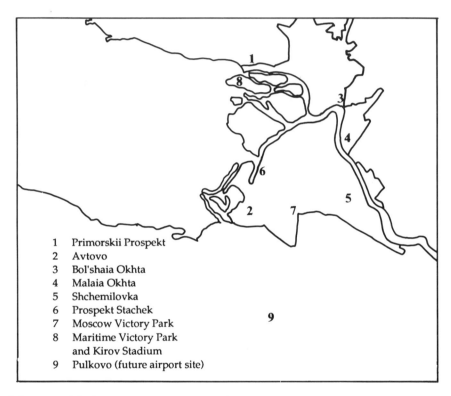

1 Primorskii Prospekt
2 Avtovo
3 Bol'shaia Okhta
4 Malaia Okhta
5 Shchemilovka
6 Prospekt Stachek
7 Moscow Victory Park
8 Maritime Victory Park
   and Kirov Stadium
9 Pulkovo (future airport site)

Map 10. *Major postwar construction projects.*

Figure 14. *Kirov Stadium.*

to grow at a rather robust pace.[14] This ability to attract migrants reflects in large measure a general transfer of population from the Soviet countryside to urban centers. Nationally, each year from 1951 to 1974, an average of 1.7 million people moved from country to city.[15] Until very recently, this national pattern was magnified in the Northwest Economic Region around Leningrad (see Map 1), where demographer Grigorii Vechkanov had found that 70 of 100 school-age residents in selected rural districts left home to pursue educational opportunities in towns and cities.[16] This large-scale out-migration from nearby rural areas may finally have come to an end during the 1980s, although more data are necessary to verify a trend.[17]

National or even regional trends do not suffice to explain the city's continued attractiveness to migrants. The city's migrant profile demonstrates several rather singular characteristics. In the late 1970s, for instance, much of the city's in-migration consisted of young people attracted by Leningrad's numerous and, by reputation, high-quality educational establishments.[18] By decade's end, over a quarter-million students from all over the USSR were enrolled in the city's institutions of higher learning.[19] The possibility that many students manage to stay in the city after graduation is suggested by available data on the skills and educational levels of the population. These data indicate that the number of specialists in Leningrad with higher or specialized secondary education doubled between 1965 and 1980 alone.[20] Moreover, the city's general level of educational achievement remained well above the national norm down through at least the 1970s.[21]

The Leningrad population's steady improvement in educational attainment may help compensate for the growing proportion who receive some form of pension or social insurance payment (nearly 25 percent, or 1,064,000 people, on January 1, 1982).[22] The city's elderly may form the core of a potential poverty problem since, nationally, a high correlation may be found between the number of pensioners and the number of residents below the official poverty level, which, during the mid-1970s, was set at a monthly per capita income of about 50 rubles.[23] The strain imposed by the large number of older dependents relative to the working population of Leningrad is apparent even in the limited summary data available on Soviet city budgets. In 1975, 0.8 percent of the average Soviet city budget went to social security payments,[24] whereas in Leningrad nearly 5 percent of the city budget was consumed by such obligations around that time.[25]

Another distinctive characteristic of Leningrad's migrant population has been that it now hails from nearly every economic region of the USSR.[26] Recent migratory data demonstrate that Moscow and Leningrad now stand alone among Soviet metropolitan centers in their sustained ability to attract new population from every corner of the Soviet Union. As the national capital, Moscow remains the single most important political, economic, educational, and cultural center for the country as a whole. In the case of Leningrad, the continued drawing power of the city's educational institutions undoubtedly explains the pattern to a considerable degree. In addition, major construction projects, such as the massive Gulf of Finland dam and flood control project, attract skilled labor from across the USSR.[27]

Ethnic Diversity

Whatever the motivation for moving to Leningrad, such continued migration has not substantially altered the Russians' overwhelming dominance of the town. Leningrad is a city where over 150,000 persons have the characteristically Russian last name Ivanov, over 300 are named Maria Krasovskaia, and over 200 are named Sergei Bobrov.[28] The city's urban diversity peaked as long ago as the time of the 1897 census, when there were over 60 ethnic groups represented in the city.[29] Still, migration throughout the postwar period has brought relatively large increases not only in the city's Russian population, but also especially in the Ukrainian, Belorussian, and Tatar populations (see Tables 2 and 3 and Map 1).

Large-scale Ukrainian and Belorussian migration to the city began over a century ago.[30] The emancipation of the serfs in 1861, combined

Table 2. *Nationality Composition of St. Petersburg Population, 1890–1910*

	1890[a]		1900[a]		1910[b]		% Change 1890–1910
Russian	791,000	(82.9%)	1,184,000	(82.2%)	1,568,000	(82.3%)	+98.2%
Jewish	15,400	(1.6%)	20,400	(1.4%)	35,100	(1.8%)	+127.9%
Ukrainian	5,000	(0.5%)	10,600	(0.7%)	17,000	(0.9%)	+240.0%
Belorussian	13,000	(1.4%)	42,000	(2.9%)	70,000	(3.7%)	+438.5%
Tatar	3,500	(0.4%)	5,800	(0.4%)	7,300	(0.4%)	+108.6%
Polish	27,300	(2.9%)	50,000	(3.5%)	65,000	(3.4%)	+138.1%
Other	98,800	(10.3%)	126,200	(8.9%)	143,200	(7.5%)	+44.9%
TOTAL	954,000	(100.0%)	1,439,000	(100.0%)	1,905,600	(100.0%)	+199.7%

[a]N. V. Iukhneva, *Etnicheskii sostav i etnosotsial'naia struktura naseleniia Peterburga* (Leningrad: Nauka—Leningradskoe otdelenie, 1984), 24.

[b]*Leningrad i Leningradskaia oblast' v tsifrakh: Statisticheskii sbornik* (Leningrad: Lenizdat, 1974), 19.

Table 3. *Nationality Composition of Leningrad Population, 1959–1979*

	1959[a]		1970[a]		1979[b]		% Change 1959–1979
Russian	2,968,300	(88.9%)	3,548,100	(89.0%)	4,098,000	(89.7%)	+38.1%
Jewish	168,700	(5.1%)	162,900	(4.1%)	143,000	(3.1%)	−15.2%
Ukrainian	68,700	(2.1%)	98,100	(2.5%)	117,000	(2.6%)	+70.3%
Belorussian	47,300	(1.4%)	64,600	(1.6%)	82,000	(1.8%)	+74.5%
Tatar	27,300	(0.8%)	33,100	(0.8%	39,000	(0.9%)	+43.4%
Polish	11,700	(0.3%)	10,900	(0.3%)	10,000	(0.2%)	−14.5%
Other	47,700	(1.4%)	69,100	(1.7%)	80,000	(1.7%)	+67.7%
TOTAL	3,339,700	(100.0%)	3,986,800	(100.0%)	4,569,000	(100.0%)	+36.8%

[a]*Leningrad i Leningradskaia oblast' v tsifrakh: Statisticheskii sbornik* (Leningrad: Lenizdat, 1974), 19.

[b]*Narodnoe khoziaistvo Leningrada i Leningradskoi oblasti v desiatoi piatiletke: Statisticheskii sbornik* (Leningrad: Lenizdat, 1981), 24–25.

with the country's burgeoning industrialization, encouraged peasants of both nationalities to move to the city. Between the 1869 and 1897 censuses, for example, St. Petersburg experienced a sharp decline in the absolute and relative numbers of migrants from the gentry of these and all other nationalities, and a concomitant increase in the absolute and relative numbers of peasant-migrants.[31] This trend was particularly pronounced among the Ukrainians and Belorussians.

Ukrainian migration to the city was relatively low throughout the late nineteenth century, in part because of the relative well-being of the Ukrainian countryside and in part because of the existence of alternative magnets—industrializing centers in the Ukraine such as the Donbas region.[32] During the twentieth century, and especially in more recent years, Leningrad's Ukrainian population began to grow more rapidly, so that by 1979 it had come to constitute the third largest ethnic group in the city behind the Russian and Jewish populations (see Table 3).

Belorussian migration to St. Petersburg/Leningrad has remained high ever since the emancipation of the serfs.[33] This pattern is a consequence of the relatively poor rural living standards in Belorussia, as well as the region's geographic proximity to the city. Prior to the Bolshevik Revolution, Roman Catholic peasant migrants from the Belorussian countryside were drawn to Polish cities, while their Orthodox brethren moved to St. Petersburg.[34]

Recent ethnographic research helps elucidate the underlying motivations for the continuing Tatar migration evident in Tables 2 and 3.[35] Tatars first arrived in the city during the late eighteenth century and, by the middle of the nineteenth, had become prominent in trade. The city continued to attract significant numbers of Tatar migrants throughout the Soviet period until the 1980s.[36] Today's Leningrad Tatars retain a strong ethnic identity across generational and educational barriers, as evidenced in widespread fluency in their native language and observance of traditional holidays. More than half migrated from rural areas, about a quarter from multiethnic cities, and the remainder from small towns scattered throughout the Tatar ASSR along the Volga River (see Map 1).[37]

The conspicuous decline over time in the local Jewish and Polish populations reverses historic trends and can be attributed in large part to the idiosyncratic status of both national groups in the contemporary Soviet scene. Their status reflects both national and international influences rather than purely local ethnic impulses and tendencies. For example, Jewish migration during the nineteenth century was adversely affected by laws and regulations governing Jewish settlement. Consequently, the largest migration of Jews to the city came during the early Soviet period, when such restrictions were removed.[38] The decline of the city's Jewish population more recently reflects local discriminatory practices that have prompted many Jews to leave Leningrad for Moscow, Israel, or the United States. A different pattern holds for the Poles, many of whom chose to return to their homeland following the establishment of an independent Poland at the close of World War I.[39]

Economic Change

The sweeping social changes just chronicled have been reflected in and are a consequence of significant economic transformations that have been taking place in Leningrad since the lifting of the blockade in 1944. To appreciate the extent of these trends, it is important to recall that St. Petersburg long served as an industrial center of considerable significance. Despite several distinct disadvantages—the city's location on the outer edges of Russia and Europe, its adverse climate, its lack of ready access to natural resources and to markets, and so on—in its early days the capital soon developed a small, primarily state-supported industrial base oriented toward the needs of the local economy and those of the emperor's army and navy.

By the late nineteenth century, the city had emerged as the focal point of one of the more powerful industrial regions in Europe. Until the Bolshevik Revolution, however, the city's industrial base continued its dependency on foreign and state capital markets, as well as on imported raw materials and finished manufactured goods brought in through its expanding port. As Steven Smith has suggested, by the outbreak of World War I, the city had come to represent a unique island of technologically sophisticated state-supported industrial production.[40] Unlike the more diversified industrial base in Moscow, St. Petersburg's industry remained heavily concentrated on such state-dependent large-scale industries as metalworking and chemical production.[41] Consequently, the city never came to hold overall sway in the Russian national market the way Moscow would.

St. Petersburg ultimately failed to retain national economic preeminence for numerous complicated reasons beyond the scope of this particular study. Certainly, the transfer of political power from the city in 1918 guaranteed Moscow's dominant position for the remainder of this century. However, other factors contributed to Moscow's relative economic power, even before the Bolsheviks moved their government. For example, by the late years of the nineteenth century it had already become apparent that St. Petersburg would not develop into an "import-replacing" city.[42] This failure was expressed in the city's historic and continuing inability to create an exuberant and productive city-region. Such areas manifest intense and diverse rural, industrial, and commercial activity tied together by the import-replacing city's overwhelming economic energy.[43] This all-encompassing dynamism can exist only when a city replaces its imports with internally produced products—a feat never accomplished on a sufficiently large scale to secure St. Petersburg/Leningrad's economic power over Moscow.

Initially, St. Petersburg's continued dependence on imported goods helped the capital emerge as a major transportation center, despite its peripheral location. By 1851, Russia's first major railroad connected the capital's port to Moscow, and the next year, 38 percent (by value) of all Russian foreign trade passed through St. Petersburg (representing five times the value of foreign goods passing through the second largest port—Riga).[44] This preeminence was challenged as early as the century's end, once new rail lines linked Moscow and Odessa, Moscow and Riga, and eventually Moscow and Warsaw (and through Warsaw, directly with the heart of Europe). These developments emphasized St. Petersburg's numerous geographic limitations.[45]

Over the years of Soviet rule, Leningrad political elites and economic and urban planners have developed four distinct strategies to overcome economic and geographic liabilities:

1. *Political laissez-faire.* Reliance on political patronage ties to secure economic resources within the context of a decentralized, mixed state-private economy (1917–1926).
2. *Skilled diversification.* Reliance on a skilled labor force, an extensive heavy and defense-related industrial base, and a major light-industrial capacity to fuel economic expansion (1926–1945).
3. *Consumer-oriented internationalism.* Reliance on expanded consumer goods production, extensive trade with the West, and a disproportionate claim to postwar reconstruction funds to lead economic recovery (1945–1948).
4. *Skilled specialization.* Reliance on a skilled labor force, an increasingly specialized heavy and defense-related industrial base, and, especially since 1951, a leading scientific infrastructure combined with a reduction in light industrial capacity to sustain economic growth (1951–present).

The fourth and most recent strategy—skilled specialization—has significantly altered the contour of the city's economy to the point where a new Leningrad economic structure may be said to have emerged over approximately the past three to four decades. The focus of this study is principally on this new Leningrad as a special case of Soviet regional management. Before discussing the fourth strategy in greater detail, however, we should briefly review its predecessors.

The initial response (1917–1926) to the city's precipitous decline during the Civil War was largely political. The city's Communist Party organization remained subjugated to the whim of Comintern Chairman Grigorii Zinov'ev. Zinov'ev, who succeeded Leon Trotsky as Petrograd city soviet chairman in 1917, attempted to use his Petrograd post and power base to challenge Joseph Stalin for party leadership during the mid-1920s.[46] By 1926 Zinov'ev had lost that quest, as Stalin had members of Zinov'ev's "Left" opposition expelled from major party positions. Control over the Leningrad party organization quickly passed to a new regional party first secretary, Sergei Kirov.

Before being removed from his Leningrad posts, Zinov'ev had paid far greater attention to the care and maintenance of a loyal political machine than to the city's economic recovery. In short, his strategy, as well as that of his planners and managers, appears to have been simply not to develop a coherent response to the threat of permanent economic decline. Although Petrograd/Leningrad slowly managed to regain its population and economic base throughout the early and mid-1920s, the lack of a sustained program of economic development severely limited the scope and durability of that recovery.

Both Kirov and, following his assassination on December 1, 1934, Andrei Zhdanov, his successor as regional party first secretary, tried to build on their city's historic economic strengths (a skilled labor force, an extensive heavy and defense-related industrial base, and a major light-industrial capacity). This second Leningrad development strategy of the Soviet period (1926–1945), which conformed closely to that of the national five-year plans, catapulted the local economy into preeminence in numerous areas of highly sophisticated industrial production. By the eve of World War II, the city had reemerged as the Soviet Union's leading center for industrial innovation.[47]

The third approach to economic development proclaimed by the city's postwar leadership proved short-lived (1945–1948), quickly becoming entangled in some of the most bitter and destructive political struggles of Soviet history.[48] Leningrad elites of the period were outspoken proponents of major policy positions that subsequently failed to gain Stalin's endorsement.[49] For example, as early as June 1945, Aleksei Kuznetsov (who had replaced Zhdanov as Leningrad regional party first secretary earlier that year) argued before a joint session of the Leningrad regional and city party committees that the Communist Party should assume full responsibility for guaranteeing "normal relaxation," now that the war was over.[50] Kuznetsov repeated this theme in an address launching the 1946 Supreme Soviet campaign in Leningrad,[51] as did Zhdanov (who was now a member of the national Central Committee Secretariat in Moscow) in a remarkable address to the residents of Leningrad's Volodarskii Election District during that same campaign.[52]

While other national leaders of the period typically ignored local concerns in their election speeches,[53] Zhdanov relied heavily on his wartime experiences in the city to advocate policies designed to improve the quality of life of Leningrad citizens. The new Leningrad economy, Zhdanov argued, would be based on consumer-goods production, extensive trade with the West, and a disproportionate claim to postwar reconstruction funds. He thus linked Leningrad's resurgence to particularly volatile leadership struggles in Moscow over the Soviet Union's peacetime relations with wartime allies and, ultimately, to his own fate.

Following Zhdanov's death in August 1948, his major rivals, Georgii Malenkov and Lavrentii Beria, set in motion a large-scale purge of Zhdanov protégés in Leningrad and elsewhere. Numerous Leningraders holding national posts together with nearly all senior city and regional officials were removed from their positions, never to be seen again, in what has become known as the Leningrad Affair.[54] Beyond Leningrad, in Gorky (previously Nizhnii Novgorod), where Zhdanov had served prior to his arrival in Leningrad, numbers of leading Communists also fell victim to the "provocative Leningrad Affair, fabricated by Malenkov."[55]

The conventional explanation of the affair interprets the events of 1948 and 1949 as a consequence of Zhdanov's protracted struggle for power with Malenkov. Robert Conquest, for example, observes that the one uncontestable outcome was for Zhdanov's men to be replaced by Malenkov's.[56] The few Soviet accounts of the Leningrad purges that have thus far come to light—including Mikhail Gorbachev's mention of these events in his address commemorating the seventieth anniversary of the Bolshevik Revolution—are not strikingly different from that offered by Conquest.[57]

Recently, Western analysts have identified policy issues within the personal struggles of the period. Werner Hahn identifies multiple and linked areas of policy concern that might underlie the purges of 1948 and 1949: the nature of Soviet relations with the West, the possibility of reorientation of the postwar Soviet economy toward consumer industries, and the distribution of a majority of reconstruction funds to "front-line" regions such as Leningrad (as opposed to "home-front" areas to the east).[58] The precise role that any one of these issues played in the Leningrad Affair is likely to remain uncertain. Nevertheless, one should note that Leningraders' ultimately unsuccessful plans for a postwar reorientation of their region's economy were tied to improved relations with the West, a reorientation of the economy toward consumer-goods production, and a disproportionate claim to postwar reconstruction funds. In this respect, Leningrad's resurgence became inexorably linked to Moscow's leadership struggles in a particularly explosive fusion of local and national politics. This blend ultimately proved the undoing not only of several senior Leningrad political officials and scores of their protégés, but also of their strategy of economic revitalization through the expansion of consumer industries and international trade.

Following the extensive purges of Zhdanov associates during 1948 and 1949, local leaders, together with their partners and sponsors in Moscow, returned to the basic strategy of the 1930s, but with several important variations. In many ways, this fourth approach (1951–present) was merely a modification of the growth strategy of the prewar five-year-plan periods, relying on heavy-industrial production and technological innovation. Nonetheless, the current strategy varied from its predecessors in being predicated on economic specialization rather than diversification. Moreover, since the Fifth Five-Year Plan (1951–1955), the strategies have relied more explicitly on the interaction of science and industry than in the past. This fourth approach to Leningrad's economic development—the focus of the policy studies to follow—remained in force from the 1950s through the 1970s and was incorporated into the Leningrad general plan for 1986–2005.[59]

Its durability suggests that we must assume this latest approach to economic development has in fact come to represent an accepted official view of Leningrad's role in the national Soviet economy. Although it would be misleading to identify this most recent Leningrad growth strategy with any single official, we can turn to the pronouncements of two Leningrad regional party first secretaries—Frol Kozlov, who held the post from 1953 until 1957, and Grigorii Romanov, the incumbent from 1970 until 1983—for comprehensive recitations of this latest strategy for the city's economic development. While this rhetorical device allows us to examine the period under consideration by focusing on two end points, it should in no way be taken to mean that Kozlov and Romanov monopolized leadership during the past three and a half decades. Regional party first secretaries Ivan Spiridonov (1957–1962), Vasili Tolstikov (1962–1970), Lev Zaikov (1983–1985), and Iurii Solov'ev (1985–1989), as well as scores of other local and national political leaders, have also played critically important roles in developing this present-day regional economic strategy.

Kozlov's Development Strategy

Throughout the 1950s, Frol' Kozlov, initially as city party first secretary, then as regional party second and first secretary, and later as first deputy prime minister of the USSR, vigorously advocated the reorientation of the Leningrad economy around technologically specialized industrial production. This orientation conformed with his views on the national economy; in fact, some Western analysts see Kozlov as having led coalitions opposing Khrushchev's plans to shift national resources from industry to agriculture and light-industrial production.[60] In addition to an emphasis on heavy-industrial production, Kozlov argued that, given Leningrad's extensive scientific research community and its famous industrial plant, the city could come to serve very specific functions within the overall Soviet economy: those of innovator, producer of high-quality industrial goods, and leader in precision-instrument making.[61] To Kozlov's mind, such a growth strategy would necessitate a phasing out of the city's light-industrial capacity—a goal quite at variance with the strategy of industrial diversity followed by previous Leningrad leaders.

Jumping ahead to the period of Grigorii Romanov's tenure as regional party first secretary, we find remarkably few changes in the rhetoric of Leningrad economic development.[62] More importantly, that strategy had come to fruition (in large part because of the specific policies examined later in this volume). The realization of this growth strategy, as seen in the growing dominance of machine and metal industries, and the accompanying decline in chemicals and petrochemicals, forestry, construction material, food processing, and other light industries, is a direct consequence of industrial investment policies.[63] The achievement of this pattern must be considered all the more striking when compared to trends in the Moscow and national Soviet economies and when taking into account the demographic trends described earlier, most of which inhibit the expansion of the workforce available for service in heavy industry (see Table 4).

Meanwhile, the role of science and related services in the Leningrad economy has expanded. By the 1970s, scientific and related institutions represented the city's second largest employer, behind industry.[64] The city's scientific research establishments and institutions of higher learning employed almost one fifth of the Leningrad workforce, and the city was second only to Moscow in the number of scientific workers employed in the local economy.[65] In 1982, one in 11 Soviet scientists worked in Leningrad, and a much higher share of the country's skilled specialists were to be found there.[66]

The close interaction between the city's enormous scientific community and its powerful industrial base is apparent in an emphasis on applied rather than basic research—an emphasis reflected in the distribution of Leningrad scientific workers by discipline during the 1970s.[67] Leningrad party leaders are quick to point out that the mission of the newly constituted Leningrad Scientific Center of the USSR Academy of Sciences, which was established in March 1983 by bringing together under a single institutional umbrella preexisting academy research institutes, was to improve the coordination of basic and fundamental research on the one hand and industrial activity on the other.[68]

The increasingly close coordination of Leningrad's scientific and industrial organizations pushed the city ahead of all other Soviet industrial centers in various measures of technological innovation. According to Leonid Bliakhman of Leningrad's Institute of Socioeconomic Problems, during the mid-1970s the city led the Soviet Union on a per capita basis in the annual economic impact of the introduction of new technologies into production, the number of new types of machines

Table 4. *Relative Distribution of Leningrad, Moscow, and USSR Industrial Capacity by Sector Based on Value of Production, 1965–1980*

Sector	1965 Leningrad[a]	Moscow[b]	USSR[c]	1970 Leningrad[a]	Moscow[b]	USSR[c]
Electricity and energy	1.2%	—	14.9%	1.2%	19.1%	17.4%
Chemical and petrochemical	8.4	—	8.3	7.3	4.4	8.9
Machine building and metalworking	32.2	—	19.0	36.1	42.5	20.0
Forestry, woodworking, and paper processing	3.4	—	5.6	3.2	2.6	5.1
Construction materials	2.7	—	6.1	2.9	6.0	5.7
Light industry	26.3	—	4.4	23.8	6.3	4.6
Food industry	20.9	—	8.2	19.1	5.3	7.5
Other	4.9	—	33.5	6.4	13.8	30.8
TOTAL	100.0%	100.0%	100.0%	100.0%	100.0%	100.0%

Sector	1975 Leningrad[a]	Moscow[b]	USSR[c]	1980 Leningrad[a]	Moscow[b]	USSR[c]
Electricity and energy	1.0%	20.5%	16.8%	1.1%	20.5%	15.9%
Chemical and petrochemical	6.6	3.7	9.4	5.7	3.1	9.9
Machine building and metalworking	40.8	47.9	21.5	48.3	48.6	23.7
Forestry, woodworking, and paper processing	2.9	2.0	4.8	2.5	1.8	4.5
Construction materials	2.7	4.8	5.8	2.3	4.1	5.3
Light industry	21.1	5.8	4.4	18.7	5.5	4.2
Food industry	17.2	5.5	7.5	14.3	5.8	6.9
Other	7.7	9.8	29.8	7.1	10.6	29.6
TOTAL	100.0%	100.0%	100.0%	100.0%	100.0%	100.0%

[a]*Narodnoe khoziaistvo Leningrada i Leningradskoi oblasti v desiatoi piatiletke: Statisticheskii sbornik* (Leningrad: Lenizdat, 1981), 41–42.

[b]*Moskva v tsifrakh (1985): Statisticheskii ezhegodnik* (Moscow: Finansy i statistika, 1985), 74.

[c]*Narodnoe khoziaistvo SSSR v 1980g.: Statisticheskii ezhegodnik* (Moscow: Finansy i statistika, 1981), 145.

generated annually, and the number of newly automated production lines.[69] By the early 1980s, 9 percent of all new Soviet production technologies were being developed in Leningrad.[70] These innovations may help explain how Leningrad plants produced 10 percent of all export machinery, 52 percent of all turbines, 52 percent of all generators and 26 percent of all printing facilities, even though the city's economy constitutes but 3 percent of the Soviet Union's total national industrial capacity.[71]

The implementation of this economic development strategy contributed to the transformation of the city's industrial profile and the emergence of linkages and cooperation among local industrial and scientific organizations. In the short term, this strategy has been a success, as the city has achieved respectable rates of economic growth.[72] We should note further that such growth has occurred in part because Leningrad's dominant economic sectors (machine construction, shipbuilding, and other heavy industries) are precisely the sectors that have expanded the most throughout the Soviet Union during the past 30 years.[73] In this sense, then, the strategy may represent nothing more than the effective local implementation of national priorities. Whichever came first, the Leningrad approach or the national goals, it is clear that Leningrad benefited from central investment and growth patterns.

Spatial Consequences

These sweeping social and economic changes of the postwar period proved to have significant consequences for the physical organization of the city and its metropolitan region long before the 1947 general plan could be revised. For example, the city's sustained ability to attract migrants, noted earlier, combined with a massive housing construction effort to meet the needs of those migrants to produce extensive urban sprawl. In 1951, an average of 3.3 families lived in *each* Leningrad apartment.[74] Beginning in the mid-1950s, Leningrad construction trusts, in accord with Khrushchev's housing program, began expanding the city's housing stock at an ever-accelerating rate.[75] During most of the 1970s, for example, the average per capita living space available in Leningrad grew at a rate exceeding that of other major Soviet urban centers.[76] Despite a slowdown later in the decade, it is obvious that the city has begun to approach the national average of 80 percent of all families living in their own apartments (see Figures 15 and 16).[77] At the end of 1979, for instance, a Leningrad family of four would occupy, on the average, 684.4 square feet of living space—the size of a moderate one-bedroom apartment in New York. While many North Americans or West Europeans would probably consider this inade-

Figure 15. *Apartment buildings along Nevskii Prospekt.*

Figure 16. *Apartment buildings seen from the Moika River Canal with the Pevchevskii Bridge in the foreground.*

Table 5. *Increase in Leningrad Housing Stock by District, 1955–1980*

District[a]	1955–1966[b]	1970–1973[c]	1976–1980[d]
Central Districts	15.6%	5.1%	0.8%
Middle Districts	47.7%	42.2%	35.6%
Outer Districts	36.7%	52.7%	63.6%
TOTAL	100.0%	100.0%	100.0%

[a]Delineation of Central Districts (Vasileostrovskii, Dzerzhinskii, Kuibyshevskii, Leninskii, Oktiabr'skii, Petrogradskii, and Smol'ninskii); Middle Districts (Kirovskii, Moskovskii, Nevskii, and Frunzenskii); and Outer Districts (Vyborgskii, Krasnogvardeiskii, Krasnosel'skii, Zhdanovskii, and Kalininskii) is based on the district classification developed by V. M. Khodachek and V. G. Alekseev, in *Kompleksnoe razvitie gorodskikh raionov: Kompleksnyi plan ekonomicheskogo i sotsial'nogo razvitiia v deistvii* (Leningrad: Lenizdat, 1980), 14–16.

[b]*Narodnoe khoziaistvo goroda Leningrada: Statisticheskii sbornik* (Moscow: Gosudarstvennoe statisticheskoe izdatel'stvo, 1957), 148–149; *Leningrad za 50 let: Statisticheskii sbornik* (Leningrad: Lenizdat, 1967), 141–159.

[c]*Leningrad i Leningradskaia oblast' v tsifrakh: Statisticheskii sbornik* (Leningrad: Lenizdat, 1974), 145.

[d]*Narodnoe khoziaistvo Leningrada i Leningradskoi oblasti v desiatoi piatiletke: Statisticheskii sbornik* (Leningrad: Lenizdat, 1981), 95.

quate, it represents an enormous improvement over the dreadful housing conditions of 1951.

Such achievements have not come without cost to the urban environment. In search of land for their gargantuan housing projects, local planners quickly turned to vacant sites beyond the city's boundaries. As the years have passed, successive layers of housing superblocks have built up, much as polyps build their coral reefs (see Table 5; Maps 8 and 10; and Figures 17–19). The city of Leningrad swelled from 323.4 square kilometers in 1957 to 570 in 1974.[78] This prodigious spatial growth transformed what had remained for many inhabitants a cozy nineteenth-century walking city of just 105.4 square kilometers in 1917 into a massive metropolitan agglomeration extending over 1,359 square kilometers in all by 1980.[79]

Unlike much of the urban sprawl in the West, local planners have relied extensively on subway-based mass transportation, rather than on the private automobile. This growth strategy inhibited the emergence of an efficient and flexible regionwide service, commercial, and cultural infrastructure. Except for Moscow and the largest cities of the People's Republic of China, no other urban center of comparable size has experienced such immense territorial expansion without reliance on the private automobile. If the historic central city could be traversed on foot, the new Leningrad of the late twentieth century must be crossed by wearisome bus, streetcar, and subway rides (see Figures 20 and 21).

Figure 17. *View of housing superblock on Vasil'evskii Island.*

Figure 18. *Minidistrict.*

Figure 19. *Small Avenue on Vasil'evskii Island. Examples of the old and new styles.*

Figure 20. *Pedestrians in front of the old Singer building, now the House of Books.*

Figure 21. *Streetcar on Middle Avenue on Vasil'evskii Island.*

And traversed it must be, for housing and population have both moved outward (see Table 6). Fleeing decrepit communal apartments downtown, both residents and recent arrivals from the countryside have filled the massive new districts ringing the former city center. As a result, the city's center increasingly is becoming a home to students and pensioners—two groups requiring less personal space—while the typical Soviet family of three (parents and a single child) are relocating further and further out (see Table 7). This trend has placed considerable pressure on the service infrastructure of Leningrad's new districts.

Industrialized Construction and Superblocks

Once one moves beyond the city's historic center into these massive new neighborhoods, Leningrad becomes a far less special—and more typically "Soviet"—city. Quite early on, postwar municipal leaders created several new institutions to streamline and improve the planning and the design of these new districts, in accord with Baranov's 1947 general plan.[80] They also sought to speed up the construction cycle. In 1955, for example, the Main Leningrad Construction Administration (Glavleningradstroi) commenced operations, with the Main Leningrad Construction Materials Administration (Glavlenstroimaterialy) following suit a year later.[81] These bodies are the Leningrad offices of the State Committee on Construction and the State Committee

Table 6. *Leningrad's Population by District, 1959–1980*

District[a]	1959[b]	1966[b]	1980[c]
Central Districts	50.7%	52.7%	26.3%
Middle Districts	28.2%	25.8%	37.7%
Outer Districts	21.1%	21.5%	36.0%
TOTAL	100.0%	100.0%	100.0%

[a]Delineation of Central Districts (Vasileostrovskii, Dzerzhinskii, Kuibyshevskii, Leninskii, Oktiabr'skii, Petrogradskii, and Smol'ninskii); Middle Districts (Kirovskii, Moskovskii, Nevskii, and Frunzenskii); and Outer Districts (Vyborgskii, Krasnogvardeiskii, Krasnosel'skii, Zhdanovskii, and Kalininskii) is based on the district classification developed by V. M. Khodachek and V. G. Alekseev, in *Kompleksnoe razvitie gorodskikh raionov: Kompleksnyi plan ekonomicheskogo i sotsial'nogo razvitiia v deistvii* (Leningrad: Lenizdat, 1980), 14–16.

[b]*Leningrad za 50 let: Statisticheskii sbornik* (Leningrad: Lenizdat, 1967), 23.

[c]Khodachek and Alekseev, *Kompleksnoe razvitie gorodskikh raionov*, 11.

Table 7. *Population Age Structure of Leningrad's Urban Zones, 1979*

District	Children[a]	Working Age[b]	Pension Age[c]
Center[d]	15.6%	58.7%	25.7%
Middle industrial belt[e]	16.4%	63.1%	20.5%
Outer new districts[f]	18.9%	64.3%	16.8%

SOURCE: G. F. Ivanova and O. M. Pakhomova, "Vlianie demograficheskikh faktorov na normirovanie kul'turno-bytovogo obsluzhivaniia naseleniia Leningrade," in A. P. Borisov, N. M. Sutyrin, eds., *Ekonomika i upravlenie sotsialisticheskim proizvodstvom* (Leningrad: Leningradskii inzhenerno-ekonomicheskii institut, 1983), 48–54; Table 2, pp. 50–51.

[a]Aged 15 and younger.
[b]Women aged 16–54, men 16–59.
[c]Women aged 55 and over, men 60 and over.
[d]The historic nineteenth-century city.
[e]Primarily to the south of the center.
[f]Primarily districts built after 960.

on Construction Materials, two agencies of the USSR and the 15 union republic councils of ministers charged with responsibility for directing the construction industry throughout the nation. In Leningrad, the trusts operate within departments and main administrations of the Leningrad city soviet. They are among the largest administrative agencies of the city soviet, with the Main Leningrad Construction Administration, for example, operating nearly two dozen smaller construction

Figure 22. *Example of the new minidistrict.*

firms. One such firm, the first Housing Construction Combinant (DSK no. 1) opened for business during the 1950s.[82] In short, Glavleningradstroi and Glavlenstroimaterialy are the Leningrad construction industry.

Leningrad quickly emerged as a pioneer in large-scale industrialized construction methods. The Soviet Union launched the world's most ambitious housing construction program after a July 1957 party and state decree on the further development of housing construction.[83] This effort relied on the introduction of assembly-line production of prefabricated building units. This so-called block-section construction technique, now used throughout the Soviet Union, was largely developed and perfected in Leningrad during the late 1950s and early 1960s.[84]

Widespread utilization of the block-section method produced a network of instant neighborhoods as enormous housing projects sprang up in a matter of months. These superblocks or minidistricts (*mikroraion*) became inexorably linked to the introduction of new construction technology.[85] The minidistrict—a planning rather than a political unit—can be traced to the European modernist tradition (see Figure 22). It represents an effort by the architects and planners involved to create safe and attractive residential districts by removing all basic neighborhood functions from the street, streets being viewed as dangerous, chaotic, and generally inhospitable environments. Urban designers therefore anticipated that developing social amenities in self-contained communities would make such services more convenient and accessible to larger numbers of citizens.[86] In the Soviet Union the concept evolved considerably, so that a complex doctrine concerning the minidistrict had emerged by the 1970s.[87]

Leningrad architects now generally view the minidistrict as an extension of the Petersburg tradition of grand ensembles. Few casual observers can distinguish Leningrad's standard new minidistricts from those found in Moscow and in such typical provincial cities as Sverdlovsk in the Urals and Vladivostok on the Pacific coast. A handful of experimental minidistricts that are spread throughout the city's new developments undeniably benefit from greater concern for aesthetics than do the typical residential districts in other Soviet communities.[88] Nonetheless, the emergence of industrialized construction techniques, the commitment to mass-scale housing, and the rigid control of construction agencies have generally produced mile upon mile of low-grade and unimaginative structures, both in Leningrad and elsewhere in the Soviet Union.

The 1966 General Plan

By the early 1960s many municipal officers saw that Baranov's 1947 plan had outgrown its usefulness. A new and more comprehensive plan was now needed for the effective management of the city's continuing development and growth, especially in the new minidistricts being built by a technology that did not exist when Baranov's plan took effect.[89] Moreover, the Soviet architectural community was slowly emerging from its Stalinist isolation. In 1958 the World Congress of Architects met in Moscow, and in 1960 the All-Union Conference on City Planning convened the first gathering of its kind in years.[90] These meetings mark the initiation of the post-Stalinist thaw in architecture and planning, a thaw that came just as work began on a new 25-year general plan for Leningrad's development that was to take effect in 1966.[91]

In 1966 the USSR Supreme Soviet enacted the General Plan of Development of Leningrad and the Leningrad Suburban Zone, in accordance with a draft prepared over a seven-year period by Leningrad city planning agencies—especially the Main Architectural Planning Administration—and endorsed by the Leningrad city and regional soviets and party committees.[92] The city soviet's Main Architectural Planning Administration was established to formulate not only the general plan for the city, but also various thematic and district plans that elaborate future construction in the city for up to 30 years. A parallel institution to Glavleningradstoi, the city soviet agency responsible for construction activities, the Main Planning Administration submits draft plans for review and approval by the city soviet. At various points in Leningrad history, there has also been an office of the chief architect subordinate to the Main Architectural Planning Administration. At present, the position of chief architect is distinct from the main administration, reporting in parallel fashion directly to the city soviet's executive committee. While the chief architect is responsible for the city's architectural integrity, the Main Architectural Planning Administration has assumed full authority over the preparation of the increasingly multipurpose general plan.

Once approved at the city level, a draft general plan must then be approved by the Leningrad regional soviet and passed as a state law by the USSR Supreme Soviet. As will become apparent in our discussion of the 1986 general plan, changes may be introduced at any stage prior to the plan's enactment as law. This review process is complicated by party oversight at every stage. Although party agencies do not have formal legislative authority, no draft general plan will be ratified by a soviet until the parallel party committee has approved it. Each review prolongs the planning process—helping to explain why it took seven years to prepare the 1966 general plan. None of these reviews are public, however, as the actual plan document is classified as secret for reasons of national security.

Once completed, the 1966 plan provided a general urban orientation to coordinate and provide direction for future regional components of national economic and technical plans—the five-year plans—during the next quarter century. Put forward and implemented under the direction of the city's chief architect, Valentin Kamenskii, the document drew explicitly on the city's planning and architectural traditions.[93] The existing historic city center was as much of a model for this new projection of Leningrad's future as were central decrees emanating from Moscow.

Seeking to create a more salubrious urban environment, the creators of the 1966 general plan shifted the focus of construction toward the Gulf of Finland. Thus, the low-lying areas near the coastline were to become the city's focal point. As noted earlier, this "movement to the sea" had first been proposed in the 1940s by Nikolai Baranov. It required the elevation of the low-lying areas by extensive landfill and flood control projects, as well as the construction of massive housing projects on reclaimed land at the western tip of Vasil'evskii Island and in the southwest.[94] The plan also provided for the development of major recreational facilities to the northwest along the Gulf of Finland. Such movement to the north and west became acceptable from a strategic point of view once the international boundary with Finland had been shifted from 22 miles away from the city to over 100 miles distant as a consequence of the Soviet victories in the 1939–1940 Winter War and World War II. More detailed plans for the city's 16 districts were developed to further refine general planning objectives (see Map 11).

The 1966 plan enumerated eight primary objectives that deserve special attention:[95]

1. Limitation of population and territorial expansion
2. Movement to the sea
3. Creation of new districts
4. Historic preservation
5. Improvement of intraurban transportation and communications
6. Development of the city's scientific traditions
7. Improvement of transportation approaches to the city
8. Satellite cities, greenbelts, and regional planning

Limitation of Population and Territorial Expansion

The chief goals of all Leningrad plans throughout the Soviet period have included the limitation of population growth, reduction of population densities, and minimization of built-up territories.[96] Despite repeated failures on each of these fronts, the 1966 general plan continued to restate population targets that had already been overtaken or would soon be. Under the provisions of the plan, municipal officials were to limit the city's population to 3.5 million residents by 1990. Gosplan, the State Planning Committee in Moscow, also projected a ceiling of some 4 million persons tied in one way or another to the city's economy. By 1970, these figures were already surpassed.[97]

During preliminary discussions of the plan, as early as 1960, Valentin Kamenskii had identified the need to limit urban sprawl by concentrating territorial development in a few areas.[98] Provisions to implement Kamenskii's proposals found their way into the 1966 general plan. Accordingly, city officials were to contain the area of urban development within 200 square miles, of which 185 were to be in use by 1990 (as opposed to 107 square miles in 1966).[99] Moreover, the city's population was to be distributed more evenly throughout Leningrad, with inner-city districts losing population to outlying regions. To a considerable degree, this last plan projection has been fulfilled.

Movement to the Sea

By the mid-1960s, Aleksandr Naumov had endorsed various proposals to redirect Leningrad's development in the direction of the Gulf of Finland.[100] Nikolai Baranov supported Naumov's efforts, characterizing this attempt "to reorient the city and to turn it into a real maritime city" as one of the most successful elements of the new general plan.[101] In its final form, the 1966 plan provided for the widespread develop-

Key to Districts

1	Zhdanovski	9	Kirovskii
2	Vyborgskii	10	Leninskii
3	Kalininskii	11	Oktiabr'skii
4	Krasnogvardeiskii	12	Kuibyshevskii
5	Nevskii	13	Dzerzhinskii
6	Frunzenski	14	Petrogradskii
7	Moskovskii	15	Vasileostrovskii
8	Krasnosel'skii	16	Smol'ninskii

Map 11. *Districts (raiony) of the city of Leningrad.*

ment of the regional shoreline—especially of the gulf's north shore—for recreational use.[102] This vision was based on extensive analysis of the region's geological conditions:[103]

1. The shoreline areas would have to be elevated, with bogs and swamps being drained in the northwest and southwest.
2. The best site for a new airport was to the city's south, a location that would limit population expansion in that direction.
3. The best lands for agricultural production were to the north, northeast, and southeast.
4. Urban development would have to be limited to landfill areas in previously undeveloped lands of the Neva floodplain.

On the basis of such surveys, the planners suggested that a combination of landfill and flood control—including the construction of the aforementioned dam across the gulf from Lomonosov through Kronstadt to Gorskaia—could prevent major flooding (see Map 12).[104] Accordingly, specific construction plans were developed for high-density experimental housing districts on the west end of Vasil'evskii and Dekabristov islands and along the Neva to Rybatskoe and the gulf north to Ol'gino.[105]

Creation of New Districts

Increasing population, combined with a policy of reduced population densities, created pressures for the rapid development of new housing stock in outlying areas. The 1966 general plan projected the construction of scores of new minidistricts with up-to-date cultural, economic, and educational amenities. Forty-five percent of all new housing was charted for areas north of the city, and 50 percent to the south, with the remaining 5 percent to be built in the existing city (primarily on Vasil'evskii and Dekabristov islands).[106] These apartment buildings were to be constructed in accordance with the most recent industrialized techniques in districts located in a circle around the historic city center. During the plan's first eight years 393,000 apartment units were completed and made available to 1.25 million residents.[107] But, as will be discussed later, local architects have criticized such massive construction efforts as lacking aesthetic standards.

Historic Preservation

The 1966 general plan emphasized preservation of the traditional city center as the focal point of Leningrad life. It acknowledged the need to preserve and to cultivate a townscape formed by "generations of Russian artists" into "one of the most beautiful cities in the world."[108] Historical preservation efforts were to extend to "Lenin

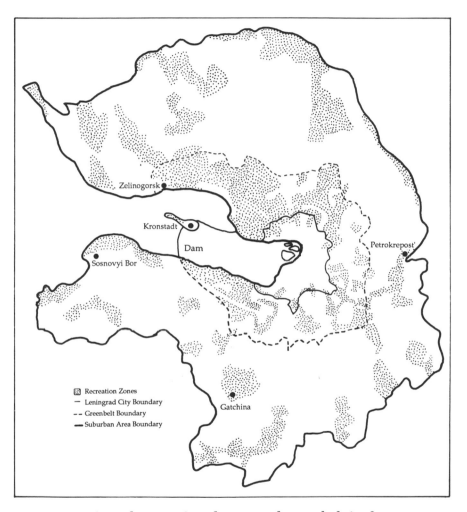

Map 12. *Projected recreational zone and greenbelt in the 1966 general plan, showing the Gulf of Finland dam.*

Places," a decision that brought large swaths of the nineteenth-century cityscape under protective measures.[109] The plan also provided for major restoration efforts at satellite palaces and parks in Pushkin, Pavlovsk, Petrodvorets, Lomonosov, and Gatchina.[110] Such concerns would become more pronounced as time passed, with entire proletarian districts from the end of the late nineteenth century coming under preservation scrutiny by the late 1980s.[111]

Improvement of Intraurban Transportation and Communications

The combined emphasis on constructing new districts and maintaining the historic city center necessitated an extensive transportation improvement program. Indeed, transportation problems have emerged as perhaps the most troublesome feature of contemporary Leningrad. Residents have moved away from the central city, but major employment sites, commercial and city services, and tourist attractions are still concentrated in the historic central core. By the early 1980s, one quarter of the pedestrians along the city's main commercial axis—Nevskii Prospekt—were visitors from out of town.[112] Moreover, approximately half of the population of the city's surrounding suburbs worked in the city center.[113] All these nonresidents of the city must rely on public transportation to move about Leningrad's major urbanized areas.

From 1950 until the early 1970s, the number of passengers using the city's public transportation system doubled, the duration of an average trip increasing to approximately 30 minutes.[114] Much of this expansion occurred after the city's subway system opened in 1955, which had a substantial impact on transportation ridership patterns throughout the Leningrad region.[115]

The 1966 general plan provided for an increase in subway and private auto use and projected declining ridership on other transportation systems.[116] Consequently, the plan recommended extensive subway and highway construction programs, as well as development of improved services for the burgeoning Soviet automobile ownership. Despite these efforts, however, highways and auto service facilities have not kept pace with auto ownership.

Development of the City's Scientific Tradition

Although Leningrad's position declined after the transfer of the headquarters of the Academy of Sciences to Moscow in 1934, the city is still a vital scientific center. The 1966 general plan called for further exploitation of such scientific resources.[117] The importance of the local scientific community for Leningrad's economic development will be discussed in greater detail in Chapter 4.

Improvement of Transportation Approaches to the City

The 1966 general plan proposed the construction of new port and airport terminals, as well as the rationalization of rail routes within the city limits.[118] Within a few years these new facilities began to be put into operation. The Moskovskii Station complex was expanded and modernized and plans are under way to phase out the operation of the Varshavskii Station, shifting all passenger traffic to the Baltiiskii Station less than a kilometer away. This consolidation of rail service constitutes a critical development for a city where more than 50 times as many people arrive by rail as by air.[119] Subsequent to the 1966 general plan, a new airport opened south of the city at Pulkovo, and a new passenger port for cruise ships was established at the western end of Vasil'evskii Island.[120]

Satellite Cities, Greenbelts, and Regional Planning

Leningrad planners began to emphasize the need for regional planning approaches during the late 1950s.[121] The plan ratified in 1966 incorporated this regional vision as it sought to govern land-use decisions for some 14,000 square kilometers beyond the city's traditional boundaries, including a 2,590-square-kilometer outer greenbelt free from all development and a 518-square-kilometer inner belt with only limited and strictly controlled use.[122] The plan also urged the full development of satellite centers at Kolpino, Pushkin, Pavlovsk, Gatchina, Petrodvorets, Lomonosov, Sestroretsk, Zelenogorsk, and Petrokrepost'-Kirovsk (see Map 2).[123]

This expansion of city planning to encompass the entire metropolitan area represented a significant innovation in Soviet planning efforts. It was permitted in part by the dominant role in Leningrad of planning agencies of regional-level party institutions that traditionally have sought to integrate the entire region (oblast) under their direct control. This pattern stands in sharp contrast to the situation in Moscow, for example, where city and region remain distinct political and administrative entities. Consequently, the city of Moscow has annexed more and more territory, never quite keeping pace with metropolitan expansion.

More significant, perhaps, was the Leningraders' strategy of planning for metropolitan expansion before development had occurred, thereby channeling growth into desired patterns. The emphasis on greenbelts and satellite cities reflected an awareness among planners of the need to keep ahead of physical growth.

Although planners were unable to stay ahead of the game—in large part because of their striking underestimation of the rate of increase in the region's population—the efficacy of their regional vision became increasingly apparent with the passage of time. By the late 1970s, several leading economic planning specialists were arguing that the entire Leningrad region—an oblast, please recall, only slightly smaller than Indiana—must be considered as part of a fully integrated unit with the city itself.[124] This conception, as we shall see in a moment, came to form the core of the proposals for the 1986–2000 general plan. It now constitutes a major Leningrad contribution to Soviet urban planning practice and philosophy.

As proposals for the regionalization of planning approaches emerged over the course of the 1970s, the regional party committee took the lead in encouraging integrated plans and, by mid-decade, secured the cooperation of republican and national planning agencies.[125] Again, as we shall see, this development has since transformed all economic and physical planning efforts.

3

Toward a New City Plan, 1966–1986

*Leningrad is celebrated as having the highest archi-
tectural culture. But for how long must we travel to
the historic center for rations of this culture?*
                                        —S. P. Zavarikhin, 1986

Aftermath of the 1966 Plan

Any evaluation of the 1966 general plan's impact should begin by
noting its calculated optimal population ceiling of 3.5 million residents
up to the year 1990. That projection bore little relationship to reality,
as Leningrad's population had passed that limit by the time the plan
was ratified in Moscow, and it continued to increase, gaining by nearly
1 million residents over the next 15 years.[1] This increase, approximately 70 percent attributable to in-migration, contradicted central
policies intended to limit population and economic growth in Leningrad, as well as in other major urban centers such as Moscow and Kiev.
The objective of such policies was to force a redistribution of rural
population to urban centers spaced more or less evenly across the
USSR.[2]

Housing plans encountered immediate difficulty, owing to the
pressure of unplanned-for population increases. The plan had specified
that only 5 percent of the new housing was to be built within the city's
traditional boundaries. As already noted, the remaining 95 percent of
projected new housing was to be distributed fairly equally among new
districts built to the south, north, and northwest of previously developed neighborhoods. Such spatial projections were designed to alle-
viate population pressures on the old city center.[3]

While the measures for reducing population densities at the city's
center were successful,[4] other creative housing programs in the 1966
general plan faced several obstacles from the start. To begin with, housing construction must conform to central standards, a requirement that
helps explain the incredibly monotonous cityscape built up across the
USSR in recent years. Leningrad planners sought and sometimes received permission to bypass these norms by designating as experimental—and therefore beyond the reach of centralized construction

Table 8. *Characteristics of Leningrad's City Center, 1980*

Indices	Percentage of Regional Total Found in City Center
Territory	0.7
Population	23.5
Industrial population	26.6
Students enrolled in institutes of higher education	78.1
Theaters	100.0
Seats in palaces and houses of culture, as well as movie theaters	40.0
Library holdings	71.7

SOURCE: A. V. Makhrovskaia and S. P. Semenov, *Puti razvitiia Leningrada* (Leningrad: Obshchestvo "Znanie"— Leningradskoe otdelenie, 1980), 14.

norms—major projects such as the one on Vasil'evskii Island mentioned earlier. Local architects wishing to apply higher design standards also confronted locally generated difficulties. For example, the new industrialized prefabricated construction developed by the Leningrad construction industry ultimately accelerated housing construction, but exacted a high aesthetic price.[5]

Competition among enterprises and municipal agencies for control of local housing and services presented additional difficulties for Leningrad planners, as it did elsewhere in the Soviet Union.[6] Ironically, the Leningrad city soviet controls a far greater percentage of consumer services and housing than do municipal authorities in virtually any other Soviet city, so that the city's government developed many of the new residential superblocks erected over the course of the past 15 years.[7] Instead of alleviating problems of social services' control and coordination, however, this jurisdiction only exacerbated the problems, as municipally controlled land was located at the city's outskirts, far from employment sites and existing service centers. For the most part, services have not moved outward from the city center along with residents (see Table 8).

Unsatiated Demand

In the final analysis, the main housing problem was simply the very heavy demand. The pressures of this unsatiated demand led the best planners and architects to drop many of their most creative designs in favor of efficiency and speed. The resulting emphasis on the pace of construction compounded long-standing difficulties in coordinating the service sector and residential development in a centrally planned economy. New Leningrad districts were served particularly poorly by consumer, health, educational, and recreational facilities.[8] During the mid-1970s, for example, the city ranked tenth among the 21 Soviet million-plus population metropolitan centers and union-republican capitals in the number of doctors available per capita, and ranked last among these same cities in the number of hospital beds per capita.[9] Concern over inadequate services led some local officials to discuss, and to a limited degree to experiment with, various schemes to place responsibility for developing social and commercial services under the same housing and construction agencies that were responsible for building the new districts in the first place.[10] While the results of these various experiments were never released, they apparently had scant impact, at least beyond the immediate neighborhoods involved. Consumer services in Leningrad remained terribly inadequate throughout the first half of the 1980s. Conceivably, this situation will improve once the small-scale cooperative stores legalized in May 1987 take hold.[11] As with several other Gorbachev-era reforms announced as this volume was going to press, such changes were not yet sufficiently developed to discern an impact. In many ways, such policy initiatives were responses to the futile experimentation of the period under examination here.

The continuing absence of services proved both psychologically detrimental and socially disruptive. Crime became acknowledged as a significant problem, especially where cultural amenities were thought to be deficient.[12] Both officials and the populace grew concerned. A major 1981 survey of popular attitudes toward the quality of urban life found that citizens' ratings of local services and general style of life consistently ranked Leningrad last among the five major cities examined (Moscow, Alma-Ata, Baku, Kiev, and Leningrad).[13]

Urban Sprawl

As might be imagined, the sprawling new residential districts also increased the demand for mass transportation. The city's transit system—particularly its subway—continued to expand rapidly (see Map 13), but the improved facilities failed to keep pace with increasing ridership. This state of affairs was due both to the city's continuing population growth and to the location of new housing construction on the city's outskirts. Meanwhile, other forms of transportation, especially the bus system, failed to meet rising demand.[14]

Local Leningrad authorities have been more successful than most Soviet municipalities in enforcing land-use laws, so that any expansion

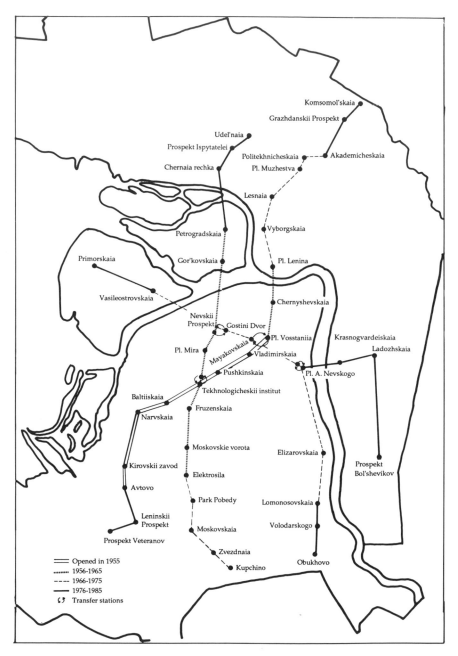

Map 13. *Development of the Leningrad subway, 1955–1985.*

of the Leningrad economy came about through more intensive development of already existing facilities, rather than through the construction of new plants.[15] Consequently, employment opportunities were still concentrated in almost precisely the same districts as before 1966, while housing migrated outward. According to one study, the central city population will decline to a half-million residents by the year 2000, while 1.4 million people will be employed by institutions located in the same area.[16] Future city residents will therefore have to travel farther to work, making the commute even longer than the present average of two hours daily.[17] Finally, slow development of service infrastructures in new residential districts required many residents to travel to the city center to shop or meet other obligations.[18]

The pressure on the city's transit system to move people from the periphery into the city center suggests yet another issue: namely, the role of the historic city core in Leningrad's future development.[19] The general plan provided for preservation of the historic center, a goal that has been attained to a remarkable degree. The urban fabric of nineteenth-century Petersburg remains largely intact, helped by the designation of 1,017 structures as architectural monuments, 1,150 as cultural monuments, and 222 as "Lenin Places" to be preserved in honor of the founder of the Soviet state. Few Leningrad planners viewed this marriage of the old city with the new as merely an issue of historic preservation.[20] Instead, discussion of the proper place of the center city in overall regional development also engendered an intense and at times bitter debate over the architectural quality of newer districts.[21]

Environmental Angst

Public concern over the region's natural environment accompanied the concern over Leningrad's man-made environment. The 1966 general plan provided for establishment of a forest-park zone devoted almost exclusively to recreational purposes as well as a suburban greenbelt restricted to carefully controlled development (see Map 13).[22] Both zones have come under tremendous developmental pressure, owing to the region's unpredicted (and therefore unplanned-for) population growth.[23] The inner recreational zone suffers particularly severe strain from overuse by city dwellers who inadvertently tear up fields and forests in pursuit of leisure pleasures. This damage raises questions, for some, of the environmental desirability of maintaining any district solely for recreational purposes.[24]

In addition to general land-use decisions, problems of pollution also must be confronted. Here, as in other industrial societies, solutions are easier to propose than to implement. Many Leningrad municipal officials and industrial managers now appreciate that the nature of pollutants has changed over time, from the biological ones in the preindustrial city, through industrial contaminants during the industrial revolution, to the ever more toxic petrochemical pollutants of late-industrial production.[25] In recognition of the problem, local officials at times have supported a variety of coordinated measures that depend on a myriad of institutional actors.[26] Authorities in Moscow and Leningrad have planned to introduce unleaded gasoline at local gas pumps and to launch more aggressive testing programs for automotive exhaust and chimney emissions. Leningrad city planners have recommended removal of the most noxious factories to outlying areas, together with the construction of suburban arterial transportation systems designed to reduce commercial traffic on city streets.[27] Moreover, in 1984, the city undertook preparation of a soil map for a region within a 100-kilometer radius of the city to chart the changing chemical composition of the area's soil, and hence the impact of industrial fallout from the atmosphere.[28] Only a half year later, the city announced a major air-pollution control program.[29]

The paucity of available data prevents us from evaluating the success of these various environmental protection programs. Officially, academic commentators claim that Leningrad's air is less polluted than that of other major Soviet industrial centers. Unofficially, one is told of "black snow" and river water made so warm by chemical pollutants that it will no longer freeze even in the coldest winter. We can hope that the *glasnost'* (openness) campaign of the Gorbachev administration will make it possible for some meaningful data to be released on the city's air, water, and soil quality. Until such data appear, we must be satisfied to report that various air-pollution control programs are being initiated.

Officials and specialists responsible for protecting Leningrad's environment have voiced concern over the quality of the region's water resources. Local water-pollution control projects have been complicated by the Neva River's relative shallowness and shortness, which limits the natural exchange of stale and fresh water throughout the river and its tributaries. By the end of 1986, local scientists were warning that the region's water resources were threatened by the previously discussed flood-control dam being built across the Gulf of Finland through Kronstadt. According to these reports, the dam would inhibit even further the limited exchange of stale with fresh water that previously had taken place in the river and its tributaries, ensuring that pollution levels would increase and water life would be seriously threatened. Despite continuing protests, these concerns appear to have fallen on deaf ears.[30] At last report, the party's Central Committee moved in March 1987 to expedite completion of the dam and flood-control system, and plans for even more massive new coastal and landfill development on Vasil'evskii Island were being discussed as this volume went to press.[31] It should be noted, however, that municipal authorities have recently taken some measures to restrict water pollution and now acknowledge the existence of an increasingly severe problem of petrochemical pollution.[32]

Controversy over the dam project refuses to die. Concern about the diversion of scarce resources to the project as well as its potentially negative environmental impact emerged as one of the most emotional issues in the Winter 1989 Leningrad district caucuses to nominate candidates for the Congress of People's Deputies. At one such meeting, Iurii Nikiforov, a Baltiiskii Plant worker and environmental candidate, declared to the voters of Election District no. 47 on Vasil'evskii Island that "Peter I Romanov hacked through a window to Europe, but Grigorii Romanov barricaded it up with a dam."[33] Nikiforov defeated all other candidates that evening but did not make it through the complicated nomination and election procedure to take a seat on the Supreme Soviet.

Specialists also became concerned with uniquely urban forms of "pollution" caused by intense human activity, such as noise pollution and the spread of infectious diseases. Leningrad city officials and their colleagues around the Soviet Union in such cities as Baku have long been aware of the health hazards of intense urban noise levels.[34] Moreover, the city's dank climate makes disease control difficult, encouraging seemingly annual massive influenza outbreaks.[35] Several Leningrad research institutions support programs studying environmental hazards and make recommendations to municipal and industrial leaders concerning environmental protection programs.[36] Finally, a lively academic discussion over the economic costs of environmental deterioration has developed in the national urbanist professional press.[37]

The Lessons of St. Petersburg

Such discussions over the quality of urban life and the city's environment increased after the accession of Mikhail Gorbachev and the initiation of his glasnost campaign. The summer 1986 conference of the 1,550-member Leningrad Division of the RSFSR Union of Architects (the main professional organization for architects) proved especially stormy as delegates excoriated their leadership for past mistakes.[38] In particular, local architects used the forum of the conference to decry what they see as the city's lost qualitative advantage in architectural design construction methods. For example, several delegates pointed to a failure in recent years to develop a sufficient variety of individual apartment unit-types to reflect changing family patterns. The quality of construction of new districts was similarly criticized. Concern was expressed that, unless a higher level of "urban planning culture" was rediscovered in the city, younger architects would lose their motivation to innovate and produce high-quality designs. Most interestingly, the architectural achievements of the city's pre- and postrevolutionary past were pointed to as possible models for future architectural development.

Just one month later, *Leningradskaia panorama* published an eloquently biting comparison of historic Petersburg and contemporary Soviet patterns of urban development under the title "Stroll along Prospect Enlightenment."[39] The author, a professional architect, began by recalling an old Russian literary form based on the author or his hero rambling through a given country, city, town, or countryside. By reporting on his impressions, the author is able to share a social critique of the scene under scrutiny. What, queried our contemporary author, would such a literary observer have to say if he were to take just such a stroll through the new districts of contemporary Leningrad? His answer was a withering attack on the visual impact of the neighborhood along Prospect Enlightenment, its substandard quality of construction, and the theoretical underpinnings that led to the design in the first place.

Upon entering the avenue in question, the author tells the reader that an inquisitive reporter would be correct in feeling as if his "soul had been seized." To begin with, the stretch of Prospect Enlightenment in question is almost 200 meters wide. This boundless space could contain within it any of Leningrad's major squares. Unfortunately, the buildings, which were erected during the 1970s, have been placed so that they contribute to the funneling of wind and the acceleration of ground-level wind speeds. Understandably, therefore, our tour leader discovers that a strong wind constantly howls throughout this enormous expanse of open space. Such extravagant use of space is all the more extraordinary when one considers, as the author urges us to, that the traffic needs of the area are served by a two-lane road no more than ten meters wide.

The literary stroll along Prospect Enlightenment continues in this vein at some length, as the author points out various aesthetic and practical difficulties created by the choice of brick color, poorly laid-out internal space of buildings and courtyards, thoughtless landscaping, repetitive use of glass, and the like. Underlying this at times shrill commentary is an explicit belief that architectural design must be freed from dogged adherence to central decrees. Instead, architects are urged to seek inspiration from the historic ensembles of central Leningrad.

Discussions of this sort dominated the local professional press for months following the Union of Architects conference, with ever more strident calls for historic preservation in the center and a learning of the "lessons of Petersburg" by those who design Leningrad's new districts. In November 1986, for example, Stepan Khrulev, chair of the Oktiabr'skii District soviet executive committee, emphasized the need to renovate, reuse, and generally protect the area's aging and substandard housing stock, 98 percent of which was constructed before the 1917 Bolshevik Revolution.[40] This plea was remarkable both for the candid manner in which it set forth the inadequacies of existing housing and for its concern for historic preservation. A month later, *Leningradskaia panorama* ran yet another article demanding the restoration and reuse of the city's prerevolutionary apartment buildings as the optimal response to the city's housing problems.[41] Here again, aesthetic considerations were among the justifications for rehabilitating existing housing, rather than simply tearing down older buildings to make way for new ones.

An even more authoritative plea for abandoning utilitarian approaches to city building appeared in January 1987 when Boris Ugarov, president of the Leningrad-based USSR Academy of Arts, demanded a *perestroika* (restructuring) of existing practices in the decorative arts and architecture. Ugarov's views, published in an interview in *Leningradskaia panorama*, praised the virtues of Petersburg classicism of the late eighteenth and early nineteenth centuries.[42] He spoke kindly of some of the architecture of the early Soviet period as well. However, he strongly denounced the finance-driven approaches to architectural and urban design of the past two decades. Such heartless functionalism, Ugarov contended, deprives the artist and architect of opportunities and destroys the city's unique appearance.

To the Street

Professional architects and even politicians were not the only Leningraders concerned about the limits of modern aesthetics and the inadequacies of current historic preservation efforts. In March 1987, scaffolding went up around two of the city's most historic hotels: the Astoria, from the bar of which John Reed and his fellow Western journalists witnessed much of the revolutions of 1917, and the Angletera where, in room no. 5, the poet Sergei Esenin committed suicide, writing a final verse in his own blood. Immediately following the first appearance of construction materials at each site, the city's morning paper, *Leningradskaia pravda*, was deluged with phone calls and letters. To quiet the storm, the editors ran a special interview with the city's chief architect, S. I. Sokolov, in which the renovation plans for the two hotels were set forth.[43]

Most of Sokolov's remarks dealt with plans for the more famous Astoria, a *style moderne* hostelry on St. Isaac's Square now reserved largely for foreigners (see Figure 23). Sokolov promised that the Astoria would be returned to its prerevolutionary magnificence, becoming a monument to the achievements of "the leading masters of Petersburg

Figure 23. *The Astoria Hotel.*

style moderne." Accordingly, particular attention would be paid to restoring the hotel's facade and major public spaces to their original appearance, while service areas would be rationalized. Individual guest rooms, "several of which do not conform to contemporary levels of comfort," would be upgraded.[44]

Sokolov continued by indicating that the future prospects for the Angletera next door were more complex. The building, located on the corner of Maiorov Prospekt and Gogol' Street in central Leningrad, is much older, having been initially constructed in the 1840s and remodeled many times to suit various purposes. Sokolov noted that it would not, therefore, be possible to restore the Angletera to its original form. Rather, the city's chief architect promised that several major elements of the building's facade would be reconstituted, and some effort would be made to preserve the room in which Esenin died. The vagueness of his statements about the Angletera was emphasized at the close of the interview when Sokolov reported that the Finnish construction firm working on the Astoria site had committed itself to completing its work by August 1989, but gave no indication as to when the Angletera reconstruction would be completed.[45]

Only four days after the appearance of Sokolov's interview—and just days after the erection of construction barriers and scaffolding around both hotels—*Leningradskaia pravda* reported that hundreds of people had been demonstrating day and night at both sites, carrying placards reading, "Friends, the History of Our City Is Our Root! Save

Our Monuments!"[46] The paper went on to publish conversations with several participants in the increasingly raucous vigil, which had begun on March 18, the day following the Sokolov interview.[47]

Aleksandr Zhuk, an honored architect of the RSFSR and a corresponding member of the Leningrad-based RSFSR Academy of Arts, defended the renovation projects by pointing out that the plans had been developed as early as 1978 at the behest of Intourist, the agency responsible for foreign tourists in the USSR, and had been approved by the USSR Council of Ministers.[48] Zhuk observed further that the buildings had become quite dangerous. Meanwhile, Iurii Andreev, editor in chief of the publication series "Library of the Poet," joined with Zhuk to argue for renovation, pointing out that every effort would be made to preserve those rooms associated with Esenin and to turn them into a special memorial to the poet.[49]

Only days later, however, the influential national literary paper *Literaturnaia gazeta* recounted the entire incident in an article by Mikhail Chulaki.[50] Chulaki excoriated city officials for their mishandling of the affair, citing extreme heavy-handedness on the part of Chief Architect Sokolov as well as Leningrad city soviet Deputy Chair Boris Surovtsev. Chulaki thought the situation would have been better managed and the fate of the Angletera more secure had Leningrad officials practiced Gorbachevian glasnost.

The ruckus refused to disappear.[51] Weekly demonstrations continued each Saturday morning, sometimes leading to confrontations with the police. Letters continued to pour into the editorial offices of *Leningradskaia pravda* (and, presumably, to other public agencies) denouncing the insensitivity of Leningrad planners and politicians to their city's cultural heritage.[52] Meanwhile, the Finnish construction crew hired to carry out the job had totally dismantled the Angletera in a matter of weeks.[53]

As time passed, the Leningrad regional and city party committees attempted to assert their control over the situation. Evidently, party leaders moved on two fronts, both of which suggest that the real crime from their point of view was public disorder rather than the destruction of an historic building. On one hand, party agencies began quite early on to lay blame for the incident at the feet of city officials. Party agencies severely criticized city soviet Chair Vladimir Khodyrev, Deputy Chair Boris Surovtsev, and others for their lack of openness in dealing with the public prior to the beginning of demolition and for their clumsy handling of the street demonstrations once public order had broken down.[54] While few commentators seemed to argue that the Angletera could not have been saved (there appears to have been a clear consensus that the building was simply beyond repair), from the party's point of view, those involved with the project should have engaged the public in various review and deliberative sessions *before* the erection of construction fences and the arrival of the wrecking crews. Within a year, such lessons may have been absorbed, as open discussions between planners and the public over the fate of the city center became more frequent.[55]

On the other hand, the party was not kind to the demonstrators. By some accounts, all students involved in the demonstrations were expelled from their institutions of higher learning (presumably non-student demonstrators suffered some form of punishment at work as well). After a process of negotiation, many students were readmitted, but their "leaders" were not permitted to return to their studies. In a more public vein, the regional party committee observed that, "under conditions of widening democracy," groups, on the whole, "performed patriotic and socially useful roles." Some groups, however, became "characterized by the display of nationalism, Slavophilism, unhealthy temper, and absence of civil maturity."[56] Such tendencies were seen by the regional party committee as manifest in the Angletera demonstrations and were clearly identified as violations of the public good.

Another important postmortem of the affair appeared in the July 1987 issue of *Leningradskaia panorama*.[57] Some architects contributing to this review reiterated those points made by Chief Architect Sokolov months before.[58] The Astoria, they argued, is one of the finest examples of Petersburg *style moderne* and is in urgent need of rehabilitation. The proposed plan will return the hotel to its previous splendor. The Angletera, on the other hand, is nearly a century and a half old, was originally constructed for other purposes, has been remodeled over and over again, suffered significant war damage, and simply can not be saved. Nevertheless, the architects involved in the project have worked closely with the Finnish construction crews to ensure that at least the facade will be restored before the construction has been completed. Additionally, the architect-commentators noted, plans for the project had been under consideration for nearly a decade, with relevant articles regularly appearing in professional publications since 1979. Therefore, they suggested, it is simply incorrect to assert that the city's architects have not been mindful of Leningrad's history and of the public interest.

Other commentators took exception to this position, pointing out that contemporary preservation methods, as internationally practiced, would permit restoration of the Angletera facade and interior.[59] If only Leningrad architects and builders were willing and able to practice their craft at the world level, they lamented, the entire issue could have been avoided. As it is, these commentators feared, Leningrad will be left with just another memorial plaque reading not even "In this building . . . ," but only "On this site stood a building in which. . . ."

Finally, some sought to separate questions of public decorum from the various architectural issues under contention.[60] "Youthful maximalism" cannot become the basis for serious professional deliberation, this argument went. Although buildings of particular merit should be protected and preserved, everyone must recognize that cities are living organisms and must change. The Angletera has little architectural merit and is historically significant only insofar as someone committed suicide there. Therefore, the planners were correct in directing their attention to the more important Astoria. In conclusion, they suggested, professionals should approach complex problems such as those posed by the Astoria-Angletera project in a fully professional manner.

The commentary in *Leningradskaia panorama* summarizing the positions captures some of the emotion encountered and many of the practical problems raised as Leningrad architects have struggled to come to terms with the rich architectural heritage of their city. Even more important, perhaps, it helps illustrate precisely why the Angletera demonstrations mark an important watershed in public concern for historic preservation in Leningrad. As the opponents to the hotel's destruction stated over and over, what was at stake was the preservation and protection of the city's history and character from the onslaught of modern architecture. Rejection of two decades or more of architectural construction design and planning practices had now moved from the pages of professional journals to the city's streets.

At their core, such critiques of Leningrad and Soviet planning, design and construction practices—like those highlighted by the stroll along Prospect Enlightenment and by the demonstrators on St. Isaac's Square—rested on a shared rejection of modernist planning theories. Leaving aside the fact that construction in Leningrad is of lower quality than in the West, Prospect Enlightenment is not significantly different in conception from Sarcelles outside of Paris or the Southwest Redevelopment Project in Washington, D.C., or other dehumanized urban spaces created during the third quarter of this century. All these projects rest on a "radical" architectural vision that sought to liberate cities and their inhabitants from the tyrannies of bourgeois industrial development. Ironically, they do so through the construction of mass-produced apartment blocks that, by virtue of their size, psychological and physical isolation, and visual monotony, only fragment the social fabric and emphasize the tyranny of the individual over that of the public.[61] A socialist state system explicitly concerned with promoting collective values clings to an urban design philosophy that elevates *res privata* over *res publica*, even after architects and planners in various capitalist societies have turned their backs on many of these aspects of the modernist "revolution."

A New Role for an Old Center

The increasingly open calls for a retreat from the architectural and city planning principles of the 1960s and 1970s and movement toward the warm embrace of traditional Leningrad design practices spurred an intense interest in historical preservation, and continued to do so for quite some time. Preservation efforts captured the public interest in Leningrad, with articles appearing in the daily press, mass magazines, and the professional press. But the actual restoration of historic monuments is only one of many interconnected issues that involve linkages of industrial and residential districts, balancing of service needs, reduction of overcrowding and population densities, and improvement in the distribution of cultural services.[62] Leningrad planners also attempted to improve communication and transportation links between old and new districts.[63] For example, by 1984 the city's streetcar lines, bus and trolleybus routes, and subway lines were carrying approximately 8.5 million passengers each day.[64] Somewhat at odds with standard Soviet practice—and despite the sustained expansion of the city's subway—the lowly streetcar remained a centerpiece of the city's transportation system.[65] In 1985 several existing streetcar routes were changed, and plans were announced for express streetcar routes from new districts to an ever-expanding subway system.[66] The subway system, in turn, had grown by year's end to extend 76 kilometers (about 47 miles), incorporating some 50 stations and carrying 2.3 million passengers on an average day.[67] To improve the distribution of services, Leningrad planners also initiated sociological studies to establish the service, housing, and occupational profiles of residential, commercial, and industrial districts.[68]

While the city's record on historical preservation is world-renowned and continues to attract tourists from around the globe,[69] complex issues like those already discussed have raised questions about the role of the central urban core. With the traditional role of the city center firmly protected by the 1966 general plan, Leningrad officials began to grapple with the problem of maintaining this preserved quarter as a vital and lively district.[70]

To begin with, the city's historic center continued to serve as the region's economic and cultural heart, and this status prevented central Leningrad from becoming a "museum city," despite its rather significant loss of population.[71] Preservation of the city center provided Leningrad's architects and planners with an alternative model of urban development to the one offered by central planning authorities in Moscow.[72] Leningrad's professional publications readily reflected the resulting preoccupation with architectural history and theory, with the psychological impact of physical structures, and with underlying aesthetic values.[73] In February 1985, in a plan designed to accentuate these values, the city announced a major effort to revamp 392 hectares of central Leningrad along and surrounding Nevskii Prospekt.[74] The plan, which was carried out in time for the celebration in 1987 of the seventieth anniversary of the Bolshevik Revolution, called for improving the design of existing commercial facades to bring them more into character with the avenue's original image. Further proposals advocated turning parts of the Nevskii into traffic-free pedestrian zones.[75] Meanwhile, as we have already noted in the discussion of Prospect Enlightenment, local architects inquired in print why the new districts were not more "cozy." How could the new districts really be called "Leningrad"?[76]

Official Responses

As we have just seen, a number of negative developments were not anticipated by the framers of the 1966 General Plan of Development of Leningrad and the Leningrad Suburban Zone. These include changing population dynamics, housing shortages, consumer service shortfalls, inadequate health care, overcrowded transportation facilities, unsatisfactory architectural aesthetic standards, and environmental deterioration. At varying times, to differing degrees and in different ways and with contrasting levels of success, numerous Leningrad publics—professional and nonprofessional—commented on these continuing urban problems. Local Leningrad authorities have also tried to deal with each of the problems mentioned thus far through official actions. The data supporting the preceding discussion are, after all, drawn almost exclusively from Soviet sources, and for the most part, generated by specialists and politicians in Leningrad itself. Furthermore, the concern of Leningrad's leaders has not been limited to mere recognition of pressing urban problems. They have relied on professional and academic specialists to identify emerging dilemmas; mobilize local resources to cope with such conditions; search the Leningrad past for possible solutions; and, when necessary, turn to central institutions for assistance.

We will now examine how Leningrad officials have sought systematic regulation of a wide range of activities carried out in their community by economic and political actors whose primary allegiance has been to central institutions in Moscow rather than to local institutions in Leningrad. The most important factors determining this process have been (1) the sustained political power of the Leningrad party organization under such national figures as Kirov, Zhdanov, Kozlov, Romanov, Zaikov, and Solov'ev; (2) the sustained presence of a cohesive and unified cohort of professional specialists; and (3) the enduring alternative urban vision of the neoclassical city built by Catherine and her grandsons, praised by turn-of-the-century architectural utopians such as the brothers Benois and Ivan Fomin, and given socialist credibility by Lev Il'in and his students such as Nikolai Baranov.

To explore these relationships further it is helpful to examine four major ways Leningrad officials have reacted to the difficulties encountered, as we noted, in implementing the 1966 general plan: (1) interjection of a social dimension into physical urban planning; (2) a series of limited policy responses to specific emerging problems; (3) regionalization of the local planning process; and (4) initiation of efforts to draft a new general plan, which took effect in 1986. Examining each of these sets of responses in greater detail should shed more light on the complex process whereby Leningrad's leaders modified and adapted public policy objectives to meet local conditions.

Interjection of the Social Dimension

Soviet urban planning encompasses the long-standing conflicts between the two complementary processes of economic planning (*planirovanie*) and physical planning (*planirovka*). Over the past several decades, both processes have been infused with the tension between the goals of economic institutions controlled by central ministries and those of local municipalities. Leningrad planners have become particularly creative in trying to deal with these fundamental strains in Soviet urban life.[77]

As the discussion in Chapter 6 will indicate, Leningrad's industrial sociologists and labor relations specialists first introduced sociological methodologies into the enterprise planning process as early as the mid-1960s. Linked to growing concern over labor productivity, such socioeconomic planning sought to integrate factory production and social plans. From these early steps there slowly emerged the concept of district, city, and regional socioeconomic planning, whereby the economic plan of a city or region is tied to plans for social, educational, and cultural services. This new interest in socioeconomic planning stimulated considerable research focused on Leningrad, which viewed the urban organization as an integrated whole—a process that created the data base local planners now use for their projections.[78] Accordingly, a good deal of work has been done on developing indices to measure social, productive, and institutional infrastructural change, as well as to assess the general quality of urban life.[79]

These ideas, many of which first emerged in Leningrad, quickly spread to other Soviet planning centers through various conferences, professional publications, and other forums of professional interaction, such as meetings sponsored by the Union of Architects. Indeed, as will be noted in Chapter 6, social scientists and planners in other communities soon contributed, along with their Leningrad colleagues, to the unfolding planning philosophy.[80] For example, during the period of the Tenth Five-Year Plan (1976–1980), Leningrad, Moscow, and Sverdlovsk all had introduced a social dimension into their city five-year economic plans.[81] Finally, in July 1979, city socioeconomic planning received the official stamp of approval of the Communist Party's Central Committee and the USSR Council of Ministers. Both central political institutions urged implementation of such planning techniques throughout the Soviet Union.[82]

According to resolutions of both bodies, the goals of socioeconomic planning in cities and regions should be (1) the proportional development of the sectorial structure of the local economy (e.g., no single sector should be promoted excessively at the expense of other spheres of economic activity); (2) the "harmonic personality development" of local citizens through improved services (e.g., the service sector, broadly defined, should promote the well-rounded development of the city's residents); (3) enhanced distribution of engineering equipment throughout the urban center (e.g., various technical services, as well as the city's general infrastructural development, should be evenly shared by all districts within the city); and (4) the rational use of material and human resources (e.g., the urban environment should be structured in such a way as to maximize economic efficiency).[83]

Over the course of the 1960s and 1970s, Leningrad's social scientists perfected a model for optimal socioeconomic plans for cities and regions.[84] According to this Leningrad model which is used as a guideline for planning practices elsewhere[85]—a city's socioeconomic plan will take some 15 years to produce and should include the following eleven sections:

1. A statement of the overall conception of a city's socioeconomic development and its goals for further growth
2. Social characteristics of the city and/or region
3. Scientific development
4. Industrial development
5. Demographic and social development
6. Branch social and engineering infrastructural development
7. Social, "life style," and educational development
8. Protection of society against antisocial influences
9. Development of external and regional economic and social ties
10. Resource utilization and protection
11. Perfection of methods of the administration of territorial economic and social development[86]

Leningraders continued to be leaders in the evolution of these planning techniques at both the factory and the city level. During approximately the past two decades Soviet planning authorities elsewhere have joined in this Leningrad concern for the need for more fully integrated and far-reaching planning approaches. Nevertheless, municipal authorities in the Soviet Union exercise relatively little control over the development of major economic institutions operating within their boundaries, let alone over those in surrounding areas. The Leningrad experience thus continues to stand out not only for its academic sophistication, but also for the attention paid to integrated planning by senior political officials, and for, to a considerable extent (at least by Soviet standards), a concern among local municipal agencies for control over the activities of central institutions operating within their jurisdictions. These developments were initiated by responses to inadequacies of the 1966 general plan's population projections, which spurred sociological and demographic research. In short, the relatively successful interjection of a social dimension into Leningrad economic and urban planning emerged as a major response to difficulties encountered in implementing the 1966 city plan. The development of new approaches and their theoretical adaptation in cities throughout the Soviet Union illustrate the manner in which local elites were able to respond to local conditions on the periphery and to alter the planning practices and policies of central elites in Moscow that had previously ignored social considerations.

Limited Planning Responses

In addition to the major restructuring of Soviet urban and economic planning methods, local planners systematically attempted to foster a series of more limited responses to the initial difficulties of implementing the 1966 general plan: for example, control of urban sprawl through increased efforts at "in-filling" (construction of new residential and commercial complexes on vacant land within previously developed districts), promotion of increased population densities, greater attention to renovation, and reduction of the rate of housing construction to allow more care for quality.[87] These diverse efforts will be discussed in the context of a single initiative that embodies many of these somewhat less ambitious planning innovations of Leningrad officials. The proposal for municipal and consumer services in central Leningrad's Dzerzhinskii District put forward by local social scientists and architects illustrates how relatively minor alterations in planning concepts and practices can in time cumulatively cause major changes in accepted approaches to comprehensive urban planning.[88] This more recent plan appears to be moving ahead, in conjunction with an earlier socioeconomic plan for the district discussed later in Chapter 6.

As will be noted in Chapter 6, the Dzerzhinskii District shares unusual problems with the rest of the historic central city (see Map 11). Ninety-seven percent of its housing stock was originally constructed before 1917. Institutions located in the district employ nearly twice as many people as live there. The population is better educated (25.6 percent having higher or specialized secondary degrees, as opposed to a city average of 19.6 percent) and has more younger individuals (students) and older ones (pensioners) than other Leningrad neighborhoods. People also live much closer together in the Dzerzhinskii District than in Leningrad as a whole (2,300 versus 400 per square kilometer). The district's historic and cultural attractions draw tourists and short-term visitors, who compete with local residents and employees for various consumer services. Finally, whatever the neighborhood's past industrial base may have been, the area is now primarily an educational, scientific, and service district, generating only 0.3 percent of Leningrad's total industrial output.

These rather unusual qualities prompted the proposal of several future socioeconomic developments. The district party committee, acting through its council on economic and social development, cooperated with various planning and academic research institutes located in the district.[89] These agencies developed short-range (5-year), medium-range (10-year), and long-range (20-year) plans for social, economic, and physical development, which were designed to maximize the district's uncommon heritage and to preserve its prominence and vitality. The result included improved recreational facilities (e.g., "vest-pocket" parks and specialized clubs), consumer services (e.g., outdoor cafes), and tourist amenities (e.g., apartment hotels located on the ground floor of residential buildings), intended to guarantee the district's social and economic well-being. The accompanying physical plans assume that the existing urban environment has proven itself to be essentially successful.[90]

Thus, official plan goals came to resemble those less official responses of architects and the public described at the outset of this chapter. Planners now seek to maximize the architectural and environmental potential of the prerevolutionary urban fabric by a variety of measures: for example, incorporating various public conveniences into one courtyard, a cafe into the next, and a small vest-pocket park into a third. This approach recognizes the existing environment as an ideal to be perfected rather than torn down and replaced. Moreover, the plan demonstrates not only a professional capacity to act on the widespread recognition of the failure of central architectural policies, but also a confidence in the ability of local officials to secure sufficient resources to implement their plans. Even on the district level, some Leningrad municipal officials have sufficient maneuvering room and adequate resources for effective responses to local conditions.

Regionalization of Urban Planning

Leningrad has been a pioneer in regional planning throughout the Soviet period, just as it was before. From the days of Peter I and Catherine II, the region's historic integration was fostered by the development of satellite palaces and cities.[91] Kolpino, Kronstadt, and Petrodvorets were all established during Peter's reign, Lomonosov and Pavlovsk during that of Catherine; Pushkin was formally incorporated in 1808, and Sestroretsk followed in 1917.[92] All these cities were brought together under the jurisdiction of the Leningrad city soviet in December 1931.[93] By the mid-1960s, another two dozen or so communities had similarly been brought under the supervision of the Leningrad city soviet.[94] Then, in 1966, city planners were able to incorporate the entire Leningrad suburban zone into the city's new general plan.[95] Nevertheless, although local elites and common citizens both recognized the presence of a large suburban region around the traditional city limits, few saw these interrelated areas as a single regional urban *system*, where urban, suburban, and rural areas were locked together as part of a functional unit.

Since the late 1950s, there has been a revolution in the thinking of Soviet urban geographers, economists, and urbanists concerning the nature of the "city."[96] Soviet scholars no longer consider the city merely a large population point. Instead, conventional wisdom has come to define cities as hubs in an agglomeration of settlements linked by various functional subsystems into a unified whole and extending across the length and breadth of the Soviet Union. These views suggest the substantial intellectual impact of the systems approaches of the West on Soviet social science.[97] We will also observe this influence in Chapter 6 when we discuss the emergence of socioeconomic planning. Such procedures combine social and economic subsystems as part of a unified and interrelated system. We can possibly detect an even more pervasive influence of systems analysis in the recent intellectual history of Soviet urban geography.

The ascendancy of systems theory in the body of Soviet thinking about cities can be seen on several different levels. An extensive body of theoretical literature has appeared in recent years describing the systemic nature of Soviet settlement patterns. Since the late 1950s, a number of geographers, including Georgii Lappo, Boris Khorev, David Khodzhaev, and Kazys Seselgis, have pioneered in establishing a distinctively Soviet outlook on urban agglomerations. This literature eventually produced the overarching concept of the Unified Settlement System (*Edinaia sistema rasseleniia*—ESR) encompassing the entire Soviet Union.[98] Several Leningrad scholars contributed both to the development of that concept and, more generally, to an emerging literature on the city as a system. Indeed, their contribution represents one of the major findings of this study.

At a more practical level, systems approaches to the city have fostered urban planning and management philosophies that seek balanced and harmonious regional development of urban centers in their entirety rather than exclusively promoting the physical development of the central cities.[99] Some authors, such as Leningraders Ivglaf Sigov, Nikolai Agafonov, and Sergei Lavrov, as well as Muscovite Boris Khorev, identify the goal of balanced development as a primary feature of Soviet settlement theory, thus differentiating it from systems approaches to urbanization emanating from the capitalist West.[100]

Moscow University geographer Khorev was for a long time a particularly prominent Soviet advocate of urban systems theory. He began vociferously to advocate systems approaches during the late 1960s and early 1970s when he first discussed the Unified Settlement System. His volume *Problemy gorodov* (*Problems of Cities*), a work that sought to demonstrate the existence of such a settlement pattern, is still a basic textbook of urban geography in Soviet undergraduate and graduate programs.[101] Khorev elaborated his notions further in more specialized works, among them a coauthored discussion arguing for the necessity of developing an effective demographic policy for the Soviet Union.[102] Khorev defines the balanced and harmonious development of interrelated industrial, transportation, resource utilization, spatial, and social policies as the primary objective of urban and regional planning efforts.

One critical element in conceptualizing the urban system has been the companion notion of the urban hierarchy. Here the Soviet penchant for putting everything in its appropriate hierarchical niche combines with the systems classifications of the West in a steady flow of efforts to assign every Soviet community to some national, republican, regional, or local settlement pyramid. In the Ukraine, for example, Petr Kovalenko has identified a three-tier urban system that is itself a subsystem of the national urban settlement pattern.[103] According to Kovalenko, this Ukrainian subsystem incorporates major population centers (Kiev, Kharkov, Donetsk, Odessa, and L'vov) and large ones (Poltava, Cherkassy, Kherson, and others), as well as medium and small ones, into a unified hierarchy. Kovalenko finds that the republic's major and large urban centers have their own extensive subsystems, with urban agglomerations growing up around such cities as Kiev, Kharkov, Dnepropetrovsk, and Odessa. He then chronicles the various functional subsystems (industrial, commercial, cultural, scientific, and so on) that become integrated through their relationship to the overall urban settlement system. He concludes by arguing that Ukrainian planners should not view the city as merely a population point. Instead, it has become the nexus of a series of multifaceted and multifunctional economic, spatial, and cultural subsystems.[104]

Oleg Litovka has been engaged in a similar study of the Leningrad urban region,[105] identifying several tiers of urban settlements around the first-tier center of Leningrad. For Litovka, Novgorod and Pskov represent second-tier centers linked to the Leningrad agglomeration, while such communities as Vyborg, Luga, and Boksitogorsk are third-tier focal points (see Map 2).

Leningrad social scientists have made significant contributions to new conceptualizations of the "city." These include the general theoretical works of such geographers and economists as Nikolai Agafonov, Evgenii Murav'ev, Sergei Uspenskii, Oleg Litovka, and Marat Mezhevich, which examine the methodological problems of investigating socialist settlement patterns. Much of this work has been based on studies of the Leningrad region.[106] One practical result of such academic endeavors has been to persuade planners that the Leningrad agglomeration in fact includes the entire area within 90 minutes' commuting time from the city center by rail, and not just those areas traditionally considered to be part of the metropolitan region or subordinate to the city soviet.[107]

The widespread acceptance of systems approaches to urban settlement patterns drastically altered Soviet urban planning practices in general and Leningrad planning approaches in particular. The central focus of planners shifted from the specific structural environment of a given urban area to the interaction of that region with its surrounding communities through various demographic, economic, spatial, transportation, communication, cultural, and environmental subsystems. This movement from a static architectural view to a dynamic systems view of the planning process marked a significant departure from traditional Soviet urban planning and managerial strategies.

In the case of Leningrad, the transformation meant that city administrators no longer saw their city merely as the urban system that was in place at the time of Alexander I. Instead they have accepted the vision of a "Leningrad" that comprises an extensive interlocking network of central, suburban, and exurban districts, many but not all of which are now under the jurisdiction of the Leningrad city soviet— rather than the regional soviet—and all within a relatively well-defined commuting radius of the city center.

The consequences of such a metamorphosis have been substantial. While the city's boundaries and direct authority were not extended outward, regional state and party agencies came to provide an integrating mechanism for the entire metropolitan region. In recreational design, for example, a new spectrum of nonurban facilities has fallen within the range of options open to Leningrad planners.[108] Similarly, industrial location policies are no longer limited by old geographic boundaries; nor, for that matter, are capital investment strategies.[109] Finally, planners have begun to consider the removal of entire urban functions from the central city to self-contained settlements on the periphery. In this last regard, Leningrad architects developed plans for self-contained academic communities, to the southwest of the city near Petrodvorets for the new campus of Leningrad State University, and to the north at Shuvalovo for the new complex of the USSR Academy of Sciences' Leningrad Scientific Center.[110]

In addition to expressing academic theories and planners' visions, expansion of the concept of the city and region conformed closely to long-standing political and institutional arrangements. Throughout the postwar period, regional institutions and officials have dominated the Leningrad Communist Party organization. Consequently, institutional and political frameworks to support regional urban management approaches were already in place long before the 1970s. Since urban management and planning decisions had previously been made on a scale larger than the boundaries of the central city and adjacent suburbs, regional political elites probably viewed the new planning approaches as the logical extension of existing institutional patterns.[111]

By the 1970s, then, the same factors that will be mentioned in our next policy studies (academic expertise, enlightened administrative responses, and regional political custom) produced an innovative response to inadequacies in public policy implementation—in this case, inadequacies in the 1966 general plan. The plan's static architectural nature and its relatively confined geographic scope came to be widely rejected in Leningrad and elsewhere.[112] As in the other policy areas, Leningrad scholars, managers, and politicians were ahead of their colleagues, their inventiveness taking the form of a series of proposals incorporating the entire oblast into a new Leningrad general plan.[113]

Proposals for a New General Plan

By the mid-1970s, it had become obvious that the 1966 general plan was giving little guidance for the future development of the Leningrad urban system. Before the decade's end, the local branches of the Soviet Sociological Association (the professional organization for sociologists) and the Union of Architects had organized and published the results of a major multidisciplinary conference focused on the city's future development until the year 2000.[114] The discussions provide ample evidence that local party, municipal, and planning authorities, along with professional architects, designers, and social scientists, all recognized the obsolescence of the 1966 plan. Initial proposals for a new plan began to be circulated.

As a new decade began, references in the professional press indicated that a new general plan would become effective as early as 1984.[115] Since the actual planning process and documents are classified as secret—and public discussion of their content, as well as informal discussion with foreigners, constitutes an illegal activity—we can only speculate about the process on the basis of a limited public record. The primary objective of all of these recommendations appears to have been the incorporation into a comprehensive document of social and economic components, along with more traditional physical planning targets. As a major factor in the proposed expansion in the scope of architectural planning, advocates of new strategies pointed to the inability of city administrators to adjust physical planning goals to changing social and economic realities.

Preparing a new general plan of development for an urban community as large and complex as Leningrad has become a mammoth undertaking, made even more complicated, of course, by the classified nature of the process. In the Soviet context, plan drafters initially consult with economic leaders to produce a statement of the region's long-term economic priorities. Such economic objectives are then established in an unpublished document, the "technical-economic foundations" (*tekhniko-ekonomicheskie osnovy*—TEO) for the future planning project. Next, architects and physical planners develop a detailed strategy to transform these economic objectives into construction and architectural design programs. The documents prepared for this second planning stage then become the basis for the proposed new general plan.[116]

A close reading of Leningrad's leading daily newspapers, *Leningradskaia pravda* and *Vechernyi Leningrad*, indicates that preparation of the new general plan moved forward with deliberate speed. In September 1983, a meeting of the city soviet executive committee's main architectural-planning administration convened to examine the status of the draft general plan's technical-economic foundations.[117] Reports published following that session indicated that the effective date for the new plan was postponed from 1984 to 1985 and that the overall planning orientation was still the city and its suburban zone. Participants expressed particular concern over the need to control urban sprawl through in-filling projects, as well as over the importance of developing more comprehensive transportation forecasts in general and subway ridership projections in particular. The following month, preparations for the new plan were discussed at a meeting of the executive committee of the Leningrad regional soviet.[118] Public reference was made at this point, and for the first time, to the possibility of expanding the general plan's scope beyond the 521-square-mile immediate Leningrad metropolitan area to incorporate projections for the Leningrad region as a whole.

In early 1984, regional party First Secretary Lev Zaikov informed delegates to the twenty-sixth Leningrad regional party conference that initial draft documents for a comprehensive regional general plan would appear before year's end.[119] By April, Zaikov was reporting further that Communist Party General Secretary Konstantin Chernenko had congratulated Leningrad officials on their preparation of a new general plan.[120] Despite all these references, no clear image of the nature of the new plan had been enunciated prior to the summary report of a session of the regional party committee in June 1984.[121] In discussions at that meeting, regional party committee members observed that the executive committees of the city and regional soviets were preparing a unified general plan for both jurisdictions.

These efforts drew on the expertise of several departments of regional, city, and district party committees throughout the oblast, as well as the planning commissions of regional and city soviet executive committees, the main architectural-planning administrations of those same institutions, the Northwestern Branch of the RSFSR State Planning Committee's (Gosplan RSFSR's) Central Scientific-Research Economics Institute, the USSR Academy of Sciences' Institute of Socioeconomic Planning, local design institutions, and several other major organizations in design, architecture, and construction.[122] The projected plan sought to define regional development for the period 1986–2005, and would be issued in two stages. First, the draft technical-economic foundations would appear prior to December 1, 1984. Next, the draft general plan would be released for discussion before November 1, 1985. Then, the final plan documents would be ratified by the appropriate local and central agencies and put into effect prior to 1986.

Shortly thereafter, the city party committee secretary, Anatolii Fateev, reported to his committee that the proposed general plan would be the first project of its kind in Soviet history to integrate both city and regional planning processes.[123] Further evidence of the genuinely regional approach adopted by plan framers may be found in the September 1984 issue of the local architectural community's professional journal, *Leningradskaia panorama*, in which Iurii Baranov, the chairman of the Boksitogorsk city soviet executive committee, reported on his city's participation in the preparation of the new regional general plan.[124]

Leningradskaia pravda and *Vechernyi Leningrad* summarized yet another session of the Leningrad city council executive committee's main architectural administration in November 1984.[125] The papers' reports of the meeting noted that nearly every Leningrad political or economic official of any consequence, including the entire regional and city party committees' bureaus, convened in joint session with the main architectural-planning administration to discuss the "Technical-Economic Foundations of the Unified General Plan of Development of Leningrad and the Leningrad Region in 1986–2005." Regional party First Secretary Zaikov and city Chief Architect Gennadii Buldakov were among the most prominent officials to address the gathering. The rather brief communiqué nonetheless offered one of the most comprehensive statements concerning the contents of the new general plan's technical-economic foundations that had yet appeared in the Soviet press. Even in this truncated form, the articles made it clear that the new 1986 plan was based on extreme concern over labor shortages and would therefore stress technological innovation, increased economic specialization, and regional integration. This statement of goals was reinforced when the entire city soviet executive committee ratified the plan's technical-economic foundations the following January.[126]

In the spring of 1985, Mikhail Gorbachev toured Leningrad and gave his blessing to the draft 1986 general plan.[127] A few weeks later, in early June, the Central Committee's Politburo also approved the document, thereby paving the way for public discussion of plan details.[128] The day after the Politburo's action, planning commission Chairman Kazimir Labetskii, in a front-page interview with *Leningradskaia pravda*, revealed that the plan's primary objectives included more balanced regional development; technological intensification of the Leningrad economy; greater efficiency in the use of water, energy, and heating; strengthened environmental protection; and improved services for transportation, health care, child care, housing, and consumers.[129] Housing and service facilities would also expand, thereby improving the region's quality of urban life.

The proposed integration of regional and city planning, Labetskii continued, would end the disproportionate concentration of the region's productive capacity in the city of Leningrad. The more balanced approach to the regional economy would be achieved by reducing the number of workplaces in the city, while local labor productivity and aggregate production would be increased by stepped-up programs of technological innovation. Labetskii's portrayal of the draft plan was echoed in Iurii Solov'ev's initial appearances as regional party committee first secretary.[130]

Next, in October 1985, Leningrad's chief architect, Gennadii Buldakov, and the chief of the general planning process, Valentin Nazarov, coauthored a lead article in the journal *Leningradskaia panorama* spelling out the overall goals and parameters of the new general plan.[131] According to Buldakov and Nazarov, the plan was based on the previously mentioned technical-economic fundamentals approved by the Politburo earlier in the year. Covering the period 1986–2005, the new plan sought (1) intensive development of the local economy; (2) improvements in the city's consumer services, water supply, energy and heating systems, and transportation network; and (3) enhanced environmental protection measures.

The 1986 General Plan

The editors of *Leningradskaia panorama* devoted the better part of their July 1986 issue to a summary of the 1986 general plan.[132] This report provided the most publicly available detailed description of what is contained in the final (and still classified) plan documents approved by various regional governing bodies in late 1985.[133] Significantly, even this overview of the 1986 general plan provides insufficient information for meaningful public participation in the planning process. Furthermore, it appeared only *after* the plan had been approved in Leningrad as well as in Moscow.

According to these articles, the 1986 plan represented a major departure from previous practices in that it included provisions for the entire Leningrad oblast.[134] This observation confirmed the previous evidence—noted earlier—that local planners had expanded the conception of the urban planning process to extend well beyond the boundaries of the city and its extensive surroundings to encompass much of Leningrad's hinterland. It also represented a strengthening of the general plan by bringing it into closer conformity with economic planning procedures, since the five-year economic plans governing Leningrad's economy are for the most part developed on a regionwide basis.[135]

The journal's editors also chided the drafters of previous Leningrad plans for not being sufficiently concerned with economic and social factors.[136] The 1986 general plan, they continued, placed prime importance on such broad social and economic contexts of urban development as the size and character of the existing workforce and the measures taken to support regional integration of science and industry. In this manner, the articles appearing in the July 1986 issue of *Leningradskaia panorama* confirmed the prominence of the various socioeconomic planning and managerial techniques that will be discussed in Part 2.

Science Dominates

Beyond these general observations, the articles focused on some of the more important provisions of the new general plan. At this point, the journal praised the "Intensification-90" campaign (to be discussed in Chapter 4) for its vision of a technology-dominated Leningrad economy by the turn of the century.[137] More specifically, the new plan called for the elimination of several smaller enterprises and the creation of a more limited number of larger and fully automated shops, assembly lines, and plants. In this manner, the previously mentioned trend toward increased concentration of the region's productive capacity in fewer and fewer institutions promised to continue.

In language that echoed the proclamations of Frol' Kozlov some three decades before, the journal's editors declared that the shift to a more scientific economic base would be accompanied by increased reliance on such sectors as machine construction, energy, shipbuilding, instrument making, electronics, and computers.[138] Infrastructural, housing, and cultural developments would be dominated by concern for the needs of these economic sectors.

Regional Integration

In preparing the new general plan, Leningrad officials concluded that labor shortages remained the fundamental factor limiting economic development in their region.[139] The plan endorsed regional integration as one means for reducing the negative impact of such shortages through improved resource allocation. In this regard, planners pointed out that 75 percent of the oblast's population lived in the immediate Leningrad metropolitan area, as opposed to 57 percent of the inhabitants of the Moscow oblast residing in metropolitan Moscow, 56 percent of the population of the Kiev oblast living in Kiev, and only 27 percent of the residents of the Sverdlovsk oblast living in and around the city of Sverdlovsk.[140] The Leningrad planners saw this concentration as restricting the possibilities for flexible regional growth strategies. Therefore, they sought to limit the metropolitan area's population growth over the next two decades to a ceiling of 5 million, with any additional population expansion being pushed off to the eastern areas of the Leningrad region.[141] To achieve this goal, the plan proposed to reduce the city's labor force from 945,000 in 1985 to 890,000 in 2005, while simultaneously increasing the population and housing stock of districts lying beyond the Leningrad metropolitan area.[142]

Despite the professed desire to expand economic activity outside the city, planners continued to view Leningrad itself as the focal point for the entire region.[143] The Leningrad neoclassical architectural tradition continued to be valued for providing both a blueprint for the restoration of existing structures and a set of principles that should govern the planning and construction of new areas.

Overall, the plan distinguished among six different urban zones within Leningrad (see Map 14):[144]

1.   A *central zone* (including such areas as Kronverk, the point of Vasilev'skii Island, and the Admiralty district), which would retain some population while serving primarily as an architectural and cultural museum

2.   A *middle urban zone* (stretching along Nevskii Prospekt roughly from the Fontanka River to the Moskovskii Station and in analogous areas elsewhere in the city), which would be subject to strict preservation regulations while continuing to have a multifunctional character

3.   A *zone of secondary urban development* encompassing both green areas (such as those on Elagin Island and in the Smolenskii cemetery and Aleksandro-Nevskaia monastery) and mixed residential-commercial areas (such as are found in the Smol'ninskii District)

4.   An *industrial/residential zone* (such as those areas on Krestovskii Island, in the Sovetskaia street system, and near the

Map 14. *Major urban zones in the 1986 general plan.*

1 Central Zone
2 Middle Urban Zone
3 Secondary Urban Development Zone
4 Industrial/Residential Zone
5 Central Residential Zone
6 New Residential Zone

technological institute), which would become the focus of efforts to modernize production facilities and to impose more stringent ecological controls

5. *A central residential zone* (including much of Petrogradskaia Storona, Dekabristov Island, and Aptekarskii Island), which would be home to large-scale industrial and scientific establishments, in addition to residential areas, smaller institutions in the area having been removed to create more open space

6. *A new residential zone* (including the west bank of the Neva and newer districts in outlying areas), which would remain residential in character while requiring significant reconstruction of apartment complexes built during the Stalin and Khrushchev eras, as well as the imposition of more stringent environmental controls to prevent future overdevelopment

Differentiated Development Strategies

To achieve the distinctive goals established for each of these zones, three different preservation/development strategies would be employed. First, the central city essentially would be preserved in its entirety. Second, the new residential zone would be subject to the "Moscow" approach, whereby all but the most significant structures are replaced. Third, the remaining areas would be developed according to the "Leningrad" strategy by making optimal use of existing structures, remodeling internal space to preserve facades whenever possible, and expanding open space while permitting new development that will not violate the essential character of a given district. This third strategy was thought to be the most expensive as it placed greatest demand on capital construction funds.[145] As the plan was for the entire Leningrad region and not just for the city and its metropolitan area, equivalent strategies were formulated for agricultural areas, as well as for the towns and cities spread out across the oblast beyond the immediate Leningrad area (such as Luga, Lodeinoe Pole, Priozersk, and Vyborg).[146]

Social Infrastructure

In addition to architectural and economic concerns, the new general plan was said to pay significant attention to the region's social infrastructure, including provisions for expanded facilities for education and health care.[147] In keeping with the regional thrust of the new plan, health care and cultural facilities were to be concentrated as much as possible away from central Leningrad. Moreover, the policy of relocating major scientific and higher education facilities in the city's suburbs (e.g., the move of Leningrad State University to Petrodvorets and that of the USSR Academy of Sciences' Leningrad Scientific Center to Shuvalovo) was to continue. These shifts were to be facilitated by transportation and infrastructural development policies (canals, energy lines, and the like) that emphasized regional interdependence.[148]

Environmental Choice

In keeping with the various responses to the insufficiencies of the 1966 general plan, over the next two decades greater attention was to be paid to environmental concerns.[149] In particular, the movement of population outward from Leningrad was to be channeled away from environmentally vulnerable areas. Furthermore, in response to intense criticism of environmental degradation, special efforts were to be made to free Lake Ladoga, the central source of fresh water in the area, from industrial pollution by 1995.[150] This last goal would be of considerable import for the city, given its location in the delta of a river, the Neva, fed by waters from the lake.

Learning from the Past

Many of these provisions of the 1986 general plan were in keeping with the nature of the popular, specialist, and political discussion of the various inadequacies of the 1966 general plan described at the outset of this chapter. It appears, then, that the new planning document was a product of several years of probing, experimentation, and debate. Furthermore, the explanations of plan objectives that have appeared in various public forums (e.g.. the print media, lectures, television, and radio) are less reticent in commenting on the plan's potential limitations than was the case in 1966.[151] For example, local specialists are skeptical of the ability of local institutions to exert authority over the activities of the ministries within their jurisdictions.[152] This new-found public appreciation of the difficulties inherent in bringing to life provisions of a city plan, plus the considerable degree to which those provisions have drawn on the shortcomings of previous plans, suggests that many of those charged with regulating Leningrad's urban environment have attempted to learn from the past.

At the most general level, then, the new general plan identifies highly specialized, technologically intensive industries as the core of all future regional development. Furthermore, the plan's technical-economic foundations emphasize the importance of increased specialization throughout the regional economy. The plan document also apparently contains several specific recommendations to reconstruct and retool the region's operating industrial plant.

As a logical consequence of this orientation toward development, the plan stresses the primacy of workforce needs. In fact, as we will see in Part 2, the draft document interjects into the physical planning process the same social variables that were developed some 15 years earlier in response to industrial planning needs during the emergence of socioeconomic planning methods. Capital investment and construction plans in the physical planning protocols will reflect the same over-arching economic priorities.

The new general plan focuses on integrated regional economic-social-infrastructural development.[153] The technical-economic foundations single out energy and transportation resources for special attention. Beyond the confines of the immediate urban agglomeration, the plan pays particular attention to long-term land reclamation projects, as well as to the vital role of the forestry and woodworking industries. Furthermore, the plan enunciates strategies for improving local living standards, and includes programs for service, health, cultural, and housing infrastructural development.

The heavy emphasis on both regional planning and balanced development reflects the strong intellectual influence of Western systems approaches on contemporary Soviet urban geographers. The sweeping pronouncements on living standards and urban infrastructural development are evidence of the extensive planning innovations of Leningrad urbanists over the past two decades. Those same pronouncements offer indirect testimony to the continuing symbolism of the traditional central city as an effective model of urban development. The incorporation of a social and an economic dimension into the physical planning process testifies to the long-term significance of the original socioeconomic planning experiments of the 1960s. To understand precisely how this is so, we now need to direct our attention to efforts to plan and manage Leningrad's socioeconomic environment.

II

The Socioeconomic Environment

4

Organizing Leningrad's Science and Industry

> *For our economic network [Leningrad and the north-west of the Russian Republic], there simply is no other way. Demographic conditions will not permit us in the foreseeable future to count on an inflow of additional workers, on whose account production has extensively expanded in the recent past.*
> —N. I. Chikovskii, 1985

Technology and Development

We saw in Part 1 how, since the early 1950s, planners in Moscow and Leningrad have implemented a development strategy for Leningrad that relies heavily on economic specialization and technological innovation. This vision of the city's economic future highlights Leningrad industry's reputation as an innovator and a producer of high-quality goods and compensates for regional labor shortages. National and local Communist Party pronouncements, along with industrial investment patterns throughout the entire post-Stalin period, demonstrate the Leningrad economy's growing reliance on technologically sophisticated industrial production (frequently defense-related) in such economic sectors as shipbuilding, machine construction, and precision-instrument making.

As noted earlier, initial attempts in Leningrad to implement this new economic vision quickly foundered on demographic constraints and labor shortages. As new labor-management schemes were incorporated into the daily industrial life of the city, local administrators wrestled with vexing organizational and institutional dilemmas confronting their new industrial order. Local planners envisioned specialized industries dependent to a large measure on interenterprise and intersectoral cooperation. Traditional Soviet organizational and institutional barriers militated against such managerial flexibility and cooperation. Accordingly, Leningrad politicians and managers were forced to turn to the center to obtain the support necessary to remove the barriers and thereby advance the city's economic performance.

By the mid-1960s, Leningraders had begun to confront the issue of how best to organize production-research and development cycles. Drawing on their own experience, as well as that of their colleagues elsewhere, many Leningrad leaders sought to devise new organizational schemes to link the city's 300 or so scientific research institutions and 40-odd institutions of higher education directly together with its nearly 500 industrial enterprises.[1]

At first, these organizational efforts focused on merging industrial establishments through unified managerial interenterprise production associations (*proizvodstvennye ob"edinenie*) linking management sites.[2] Later, Leningrad managers created interenterprise/research-institute scientific-production associations (*nauchno-proizvodstvennye ob"edinenie*) to bring entire R&D cycles under single managerial systems incorporating both production and research.[3] By the early 1980s, under the leadership of Grigorii Romanov, the Leningrad party organization took the effort one step further, bringing pressure on the USSR Academy of Sciences to reorient the research agendas of the academy's Leningrad research establishments toward the needs of local industrial production by establishing a Leningrad Scientific Center.[4] Finally, in the mid-1980s, Leningrad political leaders concerned with the innovation process once again directed their efforts toward the production end of the research-design-production cycle. In 1984, for example, regional party First Secretary Lev Zaikov launched a new program of technological innovation at the workplace.[5] This much ballyhooed "Intensification-90" campaign was endorsed by Mikhail Gorbachev immediately on his elevation to the Central Committee's general secretaryship, and contributed to Zaikov's later promotion to a Central Committee secretaryship.[6] Zaikov's skills as an administrator and his interest in technological innovation also undoubtedly played a role in his subsequent appointment as Moscow party chief.[7] Similarly, it became the central focus of Iurii Solov'ev's first secretaryship and may have been pivotal to his elevation to candidate member status on the Politburo.[8] Still, for a fuller understanding of Zaikov's and Solov'ev's innovation campaigns, one needs to look back three decades to the period during which the overall Leningrad development strategy took shape.

The Legacy of the 1950s

In the early 1950s Frol Kozlov, when he was still serving as regional party second secretary, had first expressed concern over the inadequacy of existing organizational frameworks for the promotion of technological innovation. Initially, local leaders working in consultation with central institutions established an economic development strategy for the city and region that encouraged increased reliance on technologically intensive forms of industrial production.

After experimenting with various innovations intended to improve management of the urban workforce, Leningrad officials began to advocate new organizational forms to facilitate the interinstitutional cooperation so necessary for production innovation. Managers and other specialists won the approval of municipal and party officials who, in turn, obtained permission from central institutions in Moscow to try out new forms of industrial organization, such as the interenterprise production associations. After a successful test period, Leningrad managers experimented with a variation on the associational format by creating interenterprise scientific-production associations that incorporated scientific research institutes. This new organizational approach now dominates the local R&D scene. Moreover, Leningrad experience with both forms of associational management provided an institutional prototype for similar innovations throughout the Soviet Union. Finally, innovation efforts during the mid-1980s became more concerned with the introduction of existing technologies into the production cycle than with the development of new technologies. The remainder of this chapter will examine the distinct phases in the development of the series of innovation-oriented reforms that led to the incorporation of technological innovation into the city's general plan for the period 1986–2005.

Kozlov and Innovation in Leningrad

After graduating from the Leningrad Polytechnic Institute, Frol Kozlov spent much of his early career away from Leningrad.[9] During the late 1930s, Kozlov made a name for himself as the successful chief engineer of the strategic Izhevsk Metallurgical Plant in the central Russian city of the same name. Born in a village outside of Riazan', another provincial central Russian town, Kozlov's time in Izhevsk meant that he was returning home from Leningrad. By 1940 Kozlov had become the Izhevsk city party committee's first secretary, a post he would leave in 1944 to move to defense production work with the Central Committee in Moscow. Throughout this period Kozlov was deeply involved in the defense sector. As a reward for his wartime efforts, he was elevated to second secretary of the Kuibyshev regional party committee in 1947, returning briefly to the Central Committee in 1949.

In Chapter 2 we observed that Andrei Zhdanov's major rivals to power in Moscow, Georgii Malenkov and Lavrentii Beria, set in motion a large-scale purge of Zhdanov protégés in Leningrad and elsewhere following Zhdanov's death in August 1948.[10] Before the end of March 1949, several leading Zhdanov associates, including Central Committee

Secretary Aleksei Kuznetsov and Leningrad regional and city party First Secretary Petr Popkov, were removed from their posts, never to be seen again.[11] By late summer, Joseph Stalin had engineered the appointment of a new Leningrad regional party first secretary, Vasilii Andrianov, who set about dismissing scores of leading regional, city, and factory party and government officials.[12] Beyond Leningrad, Zhdanov associates in Moscow and Gorky also fell victim to the Leningrad Affair.[13]

As part of his effort to gain control over the local party organization, Andrianov placed several non-Leningraders in critical staff positions, including Kozlov. After his brief interlude with the Central Committee in 1949, Kozlov assumed control of the prestigious and powerful party organization at Leningrad's Kirov Metallurgical Plant. The Kirov plant and its party organization had provided a base of operations for supporters of previous Leningrad party leaders, including the assassinated Sergei Kirov, the now disfavored Andrei Zhdanov, and the recently purged Aleksei Kuznetsov.[14] Therefore, Kozlov's reassignment from a national post in Moscow and a regional one in Kuibyshev to the factory position in Leningrad represented an important political promotion, despite its apparently lower-ranking position on organizational charts. Kozlov's star continued to rise when, in 1950, he assumed the first secretaryship of the Leningrad city party committee. Just two years later, Andrianov appointed Kozlov to serve as his second secretary on the Leningrad regional party committee.

Kozlov quickly became a visible presence in Leningrad political life, using his public appearances to set forth a new vision of Leningrad's economic future.[15] That image was deeply influenced by his own career experiences and preferences. Kozlov considered technologically intensive defense-related industrial production of the sort he had supervised during the war as the key to Leningrad's future prosperity.

Shortly after Stalin died in March 1953, Andrianov was demoted, dismissed, arrested, and apparently executed, for his role in the Leningrad Affair. Kozlov replaced the destroyed regional party first secretary and assumed control of the Leningrad party organization.[16] Under Kozlov's leadership, a new economic development strategy took shape. Economic development in the city and region favored specialized (in both resource demand and product), technologically intensive (as opposed to labor-intensive) industry that depended on the introduction of new technologies to enhance productivity and develop fresh product lines, and that could draw on the coordinated effort of local factories and research establishments. The Leningrad economy became ever more specialized, with traditional light industry languishing.[17] This development formula sought to push the city's production record ahead of that of other Soviet industrial centers, without undue reliance on massive infusions of scarce labor reserves.

Kozlov built on his Leningrad power base to gain national prominence. In February 1957 he became a candidate member of the party's Presidium, as the Politburo was then called, and a full member the following June. He prudently sided with Nikita Khrushchev during the pivotal events leading to the defeat in June–July 1957 of the "Antiparty Group"—Molotov, Malenkov, and Kaganovich.[18] Then, from late 1957 until 1958, he served as chair of the Russian Republic's Council of Ministers, a post he left to become first deputy chair of the USSR Council of Ministers. Kozlov retained this last post until the early signs of an ultimately fatal illness forced his resignation. Meanwhile, he became a senior Central Committee secretary with full Presidium (Politburo) status between 1960 and 1964. Despite his earlier ties with Khrushchev, however, Kozlov emerged in time as a leading spokesman for party officials resistant to Khrushchev's attempts to restructure national economic and Communist Party institutions.[19] Kozlov died in January 1965, only three months after the collective leadership of Leonid Brezhnev, Nikolai Podgorny, and Leningrader Aleksei Kosygin had overthrown Khrushchev in a Kremlin coup.[20]

Early Science-Industry Integration

The Leningrad party organization sought and obtained from central planners additional stipulations covering technological innovation from the city's 1951–1955 Five-Year Plan.[21] Precisely how this goal was achieved is lost from the public record. However, in 1951 Kozlov was able to enunciate the broad outline of a new centrally approved development strategy for the city at the tenth city and eleventh regional party conferences.[22] The policies proclaimed at these gatherings brought greater unity to a series of activities in Moscow and Leningrad alike, which encouraged the union of Leningrad's scientific and industrial establishments.

By late 1952, for example, both the regional and city party committees had organized departments to supervise the management of research and educational institutions. Further special discussion of technological innovation in the city took place at a citywide conference convened by the Leningrad city party committee during Kozlov's tenure as that body's chief executive. The conference brought together 727 leading scholars and captains of industry to examine various means for promoting technological innovation in the Leningrad economy.[23] In regard to all of these activities, the scanty available evidence indicates that the initial impetus for this development strategy originated in Leningrad, although approval from central institutions in Moscow was evidently gained quite early in the process. We do know for sure that, by June 1955, the Communist Party's Central Committee had officially endorsed this strategy.[24]

Soon, multifaceted efforts were made to expand the scope and nature of cooperation among Leningrad's research and industrial establishments. Initially, institute directors and factory managers pursued traditional contracting arrangements. By 1954, for example, the Leningrad Technological Institute had signed 57 contracts with local enterprises to advance innovation.[25] Three years later, even Leningrad State University—an educational institution further removed from the R&D cycle than most of the city's research organizations—had entered into more than 80 direct research contracts with major industrial enterprises.[26] Unfortunately, the public record tells us little about the content of these projects, although Soviet authors of the period viewed their existence as important.

At the outset of the 1960s an intricate web of interinstitutional research and technological contracts involved many local research and production centers.[27] Most of these agreements specified task assignments. The limited nature of these original compacts, however, inhibited the more far-reaching forms of cooperation required to achieve broader developmental objectives. The search for more extensive linkages between research centers and production facilities eventually merged with local attempts to introduce industrial production associations, a form of industrial organization that had been initiated elsewhere but would be quickly molded to meet Leningrad needs.

Industrial Production Associations

The industrial production association came into existence at a time when Nikita Khrushchev had destroyed the power of the central industrial ministries by replacing them with regional economic councils (*sovnarkhozy*).[28] In this policy climate one of the association's primary objectives became the integration of autonomous production units engaged in similar activities. Once the industrial ministries were reestablished in 1965, advocates of economic reforms, such as Premier Aleksei Kosygin and others, supported institutional arrangements that would enhance managerial coordination across ministerial boundaries.[29] One such arrangement, the industrial production association (*ob"edinenie*), formalized previously existing relationships by bringing under a single managerial hierarchy enterprises engaged in the manufacture of components through to finished products.

Industrial production associations eventually grew to encompass enterprises subordinate to a variety of institutional and geographic hierarchies. Their integrative capacity proved both an asset and an encumbrance. In an economic and political microclimate like Leningrad's, where development policies had been predicated on interbranch and interinstitutional cooperation, local managers encouraged this new organizational format. Elsewhere, however, associations were vulnerable to the machinations of disgruntled and insecure ministerial officials seeking to maintain their own autonomy. Although the association format originated elsewhere, it gained an immediate foothold in Leningrad, perhaps because of a local capacity to coordinate innovation across various interinstitutional (e.g., ministerial) boundaries.

The first production association was organized in L'vov in 1961, linking several local light-industrial establishments under a single organizational format.[30] A year later the same approach was used in Leningrad heavy industry. The first Leningrad production association combined four related enterprises into LOMO, the Leningrad Optico-Mechanical Association.[31] Only three years after LOMO's creation some 130 local enterprises had been joined together into 30 similar production associations, a faster rate of consolidation than found in other Soviet industrial centers. LOMO has subsequently grown into one of the largest, most prestigious and powerful production establishments of its type currently operating in the Soviet Union. The movement to establish production associations continued in Leningrad for years afterwards. By 1978, the city's 210 associations accounted for 80 to 90 percent of all its industrial production as opposed to nearly half of national industrial output.[32] The extent to which associations controlled local industry was unprecedented for the USSR, and remains so today.

To appreciate the singular success of production associations in Leningrad, we should recall that Kozlov's development strategy relied heavily on economic specialization and concentration, as well as technological innovation. By bringing scores of plants and factories under unified managerial systems, the associations enhanced the possibilities for both specialization and innovation planned from above. As smaller peripheral enterprises were absorbed by the new associations, the range of production activities changed markedly. A production shop that previously served a number of clients came to serve only one—its parent association. Possibilities for technological innovation could theoretically be exploited more efficiently as a relatively small number of conglomerates—the 200-odd associations—developed coordinated innovation plans for hundreds of production facilities.

This intense industrial centralization in Leningrad becomes ever more apparent at the level of the urban district (*raion*). For example, by the 1980s, Evgenii Mikhailov, then first secretary of the city's important Vyborgskii District party committee, reported that just 13 industrial and scientific-production associations accounted for 80 percent of the area's total industrial production.[33] Of those 13 associations, six had party committees with the full rights and responsibilities of district party committees, thereby presenting multiple challenges to the authority of Mikhailov's own district party committee (*raikom*).[34] To demonstrate that Vyborgskii was not an aberrant case, we note that 12 associations produced 90 percent of the industrial output of the Zhdanovskii District, 11 associations accounted for 80 percent of that of the Kirovskii District, and 10 produced 95 percent of that of the Leninskii District (all in 1980).[35]

Receptivity to Innovation

The production associations emerged simultaneously with the socioeconomic planning procedures (discussed in Chapter 6). This congruence was not coincidental. The success of socioeconomic planning depended on the existence of planning units sufficiently large and powerful to control a maximum number of social variables. Given the considerable degree to which local political and industrial elites staked their reputations on the success of socioeconomic planning, the advocacy among those elites of managerial centralization was almost inevitable. Shortly after the associational format had first been tried in L'vov, socioeconomic planning efforts helped create an imperative for managerial consolidation.

Conversely, creation of new organizational hierarchies cutting across traditional sectoral divisions, such as Khrushchev's *sovnarkhozy* and the industrial production associations, generated an institutional environment in which multifaceted, integrated socioeconomic planning became plausible. Both the regional economic councils and the production associations established interinstitutional forums that fostered integrated approaches to production planning. The convergence of reforms, along with the legitimation of industrial sociological research, strengthened the credibility of some form of socioeconomic planning.

Finally, both sets of reforms—production associations and socioeconomic planning—were initially implemented at many of the same enterprises. Anatoli Kirsanov, the Kalininskii District's party first secretary, has observed that the very first socioeconomic planning experiments were conducted at two of the city's first industrial production associations (LOMO and Svetlana).[36] This coincidence of innovation has several complex explanations. Party and state officials in Leningrad and Moscow considered those enterprises to be sufficiently prestigious as to serve as model sites for one set of reforms that were prominent candidates as testing-grounds for other innovations. Because of their previous reputations, these enterprises attracted some of the best-trained and most flexible managers. Once enterprises were anointed for innovation sites by higher party and state authorities, they retained managers with proven reputations as innovators, while other pro-innovation managers replaced more recalcitrant cadres. Thus, each set of reforms reinforced the other, producing an institutional climate that was more conducive to innovation than the Soviet norm.

Receptivity to innovation did not end with acceptance of policy changes, but led to interest in technological change. In Leningrad, local party officials at the time saw the establishment of associations as a critical step in their successful implementation of far-reaching managerial innovations.[37] This view was widely shared by a number of political and economic leaders around the Soviet Union, who remained resistant to more radical economic reform packages based on the decentralization of managerial decision-making or the introduction of limited price-related mechanisms into the national planning procedures. The industrial association thus came to be the form of innovation favored by leaders such as Leningrad's own Grigorii Romanov, who opposed more market-oriented approaches to economic reform. The industrial production association was a managerial reform that called for more centralization, not less. This point is an important one. Leningrad's region-oriented centralized managerial structures (i.e., managerial authority is concentrated in middle-level institutions rather than either in the ministries in Moscow or in individual enterprises) stand in opposition to more market-oriented reform packages that have emerged as dominant under Mikhail Gorbachev. Leningrad nurtured organizational forms that were intended to be activist in that they required leadership by a new set of institutions on the periphery but, at the same time, were profoundly conservative in that they preserved a centralized bureaucratic ethos. When Romanov's bid for national power was crushed in 1985 by the Gorbachev juggernaut, such centralizing reform packages fell by the wayside. Nonetheless, the Leningrad experience of the 1960s and 1970s continues to offer an important alternative economic vision to that of either Brezhnev's ministry-oriented approach or Gorbachev's focus on quasi-market enterprise reform.

Despite the kudos given the early production associations—at least as initially conceived in L'vov, Moscow, and elsewhere—they did not begin to address the question of precisely how new production technologies could be developed in the first instance. The initial reorganization efforts discussed thus far focused primarily on the production cycle rather than the R&D cycle. Leningrad managers soon addressed this oversight, by modifying the initial association concept to produce a Leningrad hybrid—the scientific-production association.

Scientific-Production Associations

The scientific-production association differs from the earlier production association in that it incorporates scientific establishments as well as production units into a single managerial system. In other words, industrial research institutes, design centers, and laboratories in a given production sphere could now merge with factories and shops active in the same sector. The scientific-production association thereby integrated R&D and production cycles much as the production association had brought together related production activities. This innovative managerial form proved itself particularly well suited to the Leningrad economy.

By the late 1960s, four industries were preeminent in the Leningrad economy: machine construction, instrument making, radio electronics, and shipbuilding. The four together produced 16 percent of local industrial output, as opposed to only an 8 percent share of national industrial production.[38] Each depends on the ability to incorporate scientific and technological advances directly into the production cycle.[39] Consequently, the very structure of the local industrial establishment encouraged Leningrad elites to advocate associational reforms designed to encompass entire R&D cycles.

Indeed, Leningrad's first four scientific-production associations—the Plastpolimer, Elektroapparat, Elektrokeramika, and Bum Mash scientific-production associations—were formed as early as 1968 and 1969.[40] By 1976, there were some 36 scientific-production associations in the city, linking production lines with more than 100 scientific and design centers. Nearly a decade later in 1985, associations of all kinds drew on the efforts of 500 industrial enterprises and 150 scientific research and design centers.[41]

For its part, the Leningrad scientific community welcomed attempts to integrate its research with the needs of industry. Over the years following removal of the headquarters of the USSR Academy of Sciences to Moscow, Leningrad-based research has evolved, shifting its center of gravity toward applied as opposed to basic research.[42] Despite the disruption accompanying the academy's move to the capital, Leningrad has remained the nation's second most important scientific center.[43] This hold on "second city" status among Soviet scientific centers generated a dramatic expansion of the city's scientific capacity in the late 1960s. Between 1965 and 1975, the local labor force employed in science and science-related endeavors increased by a phenomenal 94 percent, five times the rate of growth of the Leningrad labor force as a whole and several dozen times the increase in the Leningrad industrial workforce.[44] By the early 1970s, a full quarter of the entire Leningrad labor force was employed in the scientific sector, broadly defined.[45] This workforce represented 12 percent of all scientific workers employed in industry throughout the Soviet Union.[46]

Many of these changes have been chronicled by Leningrad social scientists. According to some of this work, at the beginning of the 1970s the Leningrad scientific labor force was tilted heavily toward applied disciplines.[47] The relatively high qualifications of scientific workers engaged in research to meet the needs of local industry were also seen as conducive to innovation.[48] Studies found that in Leningrad, as elsewhere in the Soviet Union, the scientific workforce had become a focal point of female employment.[49] Such research noted further that because the mix of disciplinary skills and skilled support staff was combined with the presence of major educational institutions and research centers, it produced a uniquely favorable environment for scientific research.

Igor Glebov and Ivglaf Sigov confirmed the importance of the local scientific infrastructure in later work examining the economic and social functions of the knowledge industry in the development of major cities.[50] Glebov and Sigov pointed to the existence of Leningrad's far-reaching library, computer, and information infrastructures as a primary reason for the city's continued leadership in Soviet science. For example, the city played a critical regional role in the creation of the national State System of Scientific Technical Information—an information network established by the USSR State Committee on Science and Technology to collect, process, store, and disseminate foreign and domestic technical data and research results.[51] Leningrad's social science community has also contributed to the creation of a national information system in the relevant branches of the social sciences and humanities.[52]

To summarize the discussion of this point, the local Leningrad scientific community offered a unique set of assets and opportunities for programs to enhance cooperation between science and industry. Moreover, the city's scientific community underwent one of its most vigorous growth periods just as the associational reforms were being put into place. The early formation of scientific-production associations linking science and industry is not at all surprising in light of (1) the strong support among local political elites for associational reforms, (2) the needs of key Leningrad industries for technological innovations, and (3) the expansion of a scientific infrastructure already oriented toward applied research.

Typical Associations

For a better sense of the organization and function of the associations, it may be useful to recount briefly the histories of three rather different Leningrad scientific-production units that have many of the most prominent features of this new organizational framework.

The *Leningrad Elektrosila Electro-Machine Building Association* traces its institutional genealogy to the prerevolutionary Siemens & Shukert Dynamo Plant.[53] By 1922, the new Soviet government had reorganized the Siemens & Shukert plant into Elektrosila, which immediately became known for a leading role in industrial innovation. By 1956 Elektrosila had established its first factory-based laboratory facility, an installation that was organizationally subordinate to the Leningrad branch of a major industrial research institute. In 1960 both that laboratory and the entire Leningrad branch institute were absorbed into the Elektrosila hierarchy. Nine years later, Elektrosila research facilities obtained organizational autonomy in the factory's hierarchy, a status that was retained in 1975 when Elektrosila was transformed into a scientific-production association linking all the stages of the research-development-production cycle. At present, Elektrosila's research institute is responsible for applied research, design, and development related to the production of turbines and generators.

The association's research facilities have become heavily involved in power-station development, including major research efforts on behalf of the Soviet Union's nuclear power industry. To a considerable degree, then, the Elektrosila association functions as the Soviet equivalent of Westinghouse or General Electric. It has continued to build on its Leningrad base to assume a major national and even international presence. Its prominence within the Soviet economy continues to be reflected in its leading role in developing Siberian hydroelectric resources, its sale of products to more than 75 countries, including Canada, India, Brazil, and Syria, and its long-sustained direct ties to the USSR Academy of Sciences and leading institutions of higher education.

For Leningrad, the urban presence of Elektrosila's central administrative, research, and production facilities helps establish the region's importance as a national economic center. The association's success, predicated to a considerable degree on its ability to integrate R&D with production, advances local interests by promoting Leningrad's role as a primary center of Soviet innovation. Nurturing of its research capacity by local political support for technological innovation helps defend Leningrad's regional economy, within the context of a centrally directed political economy.

The *Plastpolimer Scientific-Production Association*, a second Leningrad giant, shares many common development patterns with Elektrosila.[54] Like Elektrosila, Plastpolimer has always been a major innovative center within Russian and Soviet industrial life. Having evolved from a production facility that dates back to 1719, the association claims a lineage beginning with Peter the Great's orders to build munitions plants. Two centuries later, a new Soviet administration shifted the plant's focus from gunpowder toward plastics. By 1932, its main research branch, the Scientific Research Institute of Polymer Plastics, had become the first Soviet research institute devoted to plastics.

Various linkages between research and production were largely informal, however, until the period 1956–1962, when more formal contractual relations were established between the Plastpolimer research facilities and the burgeoning Soviet chemical industry. In 1969, various plastics and chemical research and production units in the Leningrad area joined to form the present-day association, which is the Soviet leader in developing and producing polyolefins, polystyrols, and fluoroplastics.

Headquartered in Leningrad, Plastpolimer operates a sprawling network of factories and laboratories stretching as far as Erevan in Armenia and Novosibirsk in Siberia. If there were a "Fortune 500"-style list of Soviet "corporations," Plastpolimer would be near the top. As is true of Elektrosila, its presence in the city advances local economic interests. The two associations have become so powerful in their respective economic sectors that central institutions in Moscow cannot ignore their needs. Operating in a metropolitan economy, however, neither Elektrosila nor Plastpolimer can dominate the local scene in a way that would threaten to turn Leningrad into a company town.

The third scientific-production association, the *All-Union Scientific Research Institute of Metrology*, represents an alternative model of institutional development whose production capacity evolved within a research environment.[55] Established in 1893 as the Main House of Weights and Measures, the institute has long led the conversion of the Soviet Union to international standards of weights and measures. The research facility's presence promoted the development in the city of a local precision-instrument industry. At the outbreak of World War II, such plants as Kalibr, Gosmetr, and Manometr guaranteed Leningrad's position as the primary center for this increasingly important industry.

With the establishment of the All-Union Committee on Standardization in Moscow in 1930, the industry's center of gravity began to shift to Moscow. By the 1950s, Leningrad's dominance of precision-instrument production had waned, resulting in several reorganizations of local research and production facilities. From this nadir, however, Leningrad precision-instrument making began to expand once more, led in large part by the research center, which doubled the number of its laboratories while increasing its research staff from a low of just 100 in 1928 to 550 employees by 1955, and 1,500 in 1971. That year various production facilities merged under institute control to form the current scientific-production association. In the case of precision instruments, the city's scientific traditions have thus sustained local industry through some rough periods. The existence and eventual expansion of research facilities provided the necessary context for further economic development. The willingness of local Leningrad elites to promote the merger of research and production facilities protected this vital sector of the city's economy. Local endorsement of associational reforms helped sustain economic development.

This discussion of the Elektrosila, Plastpolimer, and Metrology scientific-production associations illustrates many general themes in the evolution of Leningrad R&D management. Their histories document the continuing effort of local managers to gain control over the activities of related but semiautonomous research units in their jurisdictions by creating unified managerial structures. This long-standing tendency toward institutional centralization reflects similar trends among the ministries and economic planners in Moscow. A primary underlying assumption appears to be the notion that bringing all R&D under a single roof will inevitably reduce or redress traditional disincentives for innovation.

The USSR Academy of Sciences' Leningrad Scientific Center

As noted earlier, the drive toward integrated research-production management may also be seen in local support for attempts by the Academy of Sciences to unite all preexisting Leningrad operations within a single Leningrad-based scientific center. Along with wartime evacuations and losses, the prewar transfer of the Academy of Sciences' main administration to Moscow depleted Leningrad of many of its leading researchers and weakened its institutional base within the national academy structure.[56] By the mid-1950s, the relocated academy had spawned a dozen republic-level academies of sciences, as well as an embryonic network of regional scientific centers, including the prestigious Siberian Division based in Novosibirsk.[57] Two decades later, nearly every autonomous republic had an academy "scientific branch" integrating a series of research functions under local management.[58]

Meanwhile, Leningraders had only a handful of academy research facilities (e.g., institutes, laboratories, libraries, archives), most of them mere "Leningrad branches" in the hierarchy of Moscow-based research institutions. This long-standing subordination, by which Leningrad facilities were subdivisions of Moscow research institutes, placed many decisions concerning critical personnel, research, and resources in the hands of institute directors in charge of major academy installations in the capital. Such a state of affairs meant that Leningrad's local political officials had less than direct or total control over the academy's Leningrad operations. Admittedly, however, many in the city's scientific community preferred having the general political oversight function lodged with officials far away in Moscow rather than situated virtually next door in Leningrad itself.

By the mid-1970s, Grigorii Romanov had taken considerable interest in the state of the academy in Leningrad. In 1975, acting at Romanov's prompting (at least according to anecdotal evidence), the academy merged existing Leningrad divisions, as well as sections of a half-dozen Moscow-based social science research centers, to form the Institute of Socioeconomic Problems.[59] Very soon thereafter, Leningrad party officials began to agitate for a similar arrangement in the natural sciences so as to ensure that academy research would better serve the interests of local industry (and of political leaders such as Romanov).[60] As the seventies closed, Leningrad politicians were lobbying to upgrade the local presence in the academy structure, thereby recapturing some of the status lost when the academy moved to Moscow during the 1930s.

This advocacy for improved status not unexpectedly encountered bureaucratic opposition within the academy itself. To gain greater autonomy, Leningrad research centers would have to sever their long-standing affiliations with Moscow institutions, and the Muscovites naturally resisted such proposals. The academy began to relent, however, responding to pressure from an ever-more-powerful Romanov and other Leningrad-based politicians to hold local scholars accountable first and foremost to the Leningrad party organization. Considerable unofficial and unpublished evidence points to Romanov's major role in this effort. His growing stature in the national Communist Party hierarchy undoubtedly assisted the efforts of Leningraders to seize control of their local institutions. In 1979, the entire academy structure in the Northwestern RSFSR (see Map 1) was placed in the jurisdiction of a new Leningrad-based interagency coordinating council.

The new body quickly established 14 specialized subcouncils to coordinate all research in Leningrad (both the city and the region), as well as in the Arkhangelsk, Vologda, Novgorod, Murmansk, and Pskov regions and in the Karelian and Komi autonomous republics.[61] The new coordinating council did not limit itself to the Academy of Sciences, but publicly declared its intention to direct all research activities in the natural, technical, and social sciences carried out within its jurisdiction by all research centers, regardless of their institutional subordination.[62] In an article appearing in *Pravda* on August 4, 1981, Romanov emphasized the role of the council in coordinating the relationship between scientific research and economic production.[63] Thus, Romanov made it clear, as he did again in the party's leading ideological journal, *Kommunist*, that Leningrad science must serve Leningrad industry.[64] Finally, just weeks after Romanov had left Leningrad to join the Central Committee's Secretariat in Moscow, the Academy of Sciences, acting at the behest of the Central Committee, announced the formation of a new Leningrad Scientific Center, responsible for all academy activities in the Northwestern RSFSR (see Chart 4).[65]

The establishment of the academy's Leningrad Scientific Center

Chart 4. *Research system of the USSR Academy of Sciences and the Academies of Sciences of the Union Republics.*

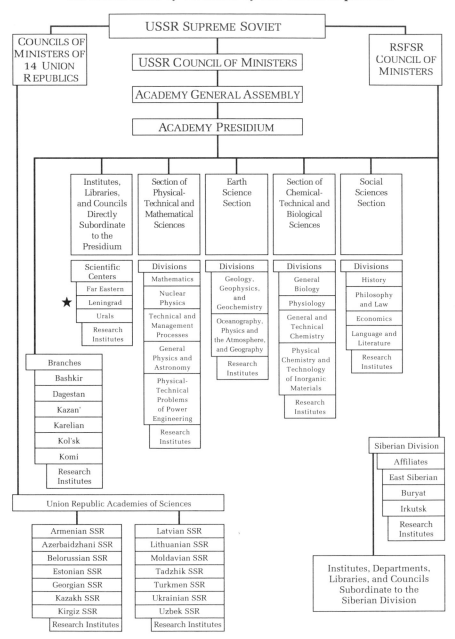

marked a new stage in the relationship between Leningrad's scientific and industrial communities (and one not necessarily welcomed by scholars concerned with basic research). Based more fully on local control than was true of previous academy arrangements in Leningrad, the center declared its primary objective to be the advancement of local economic production. In published interviews appearing at the time, the center's chief executive, Academician Igor Glebov, noted that the new organization would seek to direct all research (not just that of the academy) toward the more efficient utilization of research results in production. Glebov reported that the center had incorporated 14 academy scientific councils and 31 research institutes operating within the Leningrad region, while its presidium included the 80 full and corresponding members of the academy resident in the region.[66] The center also anticipated moving the bulk of its operations to Shuvalovo, a new satellite community on the city's northern outskirts.

Romanov, Glebov, and, later on, Lev Zaikov repeatedly observed that the center's research branches must link scientific research with economic production so as to enhance opportunities for technological innovation in local industry.[67] In this regard, the creation of the Leningrad Scientific Center is yet another stage in the continuing effort of local political elites to control and maintain the city's economy as a leading innovative center in the national economic system.

In February 1985, on the eve of Konstantin Chernenko's death, Romanov returned to Leningrad to present his election speech to the RSFSR Supreme Soviet ward in the city's Smol'ninskii District.[68] The address, which turned out to be his last major public appearance in the city, stressed the need to quicken the pace of technological innovation in Leningrad industry. He offered perhaps the most precise formulation of the Leningrad Scientific Center's role in that effort, pointing to the development of the Ukrainian Academy of Sciences as a model to be emulated in Leningrad. Romanov's references to the Ukrainian academy are noteworthy, for that institution had reoriented much of its research effort around applied research designed to enhance the republic's economic potential.[69] Significantly, one of the first major institution-building efforts of the new Leningrad Scientific Center was the formation of a new Institute of Information Sciences and Automation just one year later, in March 1986.[70] This theme of the center's role in linking science and industry has been frequently repeated since.[71]

The history of the founding of the academy's Leningrad Scientific Center, as well as the development of local scientific-production associations, illustrates long-standing themes in the Soviet approach to R&D. As Thane Gustafson has pointed out, these are that (1) science is the source of most worthwhile innovations; (2) industry is a source of most obstacles to innovation; and (3) the solution is to give scientists direct control over production facilities.[72]

The "Intensification-90" Campaign

In July 1984, First Secretary Lev Zaikov informed the Leningrad regional party committee that he had just been invited by the Central Committee to report on the activities of the Leningrad party organization in planning fundamental economic and social development throughout the Leningrad region for the periods 1985–1990 and 1985–2000.[73] In preparing his report for the Central Committee, Zaikov continued, he would pay particular attention to the role of technological innovation in increasing productivity throughout the Leningrad region. Indeed, he concluded, automation and computerization would be the foundation of local economic growth for the next two decades. At the same time, the then regional party second secretary and soon-to-be city party committee first secretary, Anatoli Dumachev, informed the RSFSR Supreme Soviet that existing labor shortages in the city dictated that all increases in the production of Leningrad industry over the next three years could take place *only* through technological innovation. In Dumachev's view, Leningrad managers had no choice but to follow the example set by their American and Japanese counterparts and force extensive automation and innovation.[74] The available data support this intense concern over labor shortages.[75]

Zaikov's speeches heralded a new stage in the efforts of Leningrad elites to spur technological innovation. This "Intensification-90" campaign, as it became known because of its goal of automating the Leningrad economy by 1990, quickly gained momentum as Leningrad politicians stressed the program's origins both in the emergence of the scientific-production associations and in the establishment of the academy's Leningrad Scientific Center.[76] Such proclamations correctly viewed "Intensification-90" as a logical extension of earlier Leningrad innovations. Moreover, local elites identified the city's labor shortages as a driving force behind the innovation campaign.[77] Soviet cities with less acute shortages could well have been less hospitable to such a massive computerization drive.

However valid these elements of the official position on the program's origins may be, such statements ignore or purposefully obscure differences between this innovation drive and previous campaigns. As we have noted, the development of scientific-production associations and the founding of the academy's Leningrad Scientific Center were both moves that reflected the view of science as the source of most worthwhile innovations. In contrast, the "Intensification-90" campaign focuses first and foremost on the ability of industry to adapt managerial systems to technologies that already exist. This accent in the most recent program falls on the management side of the innovation equation. It is important, therefore, to review precisely what Zaikov and others sought to accomplish with "Intensification-90."

Following Zaikov's report, in August 1984, the Central Committee approved the "Intensification-90" program with the explicit intention of utilizing the Leningrad experience as a prototype for similar efforts elsewhere.[78] The goal was to involve representatives of the State Planning Committee (*Gosplan*), the State Committee on Science and Technology, the RSFSR Council of Ministers, and the USSR Academy of Sciences in a joint effort, under the direction of Leningrad party leaders, to reduce manual labor through the automation and computerization of production lines and front offices. Approved with considerable fanfare a few days later by the Leningrad regional party committee, the specific program objectives soon emerged in the local press.[79]

In interviews published at the time, and in subsequent public appearances, Academician Glebov identified the campaign's goals as computerization of management, production, and design at all levels of the Leningrad economy; the creation of integrated computerized systems rather than the continued accumulation of mismatched components of such systems; a drive for energy conservation; and general support for nuclear power programs.[80] The initial computerization effort, Glebov repeated, would take place at 336 enterprises representing 99 ministries and institutions and employing more than 660,000 people. Ultimately, by the time of the program's final stages in 1990, Glebov concluded, there would be 5 totally automated plants, 69 automated shops, 152 integrated production complexes, 137 flexible production systems, 187 automated management systems, 232 integral lines of communications, and 160 other mechanized sites.

"Intensification-90" immediately gained the trappings of a major Soviet campaign, as program publicists added all the traditional bells and whistles. Articles appeared almost daily in the Leningrad press for well over a year praising this or that innovation initiative undertaken in connection with "Intensification-90".[81] More significantly, Leningrad's party chief, Lev Zaikov, began using the opportunities presented by the innovation drive to advance his own political position.

The Emergence of Lev Zaikov

Zaikov's rise to local dominance following Romanov's elevation to the Central Committee's Secretariat had been rather unpredictable. A graduate of the Leningrad Engineering-Economics Institute, Zaikov established his reputation as a dynamic and effective manager, eventually rising to the general directorship of an unspecified (though probably defense-related) scientific-production association by the mid-1970s.[82] He was appointed chair of the Leningrad city soviet in 1976, and by the end of the decade was serving as a member of the Commission on Foreign Affairs of the Supreme Soviet's Council of the Union.[83] From the time he began his career as a lathe operator in 1940 until his assumption of the Leningrad regional first secretaryship in 1983, Zaikov apparently held no major Communist Party post. With this general background, his interest in managerial innovation and economic efficiency is hardly surprising. In less than two years, Zaikov had joined Gorbachev's Secretariat in Moscow, where he assumed responsibility for defense industries and later became first secretary of the powerful Moscow party organization. His meteoric rise was facilitated by the successful promotion of the "Intensification-90" campaign in Leningrad and nationally. That promotion also generated economic resources for the city and its leaders to draw on.

Within days of the Central Committee's endorsement of the "Intensification-90" campaign, Zaikov published an article in *Pravda* stating its goals.[84] From that point forward, Zaikov's major addresses have stressed the innovation theme.[85] National publications publicized the program as well.[86] Finally, Leningrad politicians utilized opportunities afforded to them by various republic and national meetings to praise "Intensification-90."[87]

Gorbachev Comes to Town

Zaikov, a skilled manager with extensive practical experience, fit the initial mold of the new "Gorbachev Man." This image was strengthened by Gorbachev's visit to Leningrad in May 1985,[88] which was the new leader's first major foray outside of Moscow following his ascension to power. At first glance, this maneuver appeared to have been aimed at Gorbachev's chief rival of the period, Grigorii Romanov. This interpretation is bolstered by Romanov's own removal from the Politburo in July of that year.

Gorbachev's visit was extensively covered in the Soviet print and electronic media, and included stops at the Svetlana Electronic-Instrument Making Association, the Bolshevichka Sewing Association, Elektrosila, the Leningrad Metallurgical Plant, and the Kalinin Polytechnic Institute.[89] At each institution, as well as in Gorbachev's focal appearance before a meeting of Leningrad party activists, the new general secretary dwelled on the advances made by the Leningrad economy in the area of technological innovation, particularly under the "Intensification-90" campaign.[90] In his address to city party activists, Gorbachev reviewed all he had seen during his visit, stressing the positive impact of "Intensification-90" on local economic development. He noted that the Central Committee was pleased by the program's success, observing that the Leningrad party organization always played an important role in the formulation of national socioeconomic policies. The party's leadership endorsed the latest efforts in Leningrad to enhance labor productivity through scientific-technical progress, particularly in the area of computerization in management. Hence, the "Intensification-90" campaign served as a model to be emulated elsewhere.

Gorbachev's endorsement was followed by Central Committee approval a month later during a plenum that also saw the elevation of Zaikov to the Secretariat.[91] Shortly after Zaikov's departure from Leningrad to assume his new post in Moscow, his successor as regional party first secretary, Iurii Solov'ev, devoted the preponderance of his initial speech in that post to the "Intensification-90" campaign.[92] By year's end, the city party first secretary, Anatolii Dumachev, similarly chose to use the "Intensification-90" campaign as the focal point for his report to the twenty-fifth conference of the city party organization.[93] Meanwhile, local bookstores established special displays of materials relating to the campaign, an exhibit showing off its achievements opened in Moscow, and, at the behest of the Central Committee's Secretariat, the local party organization organized seminars for party leaders and economic managers from around the Soviet Union to learn more about the "Intensification-90" campaign.[94] Finally, the "Intensification-90" program was incorporated into the 1986 general development plan for the city and region.[95] Regional party Secretary Pavel Mozhaev and city party committee First Secretary Anatolii Dumachev also reported in December 1985 that the campaign, with its concomitant emphasis on increased economic specialization and centralization, had formed the keystone for the 1986–1990 regional and city five-year plans.[96] Moreover, Iurii Solov'ev chose to highlight the program upon his elevation to candidate member status on the national party's Politburo.[97] As with the effort to develop scientific-production associations, Leningrad's "Intensification-90" advanced both the economic resources and the power of the local leaders. By the time of the twenty-seventh party congress in early 1986, the program had once again secured Leningrad's image as a national leader in technological innovation.

Problems Persist

Despite the apparent success of the "Intensification-90" campaign as a vehicle for promoting the political interests of Leningrad leaders, it is worth remembering that the successful adoption of a development strategy at the local and national levels is not the same as that program's successful implementation. By October 1986 both regional party First Secretary Iurii Solov'ev and Central Committee Secretary Lev Zaikov were beginning to sound more cautious in their evaluations of the program's impact.

In response to queries from local party propagandists, Solov'ev observed that innovation programs based on managerial reorganization can have the effect of increasing the bureaucratic apparatus without increasing productivity.[98] Consequently, he reported that the Leningrad party organization was disbanding the association managerial structure in food industries in an effort to reduce administrative overhead costs by 20 percent, thereby reversing the policies of the sixties and seventies that had embraced centralization as facilitating innovation. Shortly thereafter, Solov'ev informed the Leningrad regional party committee that the region's critically important machine-construction industry was failing to meet various innovation goals.[99] The reasons for this failure were complex. At the core, Solov'ev argued, was the resistance of managers to drawing on the latest innovations generated by the scientific community. He concluded by suggesting that the "Intensification-90" campaign was a necessary means for breaking down such resistance. These sentiments were repeated by Solov'ev again just eight months later. In the interim they were echoed by city party First Secretary Anatolii Gerasimov, who in various reports to the city party committee suggested that technological innovation and enhanced labor productivity were proving more difficult goals to obtain than the architects of "Intensification-90" had ever before been willing to acknowledge.[100]

During an October 1986 speech to voters in Leningrad's Moskovskii election district, Lev Zaikov offered a more comprehensive review of the successes and failures of the "Intensification-90" campaign than did either Solov'ev or Gerasimov before or afterward.[101] Zaikov began his remarks by observing that Leningrad's political leaders had long been interested in strengthening the ties between science and industry. He proposed that a cardinal restructuring of society was required, and that the future well-being of the Soviet population lay with the economy's ability to perfect the research-development-production cycle. Further managerial reform was necessary to ensure that the Soviet economy's innovative capacity increased.

Zaikov also contended that the Soviet Union's current economic situation demanded varied responses. To begin with, Soviet scientists should work with their colleagues from other socialist countries to improve the industrial innovation process. Workers should also become involved to a greater degree in the factory innovative cycle, while the legal rights of enterprises to act as autonomous units should be expanded. By extensive restructuring of their bureaucracies, municipal agencies should attempt to reduce the bureaucratic drain on local industries. Finally, said Zaikov, the innovation problem must be viewed as, above all, a human problem.

For Zaikov, Leningrad's "Intensification-90" program provided a comprehensive format for action along all these fronts. For this reason, he viewed Leningrad as one of the Soviet Union's leading innovative centers. Despite the failure of local industries to meet all the campaign's goals, Zaikov suggested further, Leningrad was well situated to assist the entire Soviet economy as it struggled to come to terms with the innovation process.

In reviewing various attempts to enhance Leningrad industry's innovative capacity, we must remember that these programs have only been partially successful, by the standards of the world economy. Although we do not have adequate data to evaluate the efficiency of local industry in comparative terms, on the basis of what we do know, it is difficult to believe that Leningrad's factories could compete openly with those of Western Europe, North America, and Japan. As Zaikov suggested, however, within the context of the Soviet economy the 35-year effort to improve relations between the city's scientific and industrial communities is noteworthy. This core of experience provides one of the single best models in the USSR today for helping national politicians and planners understand how they can develop comprehensive strategies for dealing with the research-development-production cycle. In this last regard, the political significance of the policies discussed in this chapter may be greater than their actual economic impact.

The political impact of strategies to link science and industry transcends the careers of Leningrad politicians. Economic accomplishment has dominated Soviet politics for decades. In its most recent manifestation, the issue of economic performance has become focused on the question of innovation. Soviet reformers and conservatives—as well as Western commentators—increasingly attribute the lackluster economic performance to a perceived inability of the economy to foster innovation. Gorbachev's response to this innovation challenge has been to nurture the development and implementation of market-oriented economic mechanisms. Should these reforms take hold, the argument goes, enterprises will become more responsive to changing needs in their environment, thereby prompting a greater receptivity to innovation.

The Leningrad approach to the innovation question emphasizes centralization of managerial decision-making, rationalization, and streamlining of organizational lines of command so as to force existing institutions to operate more efficiently. Implicitly, the approach advocated by Leningrad politicians from Kozlov through Romanov to Zaikov has offered a counterpoint to the more market-oriented reform efforts of an Aleksei Kosygin during the 1960s and a Mikhail Gorbachev today. Direct research contracts, production associations, scientific-production associations, and even the "Intensification-90" campaign constitute a conservative alternative in that such mechanisms need not undermine the traditional authority of central planners, necessitate a significant redistribution of resources away from traditionally favored heavy ("Group A") industries, or present a direct challenge to the supervisory authority of Communist Party officials over economic management. The Leningrad approach to economic development thus offers an antimarket perspective that has informed national political discourse throughout the post-Stalin era.

Science and Industry: An Overview

For four decades Leningrad leaders have vigorously pursued an economic development strategy intended to reorient the Leningrad economy around technologically specialized industrial production. This effort has fostered increased investment in industry, a phaseout of light industry, and enhancement of technological innovation through strengthened ties between science and industry. Ultimately, Leningrad elites have sought to preserve their city's historic role as an innovative producer of high-quality industrial goods and as a leader of such specialized industries as precision-instrument making, machine construction, and shipbuilding. These policies have helped sustain the city's economic growth, thereby advancing the interests of several Leningrad political leaders. The resulting increase in the power and status of an influential politician, in turn, supported some of the initiatives discussed here—for example, we saw how Grigorii Romanov apparently prompted the Central Committee to instruct the USSR Academy of Sciences to establish its Leningrad Scientific Center.

The pursuit of Leningrad's postwar development strategy has rested in large measure on fostering new and more effective linkages between scientific research and industrial production. Technological innovation has been a major objective in Leningrad throughout the Soviet period. Confronting increasingly extreme labor shortages as early as the late 1950s, Leningrad managers actively sought new production techniques to increase labor productivity. Consequently, different and at times competing strategies have emerged over the years to bind the research-development-production cycle more tightly.

During the 1950s, leading Leningrad research centers entered into contractual relationships with major industrial enterprises. By the 1960s, an intricate web of interinstitutional research and technological contracts linked most major research and production centers through task-specific agreements. Within a few years, Leningrad researchers and managers attempted to broaden the range of their cooperation beyond assignment-oriented agreements. Local elites pursued the integration of autonomous but related production units engaged in similar activities. Not surprisingly, Leningraders enthusiastically encouraged the formation of inter-enterprise production associations in the hope that such a new organizational format might foster innovation. A decade later a vast preponderance of Leningrad economic output was being produced by a relatively small number of integrated production associations, which were themselves at the pinnacle of industrial empires stretching across the Soviet Union.

Managers continued to confront difficulties in implementing innovation programs. More specifically, factory administrators demanded innovations adapted to the needs of their individual plants. Local elites responded by formally merging production and research units to form scientific-production associations. Leningrad was particularly suited for such programs of integration. On the industrial front, the city's economy had come to be dominated by a handful of sectors that relied heavily on infusions of new technologies for productivity increases. With respect to the scientific community, the city had long been a major national center for applied research. Sponsored by senior local political elites, the consolidation of production and research units into unified scientific-production associations moved forward swiftly, building on this preexisting base.

The prewar transfer of the Academy of Sciences' main administration to Moscow had left Leningrad's remaining academy research facilities in an ambiguous bureaucratic status. Converted for the most part into local affiliates of Moscow-based research institutes, Leningrad's research centers often served the interests of the national capital's scientific community. In 1979, the academy's hierarchy responded to growing political pressure from Leningrad, organizing an interagency council to coordinate research efforts throughout the Northwestern RSFSR. Five years later, the academy built on that foundation to establish its Leningrad Scientific Center, an institution that immediately proclaimed its primary mission as the continued integration of local research and production programs.

Production associations, which united production facilities under single management, and scientific-production associations, which united entire research-development-production cycles under single management, shared with the Leningrad Scientific Center a common set of organizing assumptions, the most important being the notion that technological innovation could be fostered through enhanced contact between scientists and managers. This principle also underlay Lev Zaikov's subsequent initiatives in support of technological innovation—namely, the "Intensification-90" campaign, which provided for the computerization of Leningrad industrial management and the automation of core production facilities by 1990. Its goals conformed with the development strategy first set forth 30 years earlier by Frol Kozlov and pursued by Leningrad political and economic elites ever since. These goals have had a deep and lasting impact on the shape of the local economy, and hence on the shape of the city's social and even physical face.

Unlike previous efforts, however, the "Intensification-90" campaign emphasized the full utilization of existing technical capacities as much as the creation of new capacities through R&D programs. Leningrad elites had formulated an organizational model of technological progress that stood in opposition to market-oriented reform programs. Not surprisingly, some national politicians such as Lev Zaikov argued that "Intensification-90" become a model for innovation programs nationally. Thus, the program was subsequently emulated throughout the Soviet Union. Finally, the "Intensification-90" campaign was fully integrated into the 1986–2005 Leningrad general plan.

The emergence of an economic development policy predicated on innovation, together with an evolving pattern of policies designed to implement that policy, offers an opportunity to explore how local politicians and managers in the Soviet Union, at least in the case of Leningrad, maneuver behind a screen of bureaucracy to shape their city's future economic, social, and physical development. The efforts to integrate entire research-design-production cycles under a single managerial umbrella point to one of the various means employed by Soviet urban leaders to adjust central policies and constraints so as to foster new opportunities for their communities to grow, within the context of a centrally planned economy. With this observation in mind, it is time to look at policies that focus on managing the city's workforce.

5

Educating a New Workforce

Most of the qualified workers in the city at the out-
break of the war had been evacuated, many never to
return. Those workers who stayed behind had their
educations disrupted. Postwar migrants to town
were largely unskilled. A severe decline in the skills
of the local labor pool was a major price of the war.
Something had to be done.
                                      —Vladimir Polozov, 1984

Industrial Modernization

Only five and a half months before Stalin died, Frol Kozlov, then
second secretary of the Leningrad regional party committee, strode to
the podium of the tenth Leningrad city party conference and declared:
"The fundamental content of the work of the Leningrad party organization is to mobilize laborers in the struggle for technological progress."[1] With these words, Kozlov proclaimed a fundamental principle
of a new approach to Leningrad's economic development: the doctrine
of ascendent technological innovation.

As we have already seen, Kozlov's endorsement of technological
innovation has been repeated by every successive Leningrad political
figure of any consequence, with language more enthusiastic than even
the usual glowing Soviet litany of praise for science and invention.
Indeed, an unquestioning belief in technological progress constitutes a
core value in the city's development strategy, a program that features
a reorientation of the Leningrad economy around increasingly specialized and sophisticated industries.[2] Leningrad party leaders have consistently praised and vigorously pursued an economic development
strategy rooted in the expansion of communications and interchange
between science and industry.[3] Moreover, production statistics reveal
a relative decline in the city's production capacity in light industry.[4]

An earlier version of this chapter and the next appeared in *Canadian Slavonic
Papers* 24, no. 2 (June 1982): 161–174, as "Policy Innovation and the Soviet Political
Process: The Case of Socio-economic Planning in Leningrad."

The end result, as we have emphasized, has been a sustained effort over at least three decades to concentrate the city's industry in specialized, technologically intensive, and high-quality spheres of heavy-industrial production of the sort represented by machine construction, shipbuilding, precision-instrument making, and radio electronics.[5]

On the positive side, this policy of economic specialization and innovation encouraged the modernization of many of the city's most important industrial establishments.[6] Leningrad factories are demonstrably among the most productive and efficient in the Soviet Union, particularly in such vital industries as radio electronics, optics, manufacture of precision machine tools.[7] Yet, at the same time, Leningrad's share of total national investment has declined steadily throughout the postwar period. Its all-time high was achieved in the Soviet period during the Third Five-Year Plan (1933–1937), when its share was 4.6 percent of national investment funds, from which it declined to 1.9 percent during the Sixth Five-Year Plan (1956–1960), and on down to only about 1 percent during the Ninth and Tenth Five-Year Plans (1971–1975, 1976–1980).[8] Moreover, several traditional Leningrad industries in light-industrial sectors (those relegated to "Group B" status by state planners) developed at a slower rate than they had previously. Light-industrial production in Leningrad also expanded at a slower rate than the same industries did nationally.[9]

As we look back across the past three decades or so, there seems to be an air of inevitability in the gradual and sustained redirection of the Leningrad industrial effort. Such an interpretation, encouraged by local political rhetoric, would, however, overlook the innumerable difficulties encountered in attempts to reorient the local economy around a few priority sectors, bringing together both science and industry. These difficulties were the focus of Chapter 4, and they inspired two additional sets of labor policy innovations that will be discussed in this chapter and the next—professional-technical schools and socioeconomic planning.

Modernization and Workers

As we have already noted, World War II marked a momentous demographic watershed in Leningrad history.[10] During the first 18 months of the city's siege by combined German and Finnish forces, Leningrad's population plummeted by two thirds.[11] After the war, rural in-migrants and demobilized soldiers replenished the lost population, but the new residents on the whole were less educated, skilled, and disciplined than their prewar predecessors. Consequently, by the mid-1950s, Leningrad's population approached its prewar level, but the new postwar population and workforce were qualitatively different from and inferior in capabilities to those of prewar times. In the labor market, Leningrad had lost its competitive edge over many other provincial industrial centers.

At the time, Leningrad's senior political leadership apparently was either neglectful of or ill informed about the city's evolving character.[12] In the Leningrad press of the period, one finds strong endorsements of development strategies predicated on technologically sophisticated production processes. This imprimatur suggests massive ignorance among Leningrad's leaders of the demographic changes that had, in fact, taken place during the 1940s.

Factory managers could not ignore this transformation of their workforce as easily as could planners and politicians. Confronted with a divergence between the needs of the programs being promoted and the active vocational skills of a working population that was not up to the tasks required by those programs, Leningrad industrial managers and factory party officials began advocating measures to alter either the plan or the workforce.[13] Searching for strategies to maintain the plan and improve the workforce, Leningrad officials soon responded on two fronts. First, the city's political and economic leadership began advocating the massive expansion of the city's factory-based vocational education centers, to retrain experienced workers and educate local youth to fill new factory positions. Second, they began encouraging industrial-oriented sociological research.

The efforts on both fronts paid off over the next decade. An extensive network of vocational education centers transformed the city's education system, and eventually served as a model for a thorough reorganization of primary and secondary education throughout the Soviet Union during the spring of 1984. Meanwhile, the local sociological research community focused its studies to a considerable degree on issues of factory life and worker motivation. These studies supported a policy consensus that came to be shared widely among the Leningrad academic, managerial, and political leadership: namely, that factory managers needed greater flexibility in developing production plans, deploying workers, and creating a local social infrastructure to support productivity. As we shall discuss further in Chapter 6, the resulting attempt to integrate social and economic indicators into factory production plans led to the creation of a system of plant, urban district, city, and regional socioeconomic plans throughout the Soviet Union.

By the 1980s, we can clearly identify Leningrad's skilled and well-educated workforce as a major component of the city's competitive edge over most other Soviet industrial centers. An economic development strategy has come to fruition based on the dominance of a handful of very specialized—within the Soviet context—technologically advanced and critically important industrial sectors, primarily in heavy industry. When evaluated according to its stated goals, this approach to local industrial and economic development has proven dramatically successful. The city and region are of indisputable importance to the country's overall economic effort. Success was largely attributable to innovative measures taken in the 1960s and 1970s to restructure labor-management relations at factories throughout the city. That restructuring, in turn, was a consequence of changing approaches to secondary and adult education.

Khrushchev's Educational Reform

In April 1958, Nikita Khrushchev, first secretary of the Communist Party's Central Committee, leveled a blistering attack on the Soviet Union's education system.[14] Addressing the thirteenth national congress of the Young Communist League (Komsomol), Khrushchev, seeking to combat negative attitudes toward physical labor that had emerged among postwar youth, recommended making admission to higher education easier and reducing education-enforced social stratification.[15] More specifically, the following September he proposed that continuous academic education, from primary schools through institutions of higher learning, should incorporate compulsory work programs into their normal curricula, thereby reducing the national commitment to academic training.[16] By November 1958, however, the Central Committee appeared to have put considerable distance between its instititutional stance on this subject and that of its first secretary.[17] Nevertheless, in December, some eight months after Khrushchev's initial onslaught, an educational reform took effect that, though watered down, did increase the hours devoted to polytechnical education at every stage of a student's academic career. An 11-year program incorporating vocational as well as academic training was projected to replace the traditional ten-year primary and secondary general school.[18]

In July 1959, the Council of Ministers responded to passage of the final reform legislation by establishing a new ministerial level State Committee for Professional and Technical Education, to coordinate programs operated by the councils of ministers of the various union republics (state committees being responsible for activities that cut across the jurisdiction of several ministries).[19] Subsequent statutes in May 1961 and March 1962 created a network of republic-based professional-technical schools (*professional'no-tekhnicheskoe uchilishche*, PTU, in the singular) to absorb students completing the obligatory eight-year general school program. Urban PTUs theoretically became tied to future employment sites—a linkage strengthened further in 1966, 1969, 1972, and 1974—offering students four- to five-year secondary education programs combining school with on-the-job training at future employment sites.[20]

For example, the curriculum for lathe operators, metalworkers, and instrument makers at a secondary-level PTU during the mid-1970s devoted two thirds of total instruction time to vocational training (46.6 percent, on-site production instruction; 4.9 percent, special technologies; 4.6 percent, physical education; 3.4 percent, primary military training; 2.6 percent, examination of materials and machine-building technology; 2.4 percent, drawing and design; 1 percent, labor and production economics; and 0.8 percent, tolerances and measurement), while one third was spent on more traditional academic subjects (7.8 percent, mathematics; 7.1 percent, physics; 5.4 percent, history; 5.1 percent, Russian language and literature; 4.7 percent, chemistry; 1.5 percent, social studies; 1 percent, biology; 0.9 percent, geography; and 0.4 percent, astronomy).[21] This combination of job-site experience and general academic training offered a more comprehensive educational experience than many workforce training programs in the United States and, despite difficulties at times in classroom implementation, produced a better reputation for vocational education as a means for preparing students for careers as skilled workers than has generally been the case in the United States. Indeed, as British sociologist Mervyn Matthews has observed, by the mid-1970s the network of vocational schools had grown in size and complexity well beyond Khrushchev's initial legislative vision.[22]

Vocational education was hardly new to the Soviet Union, or to Leningrad for that matter. An extensive network of short- and long-term training programs had emerged during the 1920s and 1930s. In 1940 these special secondary-level technical schools (*tekhnikumy*) and primary schools were frequently attached to factories, an institution of this sort being called a plant-factory school (*fabrichno-zavodskoe uchilishche*, FZU).[23] These schools were consolidated under the central control of a new Main Administration for State Labor Reserves at that time.[24] After the war, the importance of vocational training declined in relation to academic specialties, despite a presumption on the part of the worker's state and the leading agency of the proletariat, the Communist Party, that vocational training was ideologically superior. During the brief interlude between Stalin's death in 1953 and Khrushchev's educational reform in 1958, officials in Latvia and elsewhere experimented with programs designed to lure graduates of the ten-year general schools into vocational trades.[25] Against the background of these latter tests, Khrushchev moved to reconstitute Soviet primary and secondary education.

As the level of work skills and general education rose nationwide, vocational education had lost its attraction to many Soviet youth. In Leningrad, the overall erosion of vocational programs had taken place somewhat earlier than elsewhere.[26] During the academic year 1939/1940, for example, factory training centers (FZUs) enrolled only 15,000

Leningrad youths, as opposed to 55,000 in 1931/1932. By 1982, however, the enrollment figures at the 145 somewhat analogous Leningrad PTUs would jump to over 330,000 annually.[27] To understand this dramatic reversal, we need to return to the period surrounding Khrushchev's educational reforms of 1958.

Leningrad Responds

In the available Leningrad press, there seems little that differentiates the discussion of Khrushchev's proposed reorganization of primary and secondary schools from the discussion found in other Soviet publications of the period.[28] Leningraders supported the introduction of a vocational component into the current school curriculum, but so did nearly everyone else, in one form or another. Formal interviews and informal discussions with Leningrad social scientists in early 1984 revealed, however, that the national educational reform in 1958 had come to be perceived as a turning point in that city's faltering commitment to vocational training. Thus, for really the first time it had spurred debates among local leaders about the critical relationship between the shape of educational curricula and the region's ability to meet the labor demands of local industry.[29] To determine whether this perception of the relationship between national and local events was well founded, we need to consider the state of the Leningrad industrial workforce in the late 1950s. We can then discuss the nature of the subsequent educational effort in greater detail.

As we noted earlier, the city's recent demographic transformation had diminished Leningrad's competitive edge in the national industrial labor market. While metropolitan Leningrad remained one of the most highly populated and urbanized regions in the Soviet Union, the gender, age, and occupational structure of the population did not match the economy's needs. The city's economic development strategy was directed primarily toward heavy industry, whereas the local population was now predominantly female. The population was also aging, and a rapidly increasing number of pensioners had to be supported by the working population. High rates of female participation in the labor force contributed to low birth rates, as did inadequacies in child care and in medical and housing facilities. Despite these conditions, many senior local planners, and nearly all national planners, failed at the time to recognize the growing gap between the city's demography and the dominant pattern of economic development.[30]

Within less than a decade, however, nearly all local and most national politicians were emphasizing labor shortages whenever they discussed the Leningrad economy. For example, in a 1966 campaign speech for his USSR Supreme Soviet seat from a Leningrad district, the party's Central Committee secretary, Aleksandr Shelepin, acknowledging a labor shortage in Leningrad, urged employers to hire fewer workers and fully supported the efforts of local officials to deal with the problem in a forthright manner.[31] A year later, during the RSFSR Supreme Soviet election campaign, Kirill Mazurov, then first deputy chairman of the USSR Council of Ministers, came to the city to speak to his Leningrad constituents and repeated Shelepin's positions of the previous year.[32] Meanwhile, in 1963, an article by the chiefs of the Leningrad city party committee's industrial transportation and ideological departments appeared in *Sotsialisticheskii trud* pointing to a general need to stabilize the local workforce and to do so by developing and fostering a sense of pride and responsibility among all workers.[33]

In the first half of the 1960s, numerous other speeches and articles complained about labor shortages in Leningrad. The main point is that, by the mid-1960s, the tone of Leningrad economic discussions had changed markedly from the previous decade. Leningrad social scientists such as Vladimir Polozov point to the 1958 educational reform as the single most important event of the period influencing the direction of the discussion of economic and labor issues in Leningrad.[34] Moreover, at least in Leningrad, support for the initial educational reform proposals, with their strong orientation toward manual labor, quickly translated into support for vocational reform programs.

The data available in the West can neither demonstrate nor discount contentions such as Polozov's. Given the characteristics of the Leningrad workforce, however, and the ambitious development programs being pursued by local planners and politicians, we can only assume that the issue would have arisen at some point in some other guise, even if Khrushchev had never launched his attack on the Soviet educational establishment in 1958. In any event, if Polozov is correct, one should expect vocational education to play a particularly prominent role in Leningrad's efforts to manage the local workforce, and this has indeed been the case for the past quarter-century.

Vocational Education Ascendant

During much of this period, Leningrad politicians gave more vigorous and consistent official public support for vocational education programs than national leaders did.[35] In fact, many Leningrad leaders came to view vocational education, which offered job skills such as welding, drafting, and bookkeeping, as preferable to traditional academic education oriented toward general introductory training in the humanities and natural sciences.[36] As a result of such policy preferences, Leningrad vocational education programs have outpaced similar curricula elsewhere in the Soviet Union in (1) the speed with which new professional-technical schools have been established, (2) the pressure on parents and pupils alike to channel career aspirations into polytechnical professions, (3) the linkages created between professional-technical schools and future employment sites, and (4) the number of students enrolled in vocational programs. By the early 1980s, the Leningrad party organization viewed the vocational school as the city's central institution for secondary-level education.[37] In 1984, this distinct emphasis on vocational training over traditional academic secondary education that was expressed so clearly in Leningrad came to serve as a model for national educational reforms of that year.[38] The possible retreat from the 1984 reforms under discussion as this volume goes to press in no way negates the impact of the Leningrad experience on previous policy decisions.

In a pattern that is repeated throughout our various policy studies, scientific research institutions played a critical role in the development of a distinctive Leningrad approach to primary, secondary, and post-secondary adult vocational education. In 1960, the Moscow-based USSR Academy of Pedagogical Sciences opened its Scientific Research Institute of General Adult Education in Leningrad (see Chart 5).[39] The new institute immediately began research on professional training for adults, quickly establishing its reputation as the Soviet Union's premier center for the study of advanced vocational education. Three years later, the State Committee for Professional and Technical Education created its own research institute to examine secondary vocational education.[40] This committee, like the Academy of Pedagogical Sciences before it, chose Leningrad as the site for its All-Union Scientific Research Institute of Professional-Technical Education.

Little is known about the decisions leading to the placement of both research centers in Leningrad. Undoubtedly, many factors influenced the final determination, one of which must have been the intense interest of the city's party leaders in vocational education. Whatever the reason for the final choice, making Leningrad the home of two of the USSR's leading research institutions that were perfecting professional training techniques gave Leningrad's leaders access to a powerful resource for restructuring local education. By the mid-1970s, both institutions employed a combined total of more than 300 researchers. Moreover, the All-Union Scientific Research Institute of Professional-Technical Education also housed the Soviet Union's leading research library on vocational education. In any event, installation of both centers in Leningrad clearly reflected the local interest in vocational education by providing invaluable technical support for local politicians and also reinforced local efforts to expand vocational education.[41]

In moving to implement their programs at the secondary-school level, Leningrad educators did not stop at scientific research. By 1965, already 82 professional-technical schools had opened their doors to

Chart 5. *Structure of the USSR Academy of Pedagogical Sciences.*

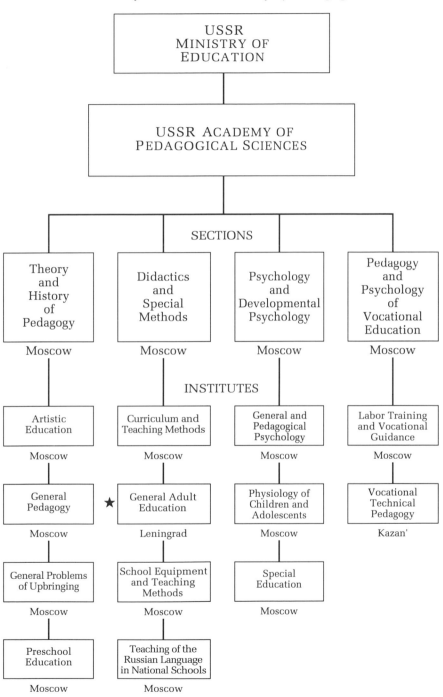

more than 35,000 Leningrad students. Over the next 15 years, the number of schools grew by 75 percent, and the number of students attending those schools increased by 158 percent.[42] It took more than voluntarism on the part of parents and students to achieve this expansion of Leningrad's vocational education programs. Considerable pressure—both positive reinforcement and negative coercion—has been applied to Leningrad children and parents alike.

On the positive side, massive youth rallies—like that held at the mammoth Lenin sports-concert complex in October 1982—brought together thousands of local youth to hear city politicians extol the virtues of vocational education.[43] Exhortations like this were and are repeated frequently, and the goal of fostering a "healthy relationship to labor" among area youth has become a constant theme in the public addresses of leading Leningrad political figures.[44] Moreover, negative pressure has also been employed, as Leningrad students have been systematically discouraged from pursuing academic educational goals. For example, on the eve of the 1983 citywide admissions tests to Leningrad institutions of higher learning, a front-page feature article in the city's leading daily newspaper, *Leningradskaia pravda*, informed applicants that a vast majority of those seeking admission to institutions of higher learning would fail their examinations.[45] Therefore, the article continued, applicants would be well advised to consider career and educational opportunities that were more readily available through vocational institutions.

Some Leningraders complain privately and with considerable passion that many parents were compelled to send their children to vocational schools upon completion of the standard eight-year general school curriculum, thereby foreclosing numerous career opportunities and ruining lives in a society where a degree from an institution of higher education is a ticket to success. For horrified parents, enrollment of their children in vocational programs precluded receipt of a full general secondary-school degree, thereby eliminating chances for post-secondary education and access to prestigious managerial and academic posts. Vocational education became synonymous in many Leningrad households with the closing down of opportunities for social advancement.

Although we have no direct published evidence of overt coercion by Leningrad educational or political officials, in June 1981 the address of regional party First Secretary Grigorii Romanov to the twenty-fifth regional party conference stopped just short of openly advocating coercion to increase vocational-school enrollment.[46] In that hard-hitting speech, the first secretary noted with considerable satisfaction that graduates of professional-technical schools accounted for more than half of the workforce of all local labor collectives. "It is the task of party organizations and pedagogical collectives," Romanov exclaimed, "to persistently inculcate in students the ability to find their bearings in present-day production."[47] Left unstated, though implied throughout, is a suggestion that such goals can and will be achieved through the forcible enrollment of Leningrad teenagers into vocational education programs.

Whether furthered by coercion or encouragement, Leningrad vocational programs have produced a generation of highly skilled workers. The key to this accomplishment is to be found in the relationship between vocational schools and future potential employers. During the 1970s, vocational programs in Leningrad and elsewhere in the Soviet Union have become more tightly linked to individual factories.[48] By 1980, students enrolled at Leningrad's professional-technical schools received free room and board, as well as a daily wage based on effort on a factory production line.[49]

At one vocational school (no. 105) third-year students were fully integrated with work brigades of the Main Leningrad Construction Administration—Glavleningradstroi.[50] *Leningradskaia pravda's* educational correspondent reported that such relationships between future employment sites and vocational schools are pivotal to the success of vocational programs, even at such relatively new schools as the three-year-old vocational school no. 137.[51] Elsewhere, in discussing the connections between school no. 147 and the Skorokhod Association, as well as school no. 6 and the Izhorsk Factory Association, the city's morning paper reported that although students frequently have slightly lower production norms than full-time workers, the gap gradually narrows as a student moves toward graduation.[52] This report concluded that vocational students are able to move directly onto the production line precisely because they have become accustomed to the rhythm of industrial labor. It concluded that such accommodation results from the direct relationship of successful vocational schools, such as nos. 147 and 6, with factories, such as Skorokhod and Izhorsk.

Thus far we have seen that Leningrad vocational education programs outpaced similar curricula elsewhere in the Soviet Union in the speed with which schools were established, the pressure brought to bear upon parents and pupils alike to channel career aspirations into industrial professions, and the linkages established between schools and future employment sites. Perhaps most important of all, Leningrad remains noteworthy in the proportion of students enrolled in vocational education programs, particularly at the secondary level. By 1984, approximately 40 percent of all Leningrad secondary-school students completing eight-year general-school programs entered professional-technical schools, a rate of entry that remains unsurpassed elsewhere in the Soviet Union.[53] In all, at that time, 211 city and regional vocational schools were offering training in over 300 industrial specialties and trades.[54] These educational patterns in Leningrad were serving as a model to be emulated throughout the nation.

Educational Reform Returns

In spring 1984, major revisions in primary and secondary educational programs were discussed in the Soviet Union. Both the draft proposals published in January 1984 and the final resolutions approved that April by the Supreme Soviet and Communist Party Central Committee remain strikingly similar despite one of the most extensive public-policy discussions in recent Soviet history.[55] In the final analysis, the 1984 reforms seek to accomplish many of the goals first enunciated in 1958 by Nikita Khrushchev: for example, an increase in vocationally oriented education and a concomitant decline in academic training. In this respect the recent reforms more closely approximate the goals Khrushchev set forth in April 1958 than did the enacting legislation in December of that year.

Six major provisions stand out among the measures recommended by the 1984 reforms:[56]

1. Nine years of compulsory education will be required of all students in both rural and urban settings.
2. A complete primary and secondary school program will require 11 years instead of 10 (the additional year of instruction being gained through a rollback in entry age from seven to six).
3. All educational programs, beginning from a pupil's first year of primary school, will offer vocational orientation curricula, with graduates of a nine-year program becoming eligible for entrance into a professional-technical school (40 percent of all ninth-year students being targeted to enter three-year vocational programs).[57]
4. The number of classroom hours devoted to academic instruction will be reduced, to provide greater opportunity for vocational training.
5. The school day will be extended through day-care and supervised study programs, thereby reducing the need for parents to leave work early to care for school children during after-school hours.
6. Vocational programs will be devoted to the needs of local industries and not to those of the overall national economy (a relationship to be strengthened by direct linkages between professional-technical schools and local factories).

Several of these objectives have been based explicitly on the previous practices of Leningrad vocational education programs, especially those emphasizing professional-technical over traditional academic skills, reducing the number of classroom hours devoted to academic subjects, extending school hours, and establishing institutional ties between district schools and industrial enterprises. Leningrad vocational schools have also been particularly active in pursuing computer training.[58] These features of the final reform would appear to confirm the contention of the director of Leningrad's professional-technical school no. 127, who told delegates to the twenty-sixth Leningrad regional party conference in January 1984 that the Central Committee openly and extensively drew on Leningrad's experience during the preparation of the draft reform.[59] The director's observations were echoed by USSR Deputy Minister of Education Vladimir Korotov during an interview on Radio Moscow's domestic service, as well as by Leningrad Supreme Soviet delegate Boris Zhuravlev in an address to the USSR's leading legislative body.[60] If implemented in full, the 1984 reform would have shaped the skills of the Soviet population as it enters the twenty-first century. The reorientation and rebuilding of an education system as large, diverse, and complex as the Soviet Union's does not take shape around any single set of experiences. Nonetheless, Leningrad's primary education and, even more so, its secondary education have long provided a de facto model for those who advocate vocation-oriented curricula.

The Leningrad Approach Goes National

To sum up, returning to the era of Khrushchev's initial proposals for educational reforms, we note again that Leningrad's industrial managers and Communist Party officials were then confronting a profound difference between the needs of an economic development policy that assumed complex work skills, on the one hand, and a working population that lacked the requisite skills to fulfill those needs on the other. Seeking strategies to maintain the development policy by ensuring the necessary skills, Leningrad elites began advocating the creation of an extensive network of factory-based vocational education centers to retrain experienced workers and educate local youth for new factory positions. In the past quarter-century those proposed vocational programs have come to fruition. Moreover, this Leningrad strategy emerged at the same time that local Communist Party officials were encouraging the development of a fledgling sociological research community to pursue industrial topics. Chapter 6 explores the consequences of this latter strategy.

The Leningrad approach to vocational education proved so successful in the eyes of its proponents that, as we have noted, local social scientists widely credited it during 1984 interviews with having transformed the city's working population and, indirectly, with having helped reorient the local economy around technology-dependent industries. This impact is not negated by the reopening of the educational reform discussion under Gorbachev. Indeed, we may note that, in early 1986, Leningrad city party committee First Secretary Anatolii Dumachev assumed full responsibility for the management of the Soviet Union's entire vocational-technical education program when he moved to Moscow to become chair of the USSR State Committee on Vocational-Technical Education.[61]

6

Industrial Sociology and the Search for Effective Urban Management

The scale and complexity of our diverse economy make it necessary to sharply increase the effectiveness of social production; the material and cultural level of the population demands the integrated and planned development of the city economy as a whole. . . . The regional party committee is attentively studying these questions, searching for ways and methods to more effectively develop Leningrad and the Leningrad region.

—Grigorii Romanov, 1972

Sociology's Rebirth

The shuffling of national political leaders after Stalin's death presaged widespread liberalization of strict ideological controls throughout Soviet society.[1] The famous "thaw" of the post-Stalin period was nowhere more evident than in the social sciences, where the removal of many party-imposed restrictions produced an immediate and far-reaching revival of nearly all disciplines. As early as 1955, the Institute of Philosophy of the USSR Academy of Sciences in Moscow established the country's first sociological research section.[2] The following year, the historic Twentieth Communist Party Congress publicly acknowledged that Marxist-Leninist theory and Soviet practice might in fact diverge, thereby providing for the first time since the 1920s an ideological breathing space for inquisitive and searching social science research in general and sociological investigations in particular.

Soviet sociology was reborn and, despite subsequent ideological vicissitudes, has grown into a major academic undertaking.[3] By 1968 the Institute of Philosophy's research section had become the core of the autonomous Institute of Concrete Social Research of the USSR Academy of Sciences which, in turn, came under attack for ideological

An earlier version of this chapter and the previous one appeared in *Canadian Slavonic Papers* 24, no. 2 (June 1982): 161–174, as "Policy Innovation and the Soviet Political Process: The Case of Socio-economic Planning in Lennigrad."

lapses and was reorganized in 1972 to form the Institute of Sociological Research.[4] By 1977 the Soviet Sociological Association, founded under the auspices of the Academy of Sciences in 1958, had grown into a vast organization supported by 2,500 individual and 460 institutional members drawn from more than 60 cities and organized into five union republic and six regional divisions, one of the most active being housed in Leningrad.[5]

Leningrad social scientists responded quickly and creatively to the new political, ideological, and academic environment emerging in Moscow. Several pioneering sociologists—Igor Kon, Vladimir Iadov, and Leonid Bliakhman, to name a few—were living and working in Leningrad, their home city, which also frequently served as the focus of their research. Leningrad State University began supporting sociological research in 1958, a sociological laboratory being formed within the university's Philosophy Faculty in 1960 and the semiautonomous Scientific Research Institute of Complex Social Research finally taking shape within the university five years later.[6] Meanwhile, local sociological research was centered within the Leningrad divisions and sections of a half-dozen Moscow-based social science research centers of the USSR Academy of Sciences. In 1974, these sections and divisions merged to form the Institute of Socioeconomic Problems, thereby becoming directly subordinate to the academy's Social Science Section, instead of under other research institutes in Moscow.

Almost simultaneously with the reemergence of this sociological community, the gap between Leningrad's labor-force skills and Leningrad's economic development policies came to the fore. Thus, when in the late 1950s Leningrad leaders set out to formulate strategies to foster economic development by upgrading local workforce skills, they naturally turned to the new academic resource being spawned in their midst. As a result of the party's interest in industrial sociology, Leningrad sociologists began to focus much of their research on issues of factory life and worker motivation.

Searching for the Worker

By the early 1960s, local researchers started to link the development of new methodologies to the study of such applied issues as labor relations.[7] In 1963 the Leningrad city party committee approved proposals for sociological research examining techniques for reducing labor turnover, thus encouraging several leading Leningrad social scientists to investigate the impact of material, technical, natural, social, and psychological factors on economic performance.[8] After 1965, local industrial sociological research was institutionalized through the creation of the above-mentioned Scientific Research Institute of Complex Social Research, which opened at Leningrad University.[9]

During a 1984 interview, Vladimir Polozov, a participating scholar in several of the studies of this early period, emphasized the importance of the new university research center in defining industrial research as predominantly interdisciplinary in nature.[10] Beyond sociologists such as himself, Polozov stressed the substantial influence of psychologist Boris Lomov (then with Leningrad University and later director of the USSR Academy of Sciences' Institute of Psychology in Moscow) and of Aleksandr Pashkov (Leningrad University's preeminent specialist in labor law, who was also director of the university's program of complex social research). Polozov maintained that the integrated and interdisciplinary nature of the industrial research effort of the 1960s generated a broad-based multifaceted approach to labor problems, which eventually permeated local efforts to deal with shortages and indiscipline. This integrated approach took on ever-greater practical significance as the new university-based center established close working relationships with several prominent local industrial firms, such as the Svetlana Electronic Instrument–Making Association.[11]

By mid-decade, through the attempts of local social scientists to examine worker motivation, a policy consensus emerged that was widely shared by Leningrad's academic, managerial, planning, and political leaders. Rather than relying on immediate coercive measures to motivate workers, politicians first evaluated the broader social and economic context in which workers must operate. Labor shortages came to be seen as problems of education and of infrastructural development, as much as a lack of discipline among workers.[12] Two important policy consequences flowed from this general conclusion: first, managers should adopt noncoercive approaches to labor discipline infractions by workers on the job; second, economic planners should adopt broad, all-encompassing approaches to production forecasting, using social and technical indicators as well as purely economic indices.[13]

The first policy option is beyond our immediate concern. Suffice it to say that Leningrad labor-law specialists have been particularly visible advocates of a broadly defined human-relations approach to labor discipline problems.[14] The second policy option requires further consideration, as it lies at the heart of the concept of socioeconomic planning. Significantly, the emerging consensus over the need for all-encompassing approaches to production forecasting took shape just as a new Brezhnev-Kosygin-Podgorny political leadership in Moscow was preparing to launch its far-reaching reorganization of industrial planning and management.

Economic Reform and Socioeconomic Planning

The 1965 economic reforms were promulgated in Moscow just as local elites in Leningrad had become aware of their labor difficulties and as Leningrad industrial sociological research was coming into its own. A consequence of this timing, at least in Leningrad, was the development of a close relationship between sociological research, the assault on low labor productivity, and economic reform proposals. This mixture eventually produced the policy innovation of socioeconomic planning.[15]

The 1965 economic reforms, spearheaded by Prime Minister Aleksei Kosygin, established three funds derived from enterprise profits, and for the first time brought under direct factory control the efforts to improve local social, health, and recreational facilities. Prior to 1965, target goals for the expansion of an enterprise's social infrastructure were established by the ministries in Moscow and incorporated by central planners into a plant's technical industrial financial plan (TIFP) with little or no local comment. Moreover, the TIFP was not considered to have the same binding character as the factory's production plan, so that some factory directors came to believe that they could ignore the social targets in the TIFP without retribution. According to Marat Mezhevich of Leningrad's Institute of Socioeconomic Problems, the new social planning procedures put into place after 1965 produced an immense psychological as well as practical transformation in factory attempts to enhance social infrastructural development.[16]

After 1965, in theory if not always in practice, a wide spectrum of services—ranging from education, health care, recreation, and social insurance to cultural programs, public transportation, communications, and commerce—fell to the supervision of municipal authorities and factory managers. To begin with, these changes in social planning procedures meant that a factory's social infrastructure—including locker rooms and stadia, food stores and day-care facilities, cafeteria and bus services—would be tied to enterprise profits. This change in funding strategy was intended to link social security firmly to implementation of the plan in the minds of workers and managers alike. Once social programs became integrated with production plans, rather than technical and financial plans, managers could no longer brusquely ignore social concerns quite as easily as they had previously. Instead, they were increasingly forced to cooperate with workers, committees, and municipal officials in planning and developing a plant's social infrastructure.

To the extent that plant and municipal managers were forced to confront one another over social planning, the 1965 economic reforms accentuated long-standing tensions and unresolved contradictions between ministerial and municipal interests.[17] Whenever questions about such services arose, Leningrad plant managers found themselves ever more subordinate to city officials who were seeking to secure their own prerogatives in the service sector. In this manner, the reforms created an administrative climate in which Leningrad leaders could argue that

managers should manipulate social services within the individual industrial enterprise so as to enhance economic rewards and performance.[18]

Early Factory Experiments

Local social scientists simultaneously got permission to experiment with various social planning techniques, their initial efforts taking
place in early 1966. A handful of industrial organizations where party
and managerial officials had been particularly supportive of managerial
innovation were selected for these experiments, including the Svetlana
Electro-Apparat, Lenin Optiko-Mekhanicheskii, Kirovskii Plant, and
Baltiiskii Plant Industrial Associations.[19]

At first, sociologists at all of these plants, and at the Svetlana
association in particular, investigated the causes of lost work time, lack
of labor discipline, and turnover.[20] Their results encouraged a series
of trial measures to upgrade the qualifications of both worker and manager (thus becoming linked with the vocational-education programs
discussed earlier); to reduce occupational diseases; and to improve the
health care, cultural life, working conditions, and living quarters of
plant workers. For example, at the Svetlana association, some shops
were completely reconstructed and refurbished with new automated
equipment; sanitary safeguards of various kinds were installed; new
shower and locker rooms were opened; and special child-care and
sports facilities were built for workers and their families. Moreover, a
prototype of a factory social plan summarized all these activities and
sought to encompass every aspect of the workforce's social, technical,
and economic development into a single document. To encourage adherence to the new social goals, party, union, and managerial officials
moved to integrate social norms and production targets in an association's production plan. They also initiated a series of reviews of plan
enforcement.

In 1966, regional party First Secretary Vasilii Tolstikov placed
these early planning initiatives at the center of his well-received address
to the Twenty-third Communist Party Congress in Moscow.[21] Tolstikov
pointed to the long-term relationship between the city's scientific and
industrial communities, also noting the role of the economic reforms
in redirecting the focus of economic life away from central ministries.
He suggested that managers learn to view their factories as social units,
and not merely as economic units. Tolstikov concluded by calling for
further study of the social dimension of labor collectives and for the
incorporation of such dimensions into the economic plan. Within a
year, Tolstikov would proudly applaud the gold medal awarded by
Moscow's Exhibition of the Achievements of the National Economy to

the Svetlana association for the increased productivity the association achieved through its social planning program.[22] Tolstikov's speech, its positive reception at the congress, and the honors bestowed by the exhibition proved critical for the further development of socioeconomic planning.[23] These accolades demonstrated widespread and powerful support for the experiments of the Leningrad social scientists and factory managers.[24]

After 1966, experiments with socioeconomic planning began to spread throughout Leningrad's industrial community. In 1968 and 1969 the Leningrad regional party committee organized a series of seminars for managers to learn more about the new techniques, and in 1970 the committee began to sponsor the publication of manuals delineating the new planning methods.[25]

The authors of these manuals recommended a planning format closely patterned after the initial Svetlana experiments.[26] By 1970 a widely duplicated five-section plan structure evolved, which has continued to function into the 1980s. Included are chapters that examine a given enterprise's social structure; working and safety conditions; income and earnings patterns; political, educational, and leisure activities; and psychological orientations toward labor (particularly among young workers enrolled in vocational education programs attached to the factory).[27]

Planners and managers base each plan chapter on quantitative analysis of eight measures of an enterprise's current operational capabilities (labor efficiency; mechanization and automation; labor turnover; education and qualifications; production quality; working conditions; housing and sociocultural conditions; and social programs).[28] Next, planners and managers, ideally acting in consultation with union officials, establish an optimal measure for each planning component, based on production goals. Finally, planners and managers devise measures to bring the plant's operations into conformity with those optimal norms, in theory, while social scientists continue to monitor progress toward those goals over time.[29]

The experimental socioeconomic plans are said to have had favorable results, with labor productivity increasing. Unfortunately, since no reliable data are available to demonstrate such increases conclusively, it is now difficult to determine precisely how favorable these initial results were. It is even more difficult to explain the causes of increased productivity, given the absence of rigorous data collection at the time. Productivity may have risen simply because more attention was being paid to the workers, therefore and would perhaps have increased whatever the actual content of the plans.[30] Alternatively, the high visibility of the initial socioeconomic planning experiments and their location within prestigious factories ensured that all necessary resources would be provided for successful implementation. Finally, however, we should not discount the possibility that the plans were a more effective management tool for integrating social and economic management than any previously existing mechanism.

Regardless of the size of the increases in production, and whatever their cause, those who were involved with the experiments were able to claim success, and on that basis achieve dramatic extensions of the experimental plans to other plants. As the experiments spread to less prestigious enterprises and economic sectors, however, complaints began to mount that social and cultural factors beyond the control of any individual factory inhibited plan fulfillment. Factory managers and social scientists alike began to urge urban district (*raion*) officials to formulate integrated socioeconomic plans that combined the efforts of all the enterprises within their jurisdiction.

District Socioeconomic Planning

By the late 1960s the party committee and soviet executive committee of Leningrad's Kalininskii District appointed a blue-ribbon commission of representatives of party and state agencies and scholars from Leningrad State University, as well as from the Leningrad (Voznesenskii) Financial-Economics Institute (see Map 11). This body assumed wide-ranging authority to investigate the feasibility of drafting a districtwide socioeconomic plan. In December 1969 the Voznesenskii Institute hosted a conference of plant managers, district officials, and social scientists to formulate a basic outline for district and citywide socioeconomic development plans during the forthcoming Ninth Five-Year Plan period (1971–1975).[31] The conferees moved to break up the labor cycle of individual enterprises and of entire districts into three discrete functions—demand, distribution, and production—each requiring distinct responses.[32]

The 1971–1975 Kalininskii District socioeconomic plan emerging from the conference sessions eventually focused upon eight primary goals: (1) scientific-technical progress and economic development; (2) optimal social and professional workforce structures (i.e., available labor skills corresponding to local labor demand); (3) improved labor conditions and reduced accident rates; (4) upgraded housing and living conditions; (5) enhanced health-care and sporting facilities; (6) enlarged educational institutions, including preschools; (7) expanded sociopolitical activities (i.e., greater participation in party meetings, political lectures, and the like); and (8) the optimal blending of Communist upbringing with the "soulful" demands of the district's population (i.e., local political programs addressing daily moral quandaries faced by the population).[33] At virtually the same time, the city's historic Oktiabr'skii

Figure 24. *Housing in the Oktiabr'skii District, near the Griboyedova Canal.*

District, under the leadership of future regional official Ratmir Bobovikov, undertook a similar effort (see Map 11).[34]

The Oktiabr'skii and Kalininskii districts' first socioeconomic plans took effect during the period of the Ninth Five-Year Plan, following the close review of relevant party and municipal agencies. The Oktiabr'skii plan took a year and a half to develop and ratify and projected severe population losses owing to the large-scale development of new districts on the periphery.[35] The reductions were generally viewed as favorable both for the district and for the city as a whole. Although the project demanded simultaneous adjustment of commercial, cultural, and transportational infrastructures, the socioeconomic planning process proved particularly well suited to this purpose (see Figures 24 and 25). Moreover, the plan for the Oktiabr'skii District sought coordinated technological innovation in area industries, compensating for the projected loss in immediately available manpower.[36] Finally, Bobovikov and his colleagues openly attempted to link local educational patterns to the needs of district industry through the tight control of entrance to vocational and nonvocational secondary schools. District local plans were drawn up at this time for the Vasileostrovskii and Vyborgskii urban districts, and the city of Boksitogorsk.[37]

Based on various addresses of Grigorii Romanov, it appears that the framers of these early district plans at first simply aggregated individual enterprise plans at a higher and more complex organizational

Figure 25. *Oktiabr'skii District scene.*

level. The straightforward logic underlying this approach was evident, for example, in a 1972 speech in which Romanov observed:

> From the beginning, everything did not occur as we had presumed, and every time, it seems, we tried to turn our attention to this or that circumstance, many of the problems—especially in smaller collectives—could not be solved within the bounds of a single enterprise independently from the development of the district and without taking into account the plans and needs of neighboring enterprises. Therefore, we logically proposed to begin work on the preparation of integrated plans of economic and social development for administrative districts.[38]

Once planners, politicians, and social scientists undertook to draft socioeconomic plans at the level of administrative districts, instead of for individual industrial enterprises, they quickly discovered that the number of variables needing to be controlled increased exponentially rather than arithmetically. Planning methodologies developed for Leningrad as a whole during the Tenth Five-Year Plan period (1976–1980) took into account the local activities of over 150 ministries and other central administrative institutions.[39] Planners responded to the new complexities by drawing on the skills of local social scientists, many of whom had by now joined the staff of the new Academy of Sciences' Institute of Socioeconomic Problems. As the decade progressed, enterprise plans focused ever more narrowly on production and financial indices, while the scope of regional plans became more ambitious.[40] The once rather simpleminded application of enterprise planning norms to the urban district, city, and region steadily evolved into an integrated hierarchy under which the level of planning determined the scope of any given plan.[41]

Among all of these new levels of social planning, the urban district should have been the least likely to succeed. An administrative unit rarely taken seriously by Western scholars, the urban district is viewed as little more than an administrative "transmission belt" between more activist plans and city offices. Nonetheless, an early and significant attempt to develop district plans took place in Leningrad's Kalininskii District and eventually assumed considerable prominence in the overall development of socioeconomic planning. Indeed, when looking back from our perspective of the 1980s, we can see that these district plans provided a vital intermediary stage between enterprise and citywide socioeconomic planning. The importance of the Kalininskii plan in particular for this overall evolutionary process was highlighted in a 1976 article by Aleksandr Netsenko.[42]

Netsenko proposed that the fundamental goal of production under socialism must be to guarantee the development of society in all its aspects. This aim requires a full investigation of existing problems and all possible solutions. Since such issues are frequently interrelated, decision-makers must look for various solutions that will satisfy all interests. Netsenko argued further that the urban district—such as the Kalininskii—has become the optimal level of organization for such measures, since it is large enough to transcend the particular interests of specific organizations, while small enough to be manageable.

In addition to Netsenko, several other Leningrad writers also singled out the district as a pivotal planning unit during this period. Writing in 1972, Vasilii El'meev, Boris Riashchenko, and Evgenii Iudin noted that district-level economic and social planning required unified action by all enterprises and organizations involved.[43] They suggested, therefore, that district socioeconomic planning depended on the coordinated development of numerous economic enterprises within a relatively limited territory. This development could be achieved only with the full support of the district party committee, since only that body could mesh the actions of all the various concerns within a single district.[44]

Leningrad's districts were able to move quickly to develop socioeconomic plans, in large part because of the active interest of key city, regional, and even national party officials. In 1971, Leonid Brezhnev had expressed his full support for Leningrad's socioeconomic planning efforts.[45] The following year, the national party leader endorsed the notion of citywide socioeconomic planning as well.[46] Closer to home, Leningrad regional party First Secretary Romanov was also busy adopting the new plan as his own, thereby ensuring its widespread use throughout Leningrad.[47] By 1972 every district and the city as a whole had become subject to socioeconomic plans drawn up to cover the periods 1974–1990 and 1976–1981 (the plan of the latter being a more detailed one, as it coincided with the Tenth Five-Year Plan).[48] While previously Soviet urban and economic planners had never totally ignored social factors, these new planning documents were innovative both in the detail of attention paid to social concerns and in the relative sophistication (by Soviet standards, at any rate) of the mathematical modeling methodologies employed.

The early Kalininskii District plan provides an illustrative example of similar efforts undertaken throughout the 1970s. By mid-decade, a typical plan came to encompass 11 planning areas:[49]

1. Plan goals
2. Social characteristics of the district, city, or region
3. Prognosis and program for development and encouragement of scientific-technical progress
4. Economic production development
5. Demographic and social development
6. Development of branch social, cultural, and engineering infrastructures
7. Social, cultural, and ideological education program
8. Prevention of antisocial influences (alcoholism, crime, etc.)
9. Development of external economic and social networks of the district, city, or region
10. Use and protection of natural resources
11. Improvement of the administration of territorial economic and social development

Over time, this general planning menu has been expanded and adapted to local conditions. We can get a fair idea of state-of-the-art socioeconomic planning in Leningrad in the early 1980s by looking at planning designs prepared at that time for the city's Dzerzhinskii District.[50]

The Dzerzhinskii District Revisited

As we noted in Chapter 3, the inner-city Dzerzhinskii District is hardly a typical Soviet urban neighborhood, even for Leningrad (see Map 11). Ironically, its idiosyncratic character sheds light on socioeconomic planning at the district level, precisely because a scheme designed for the Dzerzhinskii District must be explicitly different from the Soviet norm.

For our purposes, central among Dzerzhinskii's numerous exceptional characteristics is the current location of the USSR Academy of

Sciences' Institute of Socioeconomic Problems in the district on Voinov Street. As a result, the area is among the most-studied urban neighborhoods in the Soviet Union. Moreover, district officials can readily call on some of the country's most sophisticated academic practitioners of applied social scientific research methods, explicitly designed to support planning efforts. For example, Viktor Vorotilov, one of the institute's leading economists, served as a deputy on the district soviet, while several of his colleagues have also held district offices and consultancies.[51] The continuing cooperation between district administrators and social scientists fostered the Soviet Union's first and probably most extensive urban ecological mapping project, chronicling local air pollution, green zones, noise levels, pedestrian densities, sanitary conditions, population densities, sports, and medical facilities.[52] On the basis of the resulting maps and forecasts, Dzerzhinskii officials eventually formulated an integrated economic program. Environmental plans were subsequently incorporated into socioeconomic planning efforts elsewhere, thus illustrating that an examination of features unique to the Dzerzhinskii District may highlight more ordinary practices in other districts and cities, as well as the manner in which local activist elites may change such practices.

The Dzerzhinskii District is one of Leningrad's oldest, with 97 percent of its building stock antedating the Bolshevik Revolution of 1917.[53] Several of the city's leading cultural institutions and historic sites are located within the boundaries of this centrally located district, including the Hermitage, the Russian Museum, the Summer Gardens of Peter the Great, and a prominent "wedding palace" (see Figure 26). The area's unique architectural presence has often served as an alternative model to the new neighborhoods now circling the older city. During the 1970s, at the time of the previously noted vociferous discussions of urban aesthetics in Leningrad's professional press, several authors cited Dzerzhinskii's streets as optimal urban environments.[54] By mid-decade, the area had become a focal point for historic preservation and renovation efforts, more than 100,000 square meters of renovated housing becoming available to residents between 1976 and 1980.[55]

In addition to the Institute of Socioeconomic Problems, numerous other institutions of higher learning and research centers are housed in Dzerzhinskii (including the Leningrad Division of the Academy of Sciences' Institute of Oriental Studies and the Mukhina Higher School of Industrial Arts), as are several foreign consulates (including those of the United States, the Federal Republic of Germany, and Finland). All of these prestigious establishments crowd into Leningrad's third smallest district in area (only the island-fortress district of Kronstadt and the resort district of Sestorestsk are smaller) and the smallest in population (110,000 inhabitants in 1980).[56] Despite Dzerzhinskii's relatively mod-

Figure 26. *"Wedding palace" in the Dzerzhinskii District.*

est and declining population—it lost nearly half of its residents between 1959 and 1980—it still has one of the highest population densities in Leningrad.[57] In 1980, the area's density of 2,300 population per square kilometer was nearly six times that of the citywide average density of 400 population per square kilometer.[58]

Considering its near-total lack of industry, the Dzerzhinskii District has a remarkable economic presence. In 1980, with only 0.3 percent of Leningrad's industrial production, the district accounted for 2.4 percent of the city's retail sales and 8.3 percent of all Leningrad jobs.[59] Local employment opportunities are restricted by the district's limited industrial capacity and diminutive size, so that 30 percent of all able-bodied district inhabitants were forced to find employment elsewhere.[60]

Facing several peculiar and constraining local features, district planners during the 1980s sought to minimize the impact of the characteristics inhibiting economic growth, while maximizing those preserving the status quo or fostering economic development.[61] First, they advocated an integrated planning hierarchy of long-term (20-year), medium-term (10-year), and short-term (5-year) development, thereby providing intersector and interenterprise targets ranging from the general to the specific. Second, they urged local construction agencies, particularly those specializing in rehabilitation projects, to place new housing, commercial, and service facilities in older structures, in the handful of available lots, and in the courtyards of older buildings. They thus sought to maximize use of the district's limited open space. Third, recognizing that the district's amenities serve a population considerably larger than the area's 110,000 residents, they proposed an expansion of cultural, recreational, dining, and tourist facilities.

Perhaps most important of all, they emphasized the shortage of workers for local employers as the district's central social and economic issue. The district's planners concluded that no grand 20-year program to expand local amenities and preserve the district's architectural heritage could be effective unless district employers could hire workers who were sufficiently qualified to meet their needs. Special effort was therefore needed to develop housing units to attract singles, couples, and single-child families, and district employers were encouraged to create employment opportunities attracting younger professionals. In making their case, district planners reasserted the primacy of the labor question in socioeconomic planning. Beyond the environmental, architectural, and cultural concerns already noted, socioeconomic planning at the district level, as well as at the enterprise level, remained first and foremost a mechanism for managing the urban workforce.

Even a prestigious area like the Dzerzhinskii District faces extralocal influences that can frustrate the fulfillment of abstract plans. Despite the urban district's virtues as a manageable administrative entity, urban districts in the Soviet Union remain markedly vulnerable to outside interference. For this reason, many of the all-encompassing objectives of socioeconomic plans such as that of the Dzerzhinskii District cannot be achieved.[62]

Recalcitrant Social Problems

Despite some of the real accomplishments of district socioeconomic planning, recent public criticism of local social services, commercial facilities, and crime control underscores the durability of many social problems confronting Leningrad district managers as they seek to deal effectively with the variables in socioeconomic plans. These complaints have become so widespread that only a few representative critiques can be cited.

In his first public address in June 1983 as regional party committee first secretary, Lev Zaikov denounced the quality of housing and social services in many of the city's new districts. Zaikov called for an increase in the activity of inspectors, particularly at the level of the residential minidistrict (*mikroraion*).[63] Gennadii Bukin offered another critique, one that appeared in a monograph examining the role of commerce in socioeconomic planning, where he stressed the importance of the commercial component in urban plans, as 70 percent of all goods consumed by Leningraders were produced in the city and its surrounding region.[64]

Bukin argued that unless planners gave commercial activities and consumer goods more attention, none of the other goals of socioeconomic planning could be achieved. Commentary in *Leningradskaia panorama* took Bukin's proposals one step further, suggesting that labor performance could be directly influenced by the availability—or unavailability—of consumer goods.[65]

Critics have leveled similar charges over the inability of district planners and managers to provide adequate crime protection. In the 1980s, regional officials have been urging district officials to take crime more seriously. For example, during the early morning hours of New Year's Day, 1985, the local press reported that "rockets" were fired through the windows of at least two apartments in the older sections of the city, touching off serious fires.[66] A regional soviet resolution of September 1980 emphasized the role of alcohol and narcotics in local crime, and heralded the creation throughout the region, at both the district and the enterprise levels, of 480 "commissions for the struggle against drunkenness and alcoholism," as well as 7 narcotics divisions and 27 narcotics offices.[67] The decree continued by instructing district soviets to upgrade facilities used to combat both crime and drug abuse. Subsequent reports in the Leningrad press have linked criminality to the sterile environment of newly constructed minidistricts, much as U.S. studies have found a high correlation between public housing and crime.[68]

In a particularly striking crime account during summer 1984, the city's evening paper, *Vechernyi Leningrad*, reported that uncontrollable bands of youths poured from the stands of Kirov Stadium to destroy trams on the no. 15 line, thereby disrupting a key soccer match between Leningrad's "Zenit" and the "Dinamo" squad from Minsk.[69] The paper decried this activity much as New York tabloids might denounce unsportsmanlike conduct in the bleachers at Yankee Stadium or on the IRT no. 4 line following a game. After this apparently major incident, "cognizant organs of state security," as well as various social, party, and municipal institutions, were instructed to increase efforts to maintain order at local sporting events. This report brought protests from fans, particularly those who frequent the stadium's raucous "Section 33," who complained bitterly that their actions had been misrepresented by local reporters. They challenged claims that they had been disruptive and destructive. As the paper was quick to point out, however, someone did tear apart the trams on the no. 15 line after the match with Minsk's "Dinamo."[70] The entire controversy gained added salience when, at season's end, "Zenit" went on to earn its first national championship in years.[71]

Grievances of the kind reported about social services, commercial services, and crime control illustrate the multifaceted influences that affect the urban district. Important as the district may be for the overall socioeconomic effort, a higher level of coordination and planning is necessary if socioeconomic planning is to live up to expectations. Those presumed promises, we may recall, offered to maximize labor productivity by fostering "organic ties between economic development and the resolution of social questions."[72]

Dissemination of Socioeconomic Planning Techniques

Leningrad's advocates of socioeconomic planning next directed their attention to citywide and even regional integrated planning projects. Local administrators, planners, and scholars considered the feasibility of a citywide socioeconomic plan as early as the late 1960s, an experimental preliminary document prepared for the Eighth Five-Year Plan (1966–1970).[73] Despite the magnitude of the effort, the drafters were able to construct a full-fledged plan for Leningrad's socioeconomic development during the Ninth Five-Year Plan (1971–1975).[74] Then, in May 1972, the national State Planning Commission (Gosplan) in Moscow authorized preparation of an integrated plan for the city's social and economic development under the Tenth Five-Year Plan (1976–1980).[75] Just a short time before, the All-Union Central Council of Trade Unions had invited Leningrad State University's Scientific Research Institute of Complex Social Research to prepare manuals that could be used nationwide in implementing socioeconomic planning procedures.[76] The first of these national manuals was published in 1971. Revised manuals for enterprises and regions followed in 1978; and manuals for various economic sectors in 1981.[77] In other words, the Leningrad socioeconomic planning initiative had begun to have a national influence.

Many of Leningrad's academic participants in the development of socioeconomic planning techniques are reluctant to acknowledge their leading role in the dissemination of those techniques. Instead, they quickly point to the crucial contribution of political figures, municipal administrators, and social scientists in other cities and regions.[78] Nonetheless, the manuals on which socioeconomic plans were developed elsewhere were prepared by Leningrad scholars. Meanwhile, Leningrad politicians were trying to promote these planning techniques—and themselves. For example, in 1975 Grigorii Romanov invited regional first party secretaries from around the Soviet Union to attend a national conference devoted to sharing the Leningrad experience. Taking advantage of the forum provided by Romanov, his future rival, Mikhail Gorbachev, reported on his efforts to apply Leningrad's model in a rural context.[79] At this time, it should be recalled, Gorbachev was attempting to use his position as party first secretary in Stavropol', a region on the northern side of the Caucasus Mountains, to establish a national reputation for himself as an innovator in agricultural planning and management. This political strategy was strikingly similar to that of Romanov, who used his power base in Leningrad to gain national prestige as an innovator in industrial planning and management.

As regional and national political elites such as Romanov and Gorbachev endorsed these concepts, socioeconomic plans were drawn up by enterprises—and later, by cities—across the Soviet Union. In 1970, Soviet planners and social scientists reached out to draw on the experience of their East European colleagues who were also initiating socioeconomic planning efforts, through contacts made possible by the seventh world congress of sociologists in Bulgaria.[80] Also in 1970, the Exhibition of the Achievements of the National Economy in Moscow sponsored a "thematic exhibition" devoted to "the experience of planning and social development in enterprise and organizational collectives in Leningrad and the Leningrad Region."[81] This exhibit employed many of the city's leading younger social scientists as guides, and brought the new planning methods to the attention of a wide spectrum of national political, planning, economic, and academic elites from the capital.[82]

Soon thereafter, social scientists began refining socioeconomic planning techniques in such regional research centers as Sverdlovsk (where Vitalii Ovchinnikov, Mikhail Rutkevich, and Lev Kogan were then working at the Academy of Sciences' Urals Scientific Center's Institute of Economics and at Urals State University), Perm (where sociologists undertook research through the auspices of Perm State University and the Perm Polytechnical Institute), and L'vov (where work was focused primarily on the Ukrainian Academy's Institute of Social Sciences).[83] Grigorii Zhebit and his colleagues in Minsk concurrently developed and introduced a new research-oriented format, the "social passport," to document the sociodemographic characteristics of each unit examined. In 1982, for example, the city of Minsk was the subject of more than two dozen socioeconomic variables.[84]

It was against such a backdrop of growing national and international initiatives that Leningrad scholars became consultants for socioeconomic planning projects in various regional centers around the Soviet Union, including Al'met'evsk, Boksitogorsk, Murmansk, and Kaluga.[85] By the late 1970s, major socioeconomic planning projects had established reasonably sophisticated target programs for many Soviet cites, such as Moscow, Murmansk, Ufa, Novosibirsk, Novgorod, Orel, Tol'iatti, Sverdlovsk, Nizhnii Tagil, Donetsk, L'vov, Kiev, Kharkov, Odessa, and Zhdanov.[86] Later, during the 1980s, socioeconomic planning also began to spread to rural areas.[87]

Despite these various socioeconomic planning initiatives, Leningrad social scientists prefer to claim modesty. The available record indicates that nowhere else did local authorities attach such great significance to, and social scientists play as major a role in developing, the new planning techniques as in Leningrad. As late as 1982, the Presidium of the USSR Supreme Soviet continued to point to Leningrad as a model of socioeconomic planning to be emulated elsewhere. Moreover, the Presidium urged its daily newspaper, *Izvestiia*, and its monthly journal, *Sovety narodnykh deputatov*, to highlight Leningrad's planning efforts in forthcoming editions.[88] Why was Leningrad so cardinal for so long?

One possible explanation for the continued prominence in Leningrad of enterprise, city, and district socioeconomic planning lies with the considerable stake of local politicians in general, and Grigorii Romanov in particular, in the program's visible success. As we have noted, both Romanov and his predecessor, Tolstikov, placed the new planning techniques at the center of their reports to national party congresses in Moscow and at special conferences. Endorsement of a Romanov and a Tolstikov (to say nothing of a Brezhnev and a Kosygin) appears, however, to have been only a necessary, not a sufficient, condition for the sustained support and success of the new planning techniques. Something else was needed to assure continuing success. In Leningrad's case, this may have been the degree to which socioeconomic planning encouraged discussion of issues that were particularly salient to Leningrad planners and managers. In particular, it concentrated attention on the question of labor availability.

American political scientist William Conyngham has isolated the conditions under which socioeconomic planning emerged as a potent labor-management technique in the Soviet Union.[89] He concludes that the use of social and economic indices to integrated plans designed to enhance labor productivity had a positive, ameliorative effect on both working conditions and plant productivity, when three criteria were met: (1) labor must be in short supply; (2) local party and municipal agencies must heartily endorse socioeconomic planning; and (3) plant management must take an active interest in social issues. These conditions were rarely met in the USSR; hence the nationwide practical impact of socioeconomic planning has been marginal at best.[90] But in Leningrad, labor shortages greatly concerned local managers, party and municipal authorities strongly supported socioeconomic planning, and plant managers were as sensitive as any in the USSR to relationships between working conditions and productivity. Hence, Leningrad met Conyngham's conditions for the effective use of social and economic planning indices.

Beyond Conyngham's criteria, Leningrad is unusual for the range of expertise in the social science community and for the willingness of local political, managerial, and planning elites to accept recommendations from that community. The innovative character of local social science became more pronounced as socioeconomic planning expanded beyond the industrial enterprise to encompass the urban district and, eventually, the entire city. Local academics contributed significantly to the planning process: they used previously ignored sociological methodologies to establish the dimensions of the city's labor shortages; adapted mathematical and computer methods to social and economic forecasting; and fostered a new concept of the city as a complex integrated system. Without their methodological and conceptual breakthroughs, socioeconomic planning could never have moved beyond the rhetoric of regional party first secretaries.

Social Science and Policy-Making

We have noted how sociological research defined the scope of Leningrad's labor deficit. The computer and mathematical-modeling revolution in Soviet social science also made possible the simultaneous analysis of the many factors and variables that were now included in the modeling techniques used in socioeconomic planning.[91] By the 1970s, methodological issues such as modeling had become a paramount concern of social scientists. In October 1977 the USSR Academy of Sciences' Institute of Sociological Research organized a national conference at which 240 sociologists, economists, demographers, and statisticians from 64 research centers met to discuss methodology.[92] This growing dominance of methodological concerns testifies to the continuing institutionalization of social and economic planning by the end of the 1970s. Beginning with the Tenth Five-Year Plan (1976–1980), the general national plan had also become designated as a plan of social *and* economic development.

As socioeconomic planning moved beyond the individual enterprise, it was quickly associated with new Soviet academic definitions of the city as an integrated system. The emergence of this new conceptualization reflected the growing interest of Soviet social scientists in systems theory and approaches. The systems approach to urban analysis gained wide legitimacy following extensive discussions at a national sociological conference on quantitative research methods convened in the Georgian resort town of Sukhumi in April 1967.[93] As noted in Chapter 3, many, though not all, Soviet demographers, geographers, and sociologists have come to view the city as a social organism uniting various linked subsystems, and therefore in need of integrated planning techniques.[94] The city thus becomes a social system that requires an interdisciplinary approach to its conceptualization, planning, and management.[95] Economic and social aspects of city life cannot be distinguished and separated. Economic productivity rests in large part on the optimizing of social development.[96] Finally, it is at this point that socioeconomic planning techniques come to shape the face of the city.

The goal of harmonic and balanced urban social and economic development could be achieved through the integrated, proportional development of all subsystems within the organic urban whole. Ukrainian urbanist Anatolii Stepanenko, in a typically Soviet attempt to categorize and prioritize complex social reality, has defined no fewer than 31 subsystems constituting the single urban system (see Chart 6). Stepanenko's subsystems represent the core variables that are thought to interact with one another in shaping the totality of the city. Each subsystem is subject to measurement and analysis as social scientists develop numeric indices to capture each of these 31 urban characteristics (e.g., sex and age data for "demographic structure," number of patents and inventions for "science and scientific services," school enrollments for "education"). Ultimately, the component subsystems are analyzed in relation to one another over time. Such systems approaches, when carried by Soviet urbanists such as Stepanenko to their logical extreme, reduce the urban agglomeration to a discrete social unit, one well suited for an effective socioeconomic plan.[97] By the 1980s, Soviet theorists had moved far beyond the enterprise and the district in their approach to socioeconomic planning.

Numerous Soviet geographers and other social scientists elsewhere joined with their Leningrad colleagues in putting forth new concepts to explain the process of urbanization. While systems approaches certainly were not the only acceptable way to define and understand the socialist city, the theory proved markedly compatible with socioeconomic planning. Leningrad social scientists used systems theory to provide an intellectual justification for new urban planning methods and approaches.[98] In so doing, they developed a new ideology of socialist urbanization, which has since been institutionalized in the Academy of Sciences' Institute of Socioeconomic Problems. The institute's director, Ivglaf Sigov, once defined the city as a territorial area of labor and population, usually in the form of economic and cultural centers, serving major territorial formations such as a region or republic.[99]

The emergence and continued support of sophisticated socioeconomic planning techniques in Leningrad's policy climate of the 1960s and 1970s were largely the result of the combined effect of (1) academic breakthroughs in urban studies and mathematical methods, (2) sociological research, with the political support given the new planning approaches, and (3) the permanent labor shortage. Facing a workforce profile that did not meet the labor needs of the local development strategy, Leningrad political, economic, and academic leaders responded by developing socioeconomic planning and vocational education programs, and implementing them citywide. This response quietly reduced the labor crisis of the 1950s and 1960s. Although that crisis no longer exists, the availability of a skilled workforce remains a pressing long-term economic and policy concern.

Chart 6. *Structure of the city as a system.*

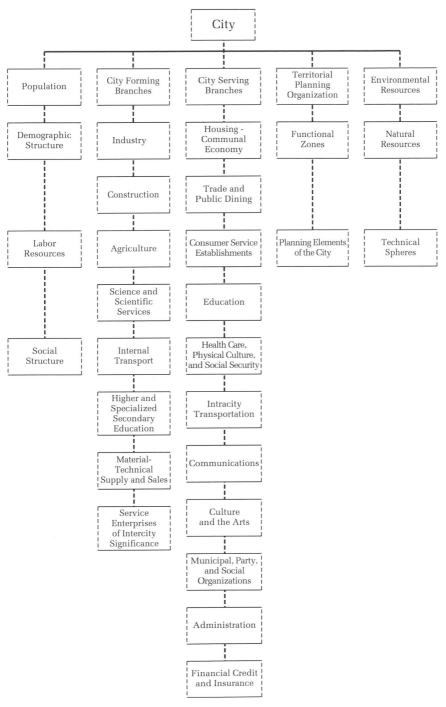

SOURCE: A. V. Stepanenko, *Goroda v usloviiakh razvitogo sotsializma* (Kiev: Naukova Dumka, 1981), pp. 48–40.

The Leningrad Approach

As noted earlier, shortly after Stalin's death, Leningrad regional party First Secretary Frol Kozlov announced a new economic development strategy for his city and region. This scheme was predicated on an unquestioning belief in technical progress, increased economic specialization and concentration, and a diminution in the relative importance of light-industrial production. Local managers saw almost immediately, however, that the available labor force could not meet the new demands. In confronting this problem, local officials moved primarily on three fronts: (1) they sought to improve the interaction of science and industry, (2) they resuscitated a dying factory-based vocational-technical education network, and (3) they launched industrial sociological investigations, which eventually generated a planning program that integrated social and economic indices. The upshot was that Leningrad elites developed an innovative and comprehensive approach to the socioeconomic dimensions of a city.

On the other hand, they were not alone in seeking to improve socioeconomic management. The Soviet Union has witnessed a cavalcade of national and local campaigns to achieve those same ends.[100] The Leningrad innovations discussed in this chapter, and in Chapters 4 and 5, were not even the most celebrated among an endless procession of labor proposals. The famous Shchekino experiments launched at a Tula chemical combine can probably lay claim to that distinction.[101] Nor have the Leningrad programs described here altered in any profound manner either the structure of the Soviet labor market or the general governmental policies that govern it.

Nevertheless, Leningrad science-industry linkages, vocational-technical education programs, and socioeconomic planning efforts had substantial local impacts. They even influenced the physical shape of contemporary Leningrad and its metropolitan region. Vocational school enrollments have increased, with two fifths of the city's secondary school students now attending vocational schools. To a degree unprecedented elsewhere in the USSR, Leningrad plant managers must now consult with district and city officials in planning factory social and cultural services. Perhaps even more important, these programs have transformed the way Leningrad's leaders look at socioeconomic problems, policies, and objectives. They have helped forge a distinctly Leningrad-oriented approach to managing the urban workforce in particular and urban socioeconomic development in general.

Conclusion

*Not only is the city an object which is perceived
(and perhaps enjoyed) by millions of people of
widely diverse class and character, but it is the
product of many builders who are constantly modifying the structure for reasons of their own. While it
may be stable in general outlines for some time, it is
ever changing in detail.*
                                        —Kevin Lynch, 1959

A Comprehensive Development Strategy

Our study has looked at several of the many ways by which Leningrad's political and economic leaders have attempted to shape the
physical and socioeconomic face of their city. We have focused on four
major policies initiated since the 1950s: physical planning innovations,
the creation of integrated scientific-production associations, vocational
education reform, and the development of enterprise and urban socioeconomic planning. These developments were anchored in attempts by
Leningrad politicians to plan and manage their city and region's environment over the past three and a half decades. Each illuminates
different aspects of a comprehensive development strategy for the region first enunciated by Frol Kozlov and those around him.

Beginning in the early 1950s, Leningrad leaders such as Kozlov
sought to overcome their city and region's distinctive economic and
geographic liabilities by accentuating local reliance on a skilled labor
force, an increasingly specialized and defense-related industrial base
(concentrated in such industries as shipbuilding, machine construction, and precision-instrument making), and a leading scientific infrastructure. These emphases were combined with a general reduction in light-industrial capacity. This strategy of skilled specialization
within the Leningrad economy significantly altered the contours of the
city and metropolitan area's economy to the point where a new Leningrad economic structure has emerged. To a considerable degree, this
structure indicates that the city and its metropolitan area serve very
specific functions within the overall Soviet economy: those of inno-

vator, producer of high-quality industrial goods, and leader in precision-instrument making. The implementation of this economic development strategy succeeded largely because of the various measures examined in our four specialized policy studies.

By concentrating on the emergence of such a limited set of policies in a rather unusual city and region, we cannot claim to offer a comprehensive analysis either of the national impact of those policies or of the full range of activities undertaken by that region's elites. Although we have examined many of the physical, economic, and social forces that have shaped the contemporary face of Leningrad, we have not sought to explain the structure and function of municipal institutions; nor have we attempted to explore the city's traumatic political history prior to the 1950s, let alone the clumsy cultural policies of local party officials during the past three decades. Instead, we have paid attention to a handful of intersections among policy initiatives that help us understand the parameters of the bureaucratic and political space within which local Soviet politicians, planners, and managers such as those in Leningrad have traditionally functioned.

Regional Integration

In pursuing Leningrad's economic strategy, local officials have increasingly relied on regional approaches to development. This regional vision resulted partially from a distinctive Leningrad configuration of political institutions and power relationships. In general, Communist Party committees throughout the Soviet Union coordinate the formulation of policy and its implementation by state agencies. Local institutions of all sorts remain subordinate to a dual system of state (ministerial) and party supervision. Within cities, municipal party institutions assume responsibility for general oversight and coordination of economic, social, political, and cultural activities in their jurisdiction. In the case of Leningrad, the party committee of the region (*obkom*)—as opposed to that of the city (*gorkom*)—has become the single most important political institution for fulfilling these oversight functions. Consequently, traditional hierarchies become murky as Leningrad's political leaders such as Frol' Kozlov, Grigorii Romanov, or Iurii Solov'ev—all being regional rather than city officials—wield greater political power than do many of their counterparts in other urban areas outside of Moscow.

Leningrad's political position is further strengthened by the city's economic domination of its region. This arrangement enhances Leningrad's power, as the future careers and reputations of influential regional officials depend more than normally on the success of the city itself.

The policy studies that form the core of this book demonstrate the extent to which Leningrad's regional party organization serves as a vital integrative force for the entire city, metropolitan area, and region. Beyond increasing the political visibility and influence of city officials, the dominance of regional party institutions facilitated the continued expansion of physical, economic, and social planning strategies from the city, where they were applied during the 1930s, to the metropolitan area in 1966 and to the region in 1986.

The introduction of regional approaches to Leningrad development was, similarly, a consequence of a long-standing local practice of conceiving of the city within a regional context. Beginning as early as the city's first architectural plan in 1717, officials, planners, and architects responsible for St. Petersburg's development assumed responsibility for directing the development of surrounding areas. Such a regional vision was further inspired by the numerous suburban royal palaces, many of which served as focal points for a growing regional rail network. The onslaught of industrialization late in the nineteenth century also prompted urban growth beyond traditional city boundaries. By the end of the imperial period two centuries later, the "New Petersburg" project set forth a vision for the city rooted in its region, albeit a much larger one than was the case in 1717.

During the Soviet period, city planners pursued regional approaches with a vengeance, going so far as to call for the abandonment of the nineteenth-century city for an expansive new socialist city to the south. By the 1960s, the focus of physical planning shifted toward integrating new outlying and older central urban areas into a single unit. The 1966 Leningrad general plan, for example, provided for the physical development of the entire metropolitan area. By the 1980s, city planning strategies had expanded to chart physical, economic, and social development throughout the Leningrad region.

The dramatic enlargement of the focus of planning throughout the 1970s and 1980s was made possible by political and administrative arrangements that favored regionwide integration and was spurred on by a 250-year tradition of planning that viewed the city within the context of its surrounding territory. It was encouraged further by an intellectual revolution within the Leningrad social-scientific and architectural communities that, as noted in Chapters 3 and 6, drew on Western systems analysis to foster the regionalization of urban planning and management.

As early as the 1950s, Soviet geographers, economists, and urbanists (especially in Leningrad, but elsewhere as well) turned to Western systems analysis for insight into the nature of the city. By the 1970s, Soviet scholars conceptualized the city as a dynamic aggregate of various subsystems that merged at a particular point in time and space. This view proved to have significant practical implications for how city planners and managers set about shaping their communities. The central focus of planning efforts shifted away from the physical development of one particular urban area to encompass a wide range of physical, economic, and social phenomena tied together within an entire region. By the 1970s, for instance, planners had come to view the Leningrad "agglomeration" as encompassing the area within a 90-minute rail-commuting range from the city center. Moreover, planners became involved in assessing not only physical trends, but demographic, economic, spatial, transportation, communications, cultural, and environmental patterns as well. The genesis of this sweeping integrative regional approach to urban physical, economic, and social planning constitutes a major empirical finding of our study.

Between Center and Periphery

Many of the regional initiatives we have identified rely on political and bureaucratic strategies to achieve economic goals. The emphasis of such approaches to development should surprise few readers. In perhaps the single most influential American study on Soviet regional administration, *The Soviet Prefects,* Jerry Hough argues that regional Communist Party agencies were originally intended to be and remain essentially administrative institutions.[1] According to Hough, extensive and complex managerial duties overwhelmed the exclusively political responsibilities of the party regional first secretary. As a result, Hough proposes, a primary function of the first secretary becomes that of regional coordinator—or prefect—for an active economic development program. The evidence of a single urban region found in this study largely supports Hough's contentions on this point.

For Hough, the concept of regional coordination becomes sufficiently broad to incorporate a diverse range of activities. The ultimate function of a regional administrator in this context must be essentially managerial. The Soviet party regional first secretary, like the French prefect, seeks the smooth operation of a complex regional bureaucracy aligned behind shared development priorities that are, for the most part, established elsewhere. Hough's Soviet prefect seeks to mobilize local resources in order to advance his community's economic position and political power.

Regional party leaders also serve as political and bureaucratic brokers between the center and the periphery. In this sense, they are intermediaries every bit as much as they impose central authority on the local scene or represent their distinctly local interests before central institutions. The fact that regional elites serve as brokers between center and periphery constitutes another of our study's major findings. It is an image, we should note, that has already been developed in relation to the contemporary West European scene.[2] Both French and Italian local political elites, for example, have been identified as key actors in processing the periphery's demands on the center.[3] This role is apparent in the allocation of policy benefits. Local elites are neither purely representatives of central authority nor traditional groupings of local notables, but rather are political, administrative, and economic intermediaries between the center and the periphery.

French and Italian regional elites fulfill their brokerage functions in distinctive manners despite the structural similarities of the two systems. Lacking strong value support for the central state, Italian local elites depend on extensive networks of clientelistic, personal, and familial ties that allow them to function *outside* of the official state and party hierarchies.[4] In France, by contrast, the entrenched Napoleonic national myth protects traditional relationships between the central state and prefectoral administration, forcing local elites to work *within* the preexisting administrative structure.[5] Consequently, Italian elites fulfill their brokerage function through political entrepreneurship, while their French colleagues rely on an administrative activism that is highly dependent on the shared values of an entrenched civil service.[6] These differences persist despite the structural similarities found in both the French and Italian state systems.

Our Leningrad studies suggest substantial differences between capitalist strategies, such as those found in France and Italy, and socialist regional efforts to maintain and enhance local productive labor and capital. In political and economic contests between center and periphery, Soviet urban leaders act through internal and frequently concealed political and bureaucratic expediencies. Recall, for example, our discussion of Grigorii Romanov's machinations that led up to the establishment of the USSR Academy of Sciences' Leningrad Scientific Center.

By the 1970s the capital cities of the 14 union republics beyond the Russian republic, the administrative centers of most of the autonomous republics, and Siberia's most prominent urban center, Novosibirsk, all claimed various divisions of the USSR Academy of Sciences system as their own. Meanwhile, Leningrad, a more important scientific center than nearly all of these competing cities, was home to local branches of Moscow-based institutions of the academy, together with a handful of self-standing research centers. Regional party First Secretary Romanov railed against this state of affairs, in part because of its symbolic diminution of Leningrad's importance and in part because of the limits it put on the authority of his party organization over local units of the academy.

In 1975, Romanov managed to cajole the academy into merging the existing Leningrad divisions and sections of a half-dozen Moscow-based social scientific research centers to form the Institute of Socioeconomic Problems. Four years later, again apparently at Romanov's bidding, the academy sponsored the establishment of a specialized coordinating council to supervise all research in the Northwestern Economic Region, which includes not only Leningrad but also several other jurisdictions. Finally, in 1983, shortly after Romanov had moved to Moscow to join the Central Committee's Secretariat, he was able to force the academy to establish the Leningrad Scientific Center, thereby bringing all academy activities in the region under a locally based division.

This example of the creation of the Leningrad Scientific Center demonstrates one way a major regional political broker operated behind the scenes to boost Leningrad's standing within the academy system (and, we might add, enhance his own control over that system). Furthermore, it supports the notion that Soviet regional and urban leaders, like their French and Italian counterparts, act as broker-activists engaged in vigorous operations between the political center and the political periphery.

Policy Innovation Cycles

The studies in this volume also demonstrate several of the ways in which elites on the political periphery have used their assets to bargain with the political center to secure resources and advance their region's economic and political interests, as well as their personal political interests. In speaking of Leningrad's "interests," one should note that urban regions are not autonomous political and economic actors.[7] Urban communities almost always exist within the larger political economy of a nation-state. Urban leaders, whether in a decentralized industrial society like Canada or a centralized one like the USSR, are limited to finite ranges of policy options in which they can pursue the interests of their communities, as well as their own. Urban governance is a governance of limits, although the particular character of those limits may be specific to individual national systems.

The operational (as opposed to geographic) boundaries of the urban polity assume a markedly different shape from those in the less restricted national policy arena. The analytically relevant focus of the structure of urban governance becomes the relationship of the city and its region to the larger political economy of the nation as a whole. Attempts to comprehend that interaction, in turn, confront the issue of how cities pursue interests—of local elites, of entire cities, and of the national political economy—as city leaders set about shaping their community's fate. Pursuit of such interests demands that local officials seek to maximize opportunities for autonomous action.

The studies in this volume highlight the methods by which Leningrad politicians, managers, and planners have been able to expand their capacity to act. We have seen that they frequently choose to move ahead with a limited policy experiment rather than with a full-fledged policy initiative. Production associations, socioeconomic planning, factory-based professional-technical schools, and new urban design strategies, for example, all found their initial expression in limited, carefully supervised, and strictly delineated policy experiments. If such trials are unsuccessful, practical and conceptual inadequacies can be corrected, or political sponsors can quietly withdraw support. If successful, the local experiments provide evidence of the periphery's leaders' need to secure the allocation of greater financial, material, and political resources from the center. A flourishing experiment is at least likely to give local officials more grounds for obtaining central endorsements and resources. In this manner, local policy experiments assist in securing economic assets within an economy of shortage.

Although the mere existence of such a cycle of regional policy innovation may surprise some readers, it is precisely at the regional level that Soviet politicians and administrators struggle to bring local conditions into conformity with central policy pronouncements. This tension between reality and pronouncement produces small-scale creative responses that may grow to reshape both local practice and central policy. In each of the cases under review at the moment, we can see how Leningrad politicians sought to recast central policy initiatives to better reflect local conditions and, in so doing, influenced future central policies.

This regional innovation cycle is perhaps most evident in the case of educational reform. We saw how local Leningrad officials responded to Nikita Khrushchev's calls for educational reform by endorsing a major restructuring of secondary education around the needs of local industries. Despite the failure of the Khrushchev program nationally, Leningrad educational managers moved ahead, aggressively pursuing vocational education programs. By the 1980s, Leningrad had created one of the largest and most efficient vocational education programs in the Soviet Union. When national leaders once again returned to something like the Khrushchev themes by demanding that secondary education be recast in accordance with the needs of industry, Leningrad's experience provided a model for doing that. In fact, almost immediately after passage of the 1984 educational reform legislation by the USSR Supreme Soviet, Leningrad already conformed to the new patterns set forth in it.

In confronting the divergence between central pronouncement and local reality, officials may create genuinely new institutional and organizational forms, as was the case with socioeconomic planning. Or, they may draw on and adapt past practices in slightly different guises, as was the case with vocational education. In either case, they are creating new policy options on which senior officials may draw in the future.

Urban Activism

The major findings just identified suggest that Leningrad politicians, planners, and managers have been able to shape to a significant degree the local physical and socioeconomic environment by effectively "working the system." Furthermore, sustained economic growth enhanced the political and bureaucratic clout of those same local leaders, as evidenced, for example, in the rise to national prominence of several Leningrad political figures during the period under examination. Underlying these successes is a set of activist political strategies.

The policy areas that have been reviewed in this volume—physical planning, technological innovation, vocational education programs, and socioeconomic planning—demonstrate the various ways in which Leningrad leaders have depended on aggressive political and bureaucratic strategies to advance their interests within the context of a centralized socialist political economy. In the area of vocational education programs, we have noted how Leningrad officials took advantage of the 1958 educational reform legislation to initiate a large-scale restructuring of the city's secondary education system. This task of reorienting the secondary school curriculum quickly fell to pedagogical specialists, many of whom were based at the city's newly created Scientific Research Institute of General Adult Education and at the All-Union Scientific Research Institute of Professional-Technical Education, who moved to recast curriculum reform as a series of technical adjustments. Meanwhile, their technical adjustments precipitated the long-term transfer of nearly half of the city's secondary school population from general academic secondary schools to vocational training programs.

By acting in this manner, Leningrad politicians have been able to define questions of major political dispute as less threatening elaborations of appropriate forms for policy implementation, thereby extending their control over events taking place within their jurisdictions. This expanded capacity to manipulate the local political arena, in turn, enhanced the national political reputations of such prominent Leningrad politicians as Kozlov, Romanov, and Zaikov. In their time, all three men occupied central positions in the ever-changing constellation of Kremlin politics. Moreover, all became vocal advocates of Leningrad policies: Kozlov vigorously proposed restructuring the local economy around technologically intensive industries; Romanov sought national visibility by promoting scientific-production associations and socio-economic planning techniques; and Zaikov became identified with technological innovation programs. These strategies offer a counter-point to various market-oriented economic reform efforts during the 1960s and 1980s. Greater economic concentration, scientific-production associations, and even the "Intensification-90" campaign constitute a conservative alternative to market-driven reformism in the Soviet political arena in that such mechanisms need not undermine the authority of central planners, redistribute resources away from traditionally favored economic sectors, or challenge the superior authority of Communist Party officials over economic management. The Leningrad approach to economic development represented by Kozlov's, Romanov's, and Zaikov's policy stances provides an antimarket perspective that has informed national political discourse throughout the post-Stalin era. The ability of local leaders such as those three politicians to assume their activist stances locally and nationally provides yet another resource for city politicians to draw on.

Alternative Policy Visions

When seeking solutions to contemporary problems in developing vocational programs and physical planning innovations, Leningrad educators and architects at times turned to earlier practices. We have seen how Leningrad politicians advocated the resurrection of expired factory-based vocational education programs, while urban planners looked to their city's neoclassical central districts as an alternative urban vision to the stark industrial style endorsed by the State Construction Committee bureaucrats in Moscow. The existence of such alternative policy vistas, be they academically generated or cast quite literally in the city's stones, affords local politicians, managers, and planners greater room to maneuver in dealing with the center. In this respect, Leningrad may of course be unrepresentative, given its size, diversity, history, and strong scientific capacity. Nevertheless, probably it is not unique since other Soviet regional entities—especially the union republics—have similar important policy models that may not be shared by central authorities in Moscow.

Leningrad's social scientists, architects, and politicians have not worked in isolation. Local industrial sociologists interact creatively with colleagues in other major research centers. Scientific-production associations headquartered in Leningrad often extend their operations into communities throughout the USSR. Leningrad's urban geographers, for their part, participated in an intellectual transformation led by their peers in Moscow and ultimately in the West. The city's architectural community collaborates extensively with fellow architects in Moscow, the Baltic republics, and elsewhere.

All this interaction among regions takes place within an essentially centralized system of political and economic management. Nevertheless, it is not always channeled through the center, as we noted in the case of the 1975 national conference on socioeconomic planning hosted by Romanov. That conference brought together party secretaries from other regions, including a young Mikhail Gorbachev, to explore various uses for the newly developed socioeconomic planning methods. By organizing the conference, Romanov created an opportunity for his fellow regional party secretaries to relate to one another outside of the centralized political environment of Moscow. Such gatherings, which take place with some regularity across the Soviet Union, provide an opportunity for regional elites to get to know one another while they are in the process of gaining national prominence. The overwhelming number of politicians from the periphery who have moved into key national positions in Moscow under the Gorbachev administration is one visible consequence of the networking that takes place among regional political leaders at sessions such as Romanov's 1975 socioeconomic planning conference.

In each of the policy areas studied, we identified distinct Leningrad approaches to regional management. Scientific-production associations emerged as a preferred institutional framework; Leningrad schoolchildren enrolled in vocational education programs in unprecedented numbers; and the city's historical preservation efforts remained unmatched in Soviet cities of comparable diversity. In the final analysis, we must conclude that an identification with Leningrad's political, managerial, and intellectual communities enabled local leaders to draw on alternative policy visions and generate innovative responses to central policy pronouncements and guidelines found inadequate or inappropriate.

The Centrality of Economic Forces

Our study has uncovered considerable local activism as it has explored various means by which Leningrad's political and economic leaders have attempted to shape the physical and socioeconomic face of their city. Our investigative task remains an enigmatic one, however, as any metropolitan area the size and complexity of Leningrad is a product of an accumulation of numerous and overlapping social, economic, cultural, and political events. The face of contemporary Leningrad thus emerges from a multitude of processes—historic and contemporary; local, regional, and national; micro- and macro-level.[8]

Part of any understanding of the current configuration of the city and metropolitan area's physical and sociological environments—and the various activities that shaped them—must be derived from an appreciation of motive forces that lie beneath the surface phenomena we wish to explain.

In a capitalist system, our analysis could well assume the underlying primacy of economic forces and emphasize various manifestations of the marketplace. In a city and metropolitan area—such as Leningrad—situated within a socialist system, there is a temptation to dismiss economic explanations for urban development and stress instead the place of planning. The evidence generated by this particular study, however, asserts the centrality of economic forces in urban incentives even within centrally planned socialist systems such as the Soviet Union.

As under capitalism, various Leningrad political, economic, and cultural leaders have sought to maintain and expand local productive capacities and enhance their access to resources of all kinds. The difference between capitalist and socialist systems lies not so much with ends as with means. In the absence of market levers, local Leningrad leaders rely solely on bureaucratic and political strategies for molding their city's physical and socioeconomic face.

Analysts of American urban affairs, of course, have long appreciated the importance of a city's economic vigor to the overall well-being of a regional urban community. Much of the available literature on the dynamics of urban growth and decline in the United States deals extensively with such questions as labor supply, industry mix, capital construction, tax rates, personal income, and consumption rates.[9] Such analyses, however, are based on the assumed operation of a free-market economy, within which urban communities compete for resources much as private corporations do.[10]

What makes the Leningrad-based studies in this volume unusual is that they illustrate the importance of the economy to urban health in nonmarket industrial economies. The frenzied promotional activities of American city governments and chambers of commerce, and the preoccupation with property taxes that so dominate the U.S. urban scene, do not at first glance seem to have a parallel in a Soviet system where land has no conventional monetary value and where local management is dominated by centralized bureaucracies. Yet our examination of Leningrad has discovered bureaucratic and political behavior analogous to that based on tax codes and real estate booms. In the USSR, the lack of market mechanisms may prevent complex policy questions from being reduced to market-oriented terms, but their absence does not prevent similar policy questions from arising in the first place.[11] Our final major conclusion, then, is that economic health appears to be vitally important to the sustenance of urban communities as much in socialist, centrally planned political economies like the Soviet Union as in market-oriented political economies like the United States.

An Economy of Shortage

The prominence in socialist political economies of bureaucratic strategies to secure productive labor and capital may be explained in part by the prevailing economy of chronic shortage.[12] In socialist systems, the survival and growth of all economic units—including cities—has not, until very recently, depended on revenues. Consequently, cost constraints are much less binding than under capitalism. Competitive demand for inputs becomes unrestrained, and the resulting disequilibrium produces a sustained state of shortage. Ultimately, the absence of cost constraints induces a voracious, near-insatiable demand that absorbs resources from both the producer and the consumer goods sectors.[13]

The behavioral consequences of chronic shortage are legend. Socialist administrators come to depend on external assistance from higher-level institutions and officials, aid that is usually not granted automatically. It must be obtained with some effort, forcing managers to exert political leverage through lobbying, personal connections, and/or hidden corruption. The directors of socialist firms—or, in the case under consideration, urban officials who serve as economic as well as political managers—do not seek to maximize profits and to balance budgets as their capitalist counterparts do. Rather, they try to maximize their access to supply by manipulating vertical linkages in the state structure, so that both economic enterprises and local communities are highly dependent on superordinate decision centers where resources are allocated and/or revenue shortfalls can be made up.[14]

Many economic organizations in an urban community such as Leningrad are vertically subordinated to extralocal units, and municipalities may exert control over their own economic subsystems only if they act, as have Leningrad officials, to maximize their operating space. If the Leningrad experience chronicled here provides reliable guidance, this struggle for resources and autonomy appears to be most frequently played out in the continuing struggle between the central ministries and the local soviets. We thus see how local autonomy depends on the ability of local communities to influence extralocal decisions concerning their economic development. In the United States such efforts may take many forms, including a mix of market manipulation and political/bureaucratic activism within and among city, county, state, and federal agencies. In the USSR, where the market is largely absent, local concerns find expression primarily through political and bureaucratic action.

One ultimate test of the results of these strategies must be an assessment of the region's economic performance during the past several decades. Leningrad politicians, managers, and planners have successfully nurtured the region's relatively scarce labor resources. Moreover, the city's industrial profile, enhanced by the various linkages established among local industrial and scientific organizations, has largely realized Frol Kozlov's nearly four-decade-old vision of the city's economic future.

In the immediate term, we can find considerable evidence that the development strategy adopted by Leningrad elites during the 1950s has proven successful. The city consistently achieved respectable rates of economic growth by both Soviet and international standards, despite some marked economic and geographic constraints. Policy innovations and resource allocation decisions originating with Leningrad elites during the period under review demonstrate the creativity employed by local elites in securing the resources necessary for their community's well-being while operating in the context of a centrally planned socialist economy.

We must acknowledge, however, that the various strategies and activities discussed in this book may not address many of Leningrad's long-term economic liabilities. The policies examined here do not deal, for instance, with the city's peripheral geographic location, hard climate, lack of resources, and absence of an active hinterland. For the most part, these vulnerabilities are so basic that they are virtually immutable. Within that context, the Leningrad strategy of increasing economic specialization may have maintained high performance levels over the short term while addressing few of the long-term restrictions on the city's development. The future economic success and general well-being of both Leningrad and its surrounding region rests more and more squarely on the sustained ability of its local elites to develop effective bureaucratic and political strategies to secure scarce resources.

Whether we choose to emphasize the short-term success of the policies under examination or their possible long-term limits, economic growth emerges as the key variable for assessing Leningrad's general vitality. Although local economic development is attributable to behind-the-scenes connections rather than market-oriented boosterism, the Soviet Union's planned economic system does not invalidate the role of urban entrepreneurship in promoting a city's—or region's—overall health.

Appendices

Appendix A:
The Structure of Leningrad's
Municipal Administration

This description of the structure of local municipal administration in the USSR generally and Leningrad more particularly, during the period of this study, is intended as a "road map" for readers who are unfamiliar with Soviet administrative structure and practices or with the Soviet and Western analytical literature about them. It does not reflect reforms in the administrative structure undertaken since 1988. The summary given here may be supplemented by referring to David T. Cattell's study of the structure of Leningrad local government during the 1960s and to Max E. Mote's doctoral dissertation examining the structure of Leningrad administration during the late 1950s and early 1960s.[1]

Soviet Federalism and the City

Soviet Russia has been a federal state ever since the formation of the Union of Soviet Socialist Republics in 1922. The structure of the Soviet federation has evolved over time, becoming enshrined in and modified by new constitutions in 1924, 1936, and 1977.[2] At present, the union consists of 15 republics that are geographical expressions of major nationality patterns. Constitutionally, each union republic must border on non-Soviet territory so that it can exercise a right of secession. Ten larger union republics are, in turn, organized into regional subunits (autonomous republics, autonomous oblasts, autonomous okrugi, and kraia) defined by officially recognized nationalities (e.g., Tatars, Jews, Mordvinians, Buryats) or by geography (oblasts). Below this intermediate regional level, there are some 50,000 local soviets that serve as the governing bodies for the territorial subunits—raiony, cities (goroda), urban districts (gorodskie raiony), workers' settlements, and villages—of smaller union republics and of the regional constituent units of larger union republics (see Table A-1).[3] Prior to Stalin's death in March 1953, most of these subregional local units appear to have been moribund, though they have gained in power and authority since that time.[4]

Table A-1. *Number and Average Size of Local Soviets, February 1980*

Type of Soviet	Total No.	Average No. of Deputies	Average No. of Registered Voters per Deputy
Autonomous oblast	8	170	961
Autonomous okrug	10	108	963
Krai	6	360	5,508
Oblast	121	240	4,115
Raion	3,075	82	315
City	2,059	137	378
City raion*	619	216	428
Workers' settlement	3,719	57	75
Village	41,374	33	45

SOURCE: Everett M. Jacobs, "Introduction: The Organizational Framework of Soviet Local Government," in Everett M. Jacobs, ed., *Soviet Local Politics and Government* (London and Boston: George Allen & Unwin, 1983), 9.
NOTE: Data for soviets of the union and autonomous republics are not included as they are not considered to be "local" soviets.
*In all cities with more than 225,000 population and in most cities with between 150,000 and 225,000 population.

Probably most Western Soviet affairs specialists dismiss the Soviet Union's alleged federalism as little more than propagandistic dressing for a highly centralized and unified system. American political scientists Donna Bahry, Philip Stewart, Roger Blough, and James Warhola, however, have each attempted in various ways to look beyond the limitations on the Soviet federal system and ask how the system may actually function.[5] Bahry, for example, argues that Western emphasis on the long arm of the center may ignore the impact of grass-roots politics on the dynamics of regional policy-making. Bahry suggests that in a system where officials in every republic capital constantly assert local interests, and where party and government decisions are presumably formulated through bargaining among such interests, policy choices ought to be intimately connected with regional politics. Meanwhile, Stewart, Blough, and Warhola demonstrate that, on the basis of a content analysis of speeches and articles presented by Politburo members between January 1, 1972, and July 1, 1979, the members display several clear regional biases, which at times are also linked to major economic issues. The work of these scholars supports the notion that the activities of regional and local elites are determined by the constitutional structure of the Soviet state, which is federal. This federal hierarchy establishes the bureaucratic, political, national, and geographic context of regional intra-elite conflict.

A major consequence of the federalist structure for Leningrad in particular is the diminution of its stature as a city. Its location in the same republic as Moscow deprives it of status as a republican capital in the federal system. The hierarchical structure of the Soviet federalist system makes it difficult, for example, for cities that are not capitals of a union republic to rise above provincial status. As noted earlier, Leningrad is a special case among such urban centers, continuing to be a city of national significance. But, Leningrad does not house republican ministries, nor does it as a matter of right maintain a vast selection of the cultural and educational amenities that are mandated in the capitals of all the union republics (a condition that increases the vulnerability of Leningrad's remarkable cultural and educational infrastructure to outside intervention).

The status of Leningrad within the USSR Academy of Sciences provides a small illustration of the ways the city has been adversely affected by its comparatively low stature as only a regional seat in the Soviet federal system. The Russian Imperial Academy of Sciences began operations in St. Petersburg in 1724 and maintained its headquarters there until 1934, when its principal administration, together with several of its more prestigious research centers, moved to Moscow.[6] Many (but not all) of the research institutes remaining in Leningrad lost their status as autonomous institutes as they were reorganized further into mere branches and affiliates of institutes in Moscow. At about the same time, the academy established integrated multidisciplinary branches in each of the union republics and in Siberia, again bypassing Leningrad as the city was not a republic capital. During the late 1940s and early 1950s, most of these republican affiliates were elevated in status to become semiautonomous republican academies.[7] Meanwhile, in 1957, the Siberian branch in Novosibirsk formed the core of the academy's Siberian Division, which by the late 1970s operated more than 50 research institutes and 70 research stations across Siberia and the Soviet Far East.[8] By 1980, regional scientific centers had been founded in Sverdlovsk and Vladivostok, and branches of the national academy were functioning in nearly every capital of the Russian Republic's autonomous republics (Kirov, Kazan', Makhachkala, Petrozavodsk, Syktyvkar, and Ufa).[9]

As capital cities of autonomous republics, such provincial nonentities as Makhachkala, Syktyvkar, and Ufa are qualified for special treatment by the academy. Leningrad, however, could make no such claim, and until 1983 simply offered a home base to research institutes directly subordinate to divisions of the academy presidium or, worse yet, subordinate to branches of Moscow-based scientific research establishments. In other words, there were no regional/republican intermediary bodies to deflect and moderate central intervention in the operation of Leningrad's academy research centers. In March 1983 the Central Committee of the Communist Party announced the long-delayed establishment of its Leningrad Scientific Center.[10] Only the Soviet Union's federal structure could justify elevating the bureaucratic stature of backwater Ufa's scientific centers over those of an international center like Leningrad.

Republican capitals also reap other institutional advantages. Central power flows through such cities as Dushanbe and Ashkhabad, capitals of the Tadzhik and Turkmen republics, on its way from Moscow to local jurisdictions. Its lower constitutional status, however, gives Leningrad less of an intermediary role and puts it in more of an overtly subordinate status in relation to Moscow. After all, Moscow is Leningrad's national and republican superior. The lack of formal status as a capital of a republic defines Leningrad's eminence as based on its own characteristics and efforts and not mandated by central policies underlying the Soviet Union's federal structure.

The Soviet Municipal Charter

In addition to reaffirming the federal nature of the Soviet state, the October 1977 Soviet constitution, as well as the constitutions of the union republics ratified over the course of the following year, proclaimed a new legal basis for Soviet municipal administration, with the role of the local soviets, or councils, being stated ever more forcefully.[11] In theory, the system of national, republican, regional, and local soviets of people's deputies set forth in the 1977 constitution is the primary instrumentality of state power.[12] Other government institutions—including such varied bodies as industrial enterprises, schools, hospitals, and shops—become subordinate at one level or another to the elected soviets, which direct all branches of state, economic, social, and cultural activities.[13] To guarantee the soviets' juridically superior position, the 1977 Constitution states in Article 105 that "The Deputy has the right to request information from the appropriate state agency or official who is obliged to respond to the inquiry at a session of the Soviet."[14]

Chapter 19 of the 1977 constitution addresses this basic conflict of Soviet local governance in a forthright manner, with Articles 146 and 147 of that chapter forming the basis of municipal attempts to assert local control over economic activities.[15] Article 146 grants local soviets the power to resolve "all questions of local importance, proceeding from the general interests of the state and the interests of citizens residing on a soviet's territory."[16] Still, the constitution's authors seem reluctant to extend the authority of local soviets over conflicts of *national* importance emerging within their territory.

At this point Article 147 assumes its significance, particularly in its final revised version, which contains new language added to the preliminary draft that had been released for public discussion. Article 147 declares, in text added after the public debate, that local soviets "ensure comprehensive economic and social development on their territory."[17] This was and still remains the boldest legislative effort to assert municipal control over the activities of national economic organizations operating within the soviets' jurisdictions. The article goes on to state that local soviets "exercise control over the observance of legislation by enterprises, institutions, and organizations of higher subordination located on the soviets' territory; and coordinate and control these entities' activity in the fields of land use, conservation, construction, the use of labor resources, the production of consumer goods, and the provision of social, cultural, consumer, and other services to the population."[18] This statute goes well beyond previous efforts to increase the authority of the soviets.

Almost immediately following the ratification of the new constitution in 1977 the Supreme Soviet began to amend and revise all existing legislation in order to bring the corpus of Soviet law into conformity with the new constitution. Many of these revisions similarly strengthened the authority of local soviets to regulate the activities of the central ministries in such areas as provision of local services, labor regulations, and environmental standards, where primary regulatory control had been ceded to the soviets.[19] The more important of these decrees was a joint resolution issued in March 1981 by the Central Committee of the Communist Party, the USSR Supreme Soviet, and the Council of Ministers; it sought to strengthen and widen the economic powers identified in Article 146 of the 1977, or "Brezhnev," Constitution.[20] Legislation enacted in June, September, and November 1980, governing the activities of local soviets,[21] and efforts during the spring and summer of 1984 by the Central Committee of the Communist Party and the supreme soviets of the union republics attempted to ensure greater local control over economic agencies operating in a given jurisdiction.[22] Consequently, the new constitution and legislation and resolutions of the past several years—taken as a whole—define the functions of the city soviet and its executive agencies.

In any given municipality or district, the soviet of people's deputies, its executive committee (*ispolnitel'nyi komitet* or *ispolkom*), administrative agencies, and commissions serve as the Soviet state's principal agent.[23] The local soviet, which is dissolved for reelection every 30 months,[24] oversees all governmental, administrative, economic, social, and cultural endeavors within its territorial domain.[25] In the city of Leningrad, the city soviet supervises the activities of over 400 industrial enterprises, 800 construction, transportation, and commercial bodies, 900 educational and scientific institutions from primary schools to advanced research centers, and 8,000 service-sector organizations, all subordinate to some 150 ministries and other state agencies.[26] Such supervision entails the coordination of interests among all of these contrasting local and national ventures, with a view to maximizing the interests of the entire community.[27] The city soviet also directs construction activity within its jurisdiction and has responsibility for enforcing environmental laws.[28]

Until 1989, the regional, city, and district soviets usually have been made up of local workers and notables such as famous actors and renowned scientists, as well as administrators who have stood unopposed in single-candidate elections organized by districts with relatively small populations.[29] For example, in 1985 the composition of the Leningrad city soviet, with a total membership of 600 deputies, was as follows:[30]

Professional Background	Percentage
Worker	54.6
Enterprise managers	11.9
Regional and city state officials	7.8
Regional and city party officials	7.3
Scientific, educational, and cultural workers	7.0
District party officials	3.3
Military and police officials	3.3
Medical workers	1.3
Pensioners	0.3
Other	3.2
Age Structure	
Under 30 years of age	37.0
30 years of age or older	63.0
Sex	
Male	50.5
Female	49.5
Party Membership	
CPSU members	50.2
Nonparty members	49.8

The deputies, who tend to meet once every quarter, select, according to Communist Party–controlled *nomenklatura* procedures to be described shortly, an executive committee to conduct the soviet's business during the intervening period. The chairman of the executive committee is also the local government's chief executive officer. The municipality's executive functions are carried out by departments and administrations that are subordinate to the soviet and its executive committee, and are supervised by citizen commissions chaired by elected deputies who are members of the local soviet.

North American observers might be struck by the relatively large number of participants at any given stage in the process of local governance.[31] The more skeptical among us might conclude that the sheer size of local soviets guarantees that they have only a most peripheral role in municipal administration, as the large numbers of deputies would presumably preclude meaningful participation in the decision-making process. In 1985, for example, the Leningrad regional soviet consisted of 280 deputies, who selected a 25-member executive committee responsible for the operation of several departments and administrations (of which 39 were reported to have been in operation in 1982), as well as for the support of standing commissions (of which there were 15 in operation in 1982).[32] The Leningrad city soviet at that time should have been even more unwieldy, with 600 deputies and a 25-member executive committee responsible for even more departments and administrations (54 at last report in 1987) and committees and commissions (28 in 1987).[33] In July 1987 the structure and membership of executive agencies were as follows:[34]

Chair of the City Soviet Executive Committee
V. Ia. Khodyrev

First Deputy Chairs of the City Soviet Executive Committee
K. I. Labetskii (also Chair, Planning Commission)
Iu. A. Maksimov (Agro-industrial Commission of Leningrad)
L. G. Perekrestov

Deputy Chairs of the City Soviet Executive Committee
A. Ia. Avdeev
N. M. Arkhipov
G. A. Bukin
V. I. Matvienko
A. S. Sokolov
B. A. Surovtsev

Secretary of the City Soviet Executive Committee
L. A. Khodchenkova

Members of the City Soviet Executive Committee
O. I. Beliakov (Secretary, Kalininskii District Party Committee)
A. A. Bol'shakov (General Director, Scientific-Production Association)
A. N. Gerasimov (First Secretary, Leningrad City Party Committee)
G. A. Grigor'eva (Doctor, City Children's Polyclinic no. 58)
V. A. Leniashin (Director, State Russian Museum)

M. V. Riabkova (Leader of Plasterers' Brigade)

T. A. Senina (Chief Engineer, All-Union Draft-Design and
Scientific Research Institute of Hydro Design)

V. I. Serova (Secretary, Leningrad Regional Trade Union
Council)

V. P. Sidel'nikov (First Secretary, Nevskii District Party
Committee)

G. G. Sintsova (General Director, May Day Dawn Association)

I. D. Spasskii (Chief, Construction-Design Bureau)

M. V. Stepanov (Brigade Leader, Sokol Association)

P. I. Timofeev (Lathe Operator, Kirov Factory)

E. A. Vasil'eva [position unidentified]

People's Control Commission Chair
E. P. Iudin

People's Court Chief
V. I. Poludniakov

Chairs of Standing Commissions of the City Soviet
Auditing: A. I. Aleksandrov (First Secretary, Moskovskii District
Party Committee)

Construction and Construction Materials Production: Iu. K.
Sevenard (Chief, Leningrad Hydro Specialized Construction
Association)

Culture: V. N. Zaitsev (Director, State Public Library)

Health: N. V. Vasil'ev (Director, Scientific Research Institute on
Trauma and Orthopedics)

Heat & Energy: G. A. Lastovkin, (General Director, Leningrad
Petrotechnical Scientific-Production Association)

Housing Accounting and Distribution: V. A. Efimov (First
Secretary, Leninskii District Party Committee)

Housing Exploitation and Repair: N. A. Ignat'ev (First Secretary,
Oktiabr'skii District Party Committee)

Improvement of Administration and Realization of the
"Intensification-90" Program: A. D. Dolbezhkin (General
Director, Printing Machine Construction Production
Association)

Industry: A. V. Chaus (General Director, Pulp Machine
Construction Production Association)

Nature Protection and Well-Being: Iu. A. Balakin (Chief,
Leningrad Civil Aviation Administration)

People's and Professional-Technical Education: B. M. Petrov
(First Secretary, Petrodvortsov District Party Committee)

Physical Culture and Sports: A. A. Arbuzov (test driver at a
scientific-production association)

Plan-Budget: V. P. Koveshnikov (general director of a scientific-production association)

Public Dining: V. F. Poliakov (Director, Leningrad Milk Combine no. 1)

Questions of Women's Labor and Style of Life: V. A. Zhelnova (Chief Doctor, City Children's Polyclinic no. 34)

Servicing of the Style of Life: L. A. Kutuzova (Director, Sewing and Clothing Repair Production Association of Vyborgskii District)

Socialist Legality and the Protection of the Social Order: A. I. Korolev (Dean, Juridical Faculty, Leningrad State University)

Social Insurance: N. Iu. Shumilova (Chief Doctor, Kalininskii District Polyclinic no. 90)

Trade: A. I. Bobrov (First Secretary, Dzerzhinskii District Party Committee)

Transportation & Communications: V. I. Karchenko (Chief, Baltic Steamship Line)

Youth Affairs: Iu. S. Vasil'ev (Rector, Leningrad Polytechnic Institute)

Leaders of Departments of the City Soviet Executive Committee
Cadres & Academic Institutions: A. A. Ponomarev
Construction & Construction Materials: A. D. Beglov
Economic Research: A. I. Denisov
General: G. A. Glukhov
Justice: M. R. Rakuta
Legal: I. A. Sobolevskii
Organizational and Instructional: V. I. Rozov
Price: Iu. V. Keleinikov
Registration of Civil Acts: G. I. Bogdanova
Veterinary: A. N. Romanov

Chiefs of Main Administrations of the City Soviet Executive Committee
Architectural Planning: V. I. Nikitin
Capital Construction: A. N. Alfimov
Construction Materials Industry: V. F. Nikulin
Construction of Engineering Structures: A. V. Veselov
Culture: A. P. Tupikin
Finance: V. N. Lomachenko
Health: G. A. Zaitsev
Heat and Energy: A. S. Khotchennov
Housing, Civil, and Industrial Construction: Iu. R. Kozhukhovskii
Internal Affairs: A. A. Kurkov

People's Education: S. A. Alekseev
Professional-Technical Education: L. A. Gorchakov
Public Dining: A. A. Tomashevich
Supply: V. Z. Grigor'ev
Trade: A. P. Zlobin
Wheat Baking and Macaroni Production: V. K. Ivanov

*Chiefs of Administrations of the City Soviet Executive
    Committee*
Archival: N. V. Ponomarev
Consumer Services: Iu. P. Filatov
Cooperative Housing Construction: A. N. Glotov
Dacha Services: A. P. Saksin
Expert: Iu. A. Ponomarev
Film: A. Ia. Vitol'
Flood Control Construction: B. P. Usanov
Foreign Relations: V. E. Kublitskii
Highway-Automotive: V. I. Shugaev
Hotels: N. M. Kazantsev
Housing: M. F. Petruk
Housing Accounting and Distribution: Iu. N. Lukanin
Individual Sewing and Clothing Repair: S. F. Molodtsova
Labor: N. Z. Amonskii
Local Industry: A. S. Vorob'ev
Municipal Services: V. V. Morozov
Parks: Iu. I. Khodakov
Pharmacy: V. M. Musatova
Protection of State Secrets in Print (Glavlit): L. N. Tsarev
Publishing and the Book Trade: E. A. Rozhnov
Servicing of Accredited Foreign Representatives: K. M. Ivanov
Social Insurance: A. A. Avseevich
Specialized Transportation and Ports: G. M. Alekseev
Streetcars and Trolleybuses: Iu. N. Gorlin
Technical: B. S. Leshukov
Technical Inventories: A. I. Zakharov
Transportation: A. A. Zorin
USSR State Savings Bank (Gostrudsberkass): V. A. Shorin

Chairs of Committees of the City Soviet Executive Committee
TV and Radio: R. V. Nikolaev
Physical Culture and Sports: N. M. Popov
Collectivized Agriculture Services: A. N. Maliutin
Capital Repair and Reconstruction of Public Buildings: E. V.
    Bozhko

*Commissions Subordinate to the City Soviet Executive
    Committee*

Superintendency: A. Ia. Avdeev (Deputy Chair, Leningrad City
    Soviet Executive Committee)
Minors' Affairs: V. I. Matvienko (Deputy Chair, Leningrad City
    Soviet Executive Committee)
Struggle with Alcoholism: L. G. Perekrestov (First Deputy Chair,
    Leningrad City Soviet Executive Committee)

Finally, jurisdictions subordinate to the Leningrad city soviet in 1987
elected 5,420 deputies to 21 district, 3 city, and 4 settlement soviets,
just one of which, that of the Vasileostrovskii District, had operated 15
standing commissions the previous year.[35] Deliberative assemblies of
such proportions are unsuited for meaningful discussion and control
of municipal affairs. For the most part, these sessions are organized
around a well-planned succession of speeches on a given set of policy
questions such as housing, the new five-year plan, or economic performance; spontaneous participation by soviet members other than
those whose remarks have been prepared in advance is discouraged.
Consequently, the soviets' executive committees, administrations, and
departments inevitably assume such supervisory functions, becoming
from necessity the central administrative agencies within this system
of local governance. Nonetheless, the deputies provide important liaison between those executive offices and the local citizenry. Inter-
changes between deputy and constituent begin during the election
process.

Local Elections

On December 11, 1984, a constitutionally mandated campaign for
local soviets was launched in Leningrad as citizens began to nominate
members of specially constituted ward election councils.[36] The events
of the subsequent two and a half months represent a reasonably typical
Soviet municipal election campaign, before Gorbachev-era proposals
for multicandidate elections and subsequent changes in elections procedures.

The campaign's first stage lasted about a month, during which
groups of citizens throughout the city met at their places of employment
to nominate candidates preselected by party-dominated commissions
and chosen from among local officials, managers, scientific and cultural
figures, and leading workers to run for seats on the regional, city, and
district soviets.[37] Next, one nomination for each available seat was
registered with election commissions established to supervise the voting process in each jurisdiction.[38] Then, on February 5, 1985, official
lists of all the candidates for all districts in every soviet were verified
by the appropriate election commission.[39] Candidates then traveled

throughout their districts, meeting with groups of constituents.[40] Voting by secret ballot took place on February 24.[41] The election commissions announced the final results on February 27: every candidate for the Leningrad regional soviet received the mandatory majority affirmative vote required for election.[42]

The establishment of dialogue between deputies and their electors takes place at the preelection meeting with voters. At the most superficial view, many such gatherings appear to be rather pro forma in character. Played out according to a script prepared by the party officials orchestrating the election in a given district, a candidate is introduced, his or her biography is praised, and there is discussion of a list of topics drawn up elsewhere (perhaps as far away as Moscow). These meetings are nonetheless models for similar discussions held periodically during a deputy's term of office. As with those subsequent postelection sessions, an important interchange can occur between representatives and represented. Such gatherings are supplemented by letters, petitions, and office visits, and provide a primary and effective forum for city residents seeking redress from municipal bureaucratic indifference.[43] In the case of the preelection meeting, this complaint function has been institutionalized in a system of electors' instructions (*nakazy izbiratelei*), which provides a much-used communication channel through which interested city administrators can actually learn about the quality of local public services.[44]

Article 102 of the 1977 constitution provides the legal foundation for electors' instructions, while a December 1980 Decree of the USSR Supreme Soviet regulates their implementation.[45] According to these regulations, the instructions are generated by individuals and groups of citizens and must be of a broad social nature (e.g., planning and construction of recreation facilities), as opposed to a purely personal one (e.g., housing allocations). Nevertheless, they can be quite specific in their content (e.g., improve the playground facilities at a neighborhood park, develop a cross-country ski course along a local river, or extend shopping hours at a local food shop). During the early 1970s, requests concerning housing, public services, and commerce dominated the instructions, and there is little reason to suspect that this earlier pattern has been substantially altered in subsequent years.[46] The executive committees of several local soviets have at times established special commissions charged with the evaluation of instructions from local voters.[47] Individual sessions of many soviets have also been set aside to deal with citizen proposals and complaints.[48] According to some Soviet sources, more than 730,000 instructions were generated by citizens nationwide during the local soviet elections of 1982, of which nearly 28 percent were responded to favorably by year's end.[49]

The issue of deputy liaison with the local populace through electors' instructions and numerous other mechanisms holds considerable significance beyond our immediate task of delineating the rules of the contest by which Leningrad elites must play in their relations with the political center in Moscow. Jeffrey Hahn has argued that political participation may be categorized by two primary modes: electoral activity and constituent contact.[50] There can be little doubt that the role of electoral activity before 1989 had been largely symbolic in the Soviet political system. Nevertheless, Hahn, Theodore Friedgut,[51] and Ronald Hill[52] have argued that constituent activity at the level of the local soviet was a major vehicle for citizen interaction with the political system of the USSR. The municipal soviet deputy in Leningrad and elsewhere fulfilled an important ombudsman function, providing a communication link between local elites and the general population. The institution of the city soviet thus partially opens up the rules of the contest of municipal administration to embrace the citizenry.

The Executive Committee

Ultimately, administrative responsibility for municipal management rests with the local soviet's executive committee and its departments, administrations, and standing commissions.[53] The executive committee retains authority to act on a daily basis to ensure that all aspects of state economic, social, and cultural policies are implemented. National legislation grants the committee a broad mandate to manage the activities of municipal and other agencies operating within its jurisdiction.[54] The executive committee (led by its chairman, deputy chairmen, and secretary, operating through its organizational-instructional department), prepares the agenda for sessions of the full soviet and informs deputies of important developments within their jurisdiction.[55] Finally, interlevel communications with other jurisdictions in the Soviet federal system are conducted through the executive committee.[56]

The executive committee varies in size according to its level of responsibility in the overall state hierarchy. Typically, the executive committee, in addition to its officers, includes the managers of major industrial enterprises and other institutions within the soviet's province, and the first secretary of its equivalent Communist Party committee.[57] In Leningrad's Kalininskii District, for example, executive committee Chairman Shekalin and party committee First Secretary Grachev frequently operated as a single managerial team for their district's development.[58] Shekalin and Grachev's cooperation was facilitated by the physical location of both institutions in a single building, an arrangement frequently found in Leningrad and elsewhere in the Soviet Union.

Officers of the executive committee share their soviet's broad competence. The executive committee's legal counsel, for example, serves deputies, departments, and commissions regardless of specific content.[59] Legal consultants to a local soviet may also provide services for local citizens. One former district legal official now residing outside the USSR described her duties to American University criminologist Louise Shelley, who reported:

> Her work was closely connected with the diverse operations of city government and the people of her community. Her job was a juggling act between the protection of the bureaucratic interests of the distant authorities and the needs of the people who appealed to her for assistance. Because the power and the financial resources of city government are limited, its ability to effect changes requested by its constituents is similarly limited.[60]

To assist officials with general responsibility for the entire scope of soviet activities, the executive committee delegates daily management in specific areas to departments and administrations, and monitors the bureaucracy through a system of standing commissions.[61] The departments and administrations constitute the managerial infrastructure for the soviet's actions. The size and number of such offices depend on the level of the jurisdiction in question. By the early 1980s, the Leningrad city soviet operated an extensive bureaucracy through more than three dozen administrations, plus another dozen departments, directly employing approximately 2 percent of the city's workforce.[62]

The executive committee oversees the work of its bureaucracy through a network of standing commissions. Each commission consists of a number of elected deputies, as well as several citizens. Such commissions are charged with general supervisory responsibility for state institutions operating within their area of competence.[63] The composition of each commission is established at the opening session of the newly elected soviet. While the number and purview of commissions will vary according to the size and needs of a given jurisdiction, nearly every soviet will establish an auditing commission; commissions for planning and budget, socialist legality and public order, and youth affairs; and more specialized bodies for specific economic, social, and cultural spheres. Commissions that are attached directly to the executive committee are usually organized to supervise council operational functions, while those serving the soviet in its entirety tend to be specialized according to substantive policy areas.[64] Both categories of commission assist the executive committee with general planning and managerial responsibilities.[65]

Despite their large constitutional mandates, local soviets have encountered persistent difficulty in asserting their authority over local institutions, whose primary loyalty is to all-union ministries in Moscow and union-republic ministries in Moscow and the republic capital. All-union ministries are directly subordinate to the USSR Council of Ministers, while union-republic ministries are subordinate to republic councils of ministers, which in turn are subordinate to the USSR Council of Ministers. In other words, all-union ministries have no republic-level counterpart and operate as a single, centralized unit for the country as a whole. Union-republic ministries, by contrast, are responsible for coordinating the work of ministries of the same name and similar purpose operating within each of the Soviet Union's constituent union republics.

Prior to 1977, for example, the Soviet community of legal-affairs specialists, as well as many regional planners and politicians, had begun to express heightened concern over the inability of existing institutions to deal effectively with the conflict between territorial interests and those of various economic branches and sectors. Jerry Hough attributed this increased anxiety in part to the higher educational levels and growing economic power of the urban sector. He also noted the limited impact of piecemeal reform attempts, such as the much-ballyhooed effort dating from the late 1950s to bestow on local soviets the responsibility of "single client" (*edinyi zakazchik*) for housing, cultural-social, and commercial services within their jurisdictions.[66] In other words, the local soviet could attain sole responsibility for ordering the necessary provisions for such services. The USSR Council of Ministers, it should be noted, reinforced that statute in 1978.[67]

A flurry of legislative activity by the Presidium of the USSR Supreme Soviet and the Communist Party's Central Committee similarly has sought to invigorate municipal agencies down to the level of the urban district (*raion*), an administration unit that, while generally regarded as powerless in confrontations with ministries, is nevertheless important in the provision of day-to-day services to the population as a whole.[68] Jeffrey Hahn reports that local governmental institutions in the Soviet Union can and do successfully represent those who elect them.[69] Hahn also notes, however, that only a few Soviet citizens take advantage of the opportunities that do exist for participation.

From a slightly different perspective, Ronald Hill indicates that a number of Soviet scholars have proposed new powers for local soviets that could alter the balance of power between municipal and ministerial operations.[70] According to Hill, specialists centered in and around the USSR Academy of Sciences' Institute of State and Law have urged that legislation specify the "competence" of municipal agencies, as well as their more traditional "rights and obligations." Such advocates, Hill continues, also argue for a strengthening of the economic powers of local state agencies as well as greater legislative attention directed toward relationships between municipal and ministerial agencies. The framers of the 1977 constitution must have been aware of these controversies and may have been among the participants.[71] This presumed

Table A-2. *Change in Revenues and Expenditures for*
Representative Municipal Services throughout the
USSR, 1966–1974

Service	Change in Revenues (in % of 1966)	Change in Expenditures (in % of 1966)
Tram transportation	− 2.9%	+ 28.6%
Trolleybus transportation	+ 64.6%	+100.8%
Water services	+230.0%	+250.0%

SOURCE: G. B. Poliak, *Biudzhet goroda* (Moscow: Finansy, 1978), 28.

knowledge accentuates the significance of provisions eventually ratified
in the so-called Brezhnev Constitution that still governs the Soviet state.

Taken together, these constitutional and legislative assertions provide the legal framework within which local officials function. They
define the juridical rules of the contest for municipal administrators.
In any legal system, of course, interpretation and actual implementation
are often more significant than published codes in influencing behavior.
This is particularly true of the Soviet Union, where legal pronouncements often represent statements of what *ought* to be, instead of reflecting what has actually come to pass. While recognizing this, we can
nevertheless conclude that legislative activity over the past two decades
or so has enlarged the bounds placed around municipal elites in their
dealings with the center, thus expanding the room for maneuvering at
the periphery.[72] The 1977 constitution, legislation, and resolutions of
the 1970s taken as a whole thus represent a loose municipal charter
defining the rules of the Soviet urban contest for such major municipal
institutions as the city soviet and its executive agencies.

City Budgets

The cost of local government has increased as Soviet cities have
grown in recent years.[73] From 1959 until 1978, the population of major
Soviet urban centers rose by 58.4 percent while city territories expanded 20 percent every five years.[74] Meanwhile, both labor costs and
demand for improved quality of city services rose, resulting in expenditures increasing faster than revenues.[75] Although the earnings gap is
more prominent in some areas than in others, it is visible across a wide
range of city services as rates of increase of expenditure for many services outstrip rates of increases in revenues (see Table A-2). Soviet
financial managers have responded by altering the profile of local expenditures and by subsidizing municipal governments through transfer

payments from other administrative levels within the Soviet state system (see Table A-3).

With transfer payments from other administrative levels have come pressures for increased financial oversight.[76] The executive committee of a local soviet is the primary responsible institution that maintains contact with other bureaucratic levels in the state hierarchy, such as the region and the republic. In recent years, executive committee concern with financial management has expanded, with the executive committee serving as a central clearinghouse for budgetary activities. The executive committee, its professional staff, and the budgetary standing commission now work year-round on financial management problems arising from past, present, and future budgets.[77] The executive committee must ratify budgets, disperse income among lower-level units (e.g., districts within cities), collect and distribute taxes, supervise capital construction funds, and also support the soviet's own considerable operations.[78] These activities inevitably involve the executive committee in consultation and negotiation with national monetary institutions as well as those of the republics and regions, and with every economic establishment within its jurisdiction. In fact, financial and budgetary control is fast becoming an executive committee's most absorbing responsibility.[79] This situation is particularly true of a city such as Leningrad, whose municipal budget approaches the size of many smaller union republic budgets. The purpose of such budgets is primarily to provide a mechanism for coordinating the individual plans of city soviet administrative departments and various sources of local income rather than to closely control expenditures or allocate revenues. Decisions on actual expenditure and allocation are made on the basis of budget projections, but frequently do not conform to budget guidelines.[80]

During 1980, some 1.2 billion rubles were scheduled to pass through the financial agencies of the Leningrad city soviet (see Table A-4). Of these funds, approximately 45 percent were generated locally, 43 percent were assigned to the soviet from general state revenues and taxes, and about 12 percent resulted from direct transfer payments from other state budgets (i.e., republic, regional, and district budgets).[81] In other words, although Leningrad is far more self-sufficient financially than most Soviet municipalities, less than half of its operating funds for 1980 were to be derived from the council's own fixed income. Consequently, the council has been drawn into an intricate financial web that not only links it downward to nearly all economic enterprises functioning within its boundaries, which provide locally generated fixed income, but also links it upward to the budgets of more senior strata within the Soviet federal system.

Slightly more than half of all projected 1980 expenditures were to be used to operate the productive capacity directly subordinate to

Table A-3. *Changes in Profile of Revenues and Expenditures of Soviet City Budgets, 1950–1975*

	1950	1960	1965	1970	1975
REVENUES					
Fixed Income	**47.1%**	**35.0%**	**27.2%**	**30.1%**	**30.5%**
Payments from enterprise profits	21.0	23.5	17.6	22.2	21.5
Local taxes and collections	21.1	7.0	5.5	4.4	3.8
Other	5.0	4.5	4.1	2.5	5.2
Transfer payments from state incomes and taxes	**48.0**	**47.2**	**54.4**	**55.2**	**53.5**
Turnover taxes	17.2	28.9	35.4	34.8	31.9
Payments from republican enterprise profits	——	——	3.0	2.2	2.6
Income taxes on enterprises	7.4	4.1	0.9	0.9	0.8
State taxes on population	13.2	13.3	14.3	15.6	16.6
State land incomes	10.0	0.2	——	0.5	0.5
Lottery income	——	0.4	0.5	0.9	0.8
Timber income	0.2	0.3	0.3	0.3	0.3
Grants from higher budgets	**0.3**	**0.7**	**1.0**	**0.4**	**0.2**
Grants from other budgets	**4.6**	**17.1**	**17.4**	**14.3**	**15.8**
TOTAL (in million rubles)	2,479.6	7,482.4	10,961.7	15,045.7	20,379.8
EXPENDITURES					
National economy	**24.4**	**44.4**	**36.2**	**38.2**	**40.7**
Sociocultural programs	**71.1**	**53.8**	**62.3**	**60.0**	**56.5**

Table A-3. (*Continued*)

	1950	1960	1965	1970	1975
Education and Science	32.6	26.0	32.8	30.3	28.8
Health and physical culture	37.5	27.1	28.7	29.1	26.9
Social security	1.0	0.7	0.8	0.6	0.8
Administration	**3.7**	**1.2**	**1.0**	**1.0**	**0.9**
Other expenditures	**0.8**	**0.6**	**0.5**	**0.8**	**1.9**
Total (in million rubles)	2,258.4	6,566.2	9,697.8	13,125.6	17,847.6

Source: G. B. Poliak, *Biudzhet goroda* (Moscow: Finansy, 1978), 21, 25–26.

the city soviet, while slightly less than half were to be expended for administration and services more closely related to traditional Western definitions of municipal functions. These latter funds were used by the city soviet's departments and administrations, with its standing commissions monitoring the expenditure of funds in specific policy areas. In this way, through the city's budgetary process the entire local economy—both managerial and productive—becomes a single integrated and interdependent financial system, with fiscal ties to the region and republic above and to the districts below via the executive committee and its financial agencies.

Linkages between a local soviet's executive committee and superior administrative levels in the government hierarchy tie local elites to national institutions, and the bond is reinforced by the reliance of local soviets on funds generated by outside state agencies. All these institutions, in turn, operate in an environment created by broad policy directions established by the Communist Party's local and national agencies.

Communist Party Agencies

Thus far we have described the national system of municipal administration. Although it is more ambitious in scale and scope than local governments in the rest of the industrialized world, it is recognizable as resembling those local government systems. Now, however, it is time to discuss the cross-cutting political and bureaucratic structure that differentiates the principles and practices of Soviet municipal gov-

Table A-4. *Leningrad City Budget, 1980*

Category	Value (in Rubles)
REVENUES	+ 1,227,922,000
Source: Turnover tax	416,365,000
Payments from profits	478,393,000
Income tax on cooperative and Social institutions and enterprises	5,001,000
State taxes from population	93,847,000
State duties, taxes on profits from film shows, local taxes and returns	23,653,000
Returns in damages of expenditures for upkeep of land	2,492,000
Savings from reduction in administrative expenditures	3,483,000
Returns of noncentral sources derived from financing of state plan expenditures	30,894,000
Other incomes	25,553,000
Transfers from republican budget	136,980,000
Transfers from surplus revenues of district (*raion*) budgets	951,000
EXPENDITURES	− 1,226,965,000
Source: City economy	659,105,000
Sociocultural measures	534,838,000
Maintenance of administrative Agencies	8,585,000
Other expenditures	21,298,000
Fund for unexpected expenses	2,188,000
Surplus of revenues transferred from the city budget	951,000
BALANCE	+ 957,000

SOURCE: "O biudzhete Leningrada na 1980 god: Reshenie Leningradskogo gorodskogo Soveta narodnykh deputatov ot 17 dekabriia 1979 goda," *Biulleten' Ispolnitel'nogo komiteta Leningradskogo gorodskogo Soveta narodnykh deputatov*, 1980, no. 3:6–9.

ernance from those of any system in the Western world. That cross-cutting structure is the Communist Party of the Soviet Union.

As noted in the introduction to this volume, local institutions in the USSR are subject to a dual system of political subordination: within the state bureaucracy just described and within a parallel network of party agencies.[82] In general, the party is a network designed to *establish policies* that are to be implemented by the state. The state bureaucracy is thus a network designed to *coordinate policy implementation*.

At the local level, municipal party institutions supervise all economic, social, political, and cultural activities within their jurisdiction. The local soviets have a rather similar role, but, in contrast to party control of the commanding heights of management, the soviets more often than not end up wrestling with petty administrative detail. In a 1965 textbook prepared for local activists by Leningrad's higher party school, Grigorii Romanov, a regional party secretary at the time, emphasized this supervisory role in discussing the party's function as leader of local social, political, and economic development.[83] In a similar volume published more than a decade later, Anatolii Gerasimov, then chief of the Leningrad regional party committee's industrial department and later city party committee first secretary, underscored the same theme of the party as system overseer. Indeed, Gerasimov perhaps went further than Romanov by noting that the effectiveness of social production rested on economic concentration and specialization, which would facilitate technological innovation, and he emphasized that such innovation was possible only through the review and intervention of a single coordinating institution in daily management: the Communist Party.[84] Other articles in the same volume, such as those by Tat'iana Zhdanova, secretary of the Leningrad city party committee, and Galina Pakhamova, chief of the regional party committee's culture department, stress that the party's helmsmanship extends across all spheres of human activity within a given jurisdiction.[85]

As noted in the introduction to this book, party supervision of local state institutions takes at least three primary forms. First, party members within state institutions are required to adhere to principles of party discipline by working to implement party policies. Second, state bodies officially cooperate with their party equivalent, and both sets of institutions prepare fully integrated plans of action. Third, through a unified system of personnel appointment, the Communist Party's *nomenklatura*, higher-ranking party and state institutions place key decision-making and leadership personnel in all subordinate organizations.

Virtually no information is available about the operations of the party's *nomenklatura* in Leningrad. But, as a surrogate source of information, here is a general outline of *nomenklatura* positions controlled by the executive committee of the Leningrad city soviet in 1980:[86]

- Chairman, Deputy Chairman, and Secretary of the Executive Committee of the Leningrad city soviet are elected by the city soviet.
- Managers of Main Administrations, Departments, and Committees of the Executive Committee are confirmed and dismissed by the city soviet, except during those periods between sessions of the city soviet when such officials are appointed to or dismissed from their positions by the Executive Committee of the city soviet.
- Deputy Managers and Chief Accountants of Administrations and Departments and employees of the bureaucracy of the Executive Committee are appointed to or dismissed from their positions by the Executive Committee.
- Employees of the bureaucracy of the Main Administrations, Administrations, and Departments of the Executive Committee and of organizations subordinate to it (appointed by the managers of such subdivisions) are appointed to or dismissed from their positions by the Executive Committee or by the *Nomenklatura* Accounting-Control of the Executive Committee.
- Managers of Main Administrations, Administrations, and Departments may appoint, dismiss, or transfer employees of the bureaucracy and subordinate organizations in which personnel actions and actions of *Nomenklatura* Accounting-Control are conducted with the approval of the Executive Committee (or its Deputy Chairman through subordinate organizations, personnel departments, and educational institutions). Such appointments must be presented for the approval of the Executive Committee within one week of assumption of duties.
- The Executive Committees of District *(Raion) soviets* approve appointments and dismissals of employees of the Executive Committees of District *(Raion)* soviets through the *Nomenklatura* Accounting-Control of the Executive Committee of the city soviet upon the approval of the Executive Committee of the city soviet while managers of Departments and Administrations of Executive Committees of District *(Raion)* soviets may appoint or dismiss employees upon the approval of the corresponding Main Administration, Administration, or Department of the Executive Committee of the city soviet.

Because the *nomenklatura* procedures utilized by the Leningrad city soviet may be different from those of the party, the data in the outline illustrate basic principles of personnel appointment according to which lower-level institutions fall under the supervision of superior agencies. For example, when the deputy manager of a city department retires or is transferred, the city soviet's executive committee—and *not* the department in question—will appoint a successor. Similarly, the appointment or dismissal of a manager of a department of a *district (raion)* soviet must be approved by the *nomenklatura* apparatus of the *city* soviet as well as by the corresponding *city* department prior to action by *district* officials. This pattern is repeated throughout the state and party hierarchies until careers fall within the domain of the most senior *nomenklatura* agency of all, the Central Committee of the Communist Party.[87]

Joel Moses has observed that little consensus can be found among the numerous Western scholars who have examined career development patterns of Soviet elites, except, perhaps, that a single integrated network of job placement encompasses state and party positions alike.[88] Examining regional elite recruitment patterns in the 1970s, Moses argues that in fact a deliberate and planned program of leadership development may be identified. This course of career advancement appears to lock personnel early in their careers into distinct functional specializations that cut across state, party, and mass organizational bureaucratic hierarchies. Moses then identifies five quite distinct functional career assignment areas: agricultural specialists, industrial specialists, ideological specialists, cadre specialists, and mixed generalists. All five career patterns may be identified within the hierarchy of appointments apparently controlled by the Leningrad regional and city party committees, although since the end of World War II both of those institutions have generally divided their areas of responsibility respectively between agricultural and urban industrial concerns.[89]

Both the integrated cross-agency nature of the *nomenklatura* system and the dominance of party institutions within that system may be seen in the pattern of appointment to the Leningrad region's senior political posts, wherein personnel move across hierarchical boundaries as they are promoted.[90] This point is illustrated by the career of Vladimir Khodyrev, who, in 1980, rose from being a secretary of the Leningrad *city* party committee to being its second secretary. In 1982, Khodyrev moved over to become Grigorii Romanov's top deputy as the Leningrad *regional* party committee's second secretary. Then, in 1983, Khodyrev was transferred outside of the party bureaucracy to become chairman of the Leningrad *city* soviet. All the while, he was responsible for city administration and was moving within a *single* personnel system, but he undertook his duties at the top of three *different* and at times competing institutions—the city *party* committee, the *regional* party committee, and the *city* soviet. Moreover, Lev Zaikov, Khodyrev's predecessor as chair of the *city* soviet, replaced Romanov as first secretary of the *regional* party committee. Although not completely analo-

Table A-5. *Composition of the Leningrad City Party Committee, 1980*

	Full Members	Candidate Members	Auditing Commission Members	Total
Party officials	35.0%	32.5%	36.9%	34.6%
Regional	8.2	0.0	0.0	5.2
City	10.3	18.9	15.8	13.1
District	13.4	8.2	15.8	12.4
Institutional	3.1	5.4	5.3	3.9
City government officials	12.4	13.5	15.8	13.1
Social organization officials	3.1	2.7	0.0	2.6
Managers	6.2	5.4	10.5	6.5
Military and police	5.2	0.0	0.0	3.3
Workers	11.3	16.2	0.0	11.1
No identification*	26.8	29.7	36.8	28.8
TOTAL	100.0%	100.0%	100.0%	100.0%
MALE	77.3%	86.5%	63.2%	77.7%
FEMALE	22.7%	13.5%	36.8%	22.3%

SOURCE: "Sostav Leningradskogo gorodskogo komiteta KPSS," *Leningradskaia pravda*, December 28, 1980, p. 1.

*Members not identified in *Leningradskaia pravda* during the period September 1980 to December 1985.

gous, this situation can be likened to one in which the U.S. Department of Health and Human Services were suddenly to become able to make all personnel decisions for federal, state, county, and city public health organizations.

Finally, in addition to these procedures and structures linking party and state agencies into a unitary administrative system, state leaders are frequently co-opted into leading party governing bodies. The Leningrad city party committee, like the city soviet, includes in its ranks many workers (see Tables A-5, A-6, and A-7). Unlike the city soviet, however, administrative personnel (party officials, city government officials, social organization officials, and the like) dominate the 169-person city party committee,[91] perhaps reflecting both the greater bureaucratic and political presence of the city party committee and the greater liaison function of the city soviet (see Chart A-1). If we look at the membership of the 1980, 1983, and 1985 Leningrad city party committees—as identified in *Leningradskaia pravda* from 1980 until 1985—it is noteworthy that city party and state officials (secretaries, department chiefs, and so on) are the two largest single groups of mem-

Table A-6. *Composition of the Leningrad City Party Committee, 1983*

	Full Members	Candidate Members	Auditing Commission Members	Total
Party officials	32.7%	20.6%	43.5%	31.4%
Regional	7.5	0.0	0.0	4.7
City	9.3	10.3	17.4	10.7
District	13.1	7.7	17.4	12.4
Institutional	2.8	2.6	8.7	3.6
City government officials	19.6	12.8	8.7	16.6
Social organization officials	2.8	2.6	4.3	2.9
Managers	4.7	2.6	0.0	3.6
Military and police	4.7	5.1	0.0	4.1
Workers	16.8	10.1	0.0	13.0
No identification[*]	18.7	46.2	43.5	28.4
TOTAL	100.0%	100.0%	100.0%	100.0%
MALE	77.6%	74.5%	56.5%	75.1%
FEMALE	22.4%	25.5%	43.5%	24.9%

SOURCE: "Sostav Leningradskogo gorodskogo komiteta KPSS," *Leningradskaia pravda*, December 18, 1983, p. 1.

[*]Members not identified in *Leningradskaia pravda* during the period September 1980 to December 1985.

bers. In other words, there are men and women who manage Leningrad's municipal affairs. This pattern is magnified if we add district (*raion*) officials who perform similar duties at their level within the Soviet federal hierarchy. Moreover, the people who actually run key municipal institutions—both party and state—are much more likely to be re-elected to successive party committees. For example, both groups dominate the ranks of the city party committee's full members reelected at party conferences in December 1983 and again in December 1985 (see Table A-8).

The Rules of the Contest

This appendix has set forth the institutional context of local governance within the Soviet system by reviewing the governing constitutional and legislative documents—the Soviet "municipal charter." It also has discussed the soviet, the institution most responsible for opening up communications between the city's governed and governors, as well as the soviet's executive agencies that link the city's administrative

Table A-7. *Composition of the Leningrad City Party Committee, 1985*

	Full Members	Candidate Members	Auditing Commission Members	Total
Party officials	35.8%	20.5%	47.8%	33.9%
Regional	8.5	0.0	0.0	5.4
City	16.0	7.7	21.7	14.8
District	10.4	12.8	17.4	11.9
Institutional	0.9	0.0	8.7	1.8
City government officials	14.1	7.7	4.3	11.3
Social organization officials	0.9	2.6	4.3	1.2
Managers	5.7	2.6	0.0	4.2
Military and police	3.8	2.6	0.0	3.0
Workers	10.4	0.0	4.3	6.5
No identification[*]	29.3	64.0	39.3	39.9
TOTAL	100.0%	100.0%	100.0%	100.0%
MALE	79.9%	84.6%	60.9%	88.0%
FEMALE	20.1%	15.4%	39.1%	22.0%

SOURCE: "Sostav Leningradskogo gorodskogo komiteta KPSS," *Leningradskaia pravda*, p. 1; December 22, 1985.

[*]Members not identified in *Leningradskaia pravda* during the period September 1980 to December 1985. The significantly larger number of unidentified members in 1985 probably is a consequence of the election of new members not previously in publicly visible positions prior to December 1985.

structure to national bureaucratic institutions. Finally, it has reviewed the role of the party committee—the only municipal institution capable of providing a broad policy framework. Taken together, these institutions and the rules of their operation establish the strictly defined limits of the institutional world within which local officials must function.

These "rules of the contest" in center-periphery relations and municipal administration in the USSR impose order on the myriad institutional and personal relationships necessary to run a modern metropolis.[92] The varied constitutional, legal, bureaucratic, political, economic, cultural, and personal norms that constitute those rules are as diverse as the relationships they seek to control. Taken as a whole, these conventions create the institutional context within which the Leningrad officials mentioned in this study have functioned.

Chart A-1. Structure of the Leningrad city party committee, December 1985.

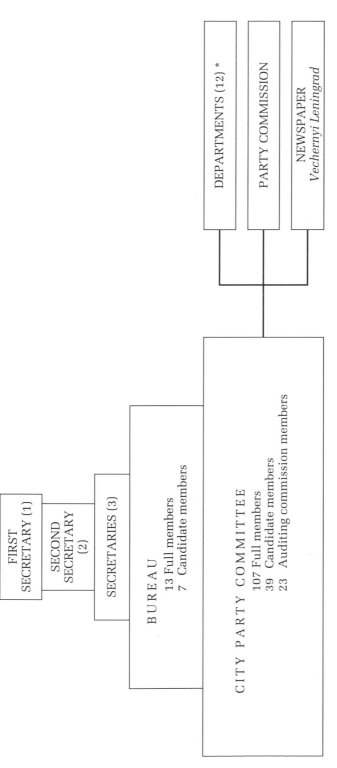

FIRST SECRETARY (1)

SECOND SECRETARY (2)

SECRETARIES (3)

B U R E A U
13 Full members
7 Candidate members

C I T Y   P A R T Y   C O M M I T T E E
107 Full members
39 Candidate members
23 Auditing commission members

DEPARTMENTS (12) *

PARTY COMMISSION

NEWSPAPER
Vechernyi Leningrad

SOURCE: "Sostav Leningradskogo komiteta KPSS," *Leningradskaia pravda*, December 22, 1985, p. 1.

* Organizational-Party Work; Propaganda and Agitation; Science and Educational Institutions; Schools; Culture; Industry; Light and Food Industries; Construction; Municipal Economy and Transportation; Trade and Consumer Services; Administration and Finance; General.

Table A-8. *Percentage of the Leningrad City Party Committee Reelected by Subsequent Party Conference, 1980–1985*

1983 Status	1980 Membership Status			
	Full Member	Candidate Member	Auditing Commission Member	Total Membership
Full member	57.7%	10.8%	15.8%	41.2%
Candidate member	0.0	40.6	10.6	11.6
Auditing commission member	0.0	0.0	36.8	4.6
Not reelected	42.2	48.6	36.8	43.1
TOTAL	100.0%	100.0%	100.0%	100.0%

1985 Status	1983 Membership Status			
	Full Member	Candidate Member	Auditing Commission Member	Total Membership
Full member	65.4%	15.4%	0.0%	45.0%
Candidate member	0.9	38.5	8.7	10.7
Auditing commission member	0.9	0.0	56.5	8.3
Not reelected	32.8	46.1	34.8	36.0
TOTAL	100.0%	100.0%	100.0%	100.0%

SOURCE: "Sostav Leningradskogo gorodskogo komiteta KPSS," *Leningradskaia pravda,* December 28, 1980, p. 1; December 18, 1983, p. 1; December 22, 1985, p. 1.

Appendix B:
Senior Leningrad Officials,
1917–1987

During the Revolution of 1917, the Civil War, and the postwar recovery period, the most powerful Bolsheviks involved in local Petrograd politics (first Leon Trotsky and then Grigorii Zinov'ev) assumed the position of chairman of the historic Petrograd soviet (see Chart B-1). With the purge of Zinov'ev and his supporters in 1926, however, prestige and power shifted to the Leningrad regional party committee's first secretaryship, where it has stayed ever since.

In December 1931, regional party institutions were separated from newly created city institutions. Nevertheless, the first secretaries of the regional party committee initially assumed both posts until 1950.

By the 1950s, a clear career pattern formed under which local leaders such as Frol Kozlov were promoted from city party second secretary to first secretary, then from regional party second secretary to first secretary. Later in the decade, regional party second secretaries Nikolai Rodionov and Georgii Popov became city party first secretary, as did Iurii Solov'ev in 1978.

The bifurcation of local party institutions into agricultural and industrial branches under Nikita Khrushchev (1963–1964) briefly obscured this hierarchy among Leningrad party institutions.[1] By the late 1960s, however, the previous pattern had been firmly reestablished.

The personnel changes following the elevation of regional party First Secretary Grigorii Romanov to the Secretariat of the Communist Party's Central Committee in June 1983, as well as the death of Romanov's second secretary, Nikolai Suslov, in an automobile accident the year before, disrupted the normal pattern of personnel advancement.[2] The June 1983 elevation of Leningrad city soviet Chairman Lev Zaikov to replace the departed Romanov would appear to defy all previously established models of Leningrad *nomenklatura* advancement.[3] No one had ever previously made such a move from the lower status city soviet post to the region's senior party position.

By mid-1985 more traditional appointment patterns had reasserted themselves. In July of that year, former Leningrad city party First Secretary Iurii Solov'ev, returning from a brief stint as USSR minister of industrial construction, was named regional party first secretary, replacing Lev Zaikov, who, in turn, had joined the Central Committee's Secretariat.[4]

Chart B-1. Leading Leningrad political officeholders, 1917–1987.

Year	Regional Party First Secretary	Regional Party Second Secretary	City Party First Secretary	City Party Second Secretary	Chairman of City Soviet	Chairman of Regional Executive Committee/Regional Soviet
1917					L. D. TROTSKY	
1918	P. S. ZASLAVSKII				G. E. ZINOV'EV	
1919	M. M. KHARITONOV S. S. ZORIN				G. E. Zinov'ev	
1920	S. S. Zorin				G. E. Zinov'ev	G. E. EVDOMIKOV
1921	S. S. Zorin N. A. UGLANOV I. N. SMIRNOV	M. M. KHARITONOV			G. E. Zinov'ev	G. E. Evdomikov
1922	I. N. Smirnov P. A. ZALUTSKII	M. M. Kharitonov I. M. MOSKVIN			G. E. Zinov'ev	G. E. Evdomikov
1923	P. A. Zalutskii	I. M. Moskvin			G. E. Zinov'ev	G. E. Evdomikov
1924	P. A. Zalutskii	I. M. Moskvin			G. E. Zinov'ev	G. E. Evdomikov
1925	P. A. Zalutskii G. E. EVDOMIKOV	N. M. SHVERNIK N. P. KOMAROV			G. E. Zinov'ev	G. E. Evdomikov N. P. KOMAROV
1926	G. E. Evdomikov S. M. KIROV	N. P. Komarov A. E. BADAEV N. M. SHVERNIK N. K. ANTYPOV			G. E. Zinov'ev N. P. KOMAROV	N. P. Komarov
1927	S. M. Kirov	N. K. Antypov			N. P. Komarov	N. P. Komarov
1928	S. M. Kirov	N. K. Antypov M. S. CHUDOV			N. P. Komarov	N. P. Komarov
1929	S. M. Kirov	M. S. Chudov	S. M. KIROV		I. F. KADATSKII	I. F. KADATSKII
1930	S. M. Kirov	M. S. Chudov			I. F. Kadatskii	I. F. Kadatskii
1931	S. M. Kirov	M. S. Chudov P. I. STRUPPE		I. I. GAZA	I. F. Kadatskii	I. F. Kadatskii F. F. TSAR'KOV

Chart B-1. Leading Leningrad political officeholders, 1917–1987.

Year	Regional Party First Secretary	Regional Party Second Secretary	City Party First Secretary	City Party Second Secretary	Chairman of City Soviet	Chairman of Regional Executive Committee/Regional Soviet
1932	S. M. Kirov	P. I. Struppe M. S. CHUDOV	S. M. Kirov	I. I. Gaza	I. F. Kadatskii	F. F. Tsar'kov P. I. STRUPPE
1933	S. M. Kirov	M. S. Chudov	S. M. Kirov	I. I. Gaza	I. F. Kadatskii	P. I. Struppe
1934	S. M. Kirov A. A. ZHDANOV	M. S. Chudov	S. M. Kirov A. A. ZHDANOV	A. I. UGAROV	I. F. Kadatskii	P. I. Struppe
1935	A. A. Zhdanov	M. S. Chudov	A. A. Zhdanov	A. I. Ugarov	I. F. Kadatskii	P. I. Struppe
1936	A. A. Zhdanov	M. S. Chudov A. S. SHCHERBAKOV	A. A. Zhdanov	A. I. Ugarov	I. F. Kadatskii	P. I. Struppe A. P. GRICHMANOV
1937	A. A. Zhdanov	A. S. Shcherbakov P. I. SMORODIN A. N. PETROVSKII	A. A. Zhdanov	A. I. Ugarov	I. F. Kadatskii V. N. SHESTAKOV	A. P. Grichmanov
1938	A. A. Zhdanov	A. N. Petrovskii A. A. KUZNETSOV T. F. SHTYKOV	A. A. Zhdanov	A. I. Ugarov A. A. KUZNETSOV	A. N. PETROVSKII A. N. KOSYGIN	N. V. SOLOV'EV
1939	A. A. Zhdanov	T. F. Shtykov	A. A. Zhdanov	A. A. Kuznetsov	A. N. Kosygin P. S. POPKOV	N. V. Solov'ev
1940	A. A. Zhdanov	T. F. Shtykov	A. A. Zhdanov	A. A. Kuznetsov	P. S. Popkov	N. V. Solov'ev
1941	A. A. Zhdanov	T. F. Shtykov	A. A. Zhdanov	A. A. Kuznetsov	P. S. Popkov	N. V. Solov'ev
1942	A. A. Zhdanov	A. A. KUZNETSOV	A. A. Zhdanov	A. A. Kuznetsov	P. S. Popkov	N. V. Solov'ev
1943	A. A. Zhdanov	A. A. Kuznetsov	A. A. Zhdanov	A. A. Kuznetsov	P. S. Popkov	N. V. Solov'ev
1944	A. A. Zhdanov	A. A. Kuznetsov	A. A. Zhdanov	A. A. Kuznetsov	P. S. Popkov	N. V. Solov'ev
1945	A. A. KUZNETSOV	A. A. Kuznetsov I. M. TURKO	A. A. KUZNETSOV	Iu. F. KAPUSTIN	P. S. Popkov	N. V. Solov'ev
1946	A. A. Kuznetsov P. S. POPKOV	I. M. Turko G. F. BADAEV	A. A. Kuznetsov P. S. POPKOV	Iu. F. Kapustin	P. S. Popkov P. G. LAZUTIN	N. V. Solov'ev I. S. KHARITNOV

Year						
1947	P. S. Popkov	G. F. Badaev	P. S. Popkov	Iu. F. Kapustin	P. G. Lazutin	I. S. Kharitonov
1948	P. S. Popkov	G. F. Badaev	P. S. Popkov	Iu. F. Kapustin	P. G. Lazutin	I. S. Kharitonov I. D. DMITRIEV
1949	P. S. Popkov V. M. ANDRIANOV	G. F. Badaev B. F. NIKOLAEV	P. S. Popkov V. M. ANDRIANOV	Iu. F. Kapustin N. A. NIKOLAEV F. R. KOZLOV	P. G. Lazutin An. Al. KUZNETSOV P. F. LADANOV	I. D. Dmitriev
1950	V. M. Andrianov	B. F. Nikolaev	F. R. KOZLOV	A. V. NOSENKO	P. F. Ladanov	I. D. Dmitriev I. P. PETROV
1951	V. M. Andrianov	B. F. Nikolaev	F. R. Kozlov	A. V. Nosenko	P. F. Ladanov	I. P. Petrov
1952	V. M. Andrianov	B. F. Nikolaev F. R. KOZLOV	F. R. Kozlov A. I. ALEKSEEV	A. V. Nosenko	P. F. Ladanov	I. P. Petrov V. N. PONOMAREV
1953	V. M. Andrianov F. R. KOZLOV	F. R. Kozlov N. G. IGNATOV G. I. VOROB'EV	A. I. Alekseev N. G. IGNATOV I. K. ZAMCHEVSKII	A. V. Nosenko A. I. ALEKSEEV	P. F. Ladanov	V. N. Ponomarev
1954	F. R. Kozlov	G. I. Vorob'ev D. D. BREZHNEV	I. K. Zamchevskii	A. I. Alekseev N. N. RODIONOV	P. F. Ladanov N. I. SMIRNOV*	V. N. Ponomarev G. I. VOROB'EV
1955	F. R. Kozlov	D. D. Brezhnev	I. K. Zamchevskii	N. N. Rodionov	N. I. Smirnov	G. I. Vorob'ev
1956	F. R. Kozlov	D. D. Brezhnev N. N. RODIONOV	I. K. Zamchevskii I. V. SPIRIDONOV	N. N. Rodionov A. P. BOIKOVA	N. I. Smirnov	G. I. Vorob'ev
1957	F. R. Kozlov I. V. SPIRIDONOV	N. N. Rodionov G. I. POPOV	I. V. Spiridonov N. N. RODIONOV	A. P. Boikova	N. I. Smirnov	G. I. Vorob'ev N. I. SMIRNOV*
1958	I. V. Spiridonov	G. I. Popov	N. N. Rodionov	A. P. Boikova	N. I. Smirnov	N. I. Smirnov
1959	I. V. Spiridonov	G. I. Popov	N. N. Rodionov	A. P. Boikova	N. I. Smirnov	N. I. Smirnov
1960	I. V. Spiridonov	G. I. Popov N. G. KORTYKOV	N. N. Rodionov G. I. POPOV	A. P. Boikova	N. I. Smirnov	N. I. Smirnov
1961	I. V. Spiridonov	V. S. TOLSTIKOV	G. I. Popov	A. P. Boikova	N. I. Smirnov	N. I. Smirnov G. I. KOZLOV
1962	I. V. Spiridonov V. S. TOLSTIKOV	V. S. Tolstikov	G. I. Popov	A. P. Boikova	N. I. Smirnov V. Ia. ISAEV	G. I. Kozlov
1963	V. S. Tolstikov(IND) G. I. KOZLOV(AG)	G. V. ROMANOV(IND) A. N. SHIBALOV(AG)	G. I. Popov	A. P. Boikova Iu. I. ZAVORUKHIN	V. Ia. Isaev	G. I. Kozlov B. A. POPOV(IND) V. G. SOMINICH(AG)**

Chart B-1. Leading Leningrad political officeholders, 1917–1987. (continued)

Year	Regional Party First Secretary	Regional Party Second Secretary	City Party First Secretary	City Party Second Secretary	Chairman of City Soviet	Chairman of Regional Executive Committee/Regional Soviet
1964	V. S. Tolstikov(IND) G. I. Kozlov(AG)	G. V. Romanov (IND) A. N. Shibalov(AG)	G. I. Popov	Iu. I. Zavorukhin	V. Ia. Isaev	B. A. Popov(IND) V. G. Sominich(AG)** G. I. KOZLOV
1965	V. S. TOLSTIKOV	G. V. ROMANOV	G. I. Popov	Iu. I. Zavorukhin	V. Ia. Isaev	G. I. Kozlov
1966	V. S. Tolstikov	G. V. Romanov	G. I. Popov	Iu. I. Zavorukhin	V. Ia. Isaev A. A. SIZOV	G. I. Kozlov
1967	V. S. Tolstikov	G. V. Romanov	G. I. Popov	Iu. I. Zavorukhin	A. A. Sizov	G. I. Kozlov
1968	V. S. Tolstikov	G. V. Romanov	G. I. Popov	Iu. I. Zavorukhin	A. A. Sizov	G. I. Kozlov A. N. SHIBALOV
1969	V. S. Tolstikov	G. V. Romanov	G. I. Popov	Iu. I. Zavorukhin	A. A. Sizov	A. N. Shibalov
1970	V. S. Tolstikov G. V. ROMANOV	G. V. Romanov V. I. KAZAKOV	G. I. Popov	Iu. I. Zavorukhin	A. A. Sizov	A. N. Shibalov
1971	G. V. Romanov	V. I. Kazakov	G. I. Popov B. I. ARISTOV	Iu. I. Zavorukhin	A. A. Sizov	A. N. Shibalov
1972	G. V. Romanov	V. I. Kazakov	B. I. Aristov	Iu. I. Zavorukhin N. V. MERENISHCHEV	A. A. Sizov	A. N. Shibalov
1973	G. V. Romanov	V. N. IGNATOV	B. I. Aristov	N. V. Merenishchev B. P. USANOV	V. I. KAZAKOV	A. N. Shibalov
1974	G. V. Romanov	V. N. Ignatov Iu. F. SOLOV'EV	B. I. Aristov	B. P. Usanov	V. I. Kazakov	A. N. Shibalov
1975	G. V. Romanov	Iu. F. Solov'ev	B. I. Aristov	B. P. Usanov	V. I. Kazakov	A. N. Shibalov
1976	G. V. Romanov	Iu. F. Solov'ev	B. I. Aristov	B. P. Usanov	V. I. Kazakov L. N. ZAIKOV	A. N. Shibalov
1977	G. V. Romanov	Iu. F. Solov'ev	B. I. Aristov	B. P. Usanov	L. N. Zaikov	A. N. Shibalov
1978	G. V. Romanov	Iu. F. Solov'ev R. S. BOBOVIKOV	B. I. Aristov Iu. F. SOLOV'EV	B. P. Usanov V. N. NIKIFOROV	L. N. Zaikov	A. N. Shibalov

1979	G. V. Romanov	R. S. Bobovikov	Iu. F. Solov'ev	V. N. Nikiforov V. I. PIMENOV	L. N. Zaikov	A. N. Shibalov
1980	G. V. Romanov	R. S. Bobovikov N. Ia. SUSLOV	Iu. F. Solov'ev	V. I. Pimencv N. Ia. SUSLOV V. Ia. KHODYREV	L. N. Zaikov	A. N. Shibalov R. S. BOBOVIKOV
1981	G. V. Romanov	N. Ia. Suslov	Iu. F. Solov'ev	V. Ia. Khodyrev	L. N. Zaikov	R. S. Bobovikov
1982	G. V. Romanov	N. Ia. Suslov V. Ia. KHODYREV	Iu. F. Solov'ev	V. Ia. Khodyrev A. F. DUBOV	L. N. Zaikov	R. S. Bobovikov
1983	G. V. Romanov L. N. ZAIKOV	V. Ia. Khodyrev A. P. DUMACHEV	Iu. F. Solov'ev	A. F. Dubov	L. N. Zaikov V. Ia. KHODYREV	R. S. Bobovikov N. I. POPOV
1984	L. N. Zaikov	A. P. Dumachev P. P. MOZHAEV	Iu. F. Solov'ev A. P. DUMACHEV	A. F. Dubov	V. Ia. Khodyrev	N. I. Popov
1985	L. N. Zaikov Iu. F SOLOV'EV	P. P. Mozhaev	A. P. Dumachev	A. F. Dubov	V. Ia. Khodyrev	N. I. Popov
1986	Iu. F. Solov'ev	P. P. Mozhaev A. M. FATEEV	A. P. Dumachev A. N. GERASIMOV	A. F. Dubov V. N. KRIKHUNOV	V. Ia. Khodyrev	N. I. Popov
1987	Iu. F. Solov'ev	A. M. Fateev	A. N. Gerasimov	V. N. Krikhunov	V. Ia. Khodyrev	N. I. Popov

SOURCE: *Petrogradskaia pravda* and *Leningradskaia pravda*. In addition, I would like to thank Mary McAuley, Werner Hahn, and Peter Gooderham for their assistance in the preparation of this chart.

NOTE: The Communist Party city committee was created as a separate entity in December 1931.

*The Nikolai Ivanovich Smirnov who served as the chairman of the Leningrad city soviet from 1954 until 1962 is not the same Nikolai Ivanovich Smirnov who was chairman of the Leningrad regional soviet from 1957 to 1961.

**During the period of the bifurcation of the Communist Party into agricultural and industrial divisions (1963 and 1964), V. S. Tolstikov and G. V. Romanov served as first and second industrial secretaries for the Leningrad region, while G. I. Kozlov and A. N. Shibalov served as first and second agricultural secretaries. B. A. Popov was chair for industry of the Leningrad Regional Soviet Executive Committee during this same period, while V. G. Sominich was chair for agriculture.

Appendix C:
Leningrad's Urban Planning Institutions

During the period of this study, the State Committee on Construction Affairs (Gosstroi) was the Soviet Union's principal national institution involved in the regional and city planning process (in addition, of course, to the economic planning agencies subordinate to the State Planning Committee [Gosplan]). Gosstroi began operations in 1950 as the successor organization to the Committee on Architectural Affairs. It was involved in one way or another with every phase of the construction process from planning to general contracting, and directed a centralized national administrative and support network for construction and related planning efforts.[1] This system included more than a dozen major research and design institutes, as well as the State Committee on Civil Construction and Architecture (Gosgrazhdanstroi).[2] As with Gosplan in economic planning, Gosstroi and Gosgrazhdanstroi were replicated at the level of the Soviet federal republics by 15 state construction committees (one for each republic). These same functions were performed at the local level by the Construction and Architectural departments and the Architectural-Planning administrations of the city and regional soviets as well as city planning institutes subordinate to Gosgrazhdanstroi. Major revision of this system at the national level is under way as this volume goes to press.

The city general plan of development is the primary instrument for physical urban planning.[3] This plan, together with accompanying detailed thematic and district plans, elaborates the broad outline of future construction in a city for a period of up to 30 years. Soviet law requires every city to adopt and implement such a general plan, and all have done so with varying degrees of practical result.[4]

Leningrad's planning structure is something of a model version of this planning system, although it is more complex than the national norm. In Leningrad, four major groups of institutions are involved in the city planning process, each containing a number of semiautonomous institutions with quite distinct ties to the policy process, both locally in Leningrad and nationally in Moscow. The first group comprises the Leningrad offices of Gosstroi and Gosgrazhdanstroi: the Architectural-Planning Administration, and the Main Administration of

Housing, Civil and Industrial Construction of the Leningrad City Soviet.[5]

The second group includes the planning and architectural organizations. The most important of these is Gosgrazhdanstroi's Leningrad
Planning Institute (LenNIIproekt), which has primary responsibility for
compliance with the city's general plan.[6] In addition, Gosgrazhdanstroi's planning center for the Northwestern RSFSR (LenZNIEP) is also
based in Leningrad, as are a number of specialized planning agencies
for housing, subway, bridge, and engineering construction projects.[7]
All these establishments are joined by several design institutes that
may be considered the functional equivalents of Western architectural
firms, as they design projects in Leningrad and elsewhere on essentially
a contract basis.[8]

The group of architectural and planning agencies also includes
the Leningrad Division of the USSR Union of Architects, which is one
of the most active branches of that organization anywhere in the Soviet
Union.[9] This 1,550-member professional association is the focal point
of the city's architectural, planning, and construction community. Its
seminars and publications are a powerful intellectual force behind the
work of local city planners and architects and provide theoretical cohesion. The union is as responsible as any other single institution for the
sustained advocacy of a distinctive Leningrad viewpoint on architectural and planning issues.

The third institutional cluster participating in the physical development of the city consists of an extensive network of contractors
headed by the Main Leningrad Construction Administration (Glavleningradstroi), which operates nearly two dozen smaller trusts that are,
in effect, construction firms.[10] Moreover, it works closely with the Leningrad-based Main Western Construction Administration (Glavzap-
stroi), which, along with its subordinate trusts assumes responsibility
for much of the construction in the Northwestern RSFSR. In addition,
a series of specialized construction agencies are charged with such
specific tasks as facade reconstruction, subway construction, bridge
construction, and university development.[11]

The city's architectural research and educational institutions com-
pose the fourth and perhaps most important institutional concentration,
providing valuable support for all the institutions we have mentioned.
The Repin Institute of Painting, Sculpture, and Architecture,[12] the Leningrad Engineering-Economics Institute,[13] the Leningrad Polytechnic
Institute, the Leningrad Engineering-Construction Institute, and the
USSR Academy of Sciences' Institute of Socioeconomic Problems all
have trained successive generations of Leningrad planners, architects,
and urbanists who share a generally uniform viewpoint on problems
of urban development. Such a linkage between common perspectives,
professional orientations, goals, and practices on the one hand and

shared educational experiences on the other is not at all surprising and has been commented on by social scientists exploring other, non-Soviet environments.[14]

These four groupings encompass dozens of institutions, and the most prominent of them are among the most influential of their kind in the Soviet Union. The system preserves a multigenerational tradition of competent and well-trained professionals who have a distinctive outlook. The cooperative partnership of Leningrad's educational, planning, design, construction, municipal, and professional institutions fosters a remarkable degree of cohesion within the local planning community on the value of historic preservation, the necessity for social planning, and the need for aesthetic harmony.

Indeed, this' consensus facilitates the efforts by Leningrad planners, architects, builders, and managers to preserve an urban environment that is unique in the world. Furthermore, it encourages them to minimize the intrusion on that environment by the standard Soviet fare of mile upon mile of prefabricated reinforced-concrete residential and industrial superblocks.[15] While such superblocks exist in Leningrad, they are kept away from the city's historic core. These features combine to produce a powerful and cohesive local architectural and planning establishment. This establishment forms a professional community and an institutional network that has access to considerable resources of its own when dealing with representatives of the centralized state from Moscow.

Notes

Foreword

1. Charles E. Lindblom, *Politics and Markets: The World's Political-Economic Systems* (New York: Basic Books, 1977), 159, 170.

Acknowledgments

1. David T. Cattell, *Leningrad: A Case Study of Soviet Urban Government* (New York: Frederick A. Praeger, 1968); Everett M. Jacobs, ed., *Soviet Local Politics and Government* (London and Boston: George Allen & Unwin, 1983); Jeffrey Hahn, *Soviet Grassroots: Citizen Participation in Local Soviet Government* (Princeton: Princeton University Press, 1988).

2. Werner G. Hahn, *Postwar Soviet Politics* (Ithaca: Cornell University Press, 1982); "Rech' tovarishcha A. N. Shelepina," *Pravda*, October 27, 1961, p. 10; Joseph Brodsky, *Less than One: Selected Essays* (New York: Farrar, Straus & Giroux, 1986).

3. Materials relevant to these reforms may be found in "XIX Vsesoiuznaia konferentsiia KPSS: Informatsionnoe soobshchenie," *Leningradskaia pravda*, June 29–July 2, 1988, p. 1; "Proekt: Zakon Soiuza Sovetskikh Sotsialisticheskikh Respublik ob izmeneniiakh i dopolneniiakh Konstitutsii (Osnovnogo Zakona) SSSR)," ibid., October 22, 1988, pp. 1–2; "Proekt: Zakon Soiuza Sovetskikh Sotsialisticheskikh Respublik o vyborakh narodnykh deputatov SSSR," ibid., October 23, 1988, pp. 1–3; "Zakon Soiuza Sovetskikh Sotsialisticheskikh Respublik ob izmeneniiakh i dopolneniiakh Konstitutsii (Osnovnogo Zakona) SSSR)," ibid., December 3, 1988 pp. 1–2; and "Zakon Soiuza Sovetskikh Sotsialisticheskikh Respublik o vyborakh narodnykh deputatov SSSR," ibid., December 4, 1988, pp. 1–3.

Introduction

1. These observations are drawn from Norton E. Long, "The Local Community as an Ecology of Games," *American Journal of Sociology* 64, no. 3 (November 1958): 251–261.

2. The concept of regional elites serving as brokers between the center

and the periphery was elaborated by Sidney Tarrow in reference to Italy and France in *Between Center and Periphery: Grassroots Politicians in Italy and France* (New Haven: Yale University Press, 1977).

3. The view of regional and municipal leaders as brokers is also consistent with Jerry Hough's portrayal of the regional party secretary as *prefect* of the Soviet administrative/political system in *The Soviet Prefects: The Local Party Organs in Industrial Decision-Making* (Cambridge: Harvard University Press, 1969).

4. The primary governmental institution at a given level within the Soviet Union's state hierarchy, consisting of elected deputies who are also leading administrators, managers, workers, and other notables. For a more complete description of the structure and function of Soviet local governance, see Appendix A.

5. M. Bliznakov, "Urban Planning in the USSR: Integrative Theories," in M. F. Hamm, ed., *The City in Russian History* (Lexington: University of Kentucky Press, 1976), 243–256; S. Frederick Starr, "Visionary Town Planning during the Cultural Revolution," in Sheila Fitzpatrick, ed., *Cultural Revolution in Russia, 1928–1931* (Bloomington: Indiana University Press, 1978), 207–240.

6. Bliznakov, "Urban Planning," 245; M. F. Parkins, *City Planning in Soviet Russia* (Chicago: University of Chicago Press, 1953), 11–12.

7. Bliznakov, "Urban Planning"; A. Kopp, *Town and Revolution* (New York: Braziller, 1970); A. Kopp, *Changer la vie, changer la ville* (Paris: U.G.E., 1975); Parkins, *City Planning*, 20–29; S. Frederick Starr, "The Revival and Schism of Urban Planning in Twentieth Century Russia," in Hamm, *City in Russian History*, 222–242; Gregory D. Andrusz, *Housing and Urban Development in the USSR* (Albany: SUNY Press, 1985), 18–19.

8. Bliznakov, "Urban Planning."

9. B. Lunin, ed., *Goroda sotsializma i sotsialisticheskaia rekonstruktsiia byta* (Moscow, 1930), 157–158.

10. Bliznakov, "Urban Planning"; Parkins, *City Planning*, 51–55.

11. James H. Bater, *The Soviet City* (London: Edward Arnold, 1980), 26–27; Henry W. Morton, "The Contemporary Soviet City," in Henry W. Morton and Robert C. Stuart, eds., *The Contemporary Soviet City* (Armonk, N.Y.: M. E. Sharpe, 1984), 15–18; and Andrusz, *Housing and Urban Development*, 114–126.

12. For a discussion of the impact of collectivization on traditional Russian patterns of seasonal migration between town and country by economic sector, see the work of Professor Shiokawa Nobuaki (e.g., his "The Collectivization of Agriculture and *Otkhodnichestvo* in the USSR, 1930," *Annals of the Institute of Social Science, University of Tokyo,* no. 24 [1982–1983], 129–158; and his "Labor Turnover in the USSR, 1929–33: A Sectorial Analysis," *Annals of the Institute of Social Science, University of Tokyo,* no. 23 [1982], 65–94).

13. The other six countries with an urban population in excess of 50 million are China, the United States, India, Japan, the Federal Republic of Germany, and Brazil (Iu. L. Pivovarov, *Sovremennaia urbanizatsiia osnovnye tendentsii rasseleniia* [Moscow: Statistika, 1976], 26). By 1980, 62 percent of the Soviet population had come to live in urban areas (M. G. Rabinovich and M. N. Shmeleva, "Gorod i etnicheskie protsessy," *Sovetskaia etnografiia,* 1984, no. 2:9), as compared to a U.S. rate of 68.8 percent of the 1975 population liv-

ing in Standard Statistical Metropolitan Areas (A. V. Dmitriev and M. N. Mezhevich, *SSSR-SShA: Sotsial'noe razvitie v gorodakh* [Leningrad: Nauka—Leningradskoe otdelenie, 1981], 42). For a listing of the 21 Soviet million-plus population centers at the time of the 1979 census, see Morton and Stuart, *Contemporary Soviet City*, 4.

14. The state committee subordinate to the USSR Council of Ministers responsible for the coordination and management of the preparation of long- and short-term economic plans.

15. The importance of the conflict can hardly be overemphasized. For recent relevant discussions, see Andrusz, *Housing and Urban Development*, 73–78, and Morton, "Contemporary Soviet City," 3–24.

16. I. M. Solodovnikov, *Mestnye sovety: Koordinatsiia i ee effektivnost'* (Moscow: Sovetskaia Rossiia, 1980), 3–14. This discussion is based on the administrative system in place during the period of our study. It illustrates some of the tensions that led to various proposals at the Nineteenth Communist Party Conference in June 1988 for a reform of local administration (Philip Taubman, "Conference Seems to Give Gorbachev a Strong Mandate," *New York Times*, July 5, 1988, pp. A1, A12–A13). The party conference resolutions led to changes in the Soviet Constitution later in 1988, which will be implemented over the coming months. These reforms include multiple candidate elections as well as a restructuring of various state institutions. A new law on the local soviets is expected as this book goes to press. For materials relevant to these reforms, see n. 3, p. 232.

17. Solodovnikov, *Mestnye sovety*, 15–23.

18. G. V. Barabashev, "Gorodskie sovety v sisteme upravleniia gorodami," in G. V. Barabashev, ed., *Rol' mestnykh sovetov v ekonomicheskom i sotsial'nom razvitii gorodov* (Moscow: Izdatel'stvo MGU, 1983), 15.

19. Carol W. Lewis, "The Economic Functions of Local Soviets," in Everett M. Jacobs, ed., *Soviet Local Politics and Government* (London and Boston: George Allen & Unwin, 1983), 38–66.

20. The hierarchical relationship among Soviet cities remains a major theme of much Soviet urban writing. For some recent discussions of this topic, see N. T. Agafonov, "Teoreticheskie i metodicheskie osnovy kontseptsii dolgostrochnogo ekonomicheskogo i sotsial'nogo razvitiia oblasti," in N. T. Agafonov, ed., *Sotsial'naia geografiia Kaliningradskoi oblast: Mezhvuzovskii sbornik trudov* (Kaliningrad: Izdanie KGU, 1982), 3–12; B. S. Khorev, *Territorial'naia organizatsiia obshchestva (aktual'nye problemy regional'nogo upravleniia i planirovaniia v SSSR)* (Moscow: Mysl', 1981), and P. S. Kovalenko, *Razvitie gorodov* (Kiev: Naukova dumka, 1980).

21. Marat Nikolaevich Mezhevich, interview, February 16, 1984.

22. N. T. Agafonov, "Strukturnye osobennosti krupnykh gorodov kak ob"ektov upravleniia," in I. I. Sigov, ed., *Upravlenie razvitiem krupnykh gorodov* (Leningrad: Nauka—Leningradskoe otdelenie, 1985), 71–72.

23. This tension was discussed with considerable frankness and in some detail by participants at the Second Scientific Conference of Sociologists of the Baltic, held at Birshtonas on October 29 and 30, 1981 (Institut filosofii, sotsiologii i prava AN Lit SSR, Pribaltiiskoe otdelenie Sovetskoi sotsiologicheskoi assotsiatsii, *Gorod kak sreda zhizdnetiatel'nosti cheloveka* [Vil'nius, 1981]). For Leningrad views concerning branch-territorial conflicts, see P. N. Lebedev,

ed., *Sistema organov gorodskogo upravleniia (opyt sotsiologicheskogo issle-dovaniia)* (Leningrad: Izdatel'stvo LGU, 1980); I. I. Sigov, *O sovershenstvovanii sochetaniia otraslevogo i territorial'nogo upravleniia* (Leningrad: Institut so-tsial'no-ekonomicheskikh problem AN SSSR, 1983); and I. I. Sigov, "Sochetanie otraslevogo i territorial'nogo upravleniia gorodom: Problemy i puti sover-shenstvovaniia," in Sigov, *Upravlenie razvitiem krupnykh gorodov*, 148–166. For some representative Western discussions, see David T. Cattell, *Leningrad: A Case Study of Soviet Urban Government* (New York: Frederick A. Praeger, 1968); Ronald J. Hill, "The Development of Soviet Local Government since Stalin's Death," in Jacobs, *Soviet Local Politics*, 18–33; and Denis J. B. Shaw, "The Soviet Urban General Plan and Recent Advances in Soviet Urban Plan-ning," *Urban Studies* 20 (1983):393–403.

24. For further discussion of soviet responsibilities for these concerns, see Gertrude E. Schroeder, "Retail Trade and Personal Services in Soviet Cities," in Morton and Stuart, *Contemporary Soviet City*, 202–220; David T. Cattell, "Local Government and the Provision of Consumer Goods and Services," in Jacobs, *Soviet Local Politics*, 172–185; and Henry W. Morton, "Local Soviets and the Attempt to Rationalize the Delivery of Urban Services: The Case of Housing," in ibid., 186–202.

25. "Pervaia sessiia Leningradskogo gorodskogo soveta," *Leningradskaia pravda*, July 3, 1982, p. 1.

26. See, for example, the discussion of "fundamental directions of the work of soviets" in A. I. Luk'ianov et al., eds., *Sovety narodnykh deputatov: Spravochnik* (Moscow: Politizdat, 1984), 210–361.

27. "Zakon ob individual'noi trudovoi deiatel'nosti," *Leningradskaia pravda*, November 21, 1986, pp. 2–3; "O proekte zakona SSSR ob individual'noi trudovoi deiatel'nosti," ibid., November 20, 1986, pp. 1–2.

28. "Eksperiment 'taksi,'" *Leningradskaia pravda*, February 24, 1987, p. 4; Iu. Trefilov, "Po sovmestitel'stva taksist: V Leningrade vladel'tsty legko-vykh avtomobilei prishli na pomoshch' gorodskomu transportu," *Sovetskaia Rossiia*, March 4, 1987, p. 4.

29. Cattell, *Leningrad*, 38–48; and Max Ethan Mote, "Leningrad Mu-nicipal Administration: Structure and Functions" (Ph.D. dissertation, Univer-sity of Washington, 1966).

30. Luk'ianov, et al., *Sovety narodnykh deputatov*, 71–75.

31. V. I. Kozlov, ed., *Ocherki istorii Leningradskoi organizatsii KPSS*, vol. 3, *1945–1985* (Leningrad: Lenizdat, 1985), 955–956.

32. See the discussion in such works as B. K. Alekseev, *Planirovanie partiinoi raboty* (Leningrad: Lenizdat, 1968); and P. P. Mozhaev, comp., *Za delovoi stil' v partiinoi rabote* (Leningrad: Lenizdat, 1981).

33. "Plenum Leningradskogo obkoma KPSS," *Leningradskaia pravda*, January 22, 1984, p. 1; "Pervaia sessiia Leningradskogo oblastnogo soveta," ibid., July 6, 1982, p. 1.

34. "Plenum Leningradskogo gorkoma KPSS," *Leningradskaia pravda*, December 18, 1983, p. 1; "Plenum Leningradskogo gorkoma KPSS," ibid., July 3, 1982, p. 1.

35. For further discussion of the *nomenklatura* system, see Rolf H. W. Theen, "Party and Bureaucracy," in Erik P. Hoffman and Robbin F. Laird, eds.,

The Soviet Polity in the Modern Era (New York: Aldine Publishing Co., 1984), 131–165, as well as the discussion found in Appendix A.

36. Leningrad is within the Russian Soviet Federated Socialist Republic (RSFSR), which has its republic capital in Moscow. Hence, Moscow is a double capital for Leningrad, being both national and republic.

37. Pavel Viacheslavovich Rusakov became Leningrader no. 5,000,000 when he was born in Maternity Hospital no. 6 on February 25, 1988. Pavel Viacheslavovich has been awarded a special gold medal commemorating his feat ("S dnem rozhdeniia, Leningradets!" *Sovetskaia Rossiia*, February 26, 1988, p. 1; "V sem'e Leningradtesev Rusakovykh: Nazvali Pavlom," ibid., February 27, 1988, p. 1).

38. *Narodnoe khoziaistvo SSSR v 1985 g.: Statisticheskii ezhegodnik* (Moscow: Finansy i statistika, 1986), p. 20; *Narodnoe khoziaistvo Leningrada i Leningradskoi oblasti v desiatoi piatiletke: Statisticheskii sbornik* (Leningrad: Lenizdat, 1981), 24.

39. *Narodnoe khoziaistvo Leningrada . . . v desiatoi piatiletke,* 39, 41–42.

40. See John Pitzer, "Gross National Product of the USSR, 1950 1980," in U.S. Congress, Joint Economic Committee, *U.S.S.R.: Measures of Economic Growth and Development, 1950–1980* (Washington: Government Printing Office, 1982), 17.

41. S. A. Kugel', B. D. Lebin, and Iu. S. Meleshchenko, eds., *Nauchnye kadry Leningrada* (Leningrad: Nauka—Leningradskoe otdelenie, 1973); and B. I. Kozlov, ed., *Organizatsiia i razvitie otraslevykh nauchno-issledovatel'skikh institutov Leningrada, 1917–1977* (Leningrad: Nauka—Leningradskoe otdelenie, 1979).

Chapter 1

1. The city was known as St. Petersburg from its establishment in May 1703 until August 1914, when its name was changed to the less Germanic Petrograd. On January 26, 1924, the city was renamed once again in honor of Vladimir Illich Lenin and has been known as Leningrad ever since.

2. Located at 59°57′ N latitude, Leningrad is the world's most northerly million-plus population center (its North American counterpart at 61°13′ N latitude is Anchorage, Alaska). As a result, the sun barely rises for just under six hours on winter's shortest day and dips below the horizon for just over five hours on summer's longest. That is, of course, when the sun is shining in Leningrad at all, for the city has only 31 "clear, cloudless" days during the average year. B. K. Dukinskii, *1000 voprosi i otvetov o Leningrade* (Leningrad: Lenizdat, 1974), 53.

3. N. F. Khomutetskii, *Peterburg-Leningrad* (Leningrad: Lenizdat, 1958), p. 9.

4. Between 1703 and 1983 there were more than 250 floods in the city, including catastrophic floods in 1772, 1777, 1824, 1903, and 1924. The city is particularly prone to floods resulting from winds backing up water in the shal-

low Gulf of Finland into the Neva, as well as from thawing ice upstream in Lake Ladoga. The worst flooding occurs when both phenomena take place simultaneously. Various proposals have been made to control flooding, including the construction of a dam across the Gulf of Finland. Construction began on such a dam in 1980 after the Central Committee of the Communist Party and the USSR Council of Ministers approved proposals put forward by the Leningrad city soviet in December 1979 ("Informatsiia o resheniiakh Ispolnitel'nogo komiteta Leningradskogo gorodskogo soveta narodnykh deputatov: Ob organizatsii upravleniia po stroitel'stvu sooruzhenii zashchity Leningrada ot navodenii, 10 Dekabria, 1979 g.," *Biulleten' Ispolnitel'nogo komiteta Leningradskogo gorodskogo soveta narodnykh deputatov*, 1980, no. 1:13). Among the numerous articles on the dam project appearing in the Leningrad press, the following provide an overview: P. A. Antonov, "Izvechnyi spor so stikhiei," *Leningradskaia panorama*, 1984, no. 5:31–33; N. Andreeva, "Most v zalive," *Leningradskaia pravda*, July 23, 1983, p. 2; "Dublery Futshtoka," ibid., April 28, 1983, p. 3; V. Volkov, "Dvoinaia nagonnaia," ibid., December 19, 1982, p. 4; Iu. Naritsyn and V. Tarasenko, "Pod natiskom uragana," ibid., November 26, 1982, p. 4; "Damby vykhodiat v more," *Leningradskaia panorama*, 1982, no. 1:12–15. For a discussion of some of the early plans for the dam project, see S. S. Agalkov, "Chtoby ne bylo navodenii," *Stroitel'stvo i arkhitektura Leningrada*, 1960, no. 10:10.

5. See, for example, the discussions in I. N. Bozherianov and E. P. Erastov, *S. Peterburg' v Petrogo vremia: Kul'turno-istoricheskie ocherki* (St. Petersburg: Kh. Krauze, 1903), 1–18; A. V. Predtechenskii, ed., *Peterburg Petrovskogo vremeni* (Leningrad: Leningradskoe gazetno-zhurnal'noe i knizhnoe izdatel'stvo, 1948), 3–38; V. N. Sashonko, *Admiralteistvo* (Leningrad: Lenizdat, 1982); L. I. Bastareva and V. I. Sidorova, *Petropavlovskaia krepost'* (Leningrad: Lenizdat, 1980); and Iu. A. Egorov, *The Architectural Planning of St. Petersburg*, trans. Eric Dlubosch (Athens: Ohio University Press, 1969).

6. A. N. Krasnova, "Traditsii vsegda sovremennyi," *Leningradskaia panorama*, 1984, no. 5:20–21.

7. George Heard Hamilton, *The Art and Architecture of Russia* (Baltimore: Penguin Books, 1975), 180–182; William Craft Brumfield, *Gold in Azure: One Thousand Years of Russian Architecture* (Boston: David R. Godine, 1983), 227–233.

8. Egorov, *Architectural Planning*, 18–20; I. N. Bozherianov, *Kul'turno-istoricheskii ocherki zhizni S-Peterburga za dva veka XVIII-XIX, 1703–1903* (St. Petersburg, 1903), vii–ix; I. Grabar', *Russkoi arkhitekture* (Moscow: Nauka, 1969), 264–283; and M. V. Iogansen, V. G. Lisovskii, and N. I. Nikulina, *Arkhitektura Vasil'evskogo ostrova v proshlom, nastoiashchem i budushchem* (Leningrad: Akademiia khudozhestv SSSR, 1969), 4–7.

9. P. N. Stolpianskii, *Staryie Peterburg i obshchestvo pooshchreniia khoduzhestv* (Leningrad: Izdanie Komiteta popularizatsii khudozhestvennykh izdanii, 1928), 23.

10. Gerald L. Burke, *The Making of Dutch Towns* (London: Cleaver-Hume Press, 1966).

11. The importance of the Copenhagen plan for the early development of St. Petersburg should not be underestimated. James Cracraft reminds us that

Peter's ambassador in Copenhagen hired Dominico Trezzini away from service to the Danish king. Trezzini, who worked in Russia from 1703 until his death in 1734, was the architect of the Church of Sts. Peter and Paul in the Peter and Paul Fortress and, as Cracraft demonstrates, perhaps the most influential architect working in Russia during the Petrine period. James Cracraft, *The Petrine Revolution in Russian Architecture* (Chicago: University of Chicago Press, 1988), 141, 154–160, 173–181.

12. D. Arkin, "Perspektivnyi plan Peterburga, 1764–1773," *Arkhitekturnoe nasledstvo*, 1955, no. 7:13–38; I. A. Bartenev, *Zodchie i stroiteli Leningrada* (Leningrad: Lenizdat, 1963), 48–67.

13. Brumfield, *Gold in Azure*, 251–274, 275–312.

14. Hamilton, *Art and Architecture*, 197–198.

15. Bozherianov, *Kul'turno-istoricheskii ocherki*; Egorov, *Architectural Planning*.

16. Egorov, *Architectural Planning*, 54–83; Bartenev, *Zodchie i stroiteli Leningrada*, 68–137.

17. Hamilton, *Art and Architecture*, 217.

18. Egorov, *Architectural Planning*, 186–196.

19. James Bater, "The Legacy of Autocracy: Environmental Quality in St. Petersburg," in R. Λ. French and F. E. Ian Hamilton, eds., *The Socialist City: Spatial Structure and Urban Policy* (New York: John Wiley & Sons, 1979), 23–48; G. B. Vasil'eva, "Vdol' ulits shumnykh . . . ," *Leningradskaia panorama*, 1984, no. 3:31–33.

20. James Bater, *St. Petersburg: Industrialization and Change* (Montreal: McGill-Queens University Press, 1976), 201–209; 366; 381–382.

21. Ibid., 335.

22. Ibid., 220–221.

23. Ibid.

24. Bater, "Legacy of Autocracy."

25. A pattern explored in the context of Moscow in Robert Eugene Johnson, "Peasant Migration and the Russian Working Class: Moscow at the End of the Nineteenth Century," *Slavic Review* 35, no. 4 (1976):652–664.

26. Bater, *St. Petersburg*, 361–362.

27. Bater, "Legacy of Autocracy."

28. V. G. Lisovskii, "Istok—drevnerusskoe zodchestvo," *Leningradskaia panorama*, 1984, no. 8:33–35.

29. Hamilton, *Art and Architecture*, 270–275.

30. Ibid., 275–283; V. G. Lisovskii, *Leningrad: Raiony novostroek* (Leningrad: Lenizdat, 1983), 26–27. These plans, in turn, would influence Fomin's work during the early Soviet period, as was the case for his designs and projects on Vasil'evskii Island. Iogansen, Lisovskii, and Nikulina, *Arkhitektura Vasil'evskogo ostrova*, 12–13; Bartenev, *Zodchie i stroiteli Leningrada*, 166–169; and Brumfield, *Gold in Azure*, 336–337.

31. S. Frederick Starr, "The Revival and Schism of Urban Planning in Twentieth Century Russia," in Michael F. Hamm, ed., *The City in Russian History* (Lexington: University of Kentucky Press, 1976), 222–242; I. Bartenev, *Arkhitektura sotsialisticheskogo Leningrada* (Leningrad: Obshchestvo "Znanie"—Leningradskaia organizatsiia, 1953), 5–10.

32. For an account of the material and social conditions of daily life in Moscow on the eve of World War I, see Diane Koenker, *Moscow Workers and the 1917 Revolution* (Princeton: Princeton University Press, 1981).

33. The differing responses of Moscow and Petrograd/Leningrad architects to the demands of socialist construction during this period are discussed in S. Frederick Starr, "Visionary Town Planning during the Cultural Revolution," in Sheila Fitzpatrick, ed., *Cultural Revolution in Russia, 1928–1931* (Bloomington: Indiana University Press, 1978), 207–240.

34. For discussion of planning and construction efforts during this period, see B. R. Rubanenko, "Razvitie goroda s 1917 po 1935 god," in Leningrad, Arkhitekturno-planirovochnoe upravlenie, *Leningrad* (Leningrad and Moscow: Iskusstvo, 1943), 45–64; V. L. Ruzhzhe, "Gradostroitel'nye problemy v krasnom Petrograde," *Stroitel'stvo i arkhitektura Leningrada*, 1967, no. 1:10–13; and V. A. Kamenskii, "Gradostroitel'noe razvitie sotsialisticheskogo Leningrada," ibid., 1967, no. 11:8–20.

35. For a discussion of the impact of the Kaganovich address on Soviet urban development, see James Bater, *The Soviet City* (London: Edward Arnold, 1980), 26–27; and Z. V. Kornil'eva, "Deiatel'nost' Leningradskoi organizatsii po osuchestvleniu general'nogo plana razvitiia goroda v semiletki (1959–1966 gg.)" (Avtoreferat dissertatsii na soiskanie uchenoi stepeni kandidata istoricheskikh nauk, Leningradskii gosudarstvennyi universitet, 1969), 4–5.

36. B. Michael Frolic, "Moscow: The Socialist Alternative," in H. Wentworth Eldredge, ed., *World Capitals: Toward Guided Urbanization* (Garden City, N.Y.: Anchor Press/Doubleday, 1975), 295–339 [309–315]; N. N. Ullas, "Novyi general'nyi razvitiia Moskvy," *Gorodskoe khoziaistvo Moskvy*, 1971, no. 8:3–25 [3–4].

37. V. A. Kamenskii and A. I. Naumov, *Leningrad: Gradostroitel'nye problemy razvitiia* (Leningrad: Stroiizdat—Leningradskoe otdelenie, 1977), 126–129; "Nashy zadachi," *Arkhitektura Leningrada*, 1936, no. 1:6–13; L. A. Il'in, "Plan razvitiia Leningrada i ego arkhitektura," ibid., 18–33; Lisovskii, *Leningrad*, 34–36.

38. Khomutetskii, *Peterburg-Leningrad*, 220; O. V. Shishkin, "Na glavnom meridiane," *Leningradskaia panorama*, 1984, no. 6:5–8; M. N. Mikishat'ev, "Doma sovetov: Obraznye resheniia," ibid., 1986, no. 11:16–18; M. E. Ivin, *Prospekt im I. V. Stalina* (Leningrad: Gosizdat. Literatury po stroitel'stva arkhitektury, 1954); *Leningrad: Vidy goroda* (Moscow: Gosizdat. Izobrazitel'nogo iskusstva, 1954), 81–99; I. Khamarev, *Za Moskovskoi zastavoi* (Leningrad: Lenizdat, 1948), 126–127.

39. G. G. Kel'kh, *Pamiatniki sovetskoi arkhitektury v Leningrade: Problemy restavratsii i okhrany* (Leningrad: Obshchestvo "Znanie" RSFSR—Leningradskaia organizatsiia, 1982).

40. M. F. Fridman, "Proekty Doma sovetov v Leningrade," *Arkhitektura Leningrada*, 1936, no. 2:8–25; N. A. Trotskii, "Dom sovetov v Leningrade," ibid., 1937, no. 2:8–19; L. V. Rudnev, "Nekotorye zamecheniia ob arkhitekture Dom Sovetov," ibid., 20–33; F. N. Pashchenko, "Stroitel'stvo zdanii administrativnogo naznacheniia v Leningrade," ibid., 1939, no. 6:9–16; L. Iu. Gal'pern, "Proekty obshchegorodskogo tsentra v Leningrade," ibid., 1940, no. 2:7–15; "Novaia sistema obshchegorodskogo tsentra Leningrada," 1941, no. 1:2–7.

41. Khomutetskii, *Peterburg-Leningrad*, 216; Lisovskii, *Leningrad*, 142–

148; V. A. Vitman et al., *Arkhitektura Leningrada* (Leningrad: Gosizdat. lit. po stroi i arkh., 1953), 228.

42. N. V. Baranov, *Siluety blokady: Zapiski glavnogo arkhitektura goroda* (Leningrad: Lenizdat, 1982).

43. *Leningrad: Entsiklopedicheskii spravochnik* (Moscow and Leningrad: Bol'shaia Sovetskaia entsiklopediia, 1957), 431; Gosudarstvennyi nauchno-issledovatel'skii muzei arkhitektury im. A. V. Shchuseva, *N. V. Baranov: Katalog vystavki osnovnykh tvorcheskikh rabot k 70-letiiu so dnia rozhdeniia i 50-letiia tvorcheskoi deiatel'nosti* (Moscow, 1979).

44. *Leningrad: Entsiklopedicheskii spravochnik*, 527–528.

45. Baranov, *Siluety blokady*, 88.

46. Ibid.

47. Ibid., 86–90; E. P. Busyreva, "Grazhdanskii podvig zodchego," *Leningradskaia panorama* 1987, no. 12:22–25.

48. N. V. Baranov, "General'nyi plan razvitiia Leningrada," in Leningrad, Arkhitekturno-planirovochnoe upravlenie, *Leningrad*, 65–84; Kamenskii and Naumov, *Leningrad*, 126–139; "O general'nom plane goroda Leningrada," *Arkhitektura Leningrada*, 1939, no. 3:2; N. V. Morozov, "Sotsialisticheskii Leningrad," ibid., 3–6.

49. Baranov, "General'nyi plan razvitiia Leningrada," 73–81.

50. Khomutetskii, *Peterburg-Leningrad*, 216; Kamenskii and Naumov, *Leningrad*, 126–139; Ivin, *Prospekt im I. V. Stalina*; V. I. Piliavskii, *Arkhitektura Leningrada* (Leningrad and Moscow: Gosizdat. lit. po stroi i arkh., 1953), 14; A. N. Kosygin, "Novoe stroitel'stvo v gorode Lenina," *Arkhitektura Leningrada*, 1938, no. 5:5–7; M. V. Morozov and N. V. Baranov, "Stroitel'stvo Leningrada v 1939 goda," ibid., 1939, no. 1:17–18; "Mezhdunarodnyi prospekt/ Moskovskoe shosse," ibid., 1938, no. 1:14–26; I. I. Fomin, "Ansambl' Moskovskogo shosse," ibid., 1938, no. 2:39–44; V. V. Popov, "Praktika zastroiki Moskovskogo shosse," ibid., 1938, no. 4:4–6; S. V. Vasil'kovskii, B. R. Rubanenko, and G. A. Simonov, "Potochno-skorotnoe stroitel'stvo na Moskovskom shosse," ibid., 1940, no. 3:25–29; V. I. Kozlov, ed., *Ocherki istorii Leningradskoi organizatsii KPSS*, vol. 3, *1945–1985* (Leningrad: Lenizdat, 1985), p. 65.

51. M. V. Posokhin et al., *Sovetskaia arkhitektura za 50 let* (Moscow: Izdat. lit. po stroitel'stvu, 1968), 79; A. K. Baratchev et al., eds., *Ezhegodnik Leningradskogo otdeleniia soiuza sovetskikh arkhitekturov*, no. 4 (Leningrad: Gosizdat lit. po stroi i arkh., 1955).

52. Leon Goure, *The Siege of Leningrad: August, 1941–January, 1944* (New York: McGraw-Hill Book Co., 1964), 4–5.

53. For accounts of this period, see ibid.; D. V. Pavlov, *Leningrad 1941: The Blockade*, trans. John C. Adams (Chicago: University of Chicago Press, 1965); Harrison E. Salisbury, *The 900 Days: The Siege of Leningrad* (New York: Harper & Row, 1969); D. Trakhtenberg, *Podvig Leningrada* (Leningrad: Khudozhnik RSFSR, 1966); E. Katerli and F. Samoilov, *Gorod v kotorom my zhivem* (Leningrad: Leningradskoe gazeto-zhurnal'noe i knizhnoe izdatel'stvo, 1945), 105–128; Alexander Werth, *Leningrad* (London: Hamish Hamilton, 1944); and Richard Bidlack, "Workers at War: Factory Workers and Labor Policy in the Siege of Leningrad" (Ph.D. dissertation, Indiana University, 1987).

54. Official data identify a low population of 639,000 in March 1943, as well as 554,000 evacuees and 632,253 civilian deaths. These figures account

for approximately 1.8 million persons in a prewar population of 3.2 million (Goure, *Siege of Leningrad*, 239; Salisbury, *The 900 Days*, 513–518).

55. M. I. Likhomanov, L. T. Pozina, and E. I. Finogenov, *Partiinoe rukovodstvo evakuatsii v pervyi period Velikoi otechestvennoi voiny, 1941–1942 gg.* (Leningrad: Izdatel'stvo Leningradskogo universiteta, 1985); Bidlack, "Workers ar War."

56. Richard Bidlack, "Worker Mobilization during the Siege of Leningrad" (Paper delivered at the annual meeting of the American Association for the Advancement of Slavic Studies, New Orleans, November 22, 1986), 1.

57. L. D. Leonov and B. K. Peiro, *Leningrad—gorod geroi* (Leningrad: Obshchestvo Znanie, 1957), 28–30; Salisbury, *The 900 Days*, 407–422, 523–528; Goure, *Siege of Leningrad*, 150–153, 217–218, 239; V. A. Ezhov, *Rabochii klass—Vedushchaia sila vosstanovleniia Leningrada 1943–1950 gg.* (Leningrad: Izdatel'stvo Leningradskogo universiteta, 1982), 19; and Bidlack, "Workers at War."

Chapter 2

1. V. A. Kamenskii, *Leningrad: General'nyi plan razvitiia goroda* (Leningrad: Lenizdat, 1972), 36–38; V. I. Piliavskii, *Arkhitektura Leningrada* (Leningrad and Moscow: Gosizdat. lit. po stroi i arkh., 1953), 45–46; M. V. Posokhin et al., *Sovetskaia arkhitektura za 50 let* (Moscow: Izdat. lit. po stroitel'stvu, 1968), 150–152; and N. V. Baranov, *Siluety blokady: Zapiski glavnogo arkhitektura goroda* (Leningrad: Lenizdat, 1982), 156–162.

2. V. A. Kamenskii and A. I. Naumov, *Leningrad: Gradostroitel'nye problemy razvitiia* (Leningrad: Stroiizdat—Leningradskoe otdelenie, 1977), 140–166; and Baranov, *Siluety blokady*, 156–162.

3. Piliavskii, *Arkhitektura Leningrada*, 45–46; I. A. Evlakhov, "O zabotakh o Vyborgskoi storone," *Leningradskaia panorama*, 1984, no. 6:18–19; E. Katerli and F. Samoilov, *Gorod v kotorom my zhivem* (Leningrad: Leningradskoe gazetno-zhurnal'noe i knizhnoe izdatel'stvo, 1945), 45–48.

4. N. F. Khomutetskii, *Peterburg-Leningrad* (Leningrad: Lenizdat, 1958), 246; Z. V. Solov'ev, "Gazifikatsiia Leningrada," *Arkhitektura i stroitel'stvo Leningrada*, 1958, no. 2:38–39; Katerli and Samoilov, *Gorod v kotorom my zhivem*, 46–48; "O meropriatiakh poulushcheniiu organizatsii gazosnabzheniia gor. Leningrada (24 marta, 1954)," *Sbornik reshenii i rasporiazhenii Ispolnitel'nogo komiteta Leningradskogo gorodskogo soveta deputatov trudiashchikhsia Leningrada* (Leningrad: Lenizdat, 1956), 524–525; and N. F. Fomicheva, "Etapy gazifikatsii," *Leningradskaia panorama*, 1985, no. 11:18–19.

5. Khomutetskii, *Peterburg-Leningrad*, 242–246; Posokhin, et al., *Sovetskaia arkhitektura*, 150–162; "Prospekt im. I. V. Stalina," *Arkhitektura i stroitel'stvo Leningrada*, 1951, no. 1:1–12.

6. Kamenskii and Naumov, *Leningrad*, 165–166; A. S. Nikol'skii and K. I. Kashin, "Stadion imeni S. M. Kirova," *Arkhitektura i stroitel'stvo Leningrada*, 1950, no. 2:5–16.

7. "Morskoi fasad Leningrada," *Leningradskaia pravda*, April 20, 1950,

p. 3; Baranov, *Siluety blokady*, 84–96; M. V. Iogansen, V. G. Lisovskii, and N. I. Nikulina, *Arkhitektura Vasil'evskogo ostrova v proshlom, nastoiashchem i budushchem* (Leningrad: Akademiia Khudozhestv SSSR, 1969).

8. Baranov, *Siluety blokady*, 84–99.

9. Ibid., 96–99.

10. V. A. Ezhov, *Rabochii klass—Vedushchaia sila vosstanovleniia Leningrada 1943–1950 gg.* (Leningrad: Izdatel'stvo Leningradskogo universiteta, 1982), 22–23. This argument is also developed in Blair A. Ruble, "The Leningrad Affair and the Provincialization of Leningrad," *Russian Review* 42, no. 3 (1983):301–320, as well as in Edward Bubis and Blair A. Ruble, "The Impact of World War II on Leningrad," in Susan J. Linz, ed., *The Impact of World War II on the Soviet Union* (Totowa, N.J.: Rowman & Allanheld, 1985), 189–206.

11. A. V. Baranov, *Sotsial'no-demograficheskoe razvitie krupnogo goroda* (Moscow: Finansy i statistika, 1981), 70–71.

12. G. S. Vechkanov, *Migratsiia trudovykh resursov v SSSR: Politiko-ekonomicheskii aspekt* (Leningrad: Leningradskii gosudarstvennyi universitet, 1981).

13. By the 1970 census, for example, 56.9 percent of the city's population was female, as opposed to 53.9 percent of the total Soviet and 53.7 percent of the Soviet urban populations (TsSU SSSR, *Itogi vsesoiuznoi perepisi naseleniia 1970 goda* [Moscow: Statistika, 1972], vol. 2, tables 1–2, pp. 5–11). Over an equivalent period, the percentage of the city's population under 20 years of age fell to just 24.9 percent in 1970 (USSR, 38.1 percent), lagging behind even the percentage of the population 50 years of age or older (Leningrad, 26.1 percent; USSR, 20.5 percent) (*Leningrad i Leningradskaia oblast' v tsifrakh: Statisticheskii sbornik* [Leningrad: Lenizdat, 1974], 18. Similar age-specific data have been omitted from subsequent statistical handbooks for the city and region of Leningrad. Soviet national data are found in Stephen Rapawy and Godfrey Baldwin, "Demographic Trends in the Soviet Union, 1950–2000," in U.S. Congress, Joint Economic Committee, *Soviet Economy in the 1980s: Problems and Prospects* [Washington: Government Printing Office, 1982], pt. 2: 288–292).

14. Throughout the postwar period Leningrad's population has been growing at a steady pace despite administrative restrictions on in-migration (the *propiska* residency permit system). The rate of population increase for both the city and the region of Leningrad during the 1959–1970 period was well below the city's peak periods of population expansion (such as the 90 percent population growth from 1869 to 1897 and the 80 percent increase from 1929 to 1939). In comparison with other Soviet cities during the entire decade of the 1970s, metropolitan Leningrad exhibited a rate of population growth of just over 13 percent, which was essentially the same as Moscow (13 + percent), but well under Minsk (39 + percent) and other such growth centers as Kiev (31 + percent), Vil'nius (29 + percent), Tashkent (28 + percent), and Alma-Ata (22 + percent). V. M. Koval'chuk, D. I. Petrikeev, and Z. V. Stepanov, eds., *Leningrad v vos'moi piatiletke, 1966–1970 gg.: Istoriko-sotsial'nyi ocherk* (Leningrad: Nauka—Leningradskoe otdelenie, 1979), 30; V. A. Mineev, E. P. Murav'ev, and L. M. Chistov, eds., *Problemy planirovaniia narodnogo khoziaistva Leningrada i Leningradskoi oblasti v tsifrakh* (Leningrad: Minvuz RSFSR, LFEI, 1971).

15. Vechkanov, *Migratsiia trudovykh resursov*, 46–47.

16. Ibid., 11–12.

17. L. V. Gracheva, *Leningradskaia oblast': Osnovnye problemy razvitiia agropromyshlennogo kompleksa i industrial'nykh tsentrov* (Leningrad: Obshchestvo "Znanie"—Leningradskaia organizatsiia, 1985), 10–11.

18. Vechkanov, *Migratsiia trudovykh resursov*, 11–12.

19. *Narodnoe khoziaistvo Leningrada i Leningradskoi oblasti v desiatoi piatiletke: Statisticheskii sbornik* (Leningrad: Lenizdat, 1981), 90–91; G. M. Romanenkova, "Sotsial'no-ekonomicheskie faktory demograficheskogo razvitiia krupnogo goroda," in N. A. Tolokontsev, G. M. Romanenkova, eds., *Demografiia i ekologiia krupnogo goroda* (Leningrad: Nauka—Leningradskoe otdelenie, 1980), 7–21.

20. Rising from 459,000 in 1965 to 912,900 in 1980. *Narodnoe khoziaistvo Leningrada . . . v desiatoi piatiletke*, 69.

21. Ibid., 26; *Narodnoe khoziaistvo Leningrada i Leningradskoi oblasti za 60 let: Statisticheskii sbornik* (Leningrad: Lenizdat, 1977), 14; *Narodnoe khoziaistvo SSSR v 1980 g.: Statisticheskii ezhegodnik* (Moscow: Finansy i statistika, 1981), 27.

22. V. M. Tareev, "Tsentr nachisleniia pensii," *Leningradskaia panorama*, 1982, no. 5:24–26.

23. Mervyn Matthews, *Poverty in the Soviet Union* (New York: Cambridge University Press, 1986), 48–51, 118–121, 176–179; and Alastair McAuley, *Economic Welfare in the Soviet Union* (Madison: University of Wisconsin Press, 1979), 16–20.

24. G. B. Poliak, *Biudzhet goroda* (Moscow: Finansy, 1978), 21.

25. *Narodnoe khoziaistvo Leningrada . . . v desiatoi piatiletke*, 34.

26. K. A. Goldman, "Migratsionnye protsessy," in Tolokontsev and Romanenkova, *Demografiia i ekologiia*, 29–36. Jane Jacobs explores the significance of a city's relative attractiveness to a national migratory pool in a discussion of the rise of Toronto in relation to Montreal during the 1950s and 1960s. For Jacobs, Toronto's ability to attract migrants from across Canada, and Montreal's failure to do so, were early indicators of the latter's relative decline. Jane Jacobs, *The Question of Separatism* (New York: Random House, 1980), 15–16.

27. "V liuboe vremia," *Vechernyi Leningrad*, January 3, 1984, p. 2.

28. V. Parshina, "Esli adres neizvesten," *Vechernyi Leningrad*, April 6, 1984, p. 2; P. Solovei, "Ostal'nyi ne prichem?" ibid., August 24, 1984, pp. 2–3.

29. N. V. Iukhneva, *Etnicheskii sostav i etnosotsial'naia struktura naseleniia Peterburga: Vtoraia polovina XIX–nachalo XX veka; Statisticheskii analiz* (Leningrad: Nauka—Leningradskoe otdelenie, 1984), 3.

30. Ibid., 129–163.

31. Ibid., 34–79.

32. Ibid., 12.

33. Ibid., 129–141.

34. Ibid., 129–163.

35. M. E. Kogan and G. V. Starovitova, "Formirovanie Tatarskoi gruppy v naselenii Leningrada i ee sovremennyi etnokulturnyi oblik," in O. V. Kibal'chik et al., *Geografiia i kul'tura etnograficheskii grupp Tatar v SSSR* (Moscow: Moskovskii filial Geograficheskogo obshchestva SSSR, 1983), 26–42.

These findings are discussed further in Blair A. Ruble, "Cultural Ethnicity among the Tatars of Leningrad: An Ethnographic Report," *Canadian Review of Studies in Nationalism* 13, no. 2 (1986):275–282.

36. Kogan and Starovitova, "Formirovanie Tatarskoi gruppy," 27–30.

37. Ibid., 28, 35–41.

38. Iukhneva, *Etnicheskii sostav*, 207–215.

39. Ibid., 200–206.

40. S. A. Smith, *Red Petrograd: Revolution in the Factories, 1917–18* (Cambridge: Cambridge University Press, 1983), 9.

41. James H. Bater, *Urban Industrialization in the Provincial Towns of Late Imperial Russia*, The Carl Beck Papers in Russian and East European Studies, no. 503 (Pittsburgh: University of Pittsburgh Center for Russian and East European Studies, 1986), 6–9.

42. For a discussion of the concept "import-replacing" city, see Jane Jacobs, *Cities and the Wealth of Nations* (New York: Random House, 1984). The absence of a densely populated suburban hinterland was also noted by David T. Cattell (*Leningrad: A Case Study of Soviet Urban Government* [New York: Frederick A. Praeger, 1968], 18–19). For a Soviet discussion of the city's continued failure to produce an active hinterland, see A. S. Shchukina, "The Interrelated Growth of Moscow, Leningrad and Other Urban Places along the October Railroad in the 1960s and 1970s," *Izvestiia Vsesoiuznogo geograficheskogo obshchestva*, 1981, no. 3:268–274, as translated in *Soviet Geography: Review and Translation* 24, no. 4 (April 1983): 297–304.

43. Jacobs, *Cities and the Wealth of Nations*.

44. James Bater, *St. Petersburg: Industrialization and Change* (Montreal: McGill-Queens University Press, 1976), 60.

45. Ibid., 139–149. E. Lopatina, *Leningrad: Ekonomiko-geograficheskii ocherk* (Moscow: Gos. Izdat. geograficheskoi literatury, 1959), 69, 120–122. For a comprehensive discussion of the difficulties encountered in transporting goods to St. Petersburg prior to the construction of Russia's rail system, see Robert E. Jones, "Getting the Goods to St. Petersburg: Water Transportation from the Interior, 1703–1811," *Slavic Review* 43, no. 3 (1984):413–433.

46. E. H. Carr, *A History of Soviet Russia*, vol. 4, *The Interregnum, 1923–24* (Harmondsworth, Middlesex, Eng.: Penguin Books, 1969).

47. *Leningrad i Leningradskaia oblast' za XX let Sovetskoi vlasti* (Leningrad: Lenoblizdat, 1937); A. R. Dzenishevich, *Rabochie Leningrada nakanune Velikoi otechestvennoi voiny, 1938–iiun, 1941 g.* (Leningrad: Nauka—Leningradskoe otdelenie, 1983), 128–172, 205–213.

48. This argument is developed further in Ruble, "The Leningrad Affair." It is based on a portrayal of Zhdanov somewhat at odds with the traditional interpretation of his political role as Stalin's "henchman" in culture.

49. Werner G. Hahn, *Postwar Soviet Politics* (Ithaca: Cornell University Press, 1982).

50. A. A. Kuznetsov, "Vazhneishie zadachi Leningradskoi partorganizatsii," *Leningradskaia pravda*, July 3, 1945, pp. 3–4. This viewpoint is also evident in Katerli and Samoilov, *Gorod v kotorom my zhivem*, 8, 58–79, 87–89.

51. A. A. Kuznetsov, "O zadachakh Leningradskoi partiinoi organizatsii v sviazi s vyborami v Verkhovnyi sovet Soiuza SSR," *Leningradskaia pravda*, December 8, 1945, pp. 2–3.

52. A. A. Zhdanov, "Na predvybornom sobranii izbiratelei Volodarskogo izbiratel'nogo okruga g. Leningrada, 6 fevraliia, 1946 g.," *Pravda*, February 8, 1946, pp. 3–4; also in *Partiinoe stroitel'stvo*, 1946, no. 3:47–53.

53. See, for example, M. I. Kalinin, "Pis'mo izbiratel'em Leningradskogo gorodskogo izbiratel'skogo okruga," *Partiinoe stroitel'stvo*, 1946, no. 3:25–28.

54. During the purges of this period some 2,000 Leningrad officials lost their jobs (and, in numerous cases, their lives), including all five regional party committee secretaries, all five city party committee secretaries, the four most senior city soviet officials, and several leading regional soviet officials. See "Doklad sekretariia Leningradskogo gorodskogo komiteta VKP(b) tov. A. I. Alekseeva," *Leningradskaia pravda*, September 23, 1952, pp. 2–3; "Doklad sekretariia Leningradskogo komiteta VKP(b) tovarishcha V. M. Andrianova," ibid., September 28, 1952, pp. 2–4; "Rech' tovarishcha Kozlova," ibid., October 16, 1952, p. 3; "Rech' tovarishcha I. V. Spiridonova," *Pravda*, October 20, 1961, p. 4; "Rech' tovarishcha N. M. Shvernika," ibid., October 26, 1961, pp. 3–4; "Rech' tovarishcha A. N. Shelepina," ibid., October 27, 1961, p. 10; "Rech' tovarishcha D. A. Lazurkinoi," ibid., October 31, 1961, p. 2; A. Afanas'ev, "Pobeditel'," *Komsomol'skaia pravda*, January 15, 1988, p. 2; and V. I. Kozlov, ed., *Ocherki istorii Leningradskoi organizatsii KPSS*, vol. 3, 1945–1985 (Leningrad: Lenizdat, 1985), 96–97.

55. These remarks were contained in the address of Gorky regional party First Secretary L. N. Efremov to the Twenty-second Party Congress in 1961 ("Rech' tovarishcha L. N. Efremova," *Pravda*, October 22, 1961, p. 3).

56. Robert Conquest, *Power and Policy in the U.S.S.R.* (New York: St. Martin's Press, 1967), 97–111.

57. In addition to the Soviet sources cited in n. 54 above, see "Gorbachev on History: 'Days That Shook the World'," *New York Times*, November 3, 1987, pp. A11–A13.

58. Hahn, *Postwar Soviet Politics*, 19–66.

59. "Strategiia griadushchikh peremen," *Leningradskaia panorama*, 1986, no. 7:3–6; "Leningradu i oblasti—Kompleksnoe razvitie," *Leningradskaia pravda*, November 24, 1984, p. 1; V. S. Kulibanov, *Problemy razvitiia narodnogo khoziaistva severo-zapada SSSR* (Leningrad: Obshchestvo "Znanie"—Leningradskaia organizatsiia, 1980), 8–10.

60. See, for example, Barbara Ann Chotiner, *Khrushchev's Party Reform: Coalition Building and Institutional Innovation* (Westport, Conn.: Greenwood Press, 1984).

61. "Rech' tovarishcha Kozlova," *Leningradskaia pravda*, September 24, 1952, p. 4. See also A. A. Smol'kina, *Deiatel'nost' KPSS po vosstanovleniiu i razvitiiu nauchno-tekhnicheskogo potentsiala Leningrada (1945–1966 gg.): Na materialakh Leningradskoi partiinoi organizatsii* (Leningrad: Leningradskii gosudarstvennyi universitet, 1983).

62. See, for example, G. V. Romanov, "Vysokii dolg kommunistov," and "Leninskim kursom—K novym pobedam v kommunisticheskom stroitel'stve," in his *Izbrannye rechi i stat'i* (Moscow: Izdat. polit. lit., 1980), 243–258, 479–501.

63. See, for example, G. I. Il'ina, "Vvedenie," and A. P. Kupaigorodskaia and Z. V. Stepanov, "V bor'be za vypolnenie narodnokhoziaistvennykh planov piatiletki," in Koval'chuk, Petrikeev, and Stepanov, *Leningrad v vos'moi pia-*

tiletke, 3–24, 53–96; A. A. Volkov, E. D. Klimenko, and V. I. Meleshchenko, eds., *Leningradskii sotsial'no-ekonomicheskii kompleks* (Leningrad: Lenizdat, 1979), 23–35; and T. G. Brodskaia, *Rol' Leningradskogo regiona v razvitii edinogo narodnokhoziaistvennogo kompleksa* (Leningrad: Obshchestvo "Znanie"—Leningradskaia organizatsiia, 1985), 7.

64. S. A. Kugel', B. D. Lebin, and Iu. S. Meleshchenko, eds., *Nauchnye kadry Leningrada* (Leningrad: Nauka—Leningradskoe otdelenie, 1973); B. I. Kozlov, ed., *Organizatsiia i razvitie otraslevykh nauchno-issledovatel'skikh institutov Leningrada, 1971–1977* (Leningrad: Nauka—Leningradskoe otdelenie, 1979); and, Volkov, Klimenko, and Meleshchenko, *Leningradskii sotsial'no-ekonomicheskii kompleks*, 142–143.

65. Kozlov, *Organizatsiia i razvitie*, 13–26; and Brodskaia, *Rol' Leningradskogo regiona*, 8.

66. Kozlov, *Organizatsiia i razvitie*, 13–26; and B. A. Kolyniuk and N. I. Chikovskii, "Kak upravliat' tekhnicheskim progressom," *Leningradskaia panorama*, 1982, no. 10:13–14.

67. Kugel', Lebin, and Meleshchenko, *Nauchnye kadry Leningrada*, 38.

68. See, for example, "Povyshat' otdacha nauchnykh uchrezhdenii," *Leningradskaia pravda*, March 31, 1983, p. 1.

69. L. S. Bliakhman, "Problemy organizatsii nauki kak elementa infrastruktury krupnogo goroda," in V. A. Vorotilov and G. N. Cherkasov, eds., *Metodologiia sotsial'no-ekonomicheskogo planirovaniia goroda* (Leningrad: Nauka—Leningradskoe otdelenie, 1980), 74–93.

70. Kh. Kh. Karimov, *Leningrad v tsifrakh i faktakh* (Leningrad: Lenizdat, 1984), 46.

71. Volkov, Klimenko, and Meleshchenko, *Leningradskii sotsial'no-ekonomicheskii kompleks*, 23–24.

72. *Narodnoe khoziaistvo Leningrada . . . v desiatoi piatiletke*, 28–30.

73. John Pitzer, "Gross National Product of the USSR, 1950–1980," in U.S. Congress, Joint Economic Committee, *USSR: Measures of Economic Growth and Development, 1950–1980* (Washington: Government Printing Office, 1982), 17.

74. Denis J. B. Shaw, "Planning Leningrad," *Geographical Review* 68, no. 2 (April 1978): 189.

75. For further discussion of Soviet housing policy, see A. J. DiMaio, Jr., *Soviet Urban Housing: Problems and Policies* (New York: Praeger Publishers, 1974).

76. *Vestnik statistiki*, 1973, no. 6:88–91; ibid., 1980, no. 12:66–68.

77. B. M. Lazarev, ed., *Grazhdanin i apparat upravleniia v SSSR* (Moscow: Nauka, 1982), 97.

78. Approximately 10 percent of the area was under water. *Leningrad: Entsiklopedicheskii spravochnik* (Moscow and Leningrad: Bol'shaia Sovetskaia entsiklopediia, 1957), 10; B. K. Dukinskii, *1000 voprosov i otvetov o Leningrade* (Leningrad: Lenizdat, 1974), 79.

79. *Leningrad: Istoriko-geograficheskii atlas*, rev. and supplemented ed. (Moscow: Glavnoe upravlenie geodezii i kartografii pri Sovete Ministrov SSSR, 1981), 114; V. M. Khodachek and V. G. Alekseev, *Kompleksnoe razvitie gorodskikh raionov: Kompleksnyi plan ekonomicheskogo i sotsial'nogo razvitiia v deistvii* (Leningrad: Lenizdat, 1980), 5.

80. For a fuller description of these institutions, see Appendix C.

81. Kamenskii and Naumov, *Leningrad*, 167–226; A. A. Sizov, "Glavlengradstroiiu—Desiat' let," *Stroitel'stvo i arkhitektura Leningrada*, 1965, no. 4:2–6; I. A. Bartenev, *Zodchie i stroiteli Leningrada* (Leningrad: Lenizdat, 1963), 274; V. S. Kulibanov et al., eds., *Nauchno-tekhnicheskii progress v stroitel'stve* (Leningrad: Lenizdat, 1984), 12.

82. Kamenskii and Naumov, *Leningrad*, 167–226; V. G. Lisovskii, *Leningrad: Raiony novostroek* (Leningrad: Lenizdat, 1983), 46–50; A. N. Afanas'ev and N. V. Kaz'micheva, eds., *10 piatiletok Leningrada* (Leningrad: Lenizdat, 1980), 288–289; Kulibanov et al., *Nauchno-tekhnicheskii progress v stroitel'stve*, 14.

83. A. J. DiMaio, Jr., *Soviet Urban Housing: Problems and Policies* (New York: Praeger Publishers, 1974); "Velikaia programma zhilishchnogo stroitel'stva," *Arkhitektura i stroitel'stvo Leningrada*, 1957, no. 4:2.

84. Shaw, "Planning Leningrad," 189; Bartenev, *Zodchie i stroiteli Leningrada*, 276–278; A. A. Liubosh, "Po tipovym proektam," in Iu. I. Zavarukhin and R. S. Zakasov, eds., *Gorodskoe khoziaistvo i stroitel'stvo Leningrada za 50 let* (Leningrad: Lenizdat, 1967), 62–79; and G. V. Troitskii, "Industrial'nymi metodami," in ibid., 80–101; "Etazhi ee zhizni," *Vechernyi Leningrad*, December 18, 1985, p. 2.

85. N. M. Trubnikova, "Sredstva i priemy arkhitekturno-prostranstvennogo postroeniia mikroraionov," in O. A. Shvidkovskii, ed., *Stroitel'stvo i arkhitektura* (Moscow: Nauka, 1967), pp. 31–44. The increasing reliance on the minidistrict concept in residential planning has touched off lively discussions over the years in the Leningrad architectural journals. For a limited sample of such discourse, see A. S. Gintsberg, "Proektirovanie kvartir novogo tipa," *Arkhitektura i stroitel'stvo Leningrada*, 1956, no. 1:9–14; L. M. Tverskoi, "Zhiloi dom, kvartal raionov, i kvartalov v Leningrade," ibid., 1956, no.2:13–16; L. M. Tverskoi, "O planirovke zhilykh kvartalov," ibid., 1955, no. 1:32–36; V. A. Kamenskii, "Praktika i perspektivy zastroiki Leningrada," ibid., 1955, no. 3:6–29; V. A. Vitman, "Novye tipy arkhitekturno-planirovochnyi organizatsii zhilnykh territorii," ibid., 1955, no. 3:30–34; B. V. Murav'ev, "Zhilishchnoe stroitel'stvo v Leningrade za gody Sovetskoi vlasti," ibid., 1957, no. 4:9–19; O. A. Ivanovna and A. V. Makhrovskaia, "Voprosy kompositsii zhilogo mikroraiona," ibid., 1959, no. 5:10–14; A. A. Liubosh, "Gradostroitel'stvo i industrializatsiia," *Stroitel'stvo i arkhitektura Leningrada*, 1960, no. 3:7–11; V. A. Vitman and A. V. Makhrovskaia, "Planirovka i zastroika krupnykh mezhmagistral'nykh territorii," ibid., 1960, no. 3:12–14; M. E. Vaitens, "Organizatsiia obshchestvennykh tsentrov," ibid., 1962, no. 4:21–25; E. M. Syrkina, "Sistema obsluzhivaniia," ibid., 1966, no. 11:26–29; and V. F. Nazarov and B. V. Nikolashchenko, "Gorod v kotorom zhit'," ibid., 1975, no. 12:9–13. One interesting Western discussion may be found in Gregory D. Andrusz, *Housing and Urban Development in the USSR* (Albany: SUNY Press, 1985), 127–132.

86. This hostility toward the street was evident in Western planning theory for much of this century. The renewed interest of recent years in the street as an urban form followed the publication during the 1960s of such works as Jane Jacobs, *The Death and Life of Great American Cities* (New York: Random House, 1961).

87. For a discussion of this debate, see J. Bater, *The Soviet City* (London:

Edward Arnold, 1980), 102–111; T. A. Reiner and R. H. Wilson, "Planning and Decision-Making in the Soviet City: Rent, Land and Urban Form," in R. A. French and F. E. Ian Hamilton, eds., *The Socialist City: Spatial Structure and Urban Policy* (New York: John Wiley & Sons, 1979), 60–61. For examples of such discussions, see V. S. Bogoliubov, "Sotsial'no-ekonomicheskaia otsena etazhnosti zhiloi zastroiki krupneishikh gorodov (na primere Leningrad)" (Avtoreferat dissertatsii na soiskanie uchenoi stepeni kandidata ekonomicheskikh nauk, Leningradskii inzhenerno-ekonomicheskii institut im. Tol'iatti, 1973); S. I. Sokolov, "Orientatsiia i dvizhenie cheloveka v mikroraione (na primere riada mikroraionov Leningrada)" (Avtoreferat dissertatsii na soiskanie uchenoi stepeni kandidata arkhitektury, Leningradskii inzhenerno-stroitel'nyi institut, 1970); G. N. Rassokhina, "Arkhitekturno-planirovochnaia organizatsiia ob-shchestvennykh tsentrov planirovochnykh raionov krupneishikh gorodov (na primere Leningrada)" (Avtoreferat dissertatsii na soiskanie uchenoi stepeni kandidata arkhitektury, Leningradskii inzhenerno-stroitel'nyi institut, 1980); and, A. N. Kolbanov, "Litso mikroraiona," *Leningradskaia Panorama*, 1985, no. 12:9–10.

88. One such district is located on the western end of Vasil'evskii Island. For the discussions leading up to the planning of that district, see Kamenskii and Naumov, *Leningrad*, 293–310; A. I. Naumov, "Vykhod goroda k moriu: Proekt planirovki severo-zapadnoi chasti Vasil'evskogo ostrova," *Arkhitektura i stroitel'stvo Leningrada*, 1958, no. 4:7–11; L. M. Tverskoi, "O vykhode Leningrada k moriu na Vasil'evskom ostrove," ibid., 1959, no. 5:14–16; N. V. Baranov, "Bol'shoi gradostroitel'nyi eksperiment: Novye primorskie ansambli Leningrada," *Stroitel'stvo i arkhitektura Leningrada*, 1966, no. 11:5–9; and B. D. Fedortsov, "Eshche raz ob eksperimente na Vasil'evskom," ibid., 1969, no. 10:17; and "Morskoi fasad goroda," *Vechernyi Leningrad*, November 9, 1984, p. 1.

89. A. I. Naumov, ed., *Gradostroitel'nye problemy razvitiia Leningrada* (Leningrad: Gosizdat lit. po stroi., arkh. i stroi-material, 1960); V. A. Kamenskii, "Gradostroitel'nye problemy razvitiia Leningrada," *Arkhitektura i stroitel'stvo Leningrada*, 1958, no. 4:1–6; K. S. Krivtsov, "Printsipy razvitiia gorodskogo transporta v proekte general'nogo plana Leningrada," ibid., 1959, no. 4:2–6; V. A. Kamenskii, "Printsipal'nye osnovy general'nogo plana razvitiia Leningrada," *Stroitel'stvo i arkhitektura Leningrada*, 1960, no. 1:4–8.

90. Posokhin et al, *Sovetskaia arkhitektura*, 257.

91. "Postanovlenie Soveta Ministrov SSSR o general'nom plane razvitiia g. Leningrada," *Sbornik postanovlenii pravitel'stva SSSR*, 1966, no. 14:275–282; "General'nyi plan razvitiia Leningrada," in Planovaia komissiia ispolkoma Lengorsoveta, Statisticheskoe upravlenie goroda Leningrada, *Leningrad za 50 let: Statisticheskii sbornik* (Leningrad: Lenizdat, 1967), 163–167; Kamenskii, *Leningrad*; and "Itogi desiatiletnogo perioda realizatsii general'nogo plana razvitiia Leningrada utverzhdennogo Soveta Ministrov SSSR v iiule 1966 goda," *Stroitel'stvo i arkhitektura Leningrada*, 1976, no. 7:1–47.

92. For a discussion of the draft plans prepared by local city planning agencies, see *Stroitel'stvo i arkhitektura Leningrada*, 1964, no. 6, entire issue.

93. A. I. Naumov, "Plan bol'shikh rabot," *Stroitel'stvo i arkhitektura Leningrada*, 1961, no. 12:1–5; Kamenskii, *Leningrad*, 5–21.

94. N. V. Baranov, *Glavnyi arkhitektor goroda: Tvorcheskaia i organi-*

zatsionnaia deiatel'nost', 2d ed. (Moscow: Stroiizdat, 1979), 29; Kamenskii and Naumov, *Leningrad*, 293–310; N. Monchadskaia, "Gosudarstvennyi chelovek," *Sovety deputatov trudiashchikhsia*, 1970, no. 6:16–20.

95. Kamenskii, *Leningrad*, 15–20.

96. "Postanovlenie . . . o general'nom plane," 275.

97. *Narodnoe khoziaistvo Leningrada . . . v desiatoi piatiletke*, 16–20.

98. V. A. Kamenskii, "Problema rasseleniia i organizatsiia territorial'nogo rosta goroda," in Naumov, *Gradostroitel'nye problemy*, 17–31.

99. "Postanovlenie . . . o general'nom plane," 275.

100. A. I. Naumov, "Osnovy general'nogo plana razvitiia Leningrada," in Naumov, *Gradostroitel'nye problemy*, 3–16; A. I. Naumov, "Leningrad vykhodit k moriu," *Stroitel'stvo i arkhitektura Leningrada*, 1960, no. 10:2–8; M. N. Sokolov, "Veliadyvaias v budushchee," ibid., 1962, no. 1:19–20.

101. Baranov, *Glavnyi arkhitektor goroda*, 49–53.

102. Kamenskii and Naumov, *Leningrad*, 293–317.

103. Kamenskii, *Leningrad*, 49–58.

104. *Leningrad bez navodenii* (Leningrad: Lenizdat, 1984). Overall, the projected dam-bridge complex will extend 25,380 meters from shoreline to with 64 shoreline, and will incorporate water-intake mechanisms to preserve natural current patterns. In addition, two passageways will be provided for ships. The first, some 200 meters wide, will facilitate the passage of ocean-going vessels, while the second, 110 meters wide, will accommodate ships from inland waterways. On top of the hydrocontrol system, a six-lane highway will run eight meters above sea level, providing a vital link for the projected Leningrad ring-road (Kh. Kh. Karimov, *Leningrad v tsifrakh i faktakh*, 15; V. N. Andreev, "More derzhit ekzamen," *Leningradskaia panorama*, 1985, no. 3:16–17). For a discussion of the original dam proposals contained in the 1966 general plan, see V. V. Smirnov, "Proekt zashchity Leningrada ot nagonnykh navodenii," *Stroitel'stvo i arkhitektura Leningrada*, 1960, no. 10:10; and Kamenskii and Naumov, *Leningrad*, 283. The project also has been followed in some detail by the city's evening paper, *Vechernyi Leningrad*, in a series of clusters of articles appearing the first Tuesday of every month entitled, "I pobezhdennaia—Shikhiia." See, for example, *Vechernyi Leningrad*, April 3, 1984, p. 2; June 3, 1984, p. 2; October 2, 1984, p. 2; December 4, 1984, p. 2; and February 5, 1985, p. 2. A discussion of the possibly negative environmental impact of the dam-bridge project appears in Chapter 3.

105. Kamenskii, *Leningrad*, 49–58; A. I. Kniazev, "Eksperimental'noe zhilye doma dlia zastroiki Vasil'evskogo ostrova," *Stroitel'stvo i arkhitektura Leningrada*, 1965, No. 1, pp. 4–9; V. A. Kamenskii, "Razvitie obshchegorodskogo tsentra i problema vykhoda Leningrada k beregam Finskogo zaliva," ibid., 1966, no. 11:10–15.

106. Kamenskii, *Leningrad*, 121.

107. Shaw, "Planning Leningrad," 189.

108. Ibid., 196; K. A. Pavlova, "Okraniaetsia gosudarstvennom pamiatniki Sovetskoi arkhitektura v Leningrade," *Stroitel'stvo i arkhitektura Leningrada*, 1970, no. 4:32–34.

109. Kamenskii, *Leningrad*, 68–72.

110. Kamenskii and Naumov, *Leningrad*, 275.

111. "Est ideia! V rabochei slobode," *Leningradskaia pravda*, April 5, 1988, p. 3.

112. Iu. N. Lobanov, "Turist v Leningrade: Krov i uslugi," *Stroitel'stvo i arkhitektura Leningrada*, 1980, no. 9:31–33.

113. Ia. Sobol', "Prigorodnye soobshcheniia: Real'nost' i problemy," *Stroitel'stvo i arkhitektura Leningrada*, 1981, no. 2:34–36.

114. Kamenskii and Naumov, *Leningrad*, 275.

115. Shaw, "Planning Leningrad," 192; V. S. Sorokin, "Samyi bystri, samyi udobnyi," in Zavarukhin and Zakasov, *Gorodskoe khoziaistvo*, 233–246.

116. Kamenskii and Naumov, *Leningrad*, 276–279.

117. "Postanovlenie . . . o general'nom plane," 277–278.

118. Ibid., 280; I. G. Iavein, "Leningrad, aerovokzal," *Stroitel'stvo i arkhitektura Leningrada*, 1966, no. 5:3.

119. *Narodnoe khoziaistvo Leningrada . . . v desiatoi piatiletke*, 52.

120. V. V. Popov, "Etapy tvorcheskikh iskanii . . . ," *Stroitel'stvo i arkhitektura Leningrada*, 1976, no. 7:11–15; V. V. Denisov, "Vse flagi v gosti . . . ," *Leningradskaia panorama*, 1983, no. 10:12–18.

121. V. A. Vitman, A. A. Afonchenko, V. K. Sveshnikov, and M. E. Vaitens, "Rasmeshchenie gorodov-sputnikov v prigorodnoi zone," in Naumov, *Gradostroitel'nye problemy*, 62–74; V. A. Vitman, A. A. Afonchenko, V. K. Sveshnikov, and V. I. Kalmykov, "Arkhitekturno-planirovochnaia struktura gorodov-sputnikov," in ibid., 75–88; G. V. Charnetskii, "Zelenyi polias Leningrada," in ibid., 141–149; G. N. Buldakov and M. P. Sokolov, "Organizatsiia massovogo zagorodnogo otdykha," in ibid., 150–158; M. P. Sokolov and I. I. Fomin, *Organizatsiia i planirovka mest massovogo otdykha trudiashchikhsia Leningrada* (Moscow: Vsesoiuznoe soveshchanie po gradostroitel'stvu, 1960).

122. Kamenskii, *Leningrad*, 78–84.

123. Shaw, "Planning Leningrad," 197–199.

124. Volkov, Klimenko, and Meleshchenko, *Leningradskii sotsial'no-ekonomicheskii kompleks*, 20–41; and Iu. V. Baranov, "V osnove—Kompleksnyi podkhod," *Leningradskaia panorama*, 1984, no. 9:3–5.

125. Volkov, Klimenko, and Meleshchenko, *Leningradskii sotsial'no-ekonomicheskii kompleks*, 56, 66.

Chapter 3

1. *Narodnoe khoziaistvo Leningrada i Leningradskoi oblasti v desiatoi piatiletke: Statisticheskii sbornik* (Leningrad: Lenizdat, 1981), 23–24.

2. A. V. Baranov, *Sotsial'no-demograficheskoe razvitie krupnogo goroda* (Moscow: Finansy i statistika, 1981), 70–71. For further discussion of the administrative measures utilized to limit population growth and economic development in Moscow, Leningrad, and Kiev, see Judith Pallot and Denis J. B. Shaw, *Planning in the Soviet Union* (Athens: University of Georgia Press, 1981), 22.

3. V. A. Kamenskii, *Leningrad: General'nyi plan razvitiia goroda* (Leningrad: Lenizdat, 1972), 121.

4. V. M. Khodachek and V. G. Alekseev, *Kompleksnoe razvitie gorodskikh raionov: Kompleksnyi plan ekonomicheskogo i sotsial'nogo razvitiia v deistvii* (Leningrad: Lenizdat, 1980).

5. N. P. Ovchinnikova, "Est' li budushchei u tipovykh zdanii?" *Leningradskaia panorama*, 1984, no. 4:20–22; "Prochnaia osnova gradostroitel'stva," ibid., 1982, no. 4:30–35; M. P. Berezin and O. V. Matiukhin, "Razvitie goroda: Tendentsii i normativy," *Stroitel'stvo i arkhitektura Leningrada*, 1981, no. 4:9–12; O. K. Zibrov, "Vopolshchaia v zhizn' zamysly zodchikh," ibid., 1976, no. 7:36–39; V. M. Tareev, "Obrazets est': Kakoi budet seriia?" *Leningradskaia panorama*, 1984, no. 8:9–11.

6. T. A. Gritsenko, "Dom za predelami kvartiry," *Leningradskaia panorama*, 1983, no. 5:26–27; B. P. Usanov, A. S. Krivov, and V. F. Nazarov, "Leningrad: Rychagi upravleniia," ibid., 1982, no. 1:8–11; V. S. Kuliabanov, "Nauka upravliat'," in B. V. Ul'ianov, comp., *Praktika sotsialisticheskogo khoziaistvovaniia: Opyt Leningradskikh predpriiatii* (Leningrad: Lenizdat, 1981), 91–104.

7. V. F. Nazarov and B. V. Nikolashchenko, "Gorod v kotorom zhit'," *Stroitel'stvo i arkhitektura Leningrada*, 1975, no. 12:9–13; V. V. Popov, "Etapy tvorcheskikh iskanii," ibid., 1976, no. 7:91–104.

8. Iu. N. Vasil'ev, A. D. Nelipa, and V. I. Pitaev, "Nuzhna edinaia sistema," *Stroitel'stvo i arkhitektura Leningrada*, 1981, no. 3:11–13; "Poliklinika meniaet adres," *Vechernyi Leningrad*, April 9, 1984, p. 1; M. Fal'pert, "V Magazin . . . po futbol'nomu polia," ibid., September 14, 1985, p. 3; B. S. Bogoliubov, "O sovershenstvovanii organizatsii kul'turno-bytovogo obsluzhivaniia naseleniia v gorodakh," in A. P. Borisov and N. M. Sutyrin, eds., *Ekonomika i upravlenie sotsialisticheskim proizvodstvom* (Leningrad: Leningradskii inzhenerno-ekonomicheskii institut, 1983), 40–47.

9. A. V. Baranov, "Sotsial'naia infrastruktura krupnogo goroda," in Leningradskaia organizatsiia ordena Lenina Soiuz arkhitekturov SSSR, Sektsiia nauchnogo prognozirovaniia LO Sovetskoi sotsiologicheskoi assotsiatsii pri AN SSSR, *Leningrad—2000: Materialy nauchno-teoreticheskogo soveshchaniia; Effektivnost' zhiloi sredy v usloviiakh gorodskogo obraza zhizni* (Leningrad: Leningradskaia organizatsiia Soiuz arkhitektorov SSSR, Leningradskoe otdelenie Sovetskoi sotsiologicheskoi assotsiatsii pri AN SSSR, 1978), 29–34.

10. N. I. Baranovskaia, "Ne zdanie a kvartal," *Stroitel'stvo i arkhitektura Leningrada*, 1981, no. 1:13–15; V. I. Kruchina-Bogdanov, "Sluzhba dobrogo nastroieniia," *Leningradskaia panorama*, 1983, no. 7:6–7; "Meditsinskomu obsluzhivaniiu-partiinuiu zabotu: Plenum Leningradskogo gorkoma KPSS," *Leningradskaia pravda*, September 13, 1984, p. 1; "K sessii Lensoveta: Dukhovnyi potentsial goroda; 'Kruglyi stol' 'Leningradskoi pravdy'," ibid., March 13, 1988, pp. 2–3; A. S. Gruzinov and V. P. Riumin, *Gorod: Upravlenie problemy* (Leningrad: Lenizdat, 1977).

11. "Zakon ob individual'noi trudovoi deiatel'nosti," *Leningradskaia pravda*, November 21, 1986, pp. 2–3; "O proekte zakona SSSR ob individual'noi trudovoi deiatel'nosti," ibid., November 20, 1986, pp. 1–2.

12. "Ukrepliat' sotsialisticheskie zakonnosti. Sessia Leninskogo oblastnogo Soveta narodnykh deputatov," *Leningradskaia pravda*, March 22, 1987, p. 1; A. Stepanova, "A u nas vo dvore . . . ," ibid., May 18, 1983, p. 2. Interestingly, this situation resembles more-global patterns of increasing crime rates

in large high-rise public housing projects in North America and Europe. In Leningrad's case, this pattern may also be explained in part by the relatively young age profile of residents of newer districts. For an account of crime problems in older central districts, see V. Tarasenko, "Bydni militsii: Pogonia v nochi," ibid., October 20, 1984, p. 4.

13. O. B. Bozhkov and V. B. Golofast, "Otsenka naseleniem uslovii zhizni v krupnykh gorodakh," *Sotsiologicheskie issledovaniia*, 1985, no. 3:95–101.

14. See, for example, such articles as O. Nosov, "Eti molchalivye avtobusy," *Vechernyi Leningrad*, July 26, 1984, p. 2; A. Kacheviavenko, "Shel po gorodu tramvai," ibid., November 1, 1984, p. 2; "V obkome KPSS," *Leningradskaia pravda*, January 29, 1986, p. 1; V. Kolesnikov and V. Efimov, "Pochemu my zhdem tramvai," ibid., May 11, 1986, p. 2.

15. In principle, no "new" industrial facilities are to be constructed in the city, although "renovation" and "expansion" of several existing plants have, in effect, resulted in the opening of factories where none previously were to be found.

16. B. V. Nikolashchenko, M. A. Sementovskaia, and N. S. Pal'chikov, "Sovershenstvuia, ne razrushat'," *Stroitel'stvo i arkhitektura Leningrada*, 1980, no. 12:20–25.

17. A. Iu. Belinskii, "Poezdi na rabotu—Kak sokratit' ikh prodolzhitel'nost'?" *Stroitel'stvo i arkhitektura Leningrada*, 1975, no. 6:24–26.

18. Ia. Sobol', "Prigorodnye soobshcheniia: Real'nosti i problemy," *Stroitel'stvo i arkhitektura Leningrada*, 1981, no. 2:24–26; B. Zuev, "Na prieme u notariusa," *Leningradskaia pravda*, March 22, 1983, p. 2.

19. M. I. Vasil'evskii, "Problemy rekonstruktsii tsentra Leningrada," *Stroitel'stvo i arkhitektura Leningrada*, 1969, No. 5, pp. 3–4; M. E. Taranovskaia, "Novoe v starom: o nekotorykh voprosakh rekonstruktsii i razvitiia," ibid., 1969, no. 8:18–21; A. I. Naumov, "Tsentr Leningrada: Problemy rekonstruktsii i razvitiia," ibid., 1971, no. 8:10–13; B. M. Pavlov, G. T. Popov, and K. A. Sharlygina, "Ot vyborochnogo remonta k kompleksnoi rekonstruktsii," 1976, no. 7:32–35; S. P. Shmakov, "Traditsii: dukh a ne bukva," 1981, no. 10:20–22; Iu. S. Iarlov, "Vysokaia missiia zodchestva," 1981, no. 12:18–19; A. Iu. Ananchenko and A. R. Shenderovich, "Sosedstvo bez konflikta," *Leningradskaia panorama*, 1984, no. 7:24–26; and Iu. M. Smirnov, "Proshloe—v griadushchem," ibid., 1984, no. 3:28–30.

20. V. M. Tareev, "Glavnaia zadacha zodchikh," *Stroitel'stvo i arkhitektura Leningrada*, 1981, no. 4:4–7.

21. N. V. Baranov, *Glavnyi arkhitektor goroda: Tvorcheskaia i organizatsionnaia deiatel'nost'*, 2d ed. (Moscow: Stroiizdat, 1979), 6–7; A. I. Gegello, "Nashi tvorcheskie zadachi," *Arkhitektura i stroitel'stvo Leningrada*, 1949, no. 1:43–47; Vasil'evskii, "Problemy rekonstruktsii tsentra Leningrada"; I. Iu. Murav'eva, L. A. Lamekin, "S nesti dom ili rekonstruirovat'?" *Stroitel'stvo i arkhitektura Leningrada*, 1969, no. 5:12; V. A. Kamenskii, "O realizatsii general'nogo plana razvitiia Leningrada," ibid., 1969, no. 6:2–10; E. M. Poltoratskii, "Gorod: Zastroika ili zhivoi organizm," ibid., 1974, no. 9:7–9; G. I. Iakovlev, "Povtoriaemost' eshche ne monotonnost'," ibid., 1975, no. 7:41–43; M. P. Berezin, "Pochemu neuiutno v novom kvartale?" ibid., 1976, no. 5:28–30; G. I. Bril'iantshchikov, "Kupchino—Eto Leningrad?" ibid., 1970, no. 1:21–22; G. Ia. Gladshtein, "Nezorazmerno cheloveka . . . ," ibid., 1970, no. 11:

22–23; A. K. Alekseevskii, "A gde zhe kompositsiia?" ibid., 1970, no. 1:25–26; A. V. Makhrovskaia, "Vasil'evskii ostrov: Problemy rekonstruktsii staroi zastroiki," ibid., 1971, no. 7:13–17; S. B. Speranskii, "Slagaemye uspekha: Ideinost' i masterstvo," ibid., 1971, no. 8:2–9. A. Shliakov, "Problemy rekonstruktsii zastroiki 1950-xx–60-xx godakh," *Arkhitektura SSSR*, 1985, no. 6:79–81.

22. Denis J. B. Shaw, *Problems of Land Use and Development in the USSR*, University of Birmingham, Working Paper Series no. 5 (Birmingham, 1980); Denis J. B. Shaw, "Planning Leningrad," *Geographical Review* 68, no. 2 (1978):197–199.

23. A. G. Dudarev and V. L. Shiffers, "Neoslabnoe vnimanie okruzhaiushchei srede," *Stroitel'stvo i arkhitektura Leningrada*, 1976, no. 7:44–45; K. I. Labetskii, "Gorod Lenina: Rubezhni piatiletki," *Leningradskaia panorama*, 1982, no. 4:8–13; Ia. Sobol', "Prigorodnye soobshcheniia: Real'nost' i problemy," *Stroitel'stvo i arkhitektura Leningrada*, 1981, no. 2:34–36; A. V. Makhrovskaia and S. P. Semenov, *Puti razvitiia Leningrada* (Leningrad: Obshchestvo "Znanie"—Leningradskaia organizatsiia, 1980), 6–7.

24. Iu. N. Lobanov, "Turist v Leningrade: Krov i uslugi," *Stroitel'stvo i arkhitektura Leningrada*, 1980, no. 9:31–33; Iu. N. Lobanov, "Zhemchuzhiny russkogo severa," ibid., 1980, no. 12:31–33; G. V. Shalabin, *Ekonomicheskie voprosy okhrany prirody v regione* (Leningrad: Leningradskii gosudarstvennyi universitet, 1983); and N. P. Malysheva, "Sokhranim usadebnye parki," *Leningradskaia panorama*, 1986, no. 10:20–23.

25. V. S. Visharenko and N. A. Tolokontsev, *Ekologicheskie problemy gorodov i zdorov'e cheloveka (v pomoshch' lektoru)* (Leningrad: Obshchestvo "Znanie" —Leningradskaia organizatsiia, 1982), 6–8; G. A. Karpova, "Puti sovershenstvovaniia upravleniia okhranoi prirodnoi sredi krupnogo goroda," in I. I. Sigov, ed., *Upravlenie razvitiem krupnykh gorodov* (Leningrad: Nauka—Leningradskoe otdelenie, 1985), 191–207; V. S. Kulibanov, *Problemy ekonomicheskogo i sotsial'nogo razvitiia Leningrada i oblasti odinnadtsatoi piatiletke* (Leningrad: Obshchestvo "Znanie"—Leningradskaia organizatsiia, 1981), 20–24; and V. Vladimirov, "Ekologiia i urbanizatsiia: Kak izbezhat' konflikta," *Leningradskaia pravda*, January 18, 1986, p. 3.

26. The following discussion is based on material collected in an interview with specialists on environmental concerns from the USSR Academy of Sciences' Institute of Socioeconomic Problems in Leningrad, conducted at that institute on March 6, 1984 (Drs. V. S. Bisharenko, B. M. Firsov, and N. A. Tolokontsev).

27. Interview cited in preceding note.

28. "Na vopros otvetit . . . pochva," *Vechernyi Leningrad*, August 16, 1984, p. 1.

29. N. Andreeva, "Okean nad gorodom," *Vechernyi Leningrad*, January 22, 1985, p. 2.

30. See, for example, L. B. Dmitriev, "Ne shagnut' li gorodu . . . v more?" *Leningradskaia panorama*, 1986, no. 8:26–28; A. Tiutnenkov, "Sval'nye techeniia v zalive i vokrug stroitel'stva kompleksa zashchity goroda ot navodnenii," *Leningradskaia pravda*, November 27, 1986, pp. 2–3; A. I. Kucher, "Zdorov'e rek i kanalov," *Leningradskaia panorama*, 1986, no. 10:16–17; B. P. Usanov, "Trekhvekovoi dialog goroda s morem," ibid., 1987, no. 2:4–7; Bill

Keller, "Storm of Protest Rages over Dam near Leningrad," *New York Times,* September 27, 1987, p.16.

31. "V obkome KPSS," *Leningradskaia pravda,* March 25, 1987, p. 1; "O vode 'zhivoi' i 'mertvoi'," ibid., April 20, 1988, p. 3; "Ne shagnut' li gorodu . . . v more?" *Leningradskaia panorama,* 1987, no. 12:15–16; and "Raion gavani: Proshloe i budushchee," ibid., 1988, no. 2:4–8.

32. See, for example, "Informatsiia o resheniiakh Ispolnitel'nogo komiteta Leningradskogo gorodskogo Soveta narodnykh deputatov 'O merakh po predotvrashcheniiu zagriazneniia vodotokov Leningrada nefteproduktami'," " *Biulleten' Ispolnitel'nogo komiteta Leningradskogo gorodskogo narodnykh deputatov,* 1983, no. 23:11–12; "V obkome KPSS," *Leningradskaia pravda,* January 14, 1987, p. 1; and "V perestroike nedopustima medlitel'nost': Tezisy doklada Ispolkoma Oblastnogo soveta," ibid., July 5, 1987, p. 2.

33. E. Vorob'ev and A. Ozhegov, "Aplodismenty v polnoch'," *Leningradskaia pravda,* February 2, 1989, pp. 2–3.

34. S. Kasumova, "Shumovaia karta goroda," *Sovety deputatov trudiashchikhsia,* 1972, no. 6:38–41; "O meropriiatiiakh po borbe s shumom v Leningrade (4 avgusta, 1960 g.)," *Sbornik ispolkoma Leningorsoveta* (Leningrad: Lenizdat, 1960), 21–23.

35. Interview cited in n. 26 above.

36. Interview cited in n. 26 above.

37. See, for example, A. K. Solov'ev, "Sotsial'no-ekonomicheskaia effektivnost' gradostroitel'nykh reshenii," *Problemy bol'shikh gorodov,* 1982, no. 12:1–23; Charles E. Ziegler, *Environmental Policy in the USSR* (Amherst: University of Massachusetts Press, 1987).

38. V. M. Tareev, "Aktivnost' pozitsii zodchikh," *Leningradskaia panorama,* 1986, no. 8:7–9.

39. S. P. Zavarikhin, "Progulka po prospekty prosveshcheniia," *Leningradskaia panorama,* 1986, no. 9:20–23.

40. S. N. Khrulev, "Pora bol'shogo obnovleniia," *Leningradskaia panorama,* 1986, no. 11:5–7.

41. D. N. Minin, "Domam—Vtoruiu zhizn'," *Leningradskaia panorama,* 1986, no. 12:8–9.

42. B. S. Ugarov, "Istochnik radosti i vdokhnoveniia: Mysliami o perestroike v sfere izobrazitel'nykh isskusstv i arkhitektury delitsia," *Leningradskaia panorama,* 1987, no. 1:1–3.

43. E. Bogoslovskaia, " 'Astoriia': Segodnia i zavtra," *Leningradskaia pravda,* March 17, 1987, p. 4.

44. Ibid.

45. Ibid.

46. "Davaite nachistotu. Protivostoianie," *Leningradskaia pravda,* March 21, 1987, p. 3.

47. Ibid.

48. Ibid.

49. Ibid.

50. Mikhail Chulaki, "Eshche ras o pol'ze glasnosti," *Literaturnaia gazeta,* March 25, 1987, p. 10.

51. Ann Husarska, "Midsummer Leningrad Dream," *New Leader,* September 7, 1987, pp. 8–9.

52. "Uchimsia glasnosti: Dolzhno stat' pravilom!" *Leningradskaia pravda*, April 12, 1987, p. 13.

53. Some reports indicate that the actual facade has been saved and will be reerected once construction of a new building has commenced.

54. "V obkome KPSS," *Leningradskaia pravda*, April 14, 1987, p. 1; "Aktivno i tvorcheskii osvaivat' novye podkhody: Plenum Leningradskogo gorkoma KPSS," ibid., June 14, 1987, p. 1.

55. See, for example, M. Monusov and O. Serdobol'skii, "Kul'tura Leningrada: Den' segodniashnii i vek griadushchii," *Leningradskaia pravda*, March 20, 1988, p. 1; and "Gorod v nasledstvo," ibid., May 4, 1988, p. 1.

56. "V obkome KPSS," *Leningradskaia pravda*, June 23, 1987, p. 1.

57. "Istoriia s 'Astoriei', ili uroki 'Angletera'," *Leningradskaia panorama*, 1987, no. 7:24–27.

58. A. I. Pribul'skii, "Po zakazu 'Inturista'," *Leningradskaia panorama*, 1987, no. 7:24–25; V. N. Pitanin, "Vokrug okhrannykh zon," ibid., 1987, no. 7:26–27; V. M. Tareev, "Eshche ne posleslovie," ibid., 1987, no. 7:27.

59. S. P. Zavarikhin, "Ne upustit' shans," *Leningradskaia panorama*, 1987, no. 7:25–26.

60. Tareev, "Eshche ne posleslovie."

61. For further discussion of this point, see Dennis' perceptive history of the evolution of French urban architectural theory and practice from the *hôtels* of the sixteenth and seventeenth centuries to the apartment blocks of this century: Michael Dennis, *Court & Garden: From the French Hôtel to the City of Modern Architecture* (Cambridge: MIT Press, 1986).

62. V. V. Aleksashina, "Kompleksnyi proizvodstvenno-salitebnyi raion goroda," in O. A. Shvidkovskii, ed., *Stroitel'stvo i arkhitektura* (Moscow: Nauka, 1967), pp. 9–18; R. A. French, "The Individuality of the Soviet City," in R. A. French and F. E. Ian Hamilton, eds., *The Socialist City: Spatial Structure and Urban Policy* (New York: John Wiley & Sons, 1979), 73–104; M. M. Vlanina and M. E. Vaitens, "Formirovanie bol'shikh gorodakh," *Problemy bol'shikh gorodov*, 1979, no. 18:1–21; A. V. Makhrovskaia, "Metodika rekonstruktsii starykh zhilykh kvartalov—Rezul'taty nauchnykh issledovanii," *Stroitel'stvo i arkhitektura Leningrada*, 1969, no. 5:5–9; K. A. Sharlygina, "V osnovu—Edinyi plan," ibid., 1976, no. 4:25–28; V. M. Tareev, "Novosel'e v starom dome," *Leningradskaia panorama*, 1984, no. 9:8–13.

63. I. A. Sobol' and A. Iu. Belinskii, "Organizatsiia dvizheniia i parkirovaniia legkovogo transporta v prigorodnoi zone bol'shogo goroda," *Problemy bol'shikh gorodov*, 1980, no. 8:1–27; A. A. Liubosh, "Transport Leningrada segodnia i zavtra," *Stroitel'stvo i arkhitektura Leningrada*, 1970, no. 4:28–31; "Transportnye sviazi: skorost', nadezhnost', komfort," ibid., 1976, no. 7:24–27; E. Petrushin, "Po rabochim marshrutom," *Vechernyi Leningrad*, January 11, 1984, p. 2; "Marshruty gorodskogo transporta," ibid., November 15, 1984, p. 2; and Makhrovskaia and Semenov, *Puti razvitiia Leningrada*, 5–23.

64. "Uluchshat' rabotu gorodskogo transporta," *Leningradskaia pravda*, May 18, 1984, p. 2.

65. Siguard Grava, "Urban Transportation in the Soviet Union," in Henry W. Morton and Robert C. Stuart, eds., *The Contemporary Soviet City* (Armonk, N.Y.: M. E. Sharpe, 1984), 191; *Narodnoe khoziaistvo Leningrada . . . v desiatoi piatiletke*, 55–56.

66. "Tramvai meniaiut marshrut," *Vechernyi Leningrad*, July 1, 1985, p. 1; Iu. Trefilov, "Skorostnaia tramvainaia," ibid., December 26, 1985, p. 1.

67. V. Elsukov, "Trinadsat' milliardov passazhirov," *Vechernyi Leningrad*, November 15, 1985, p. 1; Iu. Trefilov, "Cherez Nevu za golobykh ekspressakh," ibid., December 30, 1985, p.1; and O. V. Vasil'ev, "Bol'shaia premiera Metro," *Leningradskaia panorama*, 1986, no. 3:6–9.

68. Ia. L. Donin, L. I. Petrova, and G. N. Andreeva, "Problemy bytovogo obsluzhivaniia bol'shikh gorodov," *Problemy bol'shikh gorodov*, 1980, no. 9:1–24; A. A. Liubosh, "Gorod rastet i rasshiriaetsia: Plan stroitel'stva Leningrada na 1967–1968 gg.," *Stroitel'stvo i arkhitektura Leningrada*, 1965, no. 3:4–9; G. N. Buldakov, "Novyi etap proektirovaniia i stroitel'stva—zadachy, problemy," ibid., 1972, no. 6:8–11; G. Z. Kaganov, "Gorod v gorode," ibid., 1976, no. 4:15–18.

69. Concerning international tourism in the city, see I. Dobrosedov, "Iarko i ubeditel'na," *Vechernyi Leningrad*, September 26, 1984, p. 3. The city's preservation efforts were recognized in 1984 by the Hamburg Fund's decision to award the city of Leningrad the European Gold Medal for preservation ("Mezhdunarodnoe priznanie," *Leningradskaia panorama*, 1984, no. 8:1); "Khranim i preumnozhaem!" *Vechernyi Leningrad*, July 9, 1984, p. 1; and "Za sokhranenie pamiatniki arkhitektury," ibid., July 10, 1984, p. 1.

70. L. P. Lavrov, "Komu zhit' v tsentre?" *Stroitel'stvo i arkhitektura Leningrada*, 1981, no. 6:22–25; G. Z. Kaganov, "Vliianii planirovochnykh faktorov na nekotorye aspekty formirovaniia gorodskoi sredy (na primere tsentral'nyi raionov Leningrada)" (Avtoreferat dissertatsii na soiskanie uchenoi stepeni kandidata arkhitektury, Leningradskii inzhenerno-stroitel'nyi institut, 1980).

71. Given the early closing time of most commercial and service establishments in the city that do exist in the central area, it is difficult to characterize Leningrad's city center as "vibrant" day and night in the way one might describe districts in New York, Paris, Tokyo, or Hong Kong. Nevertheless, central Leningrad's major thoroughfares generally, and Nevskii Prospekt in particular, attract large crowds of people well into the evening hours. Knowledgeable residents of the city detect considerable seasonal fluctuations in these patterns. No urban district in the world can seem quite as deserted as a central Leningrad street on a cold wintry night, whereas during the "White Nights" of June the entire city seems alive well into the wee hours of the morning.

72. See, for example, the discussion in such articles as I. Saurov, "Palitra starykh kvartalov," *Leningradskaia pravda*, August 19, 1984, p. 2.

73. The theoretical and practical implications of the perceptions of form and beauty in architecture have been given serious consideration in the Leningrad architectural community. The psychological impact of height and urban silhouette has been studied in an attempt to understand not only how contemporary Soviet architecture might be improved but also what kind of human environment is most conducive to productive work and leisure. See, for example, L. N. Nikol'skaia, "Liniia i slovo," *Stroitel'stvo i arkhitektura Leningrada*, 1980, no. 10:35–37; V. A. Mashinskii, "Instrument masshtabnykh modelei," ibid., 1981, no. 1:26–29; B. P. Usanov, "Vse ostaetsia liudiam," 1980, no. 12:5; S. V. Sementsov and Kh. E. Shteinbakh, "Arkhitektura glazami gorozhan," 1981, no. 3:24–27; Iu. N. Vasil'ev, A. D. Nelipa, and V. L. Pitaev,

"Nuzhna edinaia sistema," 1981, no. 3:11–13; and V. A. Glinki, "Algebra tsvetnoi garmonii," 1981, no. 4:20–22.

74. A. Volodin, "Tvoe litso, gorod," *Vechernyi Leningrad,* February 4, 1985, p. 1. Specific aspects of that overall plan are described in proposals for the individual city blocks, as discussed in A. R. Shenderovich, "O nachnetsia Suvorovskii s ploshchadi," in *Leningradskaia panorama,* 1986, no. 1:17–19; and V. M. Tareev, "Novye passazhi i starykh domakh," ibid., 1986, no. 3:23–25.

75. "Predlagaiem obsudit': Peshekhodnaia zona Nevskogo," *Sovetskaia Rossiia,* July 25, 1987, p. 2.

76. E. M. Poltoratskii, "Gorod: Zastroika ili zhivoi organizm?"; Iakovlev, "Povtoriaemost' eshche ne monotonnost' "; Berezin, "Pochemu neuiutno v novom kvartale?"; and Bril'iantshchikov, "Kupchino—Eto Leningrad?"

77. Daniel R. Mandelker, "City Planning in the Soviet Union: Problems of Coordination and Control," *Urban Law and Policy* 2, no. 2 (1979):97–109.

78. The significance for planners of the expanded knowledge base produced in recent years was noted prominently by Sergei Vsevolodovich Uspenskii of the Leningrad (Voznesenskii) Financial-Economic Institute during an interview conducted by the author at that institute in Leningrad on March 5, 1984.

79. These efforts have produced an extensive body of literature. For example, see such works as: G. N. Buldakov, E. I. Izvarin, A. S. Krivov, V. F. Natarov, N. S. Pal'chikov, and V. N. Starinskii, "Gradostroitel'noe proektirovanie i upravlenie razvitiem goroda," in Sigov, *Upravlenie razvitiem krupnykh gorodov,* 137–148; E. I. Vainberg and V. Ia. Liubovnyi, "Plan kompleksnogo ekonomicheskogo i sotsial'nogo razvitiia krupnogo goroda," *Problemy bol'shikh gorodov,* 1980, no. 11:1–28; G. D. Platonov and V. I. Ruzhzhe, "Problemy rhilishcha budushchego (o sotsiologicheskhikh osnovakh proektirovaniia)," *Stroitel'stvo i arkhitektura Leningrada,* 1965, no. 8:7–13; "Kakie kvartiry stroit?" ibid., 1967, no. 5:6–9; A. G. Kharchev, "O faktorakh vazhnykh dlia arkhitekturnogo proektirovaniia," ibid., 1967, no. 8:20–21; M. E. Vaitens, "Esli chelovek zhivet v tsentre goroda: Nekotorye dannye gradostroitel'no-sotsiologicheskogo obsledovaniia," ibid., 1969, no. 5:10–11; I. V. Bestuzhev-Lada, "Sotsial'noe prognozirovanie i gradostroitel'stvo," ibid., 1969, no. 12:10–11; V. L. Ruzhzhe and V. V. Popov, "Gorod: Diagnoz i prognoz," ibid., 1969, no. 12:12–13; G. N. Forim, "Za kompleksnyi perspektivnye podkhod k proektirovaniiu gorodov," ibid., 1972, no. 6:2–3; E. P. Iudin, "Po kompleksnomu planu sotsial'nogo razvitiia," ibid., 1970, no. 11:4–7; V. A. Tikhomirov, V. I. Bochkov, and N. A. Tereshchenko, "Na osnove sotsiologicheskikh issledovanii," ibid., 1970, no. 11:11–13; M. V. Borshchevskii, "Sotsial'noe planirovanie i gorod," ibid., 1970, no. 11:16–18; A. V. Makhrovskaia, "Zhizn' v gorode: Nekotorye itogi obsledovanii novykh raionov Leningrada," ibid., 1970, no. 12:9–12; A. V. Makhrovskaia, "O putiakh kompleksnogo formirovaniia raionov Leningrada," ibid., 1971, no. 11:18–19; A. S. Pashkov and V. V. Polozov, "Na puti k kompleksnomu planu razvitiia goroda," ibid., 1972, no. 6:15–16; "Leningrad, god 2000—i," ibid., 1972, no. 10:16–20; I. Iu. Murav'eva, M. P. Berezin, and S. P. Makharevich, "Skol'ko Leningradtsev budet cherez 30–50 let? Struktura i prognoz rosta naseleniia," ibid., 1973, no. 6:6–8; V. M. Tareev, "Prognoz:

Strategiia deistviia," ibid., 1974, no. 6:22–25; "Sem'e—kvartira," ibid., 1974, no. 9:18–33; E. P. Murav'ev and S. V. Uspenskii, "Kompleksnyi prognoz razvitiia goroda," ibid., 1975, no. 4:30–32; M. D. Filonov, "Tsel'—Ekonomicheskie-sotsial'nye preobrazovaniia," ibid., 1976, no. 7:2–3; and G. N. Buldakov, "V sootvetstvii s general'nym planom," ibid., 1976, no. 7:4–10.

80. This point was frequently made during interviews with scholars at the USSR Academy of Sciences' Institute of Socioeconomic Problems in Leningrad during the period February 15 through March 7, 1984.

81. Vainberg and Liubovnyi, "Plan kompleksnogo ekonomicheskogo i sotsial'nogo razvitiia," 1–2.

82. Ibid., 9–12.

83. Ibid.

84. See, for example, A. V. Baranov, "Planirovanie sotsial'noi infrastruktury krupnogo goroda," *Problemy bol'shikh gorodov*, 1979, no. 3:1–26; and V. A. Vorotilov and G. N. Cherkasov, eds., *Metodologiia sotsial'no-ekonomicheskogo planirovaniia goroda* (Leningrad: Nauka—Leningradskoe otdelenie, 1980), 159–179.

85. This point was made by V. V. Polozov of the USSR Academy of Sciences' Institute of Socioeconomic Problems during interviews conducted by the author in Leningrad on February 27 and March 2, 1984.

86. Vorotilov and Cherkasov, *Metodologiia sotsial'no-ekonomicheskogo planirovaniia goroda*, 17–31. The 15-year duration of this process is thought sufficient to ensure adequate collection of the required social data for each of these 11 concerns.

87. Usanov, Krivov, and Nazarov, "Leningrad: Rychagi upravleniia"; M. P. Berezin and O. V. Matiukhin, "Razvitie goroda: Tendentsii i normativy," *Stroitel'stvo i arkhitektura Leningrada*, 1981, no. 4:9–12; and V. M. Tareev, "Glavnaia zadacha zodchikh," ibid., 1981, no. 4:4–7; T. A. Gritsenko, "Sud'ba 'belykh piaten,'" *Leningradskaia panorama*, 1985, no. 3:28–29; "Sud'ba belykh piaten i neskol'ko otvetov na publikatsiia zhurnala," ibid., 1985, no. 8:39.

88. V. A. Vorotilov and G. D. Platonov, "V interesakh gorozhan," *Leningradskaia panorama*, 1983, no. 3:16–19; I. V. Chekin, "Na style proshlogo s griadushchim," ibid., 1986: no. 5:7–8; A. S. Konstantinov, "Kvartaly na naberezhnoi Robespiera," ibid., 1986, no. 5:9–10.

89. Such as the Leningrad Regional Planning Institute of Gosgrazhdanstoi (LenZNIIEP) and the USSR Academy of Sciences' Institute of Socioeconomic Problems.

90. All points repeatedly made in such works as N. V. Baranov, "Razvivat' gradostroitel'nye traditsii Leningrada," *Stroitel'stvo i arkhitektura Leningrada*, 1972, no. 6:4–7; S. P. Semenov, "Kontury bol'shogo Leningrada," ibid., *Leningrada*, 1974, no. 6:26–29.

91. N. I. Kulina, ed., *Prigorody Leningrada: Arkhitektury i putevoditel'* (Leningrad: Stroiizdat, 1982).

92. *Narodnoe khoziaistvo Leningrada . . . v desiatoi piatiletke*, 22.

93. *Leningrad: Istoriko-geograficheskii atlas*, rev. and supplemented ed. (Moscow: Glavnoe upravlenie geodezii i kartografii pri Sovete Ministrov SSSR, 1981), 114.

94. *Narodnoe khoziaistvo Leningrada . . . v desiatoi piatiletke,* 22–23.

95. L. K. Panov, "Bol'shoi Leningrad, puti ego razvitiia," *Stroitel'stvo i arkhitektura Leningrada,* 1975, no. 6:22–23.

96. N. T. Agafonov, S. B. Lavrov, and B. S. Khorev, "On Some Faulty Concepts in Soviet Urban Studies," *Soviet Geography: Review and Translation* 24, no. 3 (March 1983):179–188 (translated from *Izvestiia Vsesoiuznogo geograficheskogo obshchestva,* 1982, no. 6:533–539). For a Western discussion of this process during its early years, see Chauncy Harris, *Cities of the Soviet Union: Studies in Their Functions, Size, Density and Growth* (Chicago: Rand McNally, 1970).

97. For one recent concise discussion of the Western literature in this area, see S. N. Eisenstadt and A. Shachar, *Society, Culture, and Urbanization* (Beverly Hills, Calif.: Sage Publications, 1987), 39–49.

98. Ibid.; V. I. Parol', *Sotsialisticheskii gorod* (Tallin: Valgus, 1982), 5–6.

99. See, for example, such works as G. A. Maloian, "Preobrazovanie krupnykh gorodskikh aglomeratsii v sistemy vzaimosviazannykh naselennykh mest," *Problemy bol'shikh gorodov,* 1982, no. 7:1–29; and E. Iu. Faerman and Iu. A. Oleinik-Ovod, eds., *Voprosy planirovaniia gorodskogo razvitiia* (Moscow: TsEMI, 1977).

100. Agafonov, Lavrov, and Khorev, "On Some Faulty Concepts"; I. I. Sigov, "Sotsialisticheskii gorod v sisteme upravleniia razvitiem obshchestva," in Sigov, *Upravlenie razvitiem krupnykh gorodov,* 38–51; and N. T. Agafonov, "Strukturnye osobennosti krupnykh gorodov kak ob"ektov upravleniia," in ibid., 51–64.

101. B. S. Khorev, *Problemy gorodov (urbanizatsiia i edinaia sistema rasseleniia v SSSR),* 2d rev. ed. (Moscow: Mysl', 1975).

102. B. S. Khorev and L. P. Kiseleva, *Urbanizatsiia i demograficheskie protsessy* (Moscow: Finansy i statistika, 1982). For one interesting discussion of Khorev's work on this concept, see the doctoral dissertation of Rostov-on-Don's V. N. Chapek, "Aktual'nye problemy izucheniia sotsial'no-geograficheskogo mekanizma sovremennoi migratsii naseleniia SSSR," Geograficheskii fakul'tet, Leningradskii gosudarstvennyi universitet, 1980.

103. P. S. Kovalenko, *Razvitie gorodov* (Kiev: Naukova dumka, 1980), 14–18.

104. Ibid., 41.

105. Based on an interview with Oleg Litovka of the USSR Academy of Sciences' Institute of Socioeconomic Problems, Leningrad, February 28, 1984.

106. See, for example, N. T. Agafonov, *Territorial'no-proizvodstvennoe kompleksnoobrazovanie v usloviiakh razvitogo sotsializma* (Leningrad: Nauka—Leningradskoe otdelenie, 1983); E. P. Murav'ev and S. V. Uspenskii, *Metodologicheskie problemy planirovaniia gorodskogo rasseleniia pri sotsializme* (Leningrad: Leningradskii gosudarstvennyi universitet, 1974); A. V. Dmitriev and M. N. Mezhevich, eds., *Gorod: Problemy sotsial'nogo razvitiia* (Leningrad: Nauka—Leningradskoe otdelenie, 1982); Sigov, *Upravlenie razvitiem krupnykh gorodov;* S. V. Markov, "Otsenka territorial'noi struktury goroda," *Vestnik Leningradskogo gosudarstvennogo universiteta,* 1984, no. 4:99–102; and O. P. Litovka and M. N. Mezhevich, "Sotsialisticheskaia urbanizatsiia: Tendentsii i zakonomernosti," in Institut sotsial'no-ekonomicheskikh problem

AN SSSR, *Sotsialisticheskii gorod kak ob"ekt issledovaniia i upravleniia. Materialy Vsesoiuznoi nauchnoi konferentsii sostoiavsheisia v Leningrade 21–23 Oktiabriia 1981 goda* (Leningrad: Nauka—Leningradskoe otdelenie, 1983), 17–24.

107. Interview with Sergei Vsevolodovich Uspenskii.

108. For a discussion of the importance of such recreational districts for city residents as well as their planning significance, see L. P. Lavrov, A. M. Magerramov, and V. G. Shishkov, "Ne vyezzhaia za gorod," *Leningradskaia panorama*, 1984, no. 7:21–23.

109. Interview with Oleg P. Litovka; V. N. Starinskii, *Territorial'nyi plan kapital'nykh vlozhenyii* (Leningrad: Lenizdat, 1980).

110. "Dnevnik: Zdaniia geograficheskogo i geologicheskogo fakul'tetov," *Leningradskaia panorama*, 1982, no. 2:39; A. Glebov, "Ob"edininaia usiliia uchenykh," ibid., 1983, no. 7:3–5.

111. For evidence that this indeed was the case, see A. A. Volkov, E. D. Klimenko, and V. I. Meleshchenko, eds., *Leningradskii sotsial'no-ekonomicheskii kompleks* (Leningrad: Lenizdat, 1979), 20–39, 66.

112. Denis J. B. Shaw, "The Soviet Urban General Plan and Recent Advances in Soviet Urban Planning," *Urban Studies* 20 (1983):393–403.

113. "V obkome KPSS," *Leningradskaia pravda*, June 28, 1984, p. 1.

114. Leningradskaia organizatsiia ordena Lenina Soiuz arkhitekturov SSSR, *Leningrad—2000*.

115. Usanov, Krivov, and Nazarov, "Leningrad: Ryzhagi upravleniia."

116. This discussion is based on an interview with N. T. Agafonov of the USSR Academy of Sciences' Institute of Socioeconomic Problems, Leningrad, February 20, 1984.

117. "Otvetstvennye zadachi gradostroitelei," *Leningradskaia pravda*, September 7, 1983, p. 1.

118. "Perspektivy razvitiia oblasti," *Leningradskaia pravda*, October 16, 1983, p. 1.

119. L. N. Zaikov, "Namechennoe Leninskoi partiei pretvorit' v zhizn'," *Leningradskaia pravda*, January 21, 1984, pp. 1–3.

120. "Namechennoe partiei—Vypolnim: Plenum Leningradskogo obkoma KPSS; Iz doklada tov. L. N. Zaikova," *Leningradskaia pravda*, April 18, 1984, pp. 1–3.

121. "V obkome KPSS," *Leningradskaia pravda*, June 6, 1984, p. 1.

122. Iu. I. Tsymaliakov and R. K. Abbiasov, "Metody planirovaniia sotsial'nogo razvitiia goroda," in L. A. Grigor'eva, V. A. Sukhin, and Iu. I. Tsymaliakov, eds., *Sotsial'naia infrastruktura i uroven' zhizni naseleniia krupnogo goroda*, Chelovek i obshchestvo no. 21 (Leningrad: Izdatel'stvo Leningradskogo universiteta, 1986), 165–177.

123. "Razvivaia sotsialisticheskoe sorevnovanie dosrochno vypolnim zadaniia piatiletke: Plenum Leningradskogo gorkoma KPSS," *Leningradskaia pravda*, June 22, 1984, pp. 1–2.

124. Iu. V. Baranov, "V osnove—Kompleksnyi podkhod," *Leningradskaia panorama*, 1984, no. 9:3–5.

125. "Leningradu i oblasti—Kompleksnoe razvitie," *Leningradskaia pravda*, November 24, 1984, p. 1; also in *Vechernyi Leningrad*, November 24, 1984, p. 1.

126. "Zavershen pervyi etap: Razrabotki edinogo General'nogo plana razvitiia goroda i oblasti na 1986–2005 gody," *Leningradskaia pravda*, January 12, 1985, p. 3.

127. "Gorod i oblast': Edinyi plan razvitiia," *Leningradskaia pravda*, June 8, 1985, p. 1.

128. "V Politbiuro TsK KPSS," *Leningradskaia pravda*, June 7, 1985, p. 1; also in *Vechernyi Leningrad*, June 7, 1985, p. 1; "V obkome KPSS," *Leningradskaia pravda*, July 17, 1985, p. 1; also in *Vechernyi Leningrad*, July 18, 1985, p. 1; and V. I. Kozlov, ed., *Ocherki istorii Leningradskoi organizatsii KPSS*, vol. 3, *1945–1985* (Leningrad: Lenizdat, 1985), 665.

129. "Gorod i oblast'."

130. See, for example, "Soveshchanie v Smol'nom," *Leningradskaia pravda*, August 10, 1985, p. 1.

131. G. N. Buldakov and V. F. Nazarov, "Kontury general'nogo plana," *Leningradskaia panorama*, 1985, no. 10:1–3.

132. "1986/2005," *Leningradskaia panorama*, 1986, no. 7:2–32.

133. "V obkome KPSS," *Leningradskaia pravda*, December 18, 1985, p. 1.

134. "K rubezham XXI veka," *Leningradskaia panorama*, 1986, no. 7:2.

135. This point is stressed in Buldakov and Nazarov, "Kontury general'nogo plana."

136. "K rubezham XXI veka."

137. "Strategiia griadushchikh peremen," *Leningradskaia panorama*, 1986, no. 7:3–6.

138. Ibid.

139. "Razmeshchenie proizvodstva i sistema rasseleniia," *Leningradskaia panorama*, 1986, no. 7:6–8.

140. Ibid., 7.

141. Ibid., 8.

142. Ibid., 7.

143. "Gradostroenie: V osnovoe mnogoobrazie," *Leningradskaia panorama*, 1986, no. 7:9–13.

144. "Sredotochie neprekhodiashikh tsennostei," *Leningradskaia panorama*, 1986, no. 7:13–18.

145. Ibid.

146. "Perspektivny liubye poselenie," *Leningradskaia panorama*, 1986, no. 7:19–21.

147. "Zabota o blage cheloveka," *Leningradskaia panorama*, 1986, no. 7:22–24.

148. "Skorost' nadezhnost' komfort," *Leningradskaia panorama*, 1986, no. 7:25–28; "Kompleks inzhenernogo obespecheniia," ibid., 29–30; A. L. Zhukovskii and I. A. Sobol, "Poezdki za gorod: Bystro i udobno," ibid., 1986, no. 12:14–16.

149. "Zhivitel'nye istochniki zdorov'ia," *Leningradskaia panorama*, 1986, no. 7:31–32.

150. "V Tsentral'nom komitete KPSS: Tsentral'nyi komitet KPSS rassmotrel vopros o pis'makh trudiashchikhsia, sviazannykh s ekologicheskoi obstanovkoi v basseine Ledozhskogo ozera," *Leningradskaia pravda*, May 29, 1987, p. 1; "Uroki Ladogi," *Sovetskaia Rossiia*, June 4, 1987, p. 1; "Ten' nad

belym gorodom," *Leningradskaia pravda*, June 5, 1987, p. 3; V. Viktorov, "Budut li chistymi berega?" ibid., June 20, 1987, p. 2; "V obkome KPSS," ibid., June 23, 1987, p. 1.

151. See, for example, "Chitatel' sprashivaet i predlagaet," *Leningradskaia panorama*, 1986, no. 5:25.

152. See, for example, the articles in Grigor'eva, V. A. Sukhin, and Iu. I. Tsymaliakov, *Sotsial'naia infrastruktura*.

153. A point reemphasized in early 1988 in V. F. Nazarov, "General'nyi plan—V deistvii," *Leningradskaia panorama*, 1988, no. 2:2–3.

Chapter 4

1. B. I. Kozlov, ed., *Organizatsiia i razvitie otraslevykh nauchno-issledovatel'skikh institutov Leningrada, 1917–1977* (Leningrad: Nauka—Leningradskoe otdelenie, 1979), 14; Kh. Kh. Karimov, *Leningrad v tsifrakh i faktakh* (Leningrad: Lenizdat, 1984), 19, 82.

2. A. N. Gerasimov, "Kontsentratsii proizvodstva—Povsednevnoe vnimanie," in B. K. Alekseev and V. G. Zubarev, eds., *Partiinoe rukovodstvo—Na uroven' sovremennykh trebovanii: Iz opyta raboty Leningradskoi partiinoi organizatsii* (Leningrad: Lenizdat, 1978), 85–112.

3. Karimov, *Leningrad*, 19–21.

4. Ibid., 52; "Povyshat' otdachu nauchnykh uchrezhdenii," *Leningradskaia pravda*, March 31, 1983, p. 1.

5. L. N. Zaikov, "Povyshat' uroven' partiinogo rukovodstva komsomolom," *Leningradskaia pravda*, July 21, 1984, pp. 1–2; "V Tsentral'nom komitete KPSS o rabote provodimoi Leningradskim obkomom KPSS po usileniiu intensifikatsii ekonomiki v dvenadtsatoi piatiletke na osnove uskoreniia nauchno-tekhnicheskogo progressa," ibid., August 4, 1984, p. 1; "V obkome KPSS, 'Intensifikatsiia-90' programma deistviia po povysheniiu effektivnosti ekonomiki," ibid., August 7, 1984, p. 1.

6. "Nastoichivo dvizat'sia vpered: Vystuplenie M. S. Gorbacheva na sobranii aktiva Leningradskoi partiinoi organizatsii 17 maia 1985 goda," *Kommunist*, 1985, no. 8:23–34; "Soedinenie nauki s proizvodstvom velenie vremeni: Prebyvanie M. S. Gorbacheva v Leningrade," *Leningradskaia pravda*, May 17, 1985, p. 1.

7. "Aide Who Assailed Gorbachev's Pace Ousted in Moscow," *New York Times*, November 12, 1987, pp. Al, A15; "Russia's Rising Star: Moscow's No. 3 Man Tells a Few Kremlin Secrets," *Newsweek*, April 4, 1988, pp. 32–33; "Lev Zaikov Speaks Out," *Newsweek*, April 4, 1988, pp. 33–34.

8. Solov'ev's identification with the "Intensification-90" campaign is readily apparent in his January 1986 address to the twenty-seventh conference of the Leningrad regional party organization ("Utverzhdat' novyi stil', tvorcheskii podkhod v osushchestvlenii planov kommunisticheskogo sozidaniia: Iz doklada Iu. F. Solov'eva," *Leningradskaia pravda*, January 25, 1986, pp. 1–3.)

9. *Bol'shaia Sovetskaia entsiklopediia: Ezhegodnik—1962* (Moscow: Sovetskaia entsiklopediia, 1963), 599.

10. For further discussion of the impact of the purges of the Leningrad Affair on the city and its political elite, see Blair A. Ruble, "The Leningrad Affair and the Provincialization of Leningrad," *Russian Review* 42, no. 3 (1983):301–320.

11. A. Afanas'ev, "Pobeditel'," *Komsomol'skaia pravda*, January 15, 1988, p.2. Werner Hahn reports that the main victims of the purge were probably executed in September and October 1950 (Werner Hahn, *Postwar Soviet Politics* [Ithaca: Cornell University Press, 1982], 122).

12. "Doklad sekretaria Leningradskogo gorodskogo komiteta VKP(b), tov. A. I. Alekseeva," *Leningradskaia pravda*, September 23, 1952, pp. 2–3; "Doklad sekretaria Leningradskogo komiteta VKP(b), tov. Andrianova," ibid., September 28, 1952, pp. 2–3; "Rech' tov. Kozlova," ibid., October 16, 1952, p. 3.

13. These remarks are quoted from "Rech' tovarishcha L. N. Efremova," *Pravda*, October 22, 1961, p. 3.

14. Leningrad, Institut istorii partii, *Istoriia Kirovskogo (byv. Putilovskogo) metallurgicheskogo i mashinostroitel'nogo zavoda v Leningrade* (Moscow: Izd. sotsial'no-ekonomicheskaia literatura, 1961–1966).

15. See, for example, his address to the tenth city party conference in September 1952, "Rech' tov. F. R. Kozlova," *Leningradskaia pravda*, September 24, 1952, p. 4.

16. *Leningrad: Entsiklopedicheskii spravochnik* (Moscow and Leningrad: Bol'shaia Sovetskaia entsiklopediia, 1957), 138–139, 548–549.

17. A trend documented in such regional statistical handbooks as Statisticheskoe upravlenie goroda Leningrada, *Narodnoe khoziaistvo goroda Leningrada: Statisticheskii sbornik* (Moscow: Gosudarstvennoe statisticheskoe izdatel'stvo, 1957); Planovaia komissiia ispolkoma Lengorsoveta, Statisticheskoe upravlenie goroda Leningrada, *Leningrad za 50 let: Statisticheskii sbornik* (Leningrad: Lenizdat, 1967); *Leningrad i Leningradskaia oblast' v tsifrakh: Statisticheskii sbornik* (Leningrad: Lenizdat, 1974); and *Narodnoe khoziaistvo Leningrada i Leningradskoi oblasti v desiatoi piatiletke: Statisticheskii sbornik* (Leningrad: Lenizdat, 1981). It may also be seen in the discussion found in A. A. Volkov, E. D. Klimenko, and V. I. Meleshchenko, *Leningradskii sotsial'no-ekonomicheskii kompleks* (Leningrad: Lenizdat, 1979), 215–233.

18. For a general discussion of these events, see W. Leonhard, *The Kremlin since Stalin* (New York: Oxford University Press, 1962), 193–241.

19. *Bol'shaia Sovetskaia entsiklopediia: Ezhegodnik—1966* (Moscow: Sovetskaia Entsiklopediia, 1967), 594. See, for example, the discussion in Barbara Ann Chotiner, *Khrushchev's Party Reform: Coalition Building and Institutional Innovation* (Westport, Conn.: Greenwood Press, 1984).

20. For a general overview of these events, see the discussion in Michel Tatu, *Power in the Kremlin: From Khrushchev to Kosygin*, trans. Helen Katel (New York: Viking Press, 1968), 341–351, 399–423.

21. I. V. Spiridonov, *Leningradu 250 let* (Moscow: Gos. izdat. pol. lit., 1957), 63.

22. A. A. Smol'kina, *Deiatel'nost' KPSS po vosstanovleniiu i razvitiiu nauchno-tekhnicheskogo potentsiala Leningrada (1945–1966 gg.): Na materialakh Leningradskoi partiinoi organizatsii* (Leningrad: Leningradskii gosudarstvennyi universitet, 1983), 73–75; "Rech' tov. F. R. Kozlova," September 24, 1952 (see n. 15 above).

23. Smol'kina, *Deiatel'nost'* KPSS, 75.

24. L. G. Chertov, *Leningrad kak odin iz krupneishikh ekonomicheskikh kul'turnykh tsentrov SSSR* (Leningrad: Obshchestvo "Znanie"—Leningradskaia organizatsiia, 1955), 27–28; and N. Ia. Ivanov, B. M. Kochakov, and S. B. Okun', eds., *Leningrad: Kratkii istoricheskii ocherk* (Leningrad: Lenizdat, 1964), 548–549.

25. P. Ia. Kann, *Sotsialisticheskii Leningrad* (Leningrad: Obshchestvo "Znanie"—Leningradskaia organizatsiia, 1955), 30.

26. V. El'meev, *Nauka i proizvoditel'nye sily obshchestva* (Moscow: Sotsekgiz, 1959), 33.

27. V. I. Kozlov, ed., *Ocherki istorii Leningradskoi organizatsii KPSS*, vol. 3, *1945–1985* (Leningrad: Lenizdat, 1985), 130–139, 287–291.

28. Alec Nove, "The Soviet Industrial Reorganization," in Abraham Brumberg, ed., *Russia under Khrushchev* (New York: Frederick A. Praeger, 1962), 189–204.

29. Tatu, *Power in the Kremlin*, 443–446, 461–466.

30. A. V. Bakunin, ed., *Deiatel'nost' KPSS po uskoreniiu nauchno-tekhnicheskogo progressa* (Moscow: Vysshaia shkola, 1980), 58.

31. Smol'kina, *Deiatel'nost'* KPSS, 105–106.

32. A. V. Stepanenko, *Goroda v usloviiakh razvitogo sotsializma* (Kiev: Naukova Dumka, 1981), 107; Ed A. Hewett, *Reforming the Soviet Economy: Equality versus Efficiency* (Washington, D.C.: Brookings Institution, 1988), 245–250.

33. E. V. Mikhailov, "Umelo rukovodit' sotsialisticheskim khoziaistvovaniem," in B. V. Ul'ianov, comp., *Praktika sotsialisticheskogo khoziaistvovaniia: Opyt' Leningradskikh predpriiatii* (Leningrad: Lenizdat, 1981), 57–66.

34. Ibid.

35. V. M. Khodachek and V. G. Alekseev, *Kompleksnoe razvitie gorodskikh raionov: Kompleksnyi plan ekonomicheskogo i sotsial'nogo razvitiia v deistvii* (Leningrad: Lenizdat, 1980), 50.

36. A. I. Kirsanov, "Plan ekonomicheskogo i sotsial'nogo razvitiia—v deistvii," in P. P. Mozhaev, comp., *Za delovoi stil' v partiinoi rabote* (Leningrad: Lenizdat, 1981), 8.

37. See, for example, P. P. Mozhaev, "Predislovie," in Mozhaev, *Za delovoi stil'*, 6.

38. Kozlov, *Organizatsiia i razvitie*, 16.

39. Ibid., 14.

40. Ibid., 22.

41. Ibid.; B. Ul'ianov, "Programma intensifikatsii ekonomiki Leningrada i Leningradskoi oblasti," *Planovoe khoziaistvo*, 1985, no. 2:85–90.

42. S. A. Kugel', B. D. Lebin, and Iu. S. Meleshchenko, eds., *Nauchnye kadry Leningrada* (Leningrad: Nauka—Leningradskoe otdelenie, 1973), 23.

43. Kozlov, *Organizatsiia i razvitie*, 13.

44. Ibid., 21.

45. Kugel', Lebin, and Meleshchenko, *Nauchnye kadry*, 4–5.

46. Kozlov, *Organizatsiia i razvitie*, 13–14.

47. Kugel', Lebin, and Meleshchenko, *Nauchnye kadry*, 38.

48. Ibid., 41.

49. Ibid., 42.

50. I. A. Glebov and I. I. Sigov, eds., *Sovershenstvovanie upravleniia fundamental'nymi issledovaniiami v krupnom gorode* (Leningrad: Nauka— Leningradskoe otdelenie, 1983).

51. Vsesoiuznyi institut nauchnoi i tekhnicheskoi informatsii, *Organy nauchno-tekhnicheskoi informatsii SSSR—Spravochnik* (Moscow: VINITI, 1976).

52. Blair A. Ruble (with the assistance of Mark H. Teeter, Rosemary Stuart, Eleanor B. Sutter, and Mary Giles), *Soviet Research Institutes Project*, vol. 2, *The Social Sciences* (Washington, D.C.: Kennan Institute for Advanced Russian Studies, Woodrow Wilson International Center for Scholars, 1981), 288.

53. This discussion is based on Kozlov, *Organizatsiia i razvitie*, 211– 225.

54. This discussion is based on Thane Gustafson, *Selling the Russians the Rope? Soviet Technology Policy and US Export Controls* (Santa Monica: RAND Corp., 1981), 45–49.

55. Kozlov, *Organizatsiia i razvitie*, 170–179.

56. V. V. Mavrodin, ed., *Istoriia Leningradskogo universiteta* (Leningrad: Leningradskii gosudarstvennyi universitet, 1969), 354–452; G. D. Komkov, B. V. Levshin, and L. K. Semenov, *Akademiia nauk SSSR: Kratkii istoricheskii ocherk* (Moscow: Nauka, 1974), 341–388.

57. E. A. Beliaev and N. S. Pyshkova, *Formirovanie i razvitie seti nauchnykh uchrezhdenii SSSR* (Moscow: Nauka, 1979), 52–163; M. D. Millionshchikov, "Novye nauchnye tsentry RSFSR," in *Nauka Soiuza SSR* (Moscow: Nauka, 1972), 80–106.

58. L. S. Kiuzadzhan, "Introduction," in Blair A. Ruble and Mark H. Teeter, eds., *A Scholars' Guide to Humanities and Social Sciences in the Soviet Union: The Academy of Sciences of the USSR and the Academies of Sciences of the Union Republics* (Armonk, N.Y.: M. E. Sharpe, 1985), 3–9.

59. Ibid., 65–66.

60. Beliaev and Pyshkova, *Formirovanie i razvitie*, 73.

61. P. Zvonkova and E. Ivanova, "Opyt regional'noi koordinatsii nauchnykh issledovanii," *Obshchestvennye nauki*, 1984, no. 4:162–168.

62. "O mezhvedomstvennom koordinatsionnom sovete v Leningrade," *Vestnik AN SSSR*, 1980, no. 2:3–5.

63. G. V. Romanov, "Po kompleksnym programam: Intensifikatsiia sushchnost' puti i sredstva," *Pravda*, August 4, 1981, pp. 2–3.

64. G. V. Romanov, "Doverie, vzyskatel'nost', chustvo dolga," *Kommunist*, 1981, no. 16:12–27.

65. "Povyshat' otdachu nauchnykh uchrezhdenii," *Leningradskaia pravda*, March 31, 1983, p. 1.

66. S. Grachev, "Vybor tseli," *Leningradskaia pravda*, May 29, 1983, p. 2.

67. See, for example, "Po puti nauchno-tekhnicheskogo progressa," *Leningradskaia pravda*, April 21, 1984, p. 3; and "Povyshat' otdachu ot melioriatsii zemel': Plenum Leningradskogo obkoma KPSS; Iz doklada tovarishcha L. N. Zaikova," ibid., November 2, 1984, pp. 1–3.

68. "Vo vseoruzhii opyta—k novym uspekham: Vstrecha izbiratelei

Smol'ninskogo izbiratel'nogo okruga s G. V. Romanovym," *Leningradskaia pravda*, February 15, 1985, pp. 1–2.

69. See, for example, the emphasis paid to Academician Paton's efforts in this regard in Akademiia nauk Ukrainskoi SSR, *Istoriia Akademii nauk Ukrainskoi SSR* (Kiev: Naukova Dumka, 1979).

70. "Povyshat' effektivnost' raboty nauchnykh i inzhenerno-tekhnicheskikh kadrov: Plenum Leningradskogo gorkoma KPSS," *Leningradskaia pravda*, March 27, 1986, pp. 1, 3.

71. See, for example, the editorial "Fundament nauki," *Leningradskaia pravda*, February 13, 1987, p. 1.

72. Gustafson, *Selling the Russians the Rope?*, 42–44.

73. "Povyshat' uroven' partiinogo rukovodstva Komsomolom: Plenum Leningradskogo obkoma KPSS; Iz doklada tovarishcha L. N. Zaikova," *Leningradskaia pravda*, July 21, 1984, pp. 1–2.

74. "Rech' deputata A. P. Dumacheva," *Vechernyi Leningrad*, July 7, 1984, p. 3.

75. Volkov, Klimenko, and Meleshchenko, *Leningradskii sotsial'no-ekonomicheskii kompleks*, 177–178.

76. Ul'ianov, "Programma intensifikatsii ekonomiki."

77. Ibid.; L. Zaikov, "Po programme intensifikatsii," *Leningradskaia pravda*, August 13, 1984; also in *Vechernyi Leningrad*, August 13, 1984, p. 1; T. G. Brodskaia, *Rol' Leningradskogo regiona v razvitii edinogo narodno-khoziaistvennogo kompleksa* (Leningrad: Obshchestvo "Znanie"—Leningradskaia organizatsiia, 1985), 15.

78. "V tsentral'nom komitete KPSS: O rabote provodimoi Leningradskim obkomom KPSS po usileniiu intensifikatsii ekonomiki v dvenadtsatoi piatiletke na osnove uskoreniia nauchno-tekhnicheskogo progressa," *Leningradskaia pravda*, August 4, 1984, p. 1; also in *Vechernyi Leningrad*, August 4, 1984, p. 1.

79. "V obkome KPSS: 'Intensifikatsiia-90'; programma deistviia po povysheniiu effektivnosti ekonomiki," *Leningradskaia pravda*, August 7, 1984, p. 1.

80. See, for example, "Na nauchnoi osnove," *Leningradskaia pravda*, August 8, 1984, p. 1, as well as Glebov's January 1986 remarks before the twenty-seventh conference of the Leningrad Communist Party organization, "Iz vystupleniia I. A. Glebova," *Leningradskaia pravda*, January 25, 1986, p. 3.

81. See, for some random examples, such articles as "Shag v zavtru," *Leningradskaia pravda*, August 10, 1984, p. 1; A. Tiutenkov, "Vse, chto namecheno—vypolnit!" ibid., August 15, 1984, p. 1; "Vazhnye zadachi vysshei shkoly," ibid., October 7, 1984, p. 1; "V obkome KPSS," ibid., November 21, 1984, p. 1; and "Vagon razgruzhaet . . . vozdukh," ibid., February 27, 1985, p. 1; in the city's morning paper and the series "Kursom uskoreniia nauchno-tekhnicheskogo progressa" in the city's evening paper, which includes such articles as "Bol'she lushche!" *Vechernyi Leningrad*, August 7, 1984, p. 1; "Gorodskoe khoziaistvo na plechi mashin," ibid., August 9, 1984, p. 2; "Vysokoe napriazhenie," ibid., August 3, 1984, p. 2; "Otvetstvennost' zakazchika," ibid., October 11, 1984, p. 2; and K. Kosov, "Grani obnovleniia," ibid., July 5, 1985, p. 1.

82. *Deputaty Verkhovnogo soveta SSSR: Desiatyi sozyv* (Moscow, 1979), 163.

83. Ibid.

84. Zaikov, "Po programme intensifikatsii."

85. See, for example, "Vyshe tempy nauchno-tekhnicheskogo progressa: Sobranie aktiva Leningradskoi partiinoi organizatsii; Iz doklada tovarishcha L. N. Zaikova," *Leningradskaia pravda*, September 18, 1984, pp. 1–3; also in *Vechernyi Leningrad*, September 18, 1984, pp. 1–3.

86. See, for example, Ul'ianov, "Programma intensifikatsii ekonomiki"; A. Chistov, "Leningradskii opyt: Intensifikatsiia i kollektiv," *Agitator*, 1984, no. 21:31–33; and F. Listengurt and I. Portianskii, "Krupnyi gorod v usloviiakh perekhoda k intensivnoi ekonomike," *Voprosy ekonomiki*, 1985, no. 1:108–115.

87. See, for example, "Rech' deputata Murav'eva, A. Iu. na sessii Verkhovnogo soveta RSFSR," *Leningradskaia pravda*, December 6, 1984, p. 3; and "Kursom intensifikatsii ekonomiki: Vystuplenie general'nogo direktora ob"edineniia 'Svetlana' O. V. Filatova na soveshchanii v TsK KPSS," ibid., June 14, 1985, p. 3; also in *Vechernyi Leningrad*, June 14, 1985, p. 3.

88. "Soedinenie nauki s proizvodstvom—Velenie vremeni: Prebyvanie M. S. Gorbacheva v Leningrade," *Leningradskaia pravda*, May 17, 1985, p. 1; also in *Vechernyi Leningrad*, May 17, 1985, p. 1; "Edinstvo slova i dela—Osnova uspekha: Prebyvanie M. S. Gorbacheva v Leningrade," ibid., May 18, 1985, p. 1; and Kozlov, *Ocherki istorii Leningradskoi organizatsii KPSS*, 665–667.

89. Ibid.

90. "Nastoichivo dvigat'sia vpered: Vystuplenie M. S. Gorbacheva."

91. "Uskorenie nauchno-tekhnicheskogo progressa—Trebovanie zhizni: Korennii vopros ekonomicheskoi politiki partii; Doklad tovarishcha M. S. Gorbacheva," *Leningradskaia pravda*, June 12, 1985, pp. 1–2; "Kursom intensifikatsii ekonomiki: Vystuplenie tovarishcha L. N. Zaikova na sovershchanii v TsK KPSS," ibid., June 13, 1985, p. 2; "Kursom intensifikatsii ekonomiki," ibid., June 13, 1985, p. 1.

92. "Vazhnye zadachi uskoreniia nauchno-tekhnicheskogo progressa: Sobranie partiino-khoziaistvennogo aktiva Leningrada i oblasti; Doklad tov. Iu. F. Solov'eva," *Leningradskaia pravda*, July 24, 1985, pp. 1–2.

93. "Kursom uskoreniia—k novym rubezhom; Iz doklada A. P. Dumacheva," *Vechernyi Leningrad*, December 20, 1985, pp. 1–2; *Leningradskaia pravda*, December 20, 1985, 1–2.

94. See, for example, advertisements of the stores, "Tekhnicheskaia kniga," *Vechernyi Leningrad*, October 11, 1984, p. 4; and "Dom stroitel'noi knigi," ibid., October 18, 1984, p. 4; as well as such articles and reports as "Izuchaetsia opyt intensifikatsii ekonomiki," *Leningradskaia pravda*, August 13, 1985, p. 1; "Seminar rukovodiashchikh rabotniki," ibid., August 15, 1985, p. 1; "Osnovy uskoreniia," ibid., August 11, 1985, p. 1; and "Utverzhdat' novyi stil' . . . Iz doklada Iu. F. Solov'eva"; and "Na glavnoi vystavke strany," *Leningradskaia panorama*, 1986, no. 11:12.

95. Zaikov, "Po programme intensifikatsii"; "Kursom uskoreniia, perestroiki i initsiativy," *Leningradskaia pravda*, July 3, 1986, pp. 1–2; "Nasushchye zaboty sovetov," *Leningradskaia panorama*, 1986, no. 5:1–3.

96. "Tovaram narodnogo potrebleniia—Shirokii assortiment, otlichnoe kachestvo: Plenum Leningradskogo obkoma KPSS," *Leningradskaia pravda,* November 27, 1985, pp. 1–2; "Kursom uskoreniia—k novym rubezham; Iz doklada A. P. Dumacheva," *Leningradskaia pravda,* December 21, 1985, pp. 1–2.

97. "Rech' tovarishcha Solov'eva, Iu. F.," *Leningradskaia pravda,* February 28, 1986, p. 2.

98. "Glavnoe—Chelovek," *Leningradskaia pravda,* October 4, 1986, p. 2.

99. "Vysokoe kachestvo—Kliuchevoe zveno uskoreniia: Plenum obkoma KPSS," *Leningradskaia pravda,* October 22, 1986, p. 1.

100. "Deistvovat' energichno i rezul'tativno: Plenum Leningradskogo gorkoma KPSS," *Leningradskaia pravda,* October 31, 1986, p. 1; "Prakticheskimi delami uglubliat' perestroiku," ibid., July 26, 1987, pp. 1–3; and "Sotsial'naia sfera: Kursom uskoreniia i perestroiki," ibid., July 30, 1987, p. 1.

101. "Prodvigat'sia vpered narastaiushchim tempom: Vstrecha izbiratelei Moskovskogo okruga s L. N. Zaikovym," *Leningradskaia pravda,* October 30, 1986, pp. 1–3.

Chapter 5

1. "Rech' tov. F. R. Kozlova," *Leningradskaia pravda,* September 24, 1952, p. 4.

2. See, for example, E. Lopatina, *Leningrad: Ekonomiko-geograficheskii ocherk* (Moscow: Gos. izdat. geograficheskii literatury, 1959), 13, 136–139; I. Bartenev, *Arkhitektura sotsialisticheskogo Leningrada* (Leningrad: Obshchestvo "Znanie"—Leningradskaia organizatsiia, 1953), 3–4.

3. A. A. Smol'kina, *Deiatel'nost' KPSS po vosstanovleniiu i razvitiiu nauchno-tekhnicheskogo potentsiala Leningrada (1945–1966 gg.): Na materialakh Leningradskoi partiinoi organizatsii* (Leningrad: Leningradskii gosudarstvennyi universitet, 1983).

4. See, for example, G. V. Romanov, "Rech' na XXV s"ezde KPSS," in G. V. Romanov, *Izbrannye rechi i stat'i* (Moscow: Izdatel'stvo politicheskoi literatury, 1980), 289–294.

5. The linkage of "technologically intensive" with "heavy industrial production" may appear to many Western readers to be a contradiction in terms. In the Soviet context, the expanded resource base of "Group A" heavy industries allocated by planners has meant that those industries are frequently the most technologically advanced. In other words, there are no "Silicon Valley" vs "Rust Belt" conflicts as in the United States. This preference for such industries as machine construction, metalworking, and the like reflects a distinct bias toward defense-related industries throughout the Soviet economy. In the Leningrad case, such technology-dominated industries as precision-instrument making and electronics are subsumed within the same general category as more traditional "heavy" industries.

6. *Leningradskaia promyshlennost' za 50 let* (Leningrad: Lenizdat, 1976), 29.

7. L. S. Bliakhman, "Problemy organizatsii nauki kak elementa infra-

struktury krupnogo goroda," in V. A. Vorotilov and G. N. Cherkasov, eds., *Metodologiia sotsial'no-ekonomicheskogo planirovaniia goroda* (Leningrad: Nauka—Leningradskoe otdelenie, 1980), 74–93; "Rech' tovarishcha G. V. Romanova," *Leningradskaia pravda*, December 22, 1982, p. 3.

8. *Narodnoe khoziaistvo za 60 let: Iubilenii statisticheskii sbornik* (Moscow: Statistika, 1977), 432; *Narodnoe khoziaistvo SSSR v 1980 g.: Statisticheskii ezhegodnik* (Moscow: Finansy i statistika, 1981), 333; *Leningrad i Leningradskaia oblast' v tsifrakh: Statisticheskii sbornik* (Leningrad: Lenizdat, 1971), 63; *Narodnoe khoziaistvo Leningrada i Leningradskoi oblasti za 60 let: Statisticheskii sbornik* (Leningrad: Lenizdat, 1977), 20; *Narodnoe khoziaistvo Leningrada i Leningradskoi oblasti v desiatoi piatiletke: Statisticheskii sbornik* (Leningrad: Lenizdat, 1981), 28–29.

9. *Narodnoe khoziaistvo Leningrada . . . za 60 let*, 132–133; *Leningrad i Leningradskaia oblast' v tsifrakh*, 23.

10. See the discussion in Chapters 2 and 3.

11. V. A. Ezhov, *Rabochii klass—Vedushchaia sila vosstanovleniia Leningrada 1943–1950 gg.* (Leningrad: Izdatel'stvo Leningradskogo universiteta, 1982), 22–35; L. D. Leonov and B. K. Peiro, *Leningrad—Gorod geroi* (Leningrad: Obshchestvo "Znanie"—Leningradskaia organizatsiia, 1957), 28–30; Harrison E. Salisbury, *The 900 Days: The Siege of Leningrad* (New York: Harper & Row, 1969), 407–422, 518–523; Leon Goure, *The Siege of Leningrad: August, 1941– January, 1944* (New York: McGraw-Hill Book Co., 1964), 150–153, 217–218, 239.

12. See, for example, Lopatina, *Leningrad*, 133–136.

13. A point made by Vladimir Vladimirovich Polozov of the USSR Academy of Sciences' Institute of Socioeconomic Problems during interviews conducted by the author in Leningrad on February 27 and March 2, 1984.

14. *XIII s"ezd Vsesoiuznogo Leninskogo kommunisticheskogo soiuza molodezhi: Stenograficheskii otchet* (Moscow, 1959), 278–282.

15. Joel J. Schwartz and William R. Keech, "Group Influence and the Policy Process in the Soviet Union," *American Political Science Review* 62 no. 3 (September 1968):840–851.

16. *Pravda*, September 21, 1958.

17. Rudolph Schlesinger, "The Education Reform," *Soviet Studies* 10, no. 4 (April 1959):432–444.

18. For further examination of the reform and the public discussion surrounding it, see Schwartz and Keech, "Group Influence."

19. Mervyn Matthews, *Education in the Soviet Union: Policies and Institutions since Stalin* (Boston: George Allen & Unwin, 1982), 82–84.

20. Ibid., 83–84; William J. Conyngham, *The Modernization of Soviet Industrial Management* (New York: Cambridge University Press, 1982), 164; Richard B. Dobson, "Soviet Education: Problems and Policies in the Urban Context," in Henry W. Morton and Robert C. Stuart, eds., *The Contemporary Soviet City* (Armonk, N.Y.: M. E. Sharpe, 1984), 156–179.

21. Matthews, *Education in the Soviet Union*, 87.

22. Ibid., 85; a point also evident in Communist Party Central Committee decrees in 1975 and 1979. For further discussion of those decrees, see M. N. Zinov'ev, "Formirovanie vysokikh professional'nykh kachestv," in M. N. Zi-

nov'ev, ed., *Vospitatel'naia rabota partiinykh organizatsii promyshlennykh kollektivov* (Leningrad: Izdatel'stvo Leningradskogo universiteta, 1983), 21.

23. V. I. Kozlov, ed., *Ocherki istorii Leningradskoi organizatsii KPSS*, vol. 3, *1945–1985* (Leningrad: Lenizdat, 1985), 33.

24. Matthews, *Education in the Soviet Union*, 67–74. For further discussion of the leading role played by Leningrad educators in the founding of factory schools in the early Soviet period, see A. P. Kupaigorodskaia, *Vysshaia shkola Leningrada v pervye gody Sovetskoi vlasti (1917–1925 gg.)* (Leningrad: Nauka—Leningradskoe otdelenie, 1983), 22–27; as well as N. Ia. Ivanov, B. M. Kochakov, and S. B. Okun', eds., *Leningrad: Kratkii istoricheskii ocherk* (Leningrad: Lenizdat, 1964), 415–416.

25. Matthews, *Education in the Soviet Union*, 67–74.

26. A. R. Dzeniskevich, *Rabochie Leningrada nakanune Velikoi otechestvennoi voiny, 1938–iiun' 1941 g.* (Leningrad: Nauka—Leningradskoe otdelenie, 1983), 22–27.

27. Kh. Kh. Karimov, *Leningrad v tsifrakh i faktakh* (Leningrad: Lenizdat, 1984), 84.

28. As evident from a reading of the discussion of the reforms found in the Leningrad morning newspaper *Leningradskaia pravda*.

29. These interviews and discussions took place at the USSR Academy of Sciences' Institute of Socioeconomic Problems in Leningrad between February 15 and March 7, 1984.

30. "V blizhiashchie gody dognat' Soedinennye Shtaty Ameriki po proizvodstvu miasa, masla i moloko na dushu naseleniia: Rech' tovarishcha N. S. Khrushcheva," *Pravda*, May 24, 1957, pp. 1–2; also in *Leningradskaia pravda*, May 24, 1957, pp. 2–3. For additional accounts of Khrushchev's visit to the city later that year in connection with the celebration of the city's 250th anniversary, see, for example, Iu. German, D. Granin, and E. Katerii, *Rasskaz o prazdnike* (Leningrad: Lenizdat, 1957).

31. "Doverie naroda—Vysokaia chest': Vstrecha izbiratelei goroda Lenina s A. N. Shelepinym; Rech' tovarishcha A. N. Shelepina," *Leningradskaia pravda*, June 3, 1966, pp. 1, 3.

32. "Rech' tovarishcha K. T. Mazurova," *Leningradskaia pravda*, March 4, 1967, pp. 1, 3.

33. V. Ivanovskii and N. Tikhonov, "Izuchenie prichin tekuchesti i sovershenstvovanii organizatsii truda," *Sotsialisticheskii trud*, 1963, no. 12:45–50.

34. V. R. Polozov, interviews, Leningrad, February 27 and March 2, 1984.

35. See, for example, G. V. Romanov's article in *Pravda* on January 30, 1975 ("Rabochemu klassu—Dostoinoe popolenie," in Romanov, *Izbrannye rechi i stat'i*, 236–242) as well as the writings of Leningrad city party committee Secretary T. I. Zhdanova (such as T. I. Zhdanova, "Rabochemu klassu—Dostoinoe popolenie," in B. K. Alekseev and V. G. Zubarev, eds., *Partiinoe rukovodstvo—Na uroven' sovremennykh trebovanii: Iz opyta raboty Leningradskoi partiinoi organizatsii* [Leningrad: Lenizdat, 1978], 201–223). For a discussion of other significant Leningrad regional party committee decrees and resolutions on this question, see N. B. Lebedev et al., *Partiinaia organizatsiia i rabochie Leningrada* (Leningrad: Lenizdat, 1974), 371–378.

36. See, for example, G. V. Romanov's September 1973 address to the Leningrad regional party committee on the vitally important role of vocational education for the city's and region's development ("Zavtra rabochego klassa," in Romanov, *Izbrannye rechi i stat'i*, 136–143).

37. "Putevka v rabochuiu zhizn'," *Leningradskaia pravda*, April 20, 1984, p. 1.

38. For a discussion of the manner in which Leningrad vocational education programs have served as a model for national curricula, see Kozlov, *Ocherki istorii*, 420–425, 263–266.

39. Blair A. Ruble, *Soviet Research Institutes Project: Final Report* (Washington, D.C.: Kennan Institute for Advanced Russian Studies of the Wilson Center and the United States International Communication Agency, 1981), 2:99.

40. Ibid., 2:97.

41. See, for example, "Rabochaia shkola," *Vechernyi Leningrad*, October 25, 1984, p. 2.

42. *Narodnoe khoziaistvo Leningrada . . . v desiatoi piatiletke*, 70–71.

43. "S prazdnikom, rabochaia iunost'," *Leningradskaia pravda*, October 2, 1982, p. 1.

44. See, for example, "Iz klassa shkol'nogo v rabochii klass!" *Leningradskaia pravda*, April 21, 1983, p. 1; and N. Eliseeva, "Pust' v meste idut— Ucheba i trud," *Vechernyi Leningrad*, August 31, 1984, p. 1.

45. L. Tereshchenko, "Vos'moi schastlivyi bilet," *Leningradskaia pravda*, July 31, 1983, p. 1.

46. "Leninskim kursom—k novym uspekham v stroitel'stve kommunizma: Iz doklada tovarishcha G. V. Romanova," *Leningradskaia pravda*, January 17, 1981, pp. 1–4.

47. Ibid., 3.

48. Yuri Luryi, "Economic Modernization and Legal Problems of Professional Training of Workers in the USSR," in Peter B. Maggs, Gordon B. Smith, and George Ginsburgs, eds., *Law and Economic Development in the Soviet Union* (Boulder: Westview Press, 1982), 62–63.

49. Glavnyi upravlenie proftekhobrazovaniia Leningrada i Leningradskoi oblasti, *Professional'no-tekhnicheskie i tekhnicheskie uchilishcha Leningrada i Leningradskoi oblasti: Spravochnik dlia postupaiushchikh—1980 g.* (Leningrad: Lenizdat, 1980), 18–19.

50. "V dobryi put'," *Leningradskaia pravda*, April 21, 1981, pp. 1–2.

51. I. Sidorov, "Do stupeniam vospitaniia," *Leningradskaia pravda*, January 24, 1984, p. 2.

52. I. Sidorov, "Uchit' delo masterstvu," *Leningradskaia pravda*, June 7, 1984, p. 2.

53. "Putevka v rabochuiu zhizn'," *Leningradskaia pravda*, April 20, 1984, p. 1; Kozlov, *Ocherki istorii*, 571.

54. "Rechi deputata Chicherova, V. S.," *Vechernyi Leningrad*, June 20, 1984, p. 1.

55. "Proekt TsK KPSS: Osnovnye napravleniia reformy obshcheobrazovatel'noi i professional'noi shkoly," *Leningradskaia pravda*, January 4, 1984, pp. 1–3; "Postanovlenie plenuma TsK KPSS: O dal'neishem ulushchenii raboty sovetov narodnykh deputatov," ibid., April 11, 1984, pp. 1–2; "Postanovlenie

Verkhovnogo Soveta SSSR ob osnovnykh napravleniiakh reformy obshcheo-brazovatel'noi i professional'noi shkoly," ibid., April 13, 1984, p. 1; "Osnovnye napravleniia reformy obshcheobrazovatel'noi i professional'noi shkoly (odo-breno Plenumom TsK KPSS 10 apreliia i Verkhovnym sovetom 12 apreliia)," ibid, April 14, 1984, pp. 2–3.

56. For one official discussion of the provisions of the 1984 Education Reforms, see "Ob osnovnykh napravleniiakh reformy obshcheobrazovatel'noi i professional'noi shkoly: Doklad chlena Politburo TsK KPSS, pervogo zame-stitelia Predsedatelia Soveta Ministrov SSSR deputata G. A. Alieva," *Lenin-gradskaia pravda*, April 13, 1984, pp. 2–3.

57. A balance that had already been achieved in Leningrad. See "Na-mechennoe partiei–Vypolnim: Iz doklada tov. L. N. Zaikova," *Leningradskaia pravda*, April 18, 1984, pp. 1–3.

58. "Reforma shkoly i vospitanie podrastaiushchego pokoleniia," *Le-ningradskaia pravda*, June 11, 1985, p. 1.

59. "XXVI Konferentsiia Leningradskoi oblastnoi organizatsii KPSS: Rech' M. E. Kapitonovoi," *Leningradskaia pravda*, January 22, 1984, p. 2.

60. "Deputy Minister Explains Education Changes; Moscow Domestic Service in Russian, 1100 GMT, 5 January, 1984," *Foreign Broadcast Infor-mation Service Daily Report*, January 6, 1984, pp. R14–R17; "Rech' deputata Zhuraleva, B. A.," *Leningradskaia pravda*, April 13, 1984, p. 3; also in *Ve-chernyi Leningrad*, April 13, 1984, p. 2.

61. "Plenum Leningradskogo gorkoma KPSS," *Leningradskaia pravda*, January 18, 1986, p. 1.

Chapter 6

1. The ripple effects of these changes were felt among such top Leningrad political elites as regional party First Secretary V. M. Andrianov, who had been brought in from Sverdlovsk to supervise the purges of the Leningrad Affair, and was immediately dismissed and later arrested, probably to be executed, for his leadership of the dismembering during 1949 and 1950 of the wartime Communist Party leadership. Andrianov was replaced by Frol Kozlov.

2. Z. Katz, "Sociology in the Soviet Union," *Problems of Communism* 20, no. 3 (May–June 1971):22–40; and Dimitry Shalin, "The Development of Soviet Sociology, 1956–1976," *American Review of Sociology* 4, no. 4 (1978): 171–191.

3. Paul Hollander, "The Dilemmas of Soviet Sociology," *Problems of Communism* 14, no. 6 (November–December, 1965):34–46; Alex Simirenko, "Post Stalinist Social Science," *Transaction Journal* 6, no. 7 (June 1969):37–42; and E. A. Weinberg, *The Development of Sociology in the Soviet Union* (London: Routledge & Kegan Paul, 1974).

4. B. A. Babin, "Institutu sotsiologicheskikh issledovanii AN SSSR—10 let," *Sotsiologicheskie issledovaniia*, 1979, no. 1:210–212.

5. Akademiia nauk SSSR, Institut sotsiologicheskikh issledovanii AN SSSR, Sovetskaia sotsiologicheskaia assotsiatsiia, *Sotsiologicheskie tsentry SSSR (1976 god)* (Moscow: AN SSSR, ISI AN SSSR, SSA, 1976); M. N. Opalov,

"Sovetskaia sotsiologicheskaia assotsiatsiia AN SSSR," *Sotsiologicheskie issledovaniia*, 1977, no. 4:172–175; and M. N. Opalov, "Reshenie IV otchetno-vybornoi konferentsii Sovetskoi sotsiologicheskoi assotsiatsii po otchetu pravleniia SSA," ibid., 1977, no. 3:31–34.

6. Blair A. Ruble, *Soviet Research Institutes Project: Final Report* (Washington, D.C.: The Kennan Institute for Advanced Russian Studies of the Wilson Center and the United States International Communication Agency, 1981), 2:363–366.

7. A. V. Baranov, *Sotsial'no-demograficheskoe razvitie krupnogo goroda* (Moscow: Finansy i statistika, 1981), 3–5.

8. Among the studies eventually resulting from this official prompting were such seminal works as A. G. Zdravomyslov, V. P. Rozhin, and V. A. Iadov, *Chelovek i ego rabota* (Moscow: Mysl', 1967); A. S. Pashkov and M. N. Mezhevich, eds., *Problemy sotsial'nogo planirovaniia v gorode i regione*, Chelovek i obshchestvo no. 15 (Leningrad: LGU-NIIKSI, 1976); and P. N. Lebedev and V. A. Sukhin, eds., *Sotsial'nye problemy planirovaniia sotsialisticheskogo goroda*, Chelovek i obshchestvo no. 16 (Leningrad: LGU-NIIKSI, 1977).

9. Baranov, *Sotsial'no-demograficheskoe razvitie*, 5–7.

10. V. R. Polozov, interviews, February 27 and March 2, 1984.

11. V. R. Polozov, "Slovo sotsiologii," *Ekonomicheskaia gazeta*, March 31, 1965, p. 8.

12. This viewpoint has demonstrated remarkable staying power and may be seen in works two decades later, such as economist N. I. Chikovskii's 1984 examination of regional manpower reserves, which appeared in the monthly journal of the Leningrad city and regional soviets ("Skol'ko nuzhno rabochikh mest?" *Leningradskaia panorama*, 1984, no. 3:14–16).

13. Despite certain similarities between some of the approaches to labor relations taking shape within Leningrad at this time and the set of American managerial methods generally known as "Taylorism," the emergence of new labor-relations techniques during the 1960s should be viewed primarily as a response of social scientists to local conditions. The profound impact of "Taylorism" on Soviet managerial thought of the 1920s and the rich legacy of Soviet managerial science during those early years of Soviet power were essentially destroyed in the Stalin period. Few if any of the Leningrad participants involved in the development of new approaches to industrial relations during the 1960s had anything but the most limited knowledge of "Taylorism" and its impact on Soviet managerial thought four decades before.

14. For further discussion of the emergence of a human relations style of approach to labor discipline, see Blair A. Ruble, *Soviet Trade Unions: Their Development during the 1970s* (New York: Cambridge University Press, 1981). For a Soviet summary exposition of the "Leningrad" position on these issues, see A. S. Pashkov, ed., *Sovetskoe trudovoe pravo* (Moscow: Iuridicheskaia literatura, 1976).

15. For Soviet discussions of the relationships between these developments, see A. P. Kupaigorodskaia and Z. V. Stepanov, "V bor'be za vypolnenie narodno-khoziaistvennykh planov piatiletki," in V. M. Koval'chuk, D. I. Petrikeev, and Z. V. Stepanov, *Leningrad v vos'moi piatiletke, 1966–1970: Istoriko-sotsial'nyi ocherk* (Leningrad: Nauka—Leningradskoe otdelenie, 1979), 53–96; N. Zenchenko, "Kompleksnoe planirovanie i mestnye planovye organy,"

Sovety deputatov trudiashchikhsia, 1973, no. 7:15–23; M. N. Rutkevich, "Sotsial'noe planirovanie," *Sovetskaia rossiia*, February 3, 1984, p. 1.

16. Marat Nikolaevich Mezhevich, interviews, Leningrad, February 16 and 20, 1984.

17. Baranov, *Sotsial'no-demograficheskoe razvitie*, 34–43, 131–135; "Mestnyi sovet i planirovanie," *Sovety deputatov trudiashchikhsia*, 1969, no. 9:3–6.

18. M. N. Mezhevich, "Sovershenstvovanie upravleniia v gorodakh (k postanovke voprosa)," in Pashkov and Mezhevich, *Problemy sotsial'nogo planirovaniia*, 47–62; and V. Ia. El'meev, B. R. Riashchenko, and E. P. Iudin, *Kompleksnoe planirovanie ekonomicheskogo i sotsial'nogo razvitiia raiona* (Leningrad: Lenizdat, 1972), 7–9.

19. V. R. Polozov, interviews, February 27 and March 2, 1984; A. I. Kirsanov, "Plan ekonomicheskogo i sotsial'nogo razvitie v deistvii," in P. P. Mozhaev, *Za delovoi stil' v partiinoi rabote* (Leningrad: Lenizdat, 1981), 8; V. V. Shul'deshov, "Chuvstvo novogo v partiinoi rabote," in ibid., 127–131; V. S. Kulibanov, *Problemy razvitiia narodnogo khoziaistva severo-zapada SSSR* (Leningrad: Obshchestvo "Znanie"—Leningradskaia organizatsiia, 1980), p. 19.

20. *Profsoiuzy SSSR: Dokumenty i materialy*, vol. 5 (Moscow: Profizdat, 1974), no. 203: 620–624; and A. S. Pashkov and M. N. Mezhevich, "Sotsial'noe planirovanie i territorial'nye aspekty (nekotorye voprosy teorii)," in Pashkov and Mezhevich, *Problemy sotsial'nogo planirovaniia*, 9–21.

21. V. S. Tolstikov, "Rech'" na XXIII s"ezde," in *XXIII s"ezd Kommunisticheskoi partii Sovetskogo Soiuza, 29 marta–9 apreliia, 1966 goda: Stenograficheskii otchet* (Moscow: Polit. lit., 1966), 1:140–148; A. V. Dmitriev, "Rol' Leningradskoi partiinoi organizatsii v razvitii praktiki i teorii sotsial'nogo planirovaniia," in Pashkov and Mezhevich, *Problemy sotsial'nogo planirovaniia*, 21–25.

22. M. N. Zinov'ev, "Sovetskie predpriiatiia kak tsentry vsestoronnego razvitiia rabochikh trudovykh kollektivov," in M. N. Zinov'ev, ed., *Vospitatel'naia rabota partiinykh organizatsii promyshlennykh kollektivov* (Leningrad: Izdatel'stvo Leningradskogo universiteta, 1983), 44.

23. Vasilii Tolstikov's importance in these events is a subject of considerable dispute. Many American analysts view Tolstikov as a significant political actor, many of whose initiatives came to fruition under Romanov. According to this line of reasoning, Romanov benefited politically from having co-opted policies developed by his predecessor. Some Soviet observers, both in the USSR and in emigration, take exception to this interpretation. They portray Tolstikov as a less than effective political figure ("the biggest fool among Leningrad leaders in all the city's history" is how one participant-observer expressed this point of view). Grigorii Romanov, on the other hand, emerges as a hated but highly effective political boss.

Fool or not, Tolstikov was an important political actor during the 1960s and cannot be ignored in the recounting of these events. Many of the policy positions later associated with Romanov took their initial form and gained notoriety during the period of Tolstikov's first secretaryship, even if Tolstikov was not personally responsible for their germination. His role in developing and implementing new planning initiatives may be less than that of Romanov; it was not negligible.

24. V. R. Polozov, "Napravleniia i ob"ekty sotsial'nogo planirovaniia," in Pashkov and Mezhevich, *Problemy sotsial'nogo planirovaniia*, 26–35; and E. I. Vainberg and V. Ia. Liubovnyi, "Plan kompleksnogo ekonomicheskogo i sotsial'nogo razvitiia krupnogo goroda," *Problemy bol'shikh gorodov*, 1980, no. 11:8–9.

25. V. R. Polozov, interviews, February 27 and March 2, 1984. The volume was prepared by numerous prominent Leningrad social scientists, including G. A. Bogdanov, A. P. Dumachev, and I. A. Chuev: G. A. Bogdanov et al., eds., *Kompleksnoe planirovanie sotsial'nogo razvitiia kollektiv predpriiatii Leningrada* (Leningrad: Lenizdat, 1970).

26. V. Ia. El'meev and B. R. Riashchenko, *Planirovanie sotsial'nykh protsessov na predpriiatii* (Leningrad: Lenizdat, 1969); and A. S. Pashkov, V. R. Polozov, and A. V. Dmitriev, *Plan sotsial'nogo razvitiia predpriiatiia* (Moscow: Ekonomika, 1972).

27. D. A. Kerimov, E. S. Kuz'min, A. S. Pashkov, and V. R. Polozov, eds., *Metodika planirovaniia sotsial'nogo kollektiva promyshlennogo predpriiatiia* (Leningrad: Lenizdat, 1970).

28. V. R. Polozov, ed., *Sotsial'noe planirovanie i problema ego effektivnosti* (Leningrad: Nauka—Leningradskoe otdelenie, 1978), 56–58, 73–148.

29. Ibid., 73–148.

30. This hypothesis is suggested by the experience of researchers involved in the famous Hawthorne experiments of the 1920s and 1930s conducted by Elton Mayo and his colleagues from Harvard University at the Hawthorne Works of the Western Electric Company in the United States. Elton Mayo, *The Human Problems of an Industrial Civilization* (Cambridge: Harvard University Graduate School of Business Administration, Division of Research, 1933; reprint, Salem, N.Y.: Ayer Co., 1977); Elton Mayo, *The Social Problems of an Industrial Civilization* (Cambridge: Harvard University Graduate School of Business Administration, Division of Research, 1945; reprint, Salem, N.Y.: Ayer Co., 1977); Fritz J. Roethlisberger and William J. Dickson, *Management and the Worker: An Account of a Research Program Conducted by the Western Electric Company, Hawthorne Works, Chicago* (Cambridge: Harvard University Press, 1939).

31. V. R. Polozov, ed., *Sovershenstvovanie ekonomicheskogo i sotsial'nogo planirovaniia v raione v deviatoi piatiletke* (Leningrad: Lenizdat, 1973); V. A. Mineev, E. P. Murav'ev, and L. M. Chistov, eds., *Problemy planirovaniia narodnogo khoziaistva Leningrada i Leningradskoi oblasti v tsifrakh* (Leningrad: Minvuz RSFSR, LFEI, 1971).

32. E. R. Sarukhanov, *Sotsial'no-ekonomicheskie problemy upravleniia rabochei siloi pri sotsializme* (Leningrad: Izdatel'stvo Leningradskogo universiteta, 1981).

33. Iu. Makarov, "Pervye v Leningrade, pervye v strane," *Sovety deputatov trudiashchikhsia*, 1970, no. 10:55–62.

34. R. S. Bobovikov, ed., *Ekonomicheskie i sotsial'noe planirovanie v masshtabe raione* (Leningrad: Lenizdat, 1973).

35. R. S. Bobovikov, "Kollektivnyi trud," in *ibid.*, 4–8, 3–17.

36. Iu. A. Gerasimov and V. K. Krilov, "Opiraias' na opyt kollektivov," in Bobovikov, *Ekonomicheskie i sotsial'noe planirovanie*, 39–46.

37. E. N. Vitkovskii and Iu. S. Chelpanov, "Navstrechu vseobuchu," in

Bobovikov, *Ekonomicheskie i sotsial'noe planirovanie*, 111–120; V. I. Kozlov, ed., *Ocherki istorii Leningradskoi organizatsii KPSS*, vol. 3, 1945–1985 (Leningrad: Lenizdat, 1985), 260–261.

38. G. V. Romanov, "Kompleksomu ekonomicheskomu i sotsial'nomu planirovaniiu—Partiinuiu zabotu," in G. V. Romanov, *Izbrannye rechi i stat'i* (Moscow: Izdatel'stvo politicheskoi literatury, 1980), 50.

39. V. I. Meleshchenko, *Kompleksnyi plan ekonomicheskogo i sotsial'nogo razvitiia Leningrada i Leningradskoi oblasti v desiatoi piatiletke* (Leningrad: Obshchestvo "Znanie"—Leningradskaia organizatsiia, 1977); V. S. Kulibanov, *Problemy ekonomicheskogo sotsial'nogo razvitiia Leningrada v odinnadtsatoi piatiletke* (Leningrad: Obshchestvo "Znanie"—Leningradskaia organizatsiia, 1981), 5–6.

40. A distinction readily apparent in a comparison of B. V. Ul'ianov, comp., *Praktika sotsialisticheskogo khoziaistvovaniia: Opyt Leningradskikh predpriiatii* (Leningrad: Lenizdat, 1981), with N. S. Zenchenko, ed., *Planirovanie kompleksnogo razvitiia khoziaistva oblasti, kraia ASSR* (Moscow: Ekonomika, 1974).

41. G. A. Zhebit, *Kompleksnoe-planirovanie v upravlenii razvitiem kollektivov i regionov (filosofsko-sotsiologicheskii aspekt)* (Minsk: Nauka i tekhnika, 1981); M. N. Mezhevich, "Formirovanie sistemy pokazateli kompleksnogo plana goroda: Metodologicheskii aspekt," in I. I. Sigov, ed., *Upravlenie razvitiem krupnykh gorodov* (Leningrad: Nauka—Leningradskoe otdelenie, 1985), 107–120; and V. A. Artemov, N. A. Balykov, and Z. I. Kalugina, *Vremya naseleniia goroda: Planirovanie i ispol'zovanie* (Novosibirsk: Nauka—Sibirskoe otdelenie, 1982).

42. A. V. Netsenko, "Biudzhet i balans vremeni naseleniia i ego znachenie dlia razrabotki kompleksnykh planov," in Pashkov and Mezhevich, *Problemy sotsial'nogo planirovaniia*, 97–105.

43. El'meev, Riashchenko, and Iudin, *Kompleksnoe planirovanie*, 3–6.

44. A. I. Kirsanov, "Plan ekonomicheskogo i sotsial'nogo razvitiia v deistvii," in Mozhaev, *Za delovoi stil'*, 11.

45. El'meev, Riashchenko, and Iudin, *Kompleksnoe planirovanie*, 3–6.

46. V. R. Polozov, interviews, February 27 and March 2, 1984.

47. G. V. Romanov, "Rech' tovarishcha G. V. Romanova," in *XXV s"ezd Kommunisticheskoi partii Sovetskogo soiuza, 24 fevralia–5 marta, 1976 goda: Stenograficheskii otchet* (Moscow: Polit. lit., 1976), 1:144–150.

48. V. N. Starinskii, *Territorial'nyi plan kapital'nykh vlozhenii* (Leningrad: Lenizdat, 1980), 6; L. A. Bazilevich, "Vozmozhnosti primeneniia programno-tselevogo podkhoda dlia kompleksnogo planirovaniia ekonomicheskogo i sotsial'nogo razvitiia goroda," in Pashkov and Mezhevich, *Problemy sotsial'nogo planirovaniia*, 83–88.

49. Bazilevich, "Vozmoshnosti primeneniia programmno-tselevogo podkhoda."

50. V. A. Vorotilov and G. D. Platonov, "V interesakh gorozhan: Puti sovershenstvovaniia sotsial'no-bytovogo obsluzhivaniia v Dzerzhinskom raione," *Leningradskaia panorama*, 1983, no. 3:16–19.

51. V. A. Vorotilov, interview, Leningrad, February 15, 1984.

52. N. A. Tolokontsev, N. V. Bazanov, and V. S. Visharenko, "Metodologicheskie voprosy razrabotki ekologicheskikh problem krupnykh gorodov," in

V. A. Vorotilov and G. N. Cherkasov, ed., *Metodologiia sotsial'no-ekonomicheskogo planirovaniia goroda* (Leningrad: Nauka—Leningradskoe otdelenie, 1980), 110–123.

53. Vorotilov and Platonov, "V interesakh gorozhan," 17.

54. See, for example, V. Ia. Notes, "Ni kvartala, ni dvora . . . ," *Stroitel'stvo i arkhitektura Leningrada*, 1970, no. 1:25–26; G. I. Bril'iantshchikov, "Kupchino—Eto Leningrad?" ibid., 1970, no. 1:21–22; G. I. Iakovlev, "Povtoriaemost' eshche ne monotonnost'," ibid., 1975, no. 7:42–43; and M. P. Berezin, "Pochemu neuiutno v novom kvartale?" ibid., 1976, no. 5:28–30.

55. V. M. Khodachek and V. G. Alekseev, *Kompleksnoe razvitie gorodskikh raionov: Kompleksnyi plan ekonomicheskogo i sotsial'nogo razvitiia v deistvii* (Leningrad: Lenizdat, 1980), 72.

56. Ibid., 11.

57. Ibid.; Denis J. B. Shaw, "Planning Leningrad," *Geographical Review* 68, no. 2 (1978):191.

58. Vorotilov and Platonov, "V interesakh gorozhan," 17.

59. Khodachek and Alekseev, *Kompleksnoe razvitie gorodskikh raionov*, 11.

60. Vorotilov and Platonov, "V interesakh gorozhan," 17.

61. Ibid.

62. Ibid.; I. I. Travin, *Material'no-veshchnaia sreda i sotsialisticheskii obraz zhizni* (Leningrad: Nauka—Leningradskoe otdelenie, 1979).

63. L. N. Zaikov, "Povyshat' uroven' ideologicheskoi massovo-politicheskoi raboty," *Leningradskaia pravda*, June 30, 1983, pp. 1–2.

64. G. A. Bukin, *Torgovliia v plane sotsial'no-ekonomicheskogo razvitiia goroda (opyt g. Leningrada)* (Moscow: Ekonomika, 1982), 17.

65. V. I. Kruchina-Bogdanov, "Sluzhba dobrogo nastroeniia: Dostizheniia trudnosti sfery uslugi," *Leningradskaia panorama*, 1983, no. 7:6–7.

66. "Signal po telefonu . . . 01," *Vechernyi Leningrad*, January 9, 1985, p. 3.

67. "O zadachakh mestnykh sovetov narodnykh deputatov Leningradskoi oblasti po vypolneniiu postanovleniia TsK KPSS ob uluchshenii rabotu po okhrane pravoporiadka i usilenii bor'by s pravonarusheniiami: Reshenie Leningradskogo oblastnogo soveta narodnykh deputatov (tret'ia sessiia semnadtsatogo sozyva, 29 sentiabriia, 1980 goda)," *Biulleten' Ispolkoma Leningradskogo oblastnogo soveta*, 1980, no. 11:7–13.

68. See, for example, A. Stepanova, "A u nas vo dvore . . . ," *Leningradskaia pravda*, August 4, 1983, p. 2.

69. O. Ivanov, "Vne Igry," *Vechernyi Leningrad*, July 4, 1984, p. 2.

70. P. Solovei, "Ostal'nye ne pri chem?" *Vechernyi Leningrad*, August 24, 1984, pp. 2–3.

71. "Zolotoi rubezh," *Vechernyi Leningrad*, November 22, 1985, p. 3.

72. V. Ovchinnikov, "Dlia sovetskogo cheloveka," *Leningradskaia pravda*, August 4, 1983, p. 2.

73. V. R. Polozov, Interviews, February 27 and March 2, 1984.

74. Ibid.

75. V. N. Males, E. G. Panchenko, and V. I. Senchenko, *Kompleksnoe planirovanie ekonomicheskogo i sotsial'nogo razvitiia gorodov i raionov* (Moscow: Mysl', 1978), 59.

76. Soviet trade unions, which include in their collective membership approximately 98 percent of the Soviet workforce, are organized according to the "production principle," whereby all workers in a given sector of the economy are eligible to become members of the same union, regardless of profession or rank. This organizational principle creates an organizational double helix of sectorial intraunion committees that parallel the ministerial structure, and regional interunion councils that parallel the Soviet Union's federal structure. These arrangements rendered local union officials subject both to one of the 30-plus branch unions and to various regional interunion councils. In general, the regional interunion councils, which consist of representatives of each of the trade unions operating within a given region, are viewed as serving a parallel function to that of the regional or city party committee and soviet. The All-Union Central Council of Trade Unions, for example, is the unions' partner to the Communist Party's Central Committee and the Soviet state's Supreme Soviet and Council of Ministers. Factory trade union committees represent the lowest rung on the sectorial hierarchy. For further discussion of the organization, function, and performance of Soviet trade unions, see Ruble, *Soviet Trade Unions*.

77. Polozov, *Sotsial'noe planirovanie; i problema ego effektivnosti; Planirovanie sotsial'nogo razvitiia kollektiva predpriiatiia* (Moscow: Profizdat, 1971); V. R. Polozov, ed., *Sotsial'noe planirovanie v otrasli promyshlennosti: Nekotorye voprosy metodologii* (Leningrad: Nauka—Leningradskoe otdelenie, 1981).

78. This observation is based on formal interviews and informal discussions at the USSR Academy of Sciences' Institute of Socioeconomic Problems in Leningrad between February 7 and March 7, 1984.

79. "Sotsial'no-ekonomicheskoe planirovanie i ideologicheskaia rabota: Vsesoiuznaia nauchno-prakticheskaia konferentsiia," *Leningradskaia pravda*, October 1, 1975, pp. 1, 3.

80. V. R. Polozov, interviews, February 27 and March 2, 1984.

81. Romanov, "Kompleksomu ekonomicheskomu i sotsial'nomu planirovaniiu," 47; Kozlov, *Ocherki istorii*, 261.

82. V. R. Polozov, interviews, February 27 and March 2, 1984; M. N. Mezhevich, interviews, February 16 and 20, 1984; Bobovikov, "Kollektivnyi trud," 17.

83. V. R. Polozov, interviews, February 27 and March 2, 1984. For an example of this work, see V. A. Ovchinnikov and B. S. Model', eds., *Usloviia i faktory aktivizatsii obshchestvenno-upravlencheskoi deiatel'nosti trudiashchikhsia v proizvodstvennom kollektive* (Sverdlovsk: UNTs AN SSSR, 1983).

84. G. A. Zhebit, *Pyt' i problemy razrabotki sotsial'no-ekonomicheskikh pasportov kollektivov i regionov* (Minsk: Belorusskii nauchno-issledovatel'skii institut nauchno-tekhnicheskoi informatsii i tekhniko-ekonomicheskikh issledovanii Gosplana BSSR, 1982). Interestingly, Zhebit's work on the "social passport" largely parallels attempts by Western social scientists two decades or more previously to develop "social accounts." Working in response to the policy initiatives of the Johnson administration, the U.S. social science community undertook to improve the efficacy of social measurement, planning, and analytical techniques through the development of a system of social indicators. This effort was led for a number of years by the Social Science Research Council's Committee on Social Indicators. An overview of the SSRC's activities in

this area may be found in a special issue of the council's publication, *Items* 37, no. 4, December 1983.

Although there is no suggestion that Zhebit drew on Western scholarship in general or the work of the SSRC in particular, his monograph demonstrates that he was motivated by a similar concern over the need to improve the efficacy of social measurement, particularly in those areas in which social indicators can influence public policy, at least at the level of local urban planning.

85. Ibid.; Baranov, *Sotsial'no-demograficheskie razvitie*; and Iu. A. Suslov and P. N. Lebedev, eds., *Problemy sotsial'nogo razvitiia krupnykh gorodov*, Chelovek i obshchestvo, no. 19 (Leningrad: LGU-NIIKSI, 1982).

86. N. A. Sukhomlin, "Rukovodstvo sotsial'no-ekonomicheskim razvitiem gorodov," in S. S. Dzarasov and P. A. Kudinov, eds., *Opyt' deiatel'nosti partiinykh organizatsii po rukovodstvu khoziaistvom* (Moscow: Mysl', 1979), 70; Sh. Aldasheva, "Razvitie goroda—Problema raznostoronnaia," *Sovety deputatov trudiashchikhsia*, 1973, no. 9:61–64; B. P. Shubniakov, ed., *Sotsiologicheskie issledovaniia i sotsial'noe planirovanie—Sostavnye chasti upravleniia ideologicheskim protsessom (Iz opyta sotsiologicheskoi razrabotki problemy "svoboda, otvestvennost', upravlenie")* (Iaroslavl': Iaroslavskii gosudarstvennyi universitet, 1976); and Males, Panchenko, and Senchenko, *Kompleksnoe planirovanie*, 52, 65.

87. T. I. Zaslavskaia et al., *Sotsial'no-demograficheskoe razvitie sela* (Moscow: Statistika, 1980).

88. "Ob opyte raboty sovetov narodnykh deputatov goroda Leningrada i Leningradskoi oblasti po obespecheniiu kompleksnogo ekonomicheskogo i sotsial'nogo razvitiia na svoie territori: Postanovlenie Prezidiuma Verkhovnogo Soveta SSSR. 4 maia, 1982 g.," in K. M. Bogoliubov, P. G. Mishunin, E. Z. Razumov, Ia. V. Storozhev, and N. V. Tropkin, eds., *Spravochnik partiinogo rabotnika, 1983*, no. 23 (Moscow: Polit. lit., 1983), 514–517.

89. William J. Conyngham, *The Modernization of Soviet Industrial Management* (New York: Cambridge University Press, 1982), 162–174.

90. This assertion was made orally a number of times by Leningrad social scientists at the Institute of Socioeconomic Problems during formal interviews and informal discussions held between February 15 and March 7, 1984.

91. Males, Panchenko, and Senchenko, *Kompleksnoe planirovanie*, 101–109; K. Kas'ka and Iu. Ennuste, eds., *O modeliakh normativnogo prognozirovaniia sotsial'no-ekonomicheskogo razvitiia regiona* (Tallin: Institut ekonomiki AN Est SSA, 1980).

92. G. V. Osipov, *Pokazateli sotsial'nogo razvitiia i planirovaniia* (Moscow: Nauka, 1980).

93. O. N. Ianitskii, "K probleme upravleniia gorodom kak sistemoi," in Nauchnyi sovet AN SSSR po problemu konkretnykh sotsial'nykh issledovanii, Sovetskaia sotsiologicheskaia assotsiatsiia, Otdel konkretnykh sotsiologicheskikh issledovanii, Institut filosofii AN SSSR, *Seriia materialy i soobshcheniia kolichestvennye metody v sotsial'nykh issledovaniiakh: Materialy soveshcheniia, proshedshego v g. Sukhumi, 17–20 apreliia 1967*, Informatsionnyi biulleten' no. 8 (Moscow: SSA, 1968), 116–126.

Despite the importance attached to the Sukhumi conference by some Leningrad social scientists, other participants found it less than satisfying. One attendee now recalls it as "one of the most boring [conferences] in my life—

except for the Georgian food, everything was awful." Even if this commentator's recollection accurately reflects the quality of both the intellectual and dining menus at Sukhumi, no one denies that systems approaches were becoming widespread in Soviet social science at the time the conference was held.

94. Baranov, *Sotsial'no-demograficheskoe razvitie*, 25–33, 65–66.

95. M. N. Mezhevich, *Sotsial'noe razvitie i gorod: Filosofskie i sotsiologicheskie aspekty* (Leningrad: Nauka—Leningradskoe otdelenie, 1979), 6–36.

96. A. V. Dmitriev and M. N. Mezhevich, eds., *Gorod: Problemy sotsial'nogo razvitiia* (Leningrad: Nauka—Leningradskoe otdelenie, 1982); E. S. Demidenko, *Demograficheskie problemy i perspektivy bol'shikh gorodov (urbanizatsiia pri sotsializme)* (Moscow: Statistika, 1980).

97. S. V. Uspenskii, *Planirovanie ekonomicheskogo i sotsial'nogo razvitiia sistem rasseleniia i poselenii* (Leningrad: Nauka—Leningradskoe otdelenie, 1981), 4–6.

98. "Kak ty budesh', gorod?" *Vechernyi Leningrad*, October 4, 1984, p. 2.

99. I. Sigov, "Aktual'nye problemy issledovaniia krupnykh gorodov," *Obshchestvennye nauki*, 1981, no. 6:21–30. Although Sigov's views carried considerable political weight at the time, many of his colleagues have privately questioned his integrity as a scholar. In January 1987, criticism of Sigov spilled into the press when *Leningradskaia pravda* vigorously attacked his management of the institute (N. Korkonosenko, "Nedelovye igry: Pochemu oni protsvetaiot v stenakh akademicheskogo instituta?" *Leningradskaia pravda*, January 7, 1987, pp. 2–3). None of these subsequent events detract from the authoritative nature of Sigov's remarks cited here.

100. Ann Goodman and Geoffrey Schleifer, "The Soviet Labor Market in the 1980s," in U.S. Congress, Joint Economic Committee, *Soviet Economy in the 1980s: Problems and Prospects* (Washington: Government Printing Office, 1982), pt 2:323–348.

101. Beginning in 1967 and with the full support of the USSR Council of Ministers, plant managers at the Shchekino Combine began to release redundant labor from factory payrolls. For recent accounts of the Shchekino experiment, see Peter Rutland, "The Shchekino Method and the Struggle to Raise Labour Productivity in the Soviet Union," *Soviet Studies* 36, no. 3 (1984):345–365; and Henry Norr, "Shchekino: Another Look," *Soviet Studies* 38, no. 2 (1986):141–169.

Conclusion

1. Jerry Hough, *The Soviet Prefects: The Local Party Organs in Industrial Decision-Making* (Cambridge: Harvard University Press, 1969).

2. Sidney G. Tarrow, *Between Center and Periphery: Grassroots Politicians in Italy and France* (New Haven: Yale University Press, 1977).

3. Ibid., 2–4.

4. Ibid., 63–64.

5. Ibid., 69.

6. Ibid., 7–8.

7. A point developed further in Paul E. Peterson, *City Limits* (Chicago: University of Chicago Press, 1981).

8. Norton E. Long, "The Local Community as an Ecology of Games," *American Journal of Sociology* 64, no. 3 (November 1958):251–261.

9. For example, see Katherine L. Bradbury, Anthony Downs, and Kenneth A. Small in *Urban Decline and the Future of American Cities* (Washington, D.C.: Brookings Institution, 1982).

10. David Harvey, *Consciousness and the Urban Experience: Studies in the History and Theory of Capitalist Urbanization* (Baltimore: Johns Hopkins University Press, 1985); David Harvey, *The Urbanization of Capital: Studies in the History and Theory of Capitalist Urbanization* (Baltimore: Johns Hopkins University Press, 1985).

11. A point made by Charles E. Lindblom, *Politics and Markets: The World's Political-Economic Systems* (New York: Basic Books, 1977), 66–68.

12. Janos Kornai, *Economics of Shortage* (Amsterdam and New York: North-Holland, 1980); Janos Kornai, " 'Hard' and 'Soft' Budget Constraints," *Acta Oeconomica* 25, no. 3–4 (1980):231–246. For a concise summary of Kornai's work, see Herbert S. Levine's review of this volume in *Journal of Economic Literature* 21 (March 1983):95–98.

13. This finding resembles public-choice analysis of the behavior of bureaucratic elites in market economies.

14. Jacek Tarkowski, "Local Influences in a Centralized System: Resources, Local Leadership and Horizontal Integration in Poland," in Sidney Tarrow, Peter A. Katzenstein and Luigi Graziano, eds., *Territorial Politics in Industrial Nations* (New York: Praeger Publishers, 1978), 213–244.

Appendix A

1. David T. Cattell, *Leningrad: A Case Study of Soviet Urban Government* (New York: Frederick A. Praeger, 1968); and Max Ethan Mote, "Leningrad Municipal Administration: Structure and Functions" (Ph.D. dissertation, University of Washington, 1966). Changes in the structure of the Soviet government were proposed at the Nineteenth Conference of the Communist Party in June 1988 ("XIX Vsesoiuznaia konferentsiia KPSS: Informatsionnoe soobshchenie," *Leningradskaia pravda*, June 29–July 2, 1988, p. 1). The Conference resolutions led to changes in the Soviet Constitution later in 1988, to be implemented in 1989 and 1990. These reforms include multiple candidate elections as well as a restructuring of various state institutions. Further legislative action will be required before the reforms can be implemented on the local level. Accordingly, a new law on the local soviets is expected as this book goes to press. Materials relevant to the changes in the national constitution may be found in "Proekt: Zakon Soiuza Sovetskikh Sotsialisticheskikh Respublik ob izmeneniiakh i dopolneniiakh Konstitutsii (Osnovnogo Zakona) SSSR," *Leningradskaia pravda*, October 22, 1988, pp. 1–2; "Proekt: Zakon Soiuza Sovetskikh Sotsialisticheskikh Respublik o vyborakh narodnykh deputatov SSSR," ibid., October 23, 1988 pp. 1–3; "Zakon Soiuza Sovetskikh Sotsialisticheskikh Respublik ob izmenen-

iiakh i dopolneniiakh Konstitutsii (Osnovnogo Zakona SSSR)," ibid., December 3, 1988, pp. 1–2; and "Zakon Soiuza Sovetskikh Sotsialisticheskikh Respublik o vyborakh narodnykh deputatov SSSR," ibid., December 4, 1988, pp. 1–3.

2. Robert Sharlet, *The New Soviet Constitution of 1977: Analysis and Text* (Brunswick, Ohio: King's Court Communication, 1978).

3. Everett M. Jacobs, "Introduction: The Organizational Framework of Soviet Local Government," in Everett M. Jacobs, ed., *Soviet Local Politics and Government* (London and Boston: George Allen & Unwin, 1983), 4–6.

4. A point made by Ronald Hill in his "The Development of Soviet Local Government Since Stalin's Death," in Jacobs, *Soviet Local Politics,* and illustrated by works of such Soviet authors as I. N. Ananov, *Sistema organov gosudarstvennogo upravleniia v Sovetskoi sotsialisticheskoi federatsii* (Moscow: Izdatel'stvo Akademii nauk SSSR, 1951).

5. Donna Bahry, "Political Inequality and Public Policy among the Soviet Republics," in Daniel Nelson ed., *Communism and the Politics of Inequalities* (Lexington, Mass.: D. C. Heath & Co., 1988), 109–127; Philip D. Stewart, Roger Blough, and James N. Warhola, "Soviet Regions and Economic Priorities: A Study in Politburo Perceptions," *Soviet Union/Union Soviétique* 11, pt. 1 (1984):1–30.

6. *Leningrad: Entsiklopedicheskii spravochnik* (Moscow and Leningrad: Bol'shaia Sovetskaia entsiklopediia, 1957), 411–412.

7. N. Dewitt, "Reorganization of Science and Research in the USSR," *Science* 133, no. 3469 (June 23, 1961):1981–1990; "K 250-letiiu Akademii nauk SSSR," *Vestnik statistiki,* 1974, no. 4:85–95.

8. G. I. Marchuk, "Sibirskomu otdeleniiu Akademii nauk SSSR— Dvadtsat' let," in *Oktiabr' i nauka* (Moscow: Nauka, 1977), 635–656.

9. Blair A. Ruble, "The Expansion of Soviet Science," *Knowledge: Creation, Diffusion, Utilization* 2, no. 4 (June, 1981):529–553.

10. "Povyshat' otdachu nauchnykh uchrezhdenii," *Leningradskaia pravda,* March 31, 1983, p. 1; and S. Grachev and I. A. Glebov, "Vybor tseli," ibid., May 29, 1983, p. 2.

11. L. T. Krivenko, "Rukovodstvo verkhovnykh sovetov i ikh prezidiumov deiatel'nost'iu nizhestoiashchikh organov gosudarstvennoi vlasti," in V. E. Brazhnikov, R. K. Davydov, and L. T. Krivenko, eds., *XXVI s"ezd KPSS i voprosy rukovodstva v sisteme sovetov narodnykh deputatov* (Kiev: Naukova Dumka, 1983), 100–128; P. V. Panov and V. D. Sorokin, *XXVI s"ezd KPSS i aktual'nye voprosy raboty mestnykh sovetov* (Leningrad: Lenizdat, 1982), 3–20.

12. Cattell, *Leningrad;* and Mote, "Leningrad Municipal Administration"; Panov and Sorokin, *XXVI s"ezd KPSS,* 20–31.

13. Sharlet, *New Soviet Constitution of 1977,* 104.

14. Ibid., 107.

15. Ibid., 123–124.

16. Ibid., 123; Panov and Sorokin, *XXVI s"ezd KPSS,* 111–124.

17. Sharlet, *New Soviet Constitution of 1977,* 124.

18. Ibid.

19. V. E. Brazhnikov, "Konstitutsionnye osnovy rukovodstva v sisteme sovetov narodnykh deputatov," in Brazhnikov, Davydov, and Krivenko, *XXVI*

s"ezd KPSS, 9–32; Darrell Slider, "More Power to the Soviets? Reform and Local Government in the Soviet Union," *British Journal of Political Science* 16, no. 4 (October 1986):495–515.

20. R. K. Davydov, "Sviazi rukovodstva v sisteme mestnykh sovetov narodnykh deputatov," in Brazhnikov, Davydov, and Krivenko, *XXVI s"ezd KPSS*, 150–152; I. I. Sigov, "Sovershenstvovanie struktury plana kompleksnogo razvitiia goroda," in I. I. Sigov, ed., *Upravlenie razvitiem krupnykh gorodov* (Leningrad: Nauka—Leningradskoe otdelenie, 1985), 81–83.

21. A. I. Luk'ianov et al., eds., *Sovety narodnykh deputatov: Spravochnik* (Moscow: Politizdat, 1984), 156–157.

22. "Postanovlenie plenuma TsK KPSS o dal'neishem uluchshenii raboty sovetov narodnykh deputatov," *Leningradskaia pravda*, April 11, 1984, p. 1; "Vazhnye zadachi sovetov," ibid., June 20, 1984, pp. 1, 3; "Otvetstvennaia missiia sovetov," ibid., June 21, 1984, p. 1; I. A. Nosikov, "Khoroshet' gorodu Lenina," *Leningradskaia panorama*, 1984, no. 11:4–7.

23. Mote, "Leningrad Municipal Administration," 81–116; I. M. Solodovnikov, *Mestnye sovety: Koordinatsiia i ee effektivnost'* (Moscow: Sovetskaia Rossiia, 1980), 9–10.

24. Sharlet, *New Soviet Constitution of 1977*, 103.

25. Luk'ianov et al., *Sovety narodnykh deputatov*, 161.

26. V. M. Khodachek and A. G. Alekseev, *Kompleksnoe razvitie gorodskikh raionov: Kompleksnyi plan ekonomicheskogo i sotsial'nogo razvitiia v deistvii* (Leningrad: Lenizdat, 1980), 5.

27. Solodovnikov, *Mestnye sovety*, 16–18; A. S. Gruzinov and V. P. Riumin, *Gorod: Upravlenie problemy* (Leningrad: Lenizdat, 1977), 50–55; Cattell, *Leningrad*, 27–29.

28. E. V. Kukushkin, "Okhrana gorodskimi sovetami okruzhaiushchei prirodnoi sredy," in G. V. Barabashev, ed., *Rol' mestnykh sovetov v ekonomicheskom i sotsial'nom razvitii gorodov* (Moscow: Izdatel'stvo MGU, 1983), 147–176.

29. Mote, "Leningrad Municipal Administration," 370–448. Voters may vote against any single candidate. Perhaps as many as 5 to 10 percent of the eligible voters abstain from participation in voting (see Rasma Karklins, "Soviet Elections Revisited: Voter Abstention in Non-competitive Voting," *American Political Science Review* 80, no. 2 [June 1986]:449–469). The practical impact of Mikhail Gorbachev's January 1987 proposals for the introduction of multi-candidate elections is only beginning to become apparent as this volume goes to press ("Gorbachev, Citing Party's Failures, Demands Change," *New York Times*, January 28, 1987, pp. A1, A8).

30. Data on professional background are from "Spisok deputatov Leningradskogo gorodskogo soveta narodnykh deputatov eizbrannykh, 24 Fevralia 1985 goda," *Vechernyi Leningrad*, February 27, 1985, pp. 2–4. Data on age structure, sex, and party membership are from "Soobshchenie ob itogakh vyborov v Leningradskii gorodskii sovet narodnykh deputatov, 24 Fevralia 1985 goda," ibid., p. 1.

31. This point is developed further in Jeffrey Hahn, *Soviet Grassroots: Citizen Participation in Local Soviet Government* (Princeton: Princeton University Press, 1988).

32. The 1985 election results and regional soviet reorganization were

announced in two articles ("V obstanovke edinodushniia: Soobshchenie ob itogakh vyborov v Leningradskii oblastnoi sovet narodnykh deputatov 24 fevralia 1985 goda," *Leningradskaia pravda*, February 27, 1985, p. 1; and "Pervaia sessiia Leningradskogo oblastnogo soveta," ibid., March 15, 1985, p. 2). However, in a departure from long-standing custom, the composition of soviet departments, administrations, and standing commissions was not announced at that time. Therefore, the calculations for the number of such bodies are based on the announcements following the previous local election in 1982 ("Pervaia sessiia Leningradskogo oblastnogo soveta," ibid., July 6, 1982, p. 1).

33. These figures have remained unchanged since at least the 1960s; see Cattell, *Leningrad*, 27–37. The 1985 election results and city soviet reorganization were, similarly, announced in two articles ("Soobshchenie ob itogakh vyborov v Leningradskii gorodskoi sovet narodnykh deputatov 24 fevralia, 1985 god," *Leningradskaia pravda*, February 27, 1985, p. 1; also in *Vechernyi Leningrad*, February 27, 1985, p. 1; and "Pervaia sessiia Leningradskogo gorodskogo soveta," *Leningradskaia pravda*, March 12, 1985, p. 4; also appearing as "Sessiia gorodskogo soveta," *Vechernyi Leningrad*, March 12, 1985, p. 1). More recent 1987 data for the city soviet administrative structure may be found in "Sostav Leningradskogo komiteta KPSS," *Leningradskaia pravda*, December 22, 1985, p. 1.

34. "Uskoriaia obnovlenie, rasshiriaia glasnost': Pervaia sessiia Leningradskogo Soveta narodnykh deputatov dvadtsatogo sozyva," *Leningradskaia pravda*, July 15, 1987, pp. 1, 3; "Sessiia Lengorsoveta reshila," ibid., July 17, 1987, p. 1. Extensive reorganization of the executive committee and other administrative agencies may take place during interelection periods as well. Such reorganization frequently takes the form of personnel transfers (see, for example, "Sessiia gorodskogo soveta," *Vechernyi Leningrad*, March 12, 1985, p. 4; "Leningrad v dvenadtsatii piatiletki: Sessiia gorodskogo soveta," *Leningradskaia pravda*, July 13, 1986, p. 1; and "Sessiia Leningradskogo gorodskogo soveta narodnykh deputatov," ibid., December 21, 1986, p. 1).

35. "Soobshchenie ob itogakh vyborov v raionnye, gorodskie (raionnogo podchineniia) i poselkovye sovety narodnykh deputatov po Leningradu 24 fevralia 1985 god," *Leningradskaia pravda*, February 24, 1985, p. 1. The information on the district soviet on Vasil'evskii Island is found in V. Ivanov, "Sil'nyi aktivom," ibid., June 30, 1984, p. 2. Please note that this description relates to the period under review in this study and does not reflect changes which may take place in light of Mikhail Gorbachev's January 1987 address in which he called for competitive elections within party and state institutions ("Gorbachev, Citing Party's Failures, Demands Change," *New York Times*, January 28, 1987, pp. A1, A8).

36. "V sostav izbiratel'nyi komissii," *Leningradskaia pravda*, December 12, 1984, p. 1.

37. See the articles usually entitled "Kandidaty naroda," which appeared on almost a daily basis in *Leningradskaia pravda* from December 27, 1984, until January 22, 1985.

38. See the articles entitled "Registratsiia kandidatov v deputaty," which appeared on almost a daily basis in *Leningradskaia pravda* from January 23 until February 2, 1985.

39. See, for example, "V Leningradskoi oblastnoi izbiratel'noi komissii," *Leningradskaia pravda*, February 6, 1985, p. 1.

40. Appearing under such titles as "Vysokoe doverie naroda," "Doverie—dostoinym," and "V obstanovke edinodushniia," which appeared almost on a daily basis in *Leningradskaia pravda* from January 23 until February 21, 1985.

41. "Predvybornye sobraniia trudiashchikhsia: Po puti sovershenstvovaniia razvitogo sotsializma po puti sozdaniia i mira," *Leningradskaia pravda*, February 23, 1985, p. 1.

42. In the case of the Leningrad regional soviet, see "Spisok deputatov Leningradskogo oblastnogo Soveta narodnykh deputatov vosemnadtsatogo sozyva, izbirannykh 24 fevralia 1985 goda," *Leningradskaia pravda*, February 27, 1985, pp. 2–3.

43. Luk'ianov et al., *Sovety narodnykh deputatov*, 111–119.

44. Ibid., 127–135. Mote, "Leningrad Municipal Administration," 420–427. For some illustrative examples of such instructions, see A. Kucheriavenko, "Doma, ATS, magaziny . . . ," *Vechernyi Leningrad*, February 20, 1984, p. 1; "Eto nasha sovetskaia demokratiia," ibid., March 1, 1984, p. 3; and "Vlast' Sovetskaia—Podlinno narodnaia," ibid., March 3, 1984, p. 4. For further discussion, see Hahn, *Soviet Grassroots*.

45. Luk'ianov et al., *Sovety narodnykh deputatov*, 128–130.

46. V. V. Domarev, *Nakazy izbiratelei* (Leningrad: Lenizdat, 1972).

47. Solodovnikov, *Mestnye sovety*, 66–75.

48. M. P. Shchetina, *Deputat na sessii sovetov* (Moscow: Iuridicheskaia literatury, 1980).

49. A. I. Luk'ianov et al., *Sovety narodnykh deputatov*, 127; Panov and Sorokin, *XXVI s"ezd KPSS*, 141–143.

50. Jeffrey W. Hahn, "Conceptualizing Political Participation in the USSR; Two Decades of Debate" (Paper presented at the Fifteenth Annual Meeting of the Northeastern Political Science Association, Philadelphia, November 17–19, 1984).

51. Theodore H. Friedgut, *Political Participation in the USSR* (Princeton: Princeton University Press, 1979).

52. Ronald J. Hill, *Soviet Political Elites: The Case of Tiraspol* (New York: St. Martin's Press, 1977).

53. Luk'ianov et al., *Sovety narodnykh deputatov*, 185–198; Mote, "Leningrad Municipal Administration," 116–139.

54. Luk'ianov et al., *Sovety narodnykh deputatov*, 185–187.

55. Ibid., 187–191; Z. Korin, "Ispolkom i deputaty," *Sovety deputatov trudiashchikhsia*, 1973, no. 8:99–104.

56. Luk'ianov et al., *Sovety narodnykh deputatov*, 185.

57. Cattell, *Leningrad*, 48–57; Mote, "Leningrad Municipal Administration," 81–116.

58. M. Karpovich, "Chlen Ispolkoma," *Sovety deputatov trudiashchikhsia*, 1976, no. 3:35–40.

59. M. Kiselev and V. Sivov, "Iuridicheskaia pomoshch' deputatam," *Sovety deputatov trudiashchikhsia*, 1974, no. 12:89–92.

60. Louise I. Shelley, *Lawyers in Soviet Work Life* (New Brunswick, N.J.: Rutgers University Press, 1984), 137.

61. A. I. Luk'ianov et al., *Sovety narodnykh deputatov*, 192–209; Panov and Sorokin, *XXVI s"ezd KPSS*, 183–216. For a quite different view of these institutions, see Zvi Gitelman's study based on interviews with Soviet émigrés: "Working the Soviet System: Citizens and Urban Bureaucracy," in Henry W. Morton and Robert C. Stuart, eds., *The Contemporary Soviet City* (Armonk, NY: M. E. Sharpe, 1984), 221–243.

62. "Pervaia sessiia Leningradskogo gorodskogo soveta," *Leningradskaia pravda*, July 3, 1982, p.1; *Narodnoe khoziaistvo Leningrada i Leningradskoi oblasti v desiatoi piatiletke: Statisticheskii sbornik* (Leningrad: Lenizdat, 1981), 68.

63. V. Iunevichius, "Postoiannye komissii soveta i komissii pri ispolkoma," *Sovety deputatov trudiashchikhsia*, 1976, no. 8:96–100.

64. Ibid.

65. M. Melianets, "Raiispolkom i postoiannye komissii," *Sovety deputatov trudiashchikhsia*, 1976, no. 10:79–85; N. Pirozhko, "Postoiannye komissii i obispolkom," ibid., 1976, no. 12:48–54.

66. Jerry F. Hough, "USSR: The Urban Units," in Donald C. Rowat, ed., *International Handbook on Local Government Reorganization: Contemporary Developments* (Westport, Conn.: Greenwood Press, 1980), 343–353.

67. I. I. Sigov, "Sovershenstvovanie struktury plana kompleksnogo razvitiia goroda," in Sigov, *Upravlenie razvitiem krupnykh gorodov*, 102–103; and A. P. Koshelev, L. A. Krylova, and M. N. Mezhevich, "Upravlenie sotsial'nym razvitiem krupnogo goroda: metodologicheskie voprosy," in ibid., 180–191.

68. Luk'ianov et al., *Sovety narodnykh deputatov*, 42–44; Slider, "More Power to the Soviets?"

69. Hahn, *Soviet Grassroots*.

70. Ronald J. Hill, *Soviet Politics: Political Science and Reform* (White Plains, N.Y.: M. E. Sharpe, 1980), 65–69.

71. Sharlet, *New Soviet Constitution of 1977*; Hahn, *Soviet Grassroots*.

72. Hahn, *Soviet Grassroots*; Slider, "More Power to the Soviets?"

73. G. B. Poliak, *Biudzhet goroda* (Moscow: Finansy, 1978), 7–8; Cattell, *Leningrad*; Henry J. Raimondo and Robert C. Stuart, "Financing Soviet Cities," in Morton and Stuart, *Contemporary Soviet City*, 45–64; and Carol W. Lewis, "The Economic Functions of Local Soviets," in Jacobs, *Soviet Local Politics*, 48–66.

74. Poliak, *Biudzhet goroda*, 8, 38.

75. Ibid., 17, 48.

76. Ia. Stepanov, "Kak uluchshit' biudzhetnuiu rabotu," *Sovety deputatov trudiashchikhsia*, 1971, no. 11:93–99.

77. V. Kozlova, "Planirovanie," *Sovety deputatov trudiashchikhsia*, 1969, no. 3:54–60.

78. R. K. Davydov, "Sviazi rukovodstva v sisteme mestnykh sovetov narodnykh deputatov," in Brazhnikov, Davydov, and Krivenko, eds., *XXVI s"ezd KPSS*, 129–166.

79. V. V. Finagin, "Kharakteristikh khozraschetnykh otnoshenii," in V. K. Mamutov et al., eds., *Ekonomiko-pravovye problemy upravleniia gorodom (Sbornik nauchnykh trudov)* (Donetsk: IEP AN UkSSR, 1983), 21–37.

80. Cattell, *Leningrad*, 74–80.

81. The general proportion between locally generated revenues and transfer payments in Leningrad has remained essentially unchanged since the late 1960s. See ibid.; and Mote, "Leningrad Municipal Administration," 163–186.

82. Cattell, *Leningrad,* 38–48; and Mote, "Leningrad Municipal Administration."

83. G. V. Romanov, "Leninskie printsipy partiinogo rukovodstva khoziaistvennym stroitel'stvom," in A. A. Khromov and B. F. Shilov, comps., *Voprosy partiinogo stroitel'stva* (Leningrad: Lenizdat, 1965), 427–455.

84. A. N. Gerasimov, "Kontsentratsii proizvodstva—Povsednevnoe vnimanie," in B. K. Alekseev and V. G. Zubarev, eds., *Partiinoe rukovodstvo—Na uroven' sovremennykh trebovanii: Iz opyta raboty Leningradskoi partiinoi organizatsii* (Leningrad: Lenizdat, 1978), 84–112.

85. T. I. Zhdanova, "Rabochemu klassu—Dostoinoe popolnenie," and G. S. Pakhamova, "Rukovodstvo tvorcheskimi soiuzami i uchrezhdeniiami kul'tury," in B. K. Alekseev and V. G. Zubarev, eds., *Partiinoe rukovodstvo,* 201–223 and 253–280.

86. "O nomenklature dolzhnostei rukovodiashchikh i otvetstvennykh rabotnikov sistemy Ispolkoma Lensoveta," *Biulleten' Ispolnitel'nogo komiteta Leningradskogo gorodskogo Soveta narodnykh deputatov,* 1980, no. 14:17–18. The list was approved by a resolution of the executive committee of the Leningrad city soviet on March 22, 1976.

87. For further general discussion of the *nomenklatura* personnel system, see Rolf H. W. Theen, "Party and Bureaucracy," in Erik P. Hoffman and Robbin F. Laird, eds., *The Soviet Polity in the Modern Era* (New York: Aldine Publishing Co., 1984), 131–165.

88. Joel C. Moses, "The Impact of *Nomenklatura* on Soviet Regional Elite Recruitment," *Soviet Union/Union Soviétique* 8, pt. 1 (1981):62–102.

89. Cynthia S. Kaplan, "The Communist Party of the Soviet Union and Local Policy Implementation," *Journal of Politics* 45, no. 1 (1983):2–27.

90. For further discussion of this point, see Appendix B.

91. Numbering 107 full, 39 candidate, and 23 auditing commission members.

92. This use of the concept of "rules of the contest" is borrowed from Wallace Sayre and Herbert Kaufman's classic study of metropolitan politics in New York: *Governing New York City: Politics in the Metropolis* (New York: W. W. Norton & Co., 1965).

Appendix B

1. For further discussion of this reform effort, see Barbara Ann Chotiner, *Khrushchev's Party Reform: Coalition Building and Institutional Innovation* (Westport, Conn.: Greenwood Press, 1984).

2. "Nikolai Iakovlevich Suslov" (obituary), *Pravda,* September 8, 1982, p. 3.

3. "Plenum Leningradskogo obkoma KPSS," *Leningradskaia pravda,* June 22, 1983, p. 1.

4. "Plenum Leningradskogo gorkoma KPSS," *Leningradskaia pravda*, July 9, 1985, p. 1; "Informatsionnoe soobshchenie o Plenume TsK KPSS," ibid., July 2, 1985, p. 1.

Appendix C

1. *Bol'shaia sovetskaia entsiklopediia*, 3d ed. (Moscow: Sovetskaia cntsiklopediia, 1970/1978), 7:162–163.

2. Blair A. Ruble (with the assistance of Mark H. Teeter, Rosemary Stuart, Eleanor B. Sutter, and Mary Giles), *Soviet Research Institutes Project*, vol. 1, *The Policy Sciences* (Washington, D.C.: International Communication Agency, 1980), 485–595.

3. James H. Bater, *The Soviet City* (London: Edward Arnold, 1980), 130–132.

4. For example, 720 general plans were completed during the period 1945–1977 in the RSFSR alone, of which 370 have been fundamentally revised more than once. During this period Novokuznetsk had eight plans, Volgograd—six (M. N. Mezhevich, "Upravlenie razvitiem gorodov: potrebnosti i real'nosti," in P. N. Lebedev and V. A. Sukhin, eds., *Sotsial'nye problemy planirovaniia sotsialisticheskogo goroda*, Chelovek i obshchestvo no. 16 [Leningrad: LGU-NIIKSI, 1977], 54–55). Such data suggest that attainment of plan goals may be elusive, given the number of times some city plans have been revised.

5. "Pervaia sessiia Leningradskogo gorodskogo soveta," *Leningradskaia pravda*, July 3, 1982, p. 1.

6. N. V. Baranov, *Glavnyi arkhitektor goroda: Tvorcheskaia i organizatsionnaia deiatel'nost'*, 2d ed. (Moscow: Stroiizdat, 1979).

7. Among these agencies are Lengiprogor, Lengiproproekt, Lenmetroprotrans, Promstroiproekt, and Lenzhilproekt.

8. E. N. Koshelev, "Sokrashchaia nomenklatura izdelii," *Stroitel'stvo i arkhitektura Leningrada*, 1981, no. 4:18–19; S. A. Lobko, "Kotel'naia na kryshe," ibid., 1980, no. 10:30–31.

9. S. B. Speranskii, "Aktivnost' pozitsii," *Stroitel'stvo i arkhitektura Leningrada*, 1981, no. 4:3; V. M. Tareev, "Glavnaia zadacha zodchikh," ibid., 1981, no. 4:4–7.

10. A. A. Sizov, "Glavleningradstroiiu—Desiat' let," *Stroitel'stvo i arkhitektura Leningrada*, 1965, no. 4:2–6; I. A. Bartenev, *Zodchie i stroiteli Leningrada* (Leningrad: Lenizdat, 1963), 274.

11. Among these agencies are Glavleningradinzhstroi, Leningradstroi, Lenmetrostroi, Lenuniverstroi, Fasadremstroi and Lenzaptransstroi.

12. *Leningrad: Entsiklopedicheskii spravochnik* (Moscow and Leningrad: Bol'shaia Sovetskaia entsiklopediia, 1957), 412–414; B. S. Ugarov, "Akademiia znateishikh khudochestv," *Leningradskaia panorama*, 1983, no. 1:24–29.

13. V. I. Il'in and A. S. Kirovov, "Spetsialist sovremennoi formatsii," *Leningradskaia panorama*, 1982, no. 5:11–14; B. V. Morav'ev, A. V. Badialov, and G. G. Kel'kh, "Istoki dobrykh traditsii," ibid., 15–17.

14. See, for example, Herbert Kaufman's study of state and federal foresters in the United States: *The Forest Rangers: A Study in Administrative Behavior* (Baltimore: Johns Hopkins University Press, 1960).

15. "Gosudarstvennaia inspektsiia po okhrane pamiatnikov," *Pamiatniki arkhitektury Leningrada* (Leningrad: Stroiizdat—Leningradskoe otdelenie, 1975); V. A. Kamenskii and A. I. Naumov, *Leningrad: Gradostroitel'nye problemy razvitiia* (Leningrad: Stroiizdat—Leningradskoe otdelenie, 1977); K. A. Pavlova, "Okhraniaetsia gosudarstvom pamiatniki Sovetskoe arkhitektura v Leningrade," *Stroitel'stvo i arkhitektura Leningrada*, 1980, no. 12, 20–25; S. P. Shmakov, "Traditsii: dukh, a ne bukva," ibid., 1981, no. 10:20–22.

Glossary

all-union ministry   The single, centralized agency of the USSR Council of Ministers responsible for management of an economic branch throughout the Soviet Union, usually in heavy industry or other security-related sector, such as the Ministry of Civil Aviation, the Ministry of Defense, and the Ministry of Heavy and Transport Machine Building.

autonomous republic (*avtonomnaia respublika*)   The autonomous soviet socialist republic (ASSR) forms the second tier of the Soviet Union's nationality-based regional units, subordinate only to the union republic. Sixteen of the country's 20 autonomous republics are located within the Russian Republic (RSFSR).

Central Committee (*Tsentral'nyi komitet*)   The senior agency of the Communist Party of the Soviet Union, consisting of representatives of various subordinate party organizations elected by a national party congress convened once every five years.

city party committee (*gorkom*)   The senior Communist Party agency within a city, consisting of representatives of various subordinate party organizations elected by a city party conference convened once every two to three years.

Communist International (Comintern)   A Soviet-sponsored international organization intended to support the activities of foreign Communist parties. The Comintern was established in 1919 and disbanded in 1943 as a gesture of cooperation with the Soviet Union's wartime allies.

council (*sovet*)   The primary governmental institution at a given level within the Soviet Union's state hierarchy, consisting of elected deputies who are also leading administrators, managers, workers, and other notables. The term of office varies from two and a half to five years according to the administrative level of a given soviet.

Council of Ministers (*Sovet ministrov*)   Since 1946, the highest executive and administrative body of the Soviet state system, subordinate to the Supreme Soviet but with the right to issue decrees of its own. The Council of Ministers consists of the premier of the USSR, his deputies, the premiers of the councils of ministers of the 15 union republics, and the heads of all ministries and other equivalent state agencies, such as state committees. The council's Presidium functions as an executive committee for the entire council.

Council of People's Commissars (Sovnarkom)   In existence from 1917 until 1946 as the forerunner of the Council of Ministers.

district (*raion*)   The lowest-level administrative subdivision of the Soviet state system. It is located in both rural and urban areas.

economic planning (*planirovanie*)   The planning process leading up to the preparation of quarterly, annual, five-year, and longer-term economic plans for various administrative and economic units.

executive committee (*ispolkom*)   The executive agency of a soviet, including leading administrators from the soviet staff as well as from other administrative agencies.

five-year plan (*piatiletka*)   The detailed economic plan establishing supply and growth targets and "control figures" for the Soviet economy as a whole as well as for various constituent administrative and economic units.

general plan (*general'nyi plan*)   The long-term (20- to 25-year) set of physical planning targets and norms established to guide urban and regional development in accordance with economic objectives contained in the plan's technical-economic foundations.

housing construction combine (DSK)   Construction firms responsible for prefabricated housing construction utilizing the "block-section" method of construction. This method, which was developed in Leningrad during the 1960s, relies on the on-site installation of factory-produced modular building units.

krai   A large administrative subdivision of the Russian Republic (RSFSR) based either on geographic unity or on a predominantly shared nationality background among the region's populace.

Main Leningrad Construction Administration (*Glavleningradstroi*)   The primary administrative agency of the Leningrad city and regional soviets, responsible for all construction activity in the city and region of Leningrad.

minidistrict (*mikroraion*)   A small urban planning and architectural design neighborhood unit similar to the "superblock" in West European planning practice. The minidistrict does not have formal administrative or political status.

oblast (*oblast'*)   The basic administrative subdivision of the union republics.

okrug   The smallest nationality-based administrative subdivision of a union republic.

party bureau (*partbiuro*)   The executive agency of a party committee, including leading officials from the party committee's staff as well as other selected party personnel.

personnel system (*nomenklatura*)   Literally, a term referring to the list of personnel appointments controlled directly or indirectly by a superior party or state agency through the right of confirmation of appointment. More broadly, the term has come to refer to the party-controlled integrated and unified personnel system for all responsible administrative, economic, and political positions throughout the Soviet party and state hierarchies.

physical planning (*planirovka*)   The planning process leading up to the formulation of local, district, city, and regional physical and general urban plans.

plant-factory school (*fabrichno-zavodskoe uchilishche* [FZU])   Factory-based vocational and apprenticeship programs, usually at the secondary school level, that were developed during the 1920s and remained in place until World War II.

Political Bureau (Politburo)   The Central Committee's party bureau. The most
    powerful political institution in the Soviet Union.

production association (*proizvodstvennoe ob"edinenie*)   The integrated asso-
    ciation of related production units drawn from a single or multiple set
    of economic sectors and responsible for the production of the same, simi-
    lar, or related products. Such unified administrative hierarchies are cre-
    ated to ensure a higher level of economic efficiency in each of the
    association's constituent production units.

professional-technical school (*professional'no-tekhnicheskoe uchilishche* [PTU])
    A specialized type of school established by the 1958 educational reforms.
    Such schools serve as the most important secondary and postsecondary
    specialized vocational education institutions in the Soviet Union, offering
    four- and five-year curricula that are developed in accordance with the
    needs of the economic unit to which the respective school has been at-
    tached.

region   See *krai; oblast; okrug.*

regional economic councils (*sovnarkhozy*)   Regional economic agencies re-
    sponsible from 1957 to 1965 for the economic administration of territorial
    units of approximately the size of the oblasts. The *sovnarkhozy* replaced
    centralized ministries as the basic administrative unit of the Soviet eco-
    nomic system during this period.

regional party committee (*obkom*)   The senior Communist Party agency within
    a region, consisting of representatives of various subordinate party or-
    ganizations elected by a regional party conference convened once every
    two to three years.

residency permit (*propiska*)   A system of permits designed to limit the growth
    of the Soviet Union's largest urban centers. To move to a city controlled
    by the *propiska* system, a citizen must have either employment or direct
    familial ties to that city. To obtain housing or employment in a controlled
    city, a citizen must have a residency permit.

scientific-production association (*nauchno-proizvodstvennoe ob"edinenie*)
    The integrated association of related research, development, and pro-
    duction units drawn from a single or multiple set of economic sectors
    and responsible for the development and production of the same, similar,
    or related products. Such unified administrative hierarchies are created
    to ensure a high level of efficiency throughout the research-development-
    production cycle.

Secretariat (Sekretariat)   The administrative branch of the Central Committee
    or other party committee.

secretary (*sekretar'*)   A member of the Secretariat, usually responsible for su-
    pervision of the administration of several administrative and policy areas.

state committee (*gosudarstvennyi komitet*)   An agency of the Council of Min-
    isters responsible for management of a number of activities that cut across
    several economic sectors, such as the (State) Committee on State Security
    (Komitet gosudarstvennoi bezopasnosti, KGB) and the State Committee
    for Labor and Social Problems (Goskomtrud).

State Committee on Civil Construction (Gosgrazhdanstroi)   The Gosstroi
    agency responsible for the development, planning, and design work of a

city's or region's physical planning (*planirovka*), usually on a contract basis for a client soviet.

State Committee on Construction Affairs (Gosstroi)   A state committee subordinate to the Council of Ministers. Gosstroi is responsible primarily for the coordination and management of all construction taking place in the Soviet Union. It operates through a national hierarchy of local and regional representatives.

State Planning Committee (Gosplan)   A state committee subordinate to the Council of Ministers. It is responsible for the coordination and management of the preparation of long- and short-term economic plans, including five-year plans, and for various administrative and economic units down to the level of the enterprise.

Supreme Soviet (*Verkhovnyi sovet*)   The senior legislative body of a given republic or of the entire Soviet Union, consisting of elected deputies who are also leading administrators, managers, workers, and other notables. Each deputy serves a five-year term of office.

technical-economic foundations (*tekhniko-ekonomicheskie osnovy* [TEO])   The document setting forth the long-term economic and technical projections on which the general plan is based.

technical school (*tekhnikum*)   A specialized secondary-education institution offering a program of vocational and technical training typically lasting for four years.

unified settlement system (*edinaia sistema rasseleniia* [ESR])   The analytical construct used by many Soviet geographers to describe the national integrated hierarchy of urban centers throughout the Soviet Union.

union republic (*soiuznaia respublika*)   The largest and most important nationality-based administrative subdivision of the USSR. All 15 union soviet socialist republics have an international boundary and share a theoretical right of secession from the USSR.

union-republic ministry   The agency of the USSR Council of Ministers responsible for coordinating the work of ministries of the same name and similar purpose operating within each of the Soviet Union's 15 republics, usually in a given economic sector, such as the Ministry of the Food Industry, the Ministry of Health, and the Ministry of Foreign Affairs.

urban district or ward (*gorodskii raion*)   The lowest-level urban administrative and political subdivision in the Soviet state system.

Selected Bibliography

Periodicals

A. Soviet

Agitator
Arkhitektura i stroitel'stvo Leningrada (1946–1959)
Arkhitektura Leningrada (1936–1941, 1944–1945)
Arkhitektura SSSR
Arkhitekturnoe nasledstvo
Biulleten' Ispolkoma Leningradskogo oblastnogo soveta narodnykh deputatov
Biulleten' Ispolnitel'nogo komiteta Leningradskogo gorodskogo soveta narodnykh dcputatov
Chelovek i obshchestvo
Ekonomicheskaia gazeta
Izvestiia Vsesoiuznogo geograficheskogo obshchestva
Kommunist
Komsomol'skaia pravda
Leningradskaia panorama (1982–)
Leningradskaia pravda
Obshchestvennye nauki
Partiinoe stroitel'stvo
Petrogradskaia pravda
Planovoe khoziaistvo
Pravda
Problemy bol'shikh gorodov
Sbornik postanovlenii pravitel'stva SSSR
Sotsialisticheskii trud
Sotsiologicheskie issledovaniia
Sovetskaia etnografiia
Sovetskaia Rossiia
Sovety deputatov trudiashchikhsia
Sovety narodnykh deputatov
Stroitel'stvo i arkhitektura Leningrada (1960–1981)
Stroitel'stvo Leningrada (1936–1941, 1944–1959)
Vechernyi Leningrad
Vestnik AN SSSR
Vestnik Leningradskogo gosudarstvennogo universiteta

Vestnik statistiki
Voprosy ekonomiki

B. Non-Soviet

Acta Oeconomica
American Political Science Review
Annals of the Institute of Social Science, University of Tokyo
British Journal of Political Science
Canadian Review of Studies in Nationalism
Canadian Slavonic Papers
Geographical Review
International Political Science Review
Journal of Economic Literature
Journal of Politics
New York Times
Problems of Communism
Russian Review
Science
Slavic Review
Soviet Geography: Review and Translation
Soviet Studies
Soviet Union/Union Soviétique
Transaction Journal
Urban Law and Policy
Urban Studies

Formal Interviews in the Soviet Union

Agafonov, N. T. Institute of Socioeconomic Problems, USSR Academy of Sciences, Leningrad, February 20, 1984.

Bisharenko, V. S., B. M. Firsov, and N. A. Tolokontsev. Institute of Socioeconomic Problems, USSR Academy of Sciences, Leningrad, March 6, 1984.

Litovka, O. P. Institute of Socioeconomic Problems, USSR Academy of Sciences, Leningrad, February 28, 1984.

Mezhevich,. M. N. Institute of Socioeconomic Problems, USSR Academy of Sciences, Leningrad, February 16 and 20, 1984.

Polozov, V. R. Institute of Socioeconomic Problems, USSR Academy of Sciences, Leningrad, February 27 and March 2, 1984.

Sigov, I. I. Institute of Socioeconomic Problems, USSR Academy of Sciences, Leningrad, February 15 and March 7, 1984.

Uspenskii, S. V. Leningrad (Voznesenskii) Financial-Economic Institute, Leningrad, March 5, 1984.

Vorotilov, V. A. Institute of Socioeconomic Problems, USSR Academy of Sciences, Leningrad, February 15, 1984.

Dissertations and Dissertation
Abstracts (*Avtoreferaty*)

A. Soviet

Bogoliubov, V. S. "Sotsial'no-ekonomicheskaia otsena etazhnosti zhiloi zastroiki krupneishikh gorodov (na primere Leningrada)." Avtoreferat dissertatsii
na soiskanie uchenoi stepeni kandidata ekonomicheskikh nauk, Leningradskii inzhenerno-ekonomicheskii institut im Tol'iatti, 1973.
Chapek, V. N. "Aktual'nye problemy izucheniia sotsial'no-geograficheskogo
mekanizma sovremennoi migratsii naseleniia SSSR." Avtoreferat dissertatsii
na soiskanie uchenoi stepeni kandidata geografii, Geograficheskii fakul'tet,
Leningradskii gosudarstvennyi universitet, 1980.
Kaganov, G. Z. "Vliianii planirovochnykh faktorov na nekotorye aspekty for-
mirovaniia gorodskoi sredy (na primere tsentral'nykh raionov Leningrada)."
Avtoreferat dissertatsii na soiskanie uchenoi stepeni kandidata arkhitektury,
Leningradskii inzhenerno-stroitel'nyi institut, 1980.
Kornil'eva, Z. V. "Deiatel'nost' Leningradskoi partiinoi organizatsii po osuche-
stvleniu general'nogo plana razvitiia goroda v semiletki (1959–1966 gg.)."
Avtoreferat dissertatsii na soiskanie uchenoi stepeni kandidata istoriches
kikh nauk, Leningradskii gosudarstvennyi universitet, 1969.
Rassokhina, G. N. "Arkhitekturno-planirovochnaia organizatsiia obshchestvennykh tsentrov planirovochnykh raionov krupneishikh gorodov (na primere
Leningrada)." Avtoreferat dissertatsii na soiskanie uchenoi stepeni kandidata arkhitektury, Leningradskii inzhenerno-stroitel'nyi institut, 1980.
Sokolov, S. I. "Orientatsiia i dvizhenie cheloveka v mikroraione (na primere
riada mikroraionov Leningrada)." Avtoreferat dissertatsii na soiskanie uchenoi stepeni kandidata arkhitektury, Leningradskii inzhenerno-stroitel'nyi institut, 1970.

B. Non-Soviet

Bidlack, Richard. "Workers at War: Factory Workers and Labor Policy in the
Siege of Leningrad." Ph.D. dissertation, Indiana University, 1987.
Mote, Max Ethan. "Leningrad Municipal Administration: Structure and Func-
tions." Ph.D. dissertation, University of Washington, 1966.

Books and Major Scholarly Articles

A. Russian and Soviet

Afanas'ev, A. N., and N. V. Kaz'micheva, eds. *10 piatiletok Leningrada*. Leningrad: Lenizdat, 1980.
Agafonov, N. T. *Territorial'no-proizvodstvennoe kompleksnoobrazovanie v
usloviiakh razvitogo sotsializma*. Leningrad: Nauka—Leningradskoe otdelenie, 1983.

Agafonov, N. T., S. B. Lavrov, and B. S. Khorev. "On Some Faulty Concepts in Soviet Urban Studies." *Soviet Geography: Review and Translation* 24, no. 3 (March 1983):179–188 (translated from *Izvestiia Vsesoiuznogo geograficheskogo obshchestva*, 1982, no. 6:533–539).

Akademiia nauk SSSR. Institut sotsiologicheskikh issledovanii AN SSSR. Sovetskaia sotsiologicheskaia assotsiatsiia. *Sotsiologicheskie tsentry SSSR (1976 god)*. Moscow: AN SSSR, ISI AN SSSR, SSA, 1976.

Akademiia nauk Ukrainskoi SSR. *Istoriia Akademii nauk Ukrainskoi SSR*. Kiev: Naukova Dumka, 1979.

Alekseev, B. K. *Planirovanie partiinoi raboty*. Leningrad: Lenizdat, 1968.

Alekseev, B. K., and V. G. Zubarev, eds. *Partiinoe rukovodstvo—Na uroven' sovremennykh trebovanii: Iz opyta raboty Leningradskoi partiinoi organizatsii*. Leningrad: Lenizdat, 1978.

Ananov, I. N. *Sistema organov gosudarstvennogo upravleniia v Sovetskoi sotsialisticheskoi federatsii*. Moscow: Izdatel'stvo Akademii nauk SSSR, 1951.

Arkin, D. "Perspektivnyi plan Peterburga, 1764–1773." *Arkhitekturnoe nasledstvo*, 1955, no. 7:13–38.

Artemov, V. A., N. A. Balykov, and Z. I. Kalugina. *Vremya naseleniia goroda: Planirovanie i ispol'zovanie*. Novosibirsk: Nauka—Sibirskoe otdelenie, 1982.

Babin, B. A. "Institutu sotsiologicheskikh issledovanii AN SSSR—10 let." *Sotsiologicheskie issledovaniia*, 1979, no. 1:210–212.

Bakunin, A. V., ed. *Deiatel'nost' KPSS po uskoreniiu nauchno-tekhnicheskogo progressa*. Moscow: Vysshaia shkola, 1980.

Barabashev, G. V., ed. *Rol' mestnykh sovetov v ekonomicheskom i sotsial'nom razvitii gorodov*. Moscow: Izdatel'stvo MGU, 1983.

Baranov, A. V. *Sotsial'no-demograficheskoe razvitie krupnogo goroda*. Moscow: Finansy i statistika, 1981.

Baranov, N. V. *Glavnyi arkhitektor goroda: Tvorcheskaia i organizatsionnaia deiatel'nost'*. 2d ed. Moscow: Stroiizdat, 1979.

———. *Siluety blokady: Zapiski glavnogo arkhitektura goroda*. Leningrad: Lenizdat, 1982.

Baratchev, A. K., et al., eds. *Ezhegodnik Leningradskogo otdeleniia soiuza sovetskikh arkhitekturov*. No. 4. Leningrad: Gosizdat lit. po stroi i arkh., 1955.

Bartenev, I. *Arkhitektura sotsialisticheskogo Leningrada*. Leningrad: Obshchestvo "Znanie"—Leningradskaia organizatsiia, 1953.

———. *Zodchie i stroiteli Leningrada*. Leningrad: Lenizdat, 1963.

Bastareva, L. I., and V. I. Sidorova. *Petropavlovskaia krepost'*. Leningrad: Lenizdat, 1980.

Beliaev, E. A., and N. S. Pyshkova. *Formirovanie i razvitie seti nauchnykh uchrezhdenii SSSR*. Moscow: Nauka, 1979.

Bobovikov, R. S., ed. *Ekonomicheskie i sotsial'noe planirovanie v masshtabe raione*. Leningrad: Lenizdat, 1973.

Bogdanov, G. A., et al., eds. *Kompleksnoe planirovanie sotsial'nogo razvitiia kollektiv predpriiatii Leningrada*. Leningrad: Lenizdat, 1970.

Bogoliubov, K. M., P. G. Mishunin, E. Z. Razumov, Ia. V. Storozhev, and N. V. Tropkin, eds. *Spravochnik partiinogo rabotnika, 1983, no. 23*. Moscow: Polit. lit., 1983.

Borisov, A. P., and N. M. Sutyrin, eds. *Ekonomika i upravlenie sotsialisticheskim proizvodstvom.* Leningrad: Leningradskii inzhenerno-ekonomicheskii institut, 1983.

Bozherianov, I. N. *Kul'turno-istoricheskii ocherki zhizni S-Peterburga za dva veka XVIII–XIX, 1703–1903.* St. Petersburg, 1903.

Bozherianov, I. N., and E. P. Erastov. *S. Peterburg' v Petrogo vremia: Kul'turno-istoricheskie ocherki.* St. Petersburg: Kh. Krauze, 1903.

Bozhkov, O. B., and V. B. Golofast. "Otsenka naseleniem uslovii zhizni v krupnykh gorodakh." *Sotsiologicheskie issledovaniia,* 1985, no. 3:95–101.

Brazhnikov, V. E., R. K. Davydov, and L. T. Krivenko, eds. *XXVI s"ezd KPSS i voprosy rukovodstva v sisteme sovetov narodnykh deputatov.* Kiev: Naukova Dumka, 1983.

Brodskaia, T. G. *Rol' Leningradskogo regiona v razvitii edinogo narodno-khoziaistvennogo kompleksa.* Leningrad: Obshchestvo "Znanie"—Leningradskaia organizatsiia, 1985.

Bubis, E., G. Popov, and K. Sharligina. *Optimal'noe perspektivnoe planirovanie kapital'nogo remonta i rekonstruktsii zhilishchnogo fonda.* Leningrad: Stroiizdat, 1980.

Bukin, G. A. *Torgovliia v plane sotsial'no-ekonomicheskogo razvitiia goroda (opyt g. Leningrada).* Moscow: Ekonomika, 1982.

Chertov, L. G. *Leningrad kak odin iz krupneishikh ekonomicheskikh kul'turnykh tsentrov SSSR.* Leningrad: Obshchestvo "Znanie"—Leningradskaia organizatsiia, 1955.

Darinskii, A. V. *Geografiia Leningrada.* Leningrad: Lenizdat, 1982.

Demidenko, E. S. *Demograficheskie problemy i perspektivy bol'shikh gorodov (urbanizatsiia pri sotsializme).* Moscow: Statistika, 1980.

Dmitriev, A. V., and M. N. Mezhevich. *SSSR-SShA: Sotsial'noe razvitie v gorodakh.* Leningrad: Nauka—Leningradskoe otdelenie, 1981.

———, eds. *Gorod: Problemy sotsial'nogo razvitiia.* Leningrad: Nauka—Leningradskoe otdelenie, 1982.

Dukinskii, B. K. *1000 voprosov i otvetov o Leningrade.* Leningrad: Lenizdat, 1974.

Dzarasov, S. S., and P. A. Kudinov, eds. *Opyt deiatel'nosti partiinykh organizatsii po rukovodstvu khoziaistvom.* Moscow: Mysl', 1979.

Dzenishevich, A. R. *Rabochie Leningrada nakanune Velikoi otechestvennoi voiny, 1938–iiun' 1941 g.* Leningrad: Nauka—Leningradskoe otdelenie, 1983.

Egorov, Iu. A. *The Architectural Planning of St. Petersburg.* Translated by Eric Dlubosch. Athens: Ohio University Press, 1969.

El'meev, V. *Nauka i proizvoditel'nye sily obshchestva.* Moscow: Sotsekgaz, 1959.

El'meev, V. Ia., and B. R. Riashchenko. *Planirovanie sotsial'nykh protsessov na predpriiatii.* Leningrad: Lenizdat, 1969.

El'meev, V. Ia., B. R. Riashchenko, and E. P. Iudin. *Kompleksnoe planirovanie ekonomicheskogo i sotsial'nogo razvitiia raiona.* Leningrad: Lenizdat, 1972.

Ezhov, V. A. *Rabochii klass—Vedushchaia sila vosstanovleniia Leningrada 1943–1950 gg.* Leningrad: Izdatel'stvo Leningradskogo universiteta, 1982.

Faerman, E. Iu., and Iu. A. Oleinik-Ovod, eds. *Voprosy planirovaniia gorodskogo razvitiia.* Moscow: TsEMI, 1977.

German, Iu., D. Granin, and E. Katerii. *Rasskaz o prazdnike.* Leningrad: Lenizdat, 1957.

Glavnyi upravlenie proftekhobrazovaniia Leningrada i Leningradskoi oblasti. *Professional'no-tekhnicheskie i tekhnicheskie uchilishcha Leningrada i Leningradskoi oblasti: Spravochnik dlia postupaiushchikh—1980 g.* Leningrad: Lenizdat, 1980.

Glebov, I. A., and I. I. Sigov, eds. *Sovershenstvovanie upravleniia fundamental'nymi issledovaniiami v krupnom gorode.* Leningrad: Nauka—Leningradskoe otdelenie, 1983.

Gosudarstvennyi nauchno-issledovatel'skii muzei arkhitektury im. A. V. Shchuseva. *N. V. Baranov: Katalog vystavki osnovnykh tvorcheskikh rabot k 70-letiiu so dnia rozhdeniia i 50-letiia tvorcheskoi deiatel'nosti.* Moscow, 1979.

Grabar', I. *Russkoi arkhitekture.* Moscow: Nauka, 1969.

Gracheva, L. V. *Leningradskaia oblast': Osnovnye problemy razvitiia agropromyshlennogo kompleksa i industrial'nykh tsentrov.* Leningrad: Obshchestvo "Znanie"—Leningradskaia organizatsiia, 1985.

Grigor'eva, L. A., V. A. Sukhin, and Iu. I. Tsymaliakov, eds. *Sotsial'naia infrastruktura i uroven' zhizni naseleniia krupnogo goroda.* Chelovek i obshchestvo no. 21. Leningrad: Izdatel'stvo Leningradskogo universiteta, 1986.

Gruzinov, A. S., and V. P. Riumin. *Gorod: Upravlenie problemy.* Leningrad: Lenizdat, 1977.

Institut filosofii, sotsiologii i prava AN Lit SSR. Pribaltiiskoe otdelenie Sovetskoi sotsiologicheskoi assotsiatsii. *Gorod kak sreda zhizndetiatel'nosti cheloveka.* Vil'nius, 1981.

Institut sotsial'no-ekonomicheskikh problem An SSSR. *Sotsialisticheskii gorod kak ob″ekt issledovaniia i upravleniia: Materialy Vsesoiuznoi nauchnoi konferentsii sostoiavsheisia v Leningrade 21–23 Oktiabriia 1981 goda.* Leningrad: Nauka—Leningradskoe otdelenie, 1983.

Iogansen, M. V., V. G. Lisovskii, and N. I. Nikulina. *Arkhitektura Vasil'evskogo ostrova v proshlom, nastoiashchem i budushchem.* Leningrad: Akademiia khudozhestv SSSR, 1969.

Iukhneva, N. V. *Etnicheskii sostav i etnosotsial'naia struktura naseleniia Peterburga: Vtoraia polovina XIX–nachalo XX veka; Statisticheskii analiz.* Leningrad: Nauka—Leningradskoe otdelenie, 1984.

Ivanov, N. Ia., B. M. Kochakov, and S. B. Okun', eds. *Leningrad: Kratkii istoricheskii ocherk.* Leningrad: Lenizdat, 1964.

Ivin, M. E. *Prospekt im I. V. Stalina.* Leningrad: Gosizdat. Literatury po stroitel'stva arkhitektury, 1954.

Kamenskii, V. A. *Leningrad: General'nyi plan razvitiia goroda.* Leningrad: Lenizdat, 1972.

Kamenskii, V. A., and A. I. Naumov. *Leningrad: Gradostroitel'nye problemy razvitiia.* Leningrad: Stroiizdat—Leningradskoe otdelenie, 1977.

Kann, P. Ia. *Sotsialisticheskii Leningrad.* Leningrad: Obshchestvo "Znanie"—Leningradskaia organizatsiia, 1955.

Karimov, Kh. Kh. *Leningrad v tsifrakh i faktakh.* Leningrad: Lenizdat, 1984.

Kas'ka, K., and Iu. Ennuste, eds. *O modeliakh normativnogo prognozirovaniia sotsial'no-ekonomicheskogo razvitiia regiona.* Tallin: Institut ekonomiki AN Est SSA, 1980.

Katerli, E., and F. Samoilov. *Gorod v kotorom my zhivem*. Leningrad: Leningradskoe gazetno-zhurnal'noe i knizhnoe izdatel'stvo, 1945.

Kel'kh, G. G. *Pamiatniki sovetskoi arkhitektury v Leningrade: Problemy restavratsii i okhrany*. Leningrad: Obshchestvo "Znanie" RSFSR—Leningradskaia organizatsiia, 1982.

Kerimov, D. A., E. S. Kuz'min, A. S. Pashkov, and V. R. Polozov, eds. *Metodika planirovaniia sotsial'nogo kollektiva promyshlennogo predpriiatiia*. Leningrad: Lenizdat, 1970.

Khamarev, I. *Za Moskovskoi zastavoi*. Leningrad: Lenizdat, 1948.

Khodachek, V. M., and V. G. Alekseev. *Kompleksnoe razvitie gorodskikh raionov: Kompleksnyi plan ekonomicheskogo i sotsial'nogo razvitiia v deistvii*. Leningrad: Lenizdat, 1980.

Khomutetskii, N. F. *Peterburg-Leningrad*. Leningrad: Lenizdat, 1958.

Khorev, B. S. *Problemy gorodov (urbanizatsiia i edinaia sistema rasseleniia v SSSR)*. 2d, rev. ed. Moscow: Mysl', 1975.

———. *Territorial'naia organizatsiia obshchestva (aktual'nye problemy regional'nogo upravleniia i planirovaniia v SSSR)*. Moscow: Mysl', 1981.

Khorev, B. S., and L. P. Kiseleva. *Urbanizatsiia i demograficheskie protsessy*. Moscow: Finansy i statistika, 1982.

Khromov, A. A., and B. F. Shilov, comps. *Voprosy partiinogo stroitel'stva*. Leningrad: Lenizdat, 1965.

Kibal'chik, O. V., et al. *Geografiia i kul'tura etnograficheskii grupp Tatar v SSSR*. Moscow: Moskovskii filial Geograficheskogo obshchestva SSSR, 1983.

Komkov, G. D., B. V. Levshin, and L. K. Semenov. *Akademiia nauk SSSR: Kratkii istoricheskii ocherk*. Moscow: Nauka, 1974.

Kondrat'ev, R. I. *Lokal'nye normy trudovogo prava i material'noe stimulirovanie*. L'vov: Vishcha shkola, 1973.

———. *Sochetanie tsentralizovannogo i lokal'nogo pravovogo regulirovaniia trudovykh otnoshenii*. L'vov: Vishcha shkola, 1977.

Koval'chuk, V. M., D. I. Petrikeev, and Z. V. Stepanov, eds. *Leningrad v vos'moi piatiletke, 1966–1970 gg.: Istoriko-sotsial'nyi ocherk*. Leningrad: Nauka—Leningradskoe otdelenie, 1979.

Kovalenko, P. S. *Razvitie gorodov*. Kiev: Naukova Dumka, 1980.

Kozlov, A. A., E. D. Klimenko, and V. I. Meleshchenko. *Leningradskii sotsial'no-ekonomicheskii kompleks*. Leningrad: Lenizdat, 1979.

Kozlov, B. I., ed. *Organizatsiia i razvitie otraslevykh nauchno-issledovatel'skikh institutov Leningrada, 1917–1977*. Leningrad: Nauka—Leningradskoe otdelenie, 1979.

Kozlov, V. I., ed. *Ocherki istorii Leningradskoi organizatsii KPSS*. Vol. 3, 1945–1985. Leningrad: Lenizdat, 1985.

Kugel', S. A., B. D. Lebin, and Iu. S. Meleshchenko, eds. *Nauchnye kadry Leningrada*. Leningrad: Nauka—Leningradskoe otdelenie, 1973.

Kulibanov, V. S. *Problemy ekonomicheskogo i sotsial'nogo razvitiia Leningrada i oblasti odinnadtsatoi piatiletke*. Leningrad: Obshchestvo "Znanie"—Leningradskaia organizatsiia, 1981.

———. *Problemy razvitiia narodnogo khoziaistva Severo-zapada SSSR*. Leningrad: Obshchestvo "Znanie"—Leningradskaia organizatsiia, 1980.

Kulibanov, V. S., et al., eds. *Nauchno-tekhnicheskii progress v stroitel'stve*. Leningrad: Lenizdat, 1984.

Kulina, N. I., ed. *Prigorody Leningrada: Arkhitektury i putevoditel'*. Leningrad: Stroiizdat, 1982.

Kupaigorodskaia, A. P. *Vysshaia shkola Leningrada v pervye gody Sovetskoi vlasti (1917–1925 gg.)*. Leningrad: Nauka—Leningradskoe otdelenie, 1983.

Lazarev, B. M., ed. *Grazhdanin i apparat upravleniia v SSSR*. Moscow: Nauka, 1982.

Lebedev, P. N., et al. *Partiinaia organizatsiia i rabochie Leningrada*. Leningrad: Lenizdat, 1974.

————, eds., *Sistema organov gorodskogo upravleniia (opyt sotsiologicheskogo issledovaniia)*. Leningrad: Izdatel'stvo LGU, 1980.

Lebedev, P. N., and V. A. Sukhin, eds. *Sotsial'nye problemy planirovaniia sotsialisticheskogo goroda*. Chelovek i obshchestvo no. 16. Leningrad: LGU-NIIKSI, 1977.

Leningrad. Arkhitekturno-planirovochnoe upravlenie. *Leningrad*. Leningrad and Moscow: Iskusstvo, 1943.

Leningrad. Institut istorii partii. *Istoriia Kirovskogo (byv. Putilovskogo) metallurgicheskogo i mashinostroitel'nogo zavoda v Leningrade*. Moscow: Izd. sotsial'no-ekonomicheskaia literatura, 1961–1966.

Leningradskaia organizatsiia ordena Lenina Soiuz arkhitekturov SSSR. Sektsiia nauchnogo prognozirovaniia LO Sovetskoi sotsiologicheskoi assotsiatsii pri AN SSSR. *Leningrad—2000: Materialy nauchno-teoreticheskogo soveshchaniia; Effektivnost' zhiloi sredy v usloviiakh gorodskogo obraza zhizni*. Leningrad: Leningradskaia organizatsiia Soiuz arkhitektorov SSSR, Leningradskoe otdelenie Sovetskoi sotsiologicheskoi assotsiatsii pri AN SSSR, 1978.

Leningrad bez navodenii. Leningrad: Lenizdat, 1984.

Leningrad: Entsiklopedicheskii spravochnik. Moscow and Leningrad: Bol'shaia Sovetskaia entsiklopediia, 1957.

Leningrad i Leningradskaia oblast' v tsifrakh: Statisticheskii sbornik. Leningrad: Lenizdat, 1971.

Leningrad i Leningradskaia oblast' v tsifrakh: Statisticheskii sbornik. Leningrad: Lenizdat, 1974.

Leningrad i Leningradskaia oblast' za XX let Sovetskoi vlasti. Leningrad: Lenoblizdat, 1937.

Leningrad: Istoriko-geograficheskii atlas. Rev. and supplemented ed. Moscow: Glavnoe upravlenie geodezii i kartografii pri Sovete Ministrov SSSR, 1981.

Leningradskaia promyshlennost' za 50 let. Leningrad: Lenizdat, 1976.

Leningrad: Vidy goroda. Moscow: Gosizdat. Izobrazitel'nogo iskusstva, 1954.

Leningrad za 50 let: Statisticheskii sbornik. Leningrad: Lenizdat, 1967.

Leonov, L. D., and B. K. Peiro. *Leningrad—Gorod geroi*. Leningrad: Obshchestvo "Znanie"—Leningradskaia organizatsiia, 1957.

Likhomanov, M. I., L. T. Pozina, and E. I. Finogenov. *Partiinoe rukovodstvo evakuatsii v pervyi period Velikoi otechestvennoi voiny, 1941–1942 gg.* Leningrad: Izdatel'stvo Leningradskogo universiteta, 1985.

Lisovskii, V. G. *Leningrad: Raiony novostroek*. Leningrad: Lenizdat, 1983.

Listengurt, F., and I. Portianskii. "Krupnyi gorod v usloviiakh perekhoda k intensivnoi ekonomike." *Voprosy ekonomiki*, 1985, no. 1:108–115.

Lopatina, E. *Leningrad: Ekonomiko-geograficheskii ocherk*. Moscow: Gos. izdat. geograficheskoi literatury, 1959.

Luk'ianov, A. I., et al., eds. *Sovety narodnykh deputatov: Spravochnik.* Moscow: Politizdat, 1984.

Lunin, B., ed. *Goroda sotsializma i sotsialisticheskaia rekonstruktsiia byta.* Moscow, 1930.

Makhrovskaia, A. V., and S. P. Semenov. *Puti razvitiia Leningrada.* Leningrad: Obshchestvo "Znanie"—Leningradskaia organizatsiia, 1980.

Males, V. N., E. G. Panchenko, and V. I. Senchenko. *Kompleksnoe planirovanie ekonomicheskogo i sotsial'nogo razvitiia gorodov i raionov.* Moscow: Mysl', 1978.

Mamutov, V. K., et al., eds. *Ekonomiko-pravovye problemy upravleniia gorodom (Sbornik nauchnykh trudov).* Donetsk: IEP AN UkSSR, 1983.

Mavrodin, V. V., ed. *Istoriia Leningradskogo universiteta.* Leningrad: Leningradskii gosudarstvennyi universitet, 1969.

Meleshchenko, V. I. *Kompleksnyi plan ekonomicheskogo i sotsial'nogo razvitiia Leningrada i Leningradskoi oblasti v desiatoi piatiletke.* Leningrad: Obshchestvo "Znanie" —Leningradskaia organizatsiia, 1977.

Mezhevich, M. N. *Sotsial'noe razvitie i gorod: Filosofskie i sotsiologicheskie aspekty.* Leningrad: Nauka—Leningradskoe otdelenie, 1979.

Mineev, V. A., E. P. Murav'ev, and L. M. Chistov, eds. *Problemy planirovaniia narodnogo khoziaistva Leningrada i Leningradskoi oblasti v tsifrakh* (Leningrad: Minvuz RSFSR, LFEI, 1971.

Mozhaev, P. P., comp. *Za delovoi stil' v partiinoi rabote.* Leningrad: Lenizdat, 1981.

Murav'ev, E. P., and S. V. Uspenskii. *Metodologicheskie problemy planirovaniia gorodskogo rasseleniia pri sotsializme.* Leningrad: Leningradskii gosudarstvennyi universitet, 1974.

Narodnoe khoziaistvo Leningrada i Leningradskoi oblasti v desiatoi piatiletke: Statisticheskii sbornik. Leningrad: Lenizdat, 1981.

Narodnoe khoziaistvo Leningrada i Leningradskoi oblasti za 60 let: Statisticheskii sbornik. Leningrad: Lenizdat, 1977.

Narodnoe khoziaistvo SSSR v 1980 g.: Statisticheskii ezhegodnik. Moscow: Finansy i statistika, 1981.

Narodnoe khoziaistvo SSSR v 1985 g.: Statisticheskii ezhegodnik. Moscow: Finansy i statistika, 1986.

Narodnoe khoziaistvo za 60 let: Iubilenii statisticheskii sbornik. Moscow: Statistika, 1977.

Nauchnyi sovet AN SSSR po problemu konkretnykh sotsial'nykh issledovanii. Sovetskaia sotsiologicheskaia assotsiatsiia. Otdel' konkretnykh sotsiologicheskikh issledovanii. Institut filosofii AN SSSR. *Seriia materialy i soobshcheniia kolichestvennye metody v sotsial'nykh issledovaniiakh: Materialy soveshcheniia, proshedshego v g. Sukhumi, 17–20 apreliia 1967.* Informatsionnyi biulleten', no. 8. Moscow: SSA, 1968.

Nauka Soiuza SSR. Moscow: Nauka, 1972.

Naumov, A. I., ed. *Gradostroitel'nye problemy razvitiia Leningrada.* Leningrad: Gosizdat lit. po stroi., arkh. i stroi-material, 1960.

"Ob opyte raboty sovetov narodnykh deputatov goroda Leningrada i Leningradskoi oblasti po obespecheniiu kompleksnogo ekonomicheskogo i sotsial'nogo razvitiia na svoie territori: Postanovlenie Prezidiuma Verkhovnogo Soveta SSSR. 4 maia, 1982 g." In K. M. Bogoliubov, P. G. Mishunin, E. Z.

Razumov, Ia. V. Storozhev, and N. V. Tropkin, eds., *Spravochnik partiinogo rabotnika, 1983 (vypusk dvadtsat' tretii),* 514–517. Moscow: Polit. lit., 1983.

Opalov, M. N. "Reshenie IV otchetno-vybornoi konferentsii Sovetskoi sotsiologicheskoi assotsiatsii po otchetu pravleniia SSA." *Sotsiologicheskie issledovaniia,* 1977, no. 3:31–34.

———. "Sovetskaia sotsiologicheskaia assotsiatsiia AN SSSR." *Sotsiologicheskie issledovaniia,* 1977, no. 4:172–175.

Osipov, G. V. *Pokazateli sotsial'nogo razvitiia i planirovaniia.* Moscow: Nauka, 1980.

Ovchinnikov, V. A., and B. S. Model', eds. *Usloviia i faktory aktivizatsii obshchestvenno-upravlencheskoi deiatel'nosti trudiashchikhsia v proizvodstvennom kollektive.* Sverdlovsk: UNTs AN SSSR, 1983.

Pamiatniki arkhitektury Leningrada. Leningrad: Stroiizdat—Leningradskoe otdelenie, 1975.

Panov, P. V., and V. D. Sorokin. *XXVI s"ezd KPSS i aktual'nye voprosy raboty mestnykh sovetov.* Leningrad: Lenizdat, 1982.

Parol', V. I. *Sotsialisticheskii gorod.* Tallin: Valgus, 1982.

Pashkov, A. S., ed. *Sovetskoe trudovoe pravo.* Moscow: Iuridicheskaia literatura, 1976.

Pashkov, A. S., and M. N. Mezhevich, eds. *Problemy sotsial'nogo planirovaniia v gorode i regione.* Chelovek i obshchestvo no. 15. Leningrad: LGU-NIIKSI, 1976.

Pashkov, A. S., V. R. Polozov, and A. V. Dmitriev. *Plan sotsial'nogo razvitiia predpriiatiia.* Moscow: Ekonomika, 1972.

Pavlov, D. V. *Leningrad 1941: The Blockade.* Translated by John C. Adams. Chicago: University of Chicago Press, 1965.

Piliavskii, V. I. *Arkhitektura Leningrada.* Leningrad and Moscow: Gosizdat. lit. po stroi i arkh., 1953.

Pivovarov, Iu. L. *Sovremennaia urbanizatsiia osnovnye tendentsii rasseleniia.* Moscow: Statistika, 1976.

Planirovanie sotsial'nogo razvitiia kollektiva predpriiatiia. Moscow: Profizdat, 1971.

Poliak, G. B. *Biudzhet goroda.* Moscow: Finansy, 1978.

Polozov, V. R., ed. *Sotsial'noe planirovanie i problema ego effektivnosti.* Leningrad: Nauka—Leningradskoe otdelenie, 1978.

———, ed. *Sotsial'noe planirovanie v otrasli promyshlennosti: Nekotorye voprosy metodologii.* Leningrad: Nauka—Leningradskoe otdelenie, 1981.

———, ed. *Sovershenstvovanie ekonomicheskogo i sotsial'nogo planirovaniia v raione v deviatoi piatiletke.* Leningrad: Lenizdat, 1973.

Posokhin, M. V., et al. *Sovetskaia arkhitektura za 50 let.* Moscow: Izdat. lit. po stroitel'stvu, 1968.

Predtechenskii, A. V., ed. *Peterburg Petrovskogo vremeni.* Leningrad: Leningradskoe gazetno-zhurnal'noe i knizhnoe izdatel'stvo, 1948.

Profsoiuzy SSSR: Dokumenty i materialy. Vol. 5. Moscow: Profizdat, 1974.

Rabinovich, M. G., and M. N. Shmeleva. "K etnograficheskomu izucheniiu goroda." *Sovetskaia etnografiia,* 1981, no. 3:23–34.

———. "Gorod i etnicheskie protsessy." *Sovetskaia etnografiia,* 1984, no. 2:3–14.

Romanov, G. V. "Doverie, vzyskatel'nost', chustvo dolga." *Kommunist*, 1981, no. 16:12–27.

―――. *Izbrannye rechi i stat'i*. Moscow: Izdatel'stvo politicheskoi literatury, 1980.

―――. "Leninskie printsipy partiinogo rukovodstva khoziaistvennym stroitel'stvom." In A. A. Khromov and B. F. Shilov, comps., *Voprosy partiinogo stroitel'stva*, 427–455. Leningrad: Lenizdat, 1965.

―――. "Rech' tovarishcha G. V. Romanova." In *XXV s''ezd Kommunisticheskoi partii Sovetskogo soiuza, 24 fevralia–5 marta, 1976 goda: Stenograficheskii otchet*, 1:144–150. Moscow: Polit. lit., 1976.

Sarukhanov, E. R. *Sotsial'no-ekonomicheskie problemy upravleniia rabochei siloi pri sotsializme*. Leningrad: Izdatel'stvo Leningradskogo universiteta, 1981.

Sbornik ispolkoma Lengorsoveta. Leningrad: Lenizdat, 1960.

Sbornik reshenii i rasporiazhenii Ispolnitel'nogo komiteta Leningradskogo gorodskogo soveta deputatov trudiashchikhsia. Leningrad: Lenizdat, 1956, 1958, 1960.

Shalabin, G. V. *Ekonomicheskie voprosy okhrany prirody v regione*. Leningrad: Leningradskii gosudarstvennyi universitet, 1983.

Shchukina, A. S. "The Interrelated Growth of Moscow, Leningrad and Other Urban Places along the October Railroad in the 1960s and 1970s." *Izvestiia Vsesoiuznogo geograficheskogo obshchestva*, 1981, no. 3:268–274, as translated in *Soviet Geography: Review and Translation* 24, no. 4 (April 1983):297–304.

Shubniakov, B. P., ed. *Sotsiologicheskie issledovaniia i sotsial'noe planirovanie—sostavnye chasti upravleniia ideologicheskim protsessom (Iz opyta sotsiologicheskoi razrabotki problemy "svoboda, otvestvennost', upravlenie")*. Iaroslavl': Iaroslavskii gosudarstvennyi universitet, 1976.

Shvidkovskii, O. A., ed. *Stroitel'stvo i arkhitektura*. Moscow: Nauka, 1967.

Sigov, I. I. "Aktual'nye problemy issledovaniia krupnykh gorodov." *Obshchestvennye nauki*, 1981, no. 6:21–30.

―――. *O sovershenstvovanii sochetaniia otraslevogo i territorial'nogo upravleniia*. Leningrad: Institut sotsial'no-ekonomicheskikh problem AN SSSR, 1983.

―――, ed. *Upravlenie razvitiem krupnykh gorodov*. Leningrad: Nauka—Leningradskoe otdelenie, 1985.

Smol'kina, A. A. *Deiatel'nost' KPSS po vosstanovleniiu i razvitiiu nauchno-tekhnicheskogo potentsiala Leningrada (1945–1966 gg.): Na materialakh Leningradskoi partiinoi organizatsii*. Leningrad: Leningradskii gosudarstvennyi universitet, 1983.

Sokolov, M. P., and I. I. Fomin. *Organizatsiia i planirovka mest massovogo otdykha trudiashchikhsia Leningrada*. Moscow: Vsesoiuznoe soveshchanie po gradostroitel'stvu, 1960.

Solodovnikov, I. M. *Mestnye sovety: Koordinatsiia i ee effektivnost'*. Moscow: Sovetskaia Rossiia, 1980.

Spiridonov, I. V. *Leningradu 250 let*. Moscow: Gos. izdat. pol. lit., 1957.

Starinskii, V. N. *Territorial'nyi plan kapital'nykh vlozhenii*. Leningrad: Lenizdat, 1980.

Statisticheskoe upravlenie goroda Leningrada. *Narodnoe khoziaistvo goroda*

Leningrada: Statisticheskii sbornik. Moscow: Gosudarstvennoe statisti-cheskoe izdatel'stvo, 1957.

Stepanenko, A. V. *Goroda v usloviiakh razvitogo sotsializma.* Kiev: Naukova Dumka, 1981.

Stolpianskii, P. N. *Staryie Peterburg i obshchestvo pooshchreniia khoduzhestv.* Leningrad: Izdanie Komiteta popularizatsii khudozhestvennykh izdanii, 1928.

Suslov, Iu. A., and P. N. Lebedev, eds. *Problemy sotsial'nogo razvitiia krup-nykh gorodov.* Chelovek i obshchestvo no. 19. Leningrad: LGU-NIIKSI, 1982.

Tolokontsev, N. A., and G. M. Romanenkova, eds. *Demografiia i ekologiia krup-nogo goroda.* Leningrad: Nauka—Leningradskoe otdelenie, 1980.

Tolstikov, V. S. "Rech' na XXIII s″ezde." In *XXIII s″ezd Kommunisticheskoi partii Sovetskogo Soiuza, 29 marta–9 apreliia, 1966 goda: Stenograficheskii otchet,* 1:140–148. Moscow: Polit. lit., 1966.

Trakhtenberg, D. *Podvig Leningrada.* Leningrad: Khudozhnik RSFSR, 1966.

Travin, I. I. *Material'no-veshchnaia sreda i sotsialisticheskii obraz zhizni.* Le-ningrad: Nauka—Leningradskoe otdelenie, 1979.

XIII s″ezd Vsesoiuznogo leninskogo kommunisticheskogo soiuza molodezhi: Stenograficheskii otchet. Moscow, 1959.

TsSU SSSR. *Itogi vsesoiuznoi perepisi naseleniia 1970 goda.* Moscow: Stati-stika, 1972.

Ul'ianov, B. V., comp. *Praktika sotsialisticheskogo khoziaistvovaniia: Opyt Leningradskikh predpriiatii.* Leningrad: Lenizdat, 1981.

Uspenskii, S. V. *Planirovanie ekonomicheskogo i sotsial'nogo razvitiia sistem rasseleniia i poselenii.* Leningrad: Nauka—Leningradskoe otdelenie, 1981.

Vainberg, E. I., and V. Ia. Liubovnyi. "Plan kompleksnogo ekonomicheskogo i sotsial'nogo razvitiia krupnogo goroda." *Problemy bol'shikh gorodov,* 1980, no. 11:1–28.

Vechkanov, G. S. *Migratsiia trudovykh resursov v SSSR: Politiko-ekonomi-cheskii aspekt.* Leningrad: Leningradskii gosudarstvennyi universitet, 1981.

Visharenko, V. S., and N. A. Tolokontsev. *Ekologicheskie problemy gorodov i zdorov'e cheloveka (v pomoshch' lektoru).* Leningrad: Obshchestvo "Znanie" —Leningradskaia organizatsiia, 1982.

Vitman, V. A., et al. *Arkhitektura Leningrada.* Leningrad: Gosizdat. lit. po stroi i arkh., 1953.

Volkov, A. A., E. D. Klimenko, and V. I. Meleshchenko, eds. *Leningradskii sotsial'no-ekonomicheskii kompleks.* Leningrad: Lenizdat, 1979.

Vorotilov, V. A., and G. N. Cherkasov, eds. *Metodologiia sotsial'no-ekonomi-cheskogo planirovaniia goroda.* Leningrad: Nauka—Leningradskoe otde-lenie, 1980.

Vsesoiuznyi institut nauchnoi i tekhnicheskoi informatsii. *Organy nauchno-tekhnicheskoi informatsii SSSR—Spravochnik.* Moscow: VINITI, 1976.

Zaslavskaia, T. I., et al. *Sotsial'no-demograficheskoe razvitie sela.* Moscow: Statistika, 1980.

Zavarukhin, Iu. I., and R. S. Zakasov, eds. *Gorodskoe khoziaistvo i stroitel'stvo Leningrada za 50 let.* Leningrad: Lenizdat, 1967.

Zdravomyslov, A. G., V. P. Rozhin, and V. A. Iadov. *Chelovek i ego rabota.* Moscow: Mysl', 1967.

Zenchenko, N. S., ed. *Planirovanie kompleksnogo razvitiia khoziaistva oblasti, kraia ASSR.* Moscow: Ekonomika, 1974.

Zhebit, G. A. *Kompleksnoe-planirovanie v upravlenii razvitiem kollektivov i regionov (filosofsko-sotsiologicheskii aspekt).* Minsk: Nauka i tekhnika, 1981.

―――. *Put' i problemy razrabotki sotsial'no-ekonomicheskikh pasportov kollektivov i regionov.* Minsk: Belorusskii nauchno-issledovatel'skii institut nauchno-tekhnicheskoi informatsii i tekhniko-ekonomicheskikh issledovanii Gosplana BSSR, 1982.

Zinov'ev, M. N., ed. *Vospitatel'naia rabota partiinykh organizatsii promyshlennykh kollektivov.* Leningrad: Izdatel'stvo Leningradskogo universiteta, 1983.

Zvonkova, P., and E. Ivanova. "Opyt regional'noi koordinatsii nauchnykh issledovanii." *Obshchestvennye nauki,* 1984, no. 4:162–168.

B. Non-Soviet

Andrusz, Gregory D. *Housing and Urban Development in the USSR.* Albany: SUNY Press, 1985.

Bahry, Donna. "Political Inequality and Public Policy among the Soviet Republics." In Daniel Nelson ed., *Communism and the Politics of Inequalities,* 109–127. Lexington, Mass.: D. C. Heath & Co., 1988.

Bater, James H. "The Legacy of Autocracy: Environmental Quality in St. Petersburg." In R. A. French and F. E. Ian Hamilton, eds., *The Socialist City: Spatial Structure and Urban Policy,* 23–48. New York: John Wiley & Sons, 1979.

―――. *St. Petersburg: Industrialization and Change.* Montreal: McGill-Queens University Press, 1976.

―――. *The Soviet City.* London: Edward Arnold, 1980.

―――. *Urban Industrialization in the Provincial Towns of Late Imperial Russia.* The Carl Beck Papers in Russian and East European Studies, no. 503. Pittsburgh: University of Pittsburgh Center for Russian and East European Studies, 1986.

Bidlack, Richard. "Worker Mobilization during the Siege of Leningrad." Paper presented at the annual meeting of the American Association for the Advancement of Slavic Studies, New Orleans, November 22, 1986.

Bliznakov, M. "Urban Planning in the USSR: Integrative Theories." In M. F. Hamm, ed., *The City in Russian History,* 243–256. Lexington: University of Kentucky Press, 1976.

Bradbury, Katherine L., Anthony Downs, and Kenneth A. Small. *Urban Decline and the Future of American Cities.* Washington, D.C.: Brookings Institution, 1982.

Brodsky, Joseph. *Less than One: Selected Essays.* New York: Farrar, Straus & Giroux, 1986.

Brumberg, Abraham, ed. *Russia under Khrushchev.* New York: Frederick A. Praeger, 1962.

Brumfield, William Craft. *Gold in Azure: One Thousand Years of Russian Architecture.* Boston: David R. Godine, 1983.

Bubis, Edward, and Blair A. Ruble. "The Impact of World War II on Leningrad." In Susan J. Linz, ed., *The Impact of World War II on the Soviet Union*, 189–206. Totowa, N.J.: Rowman & Allanheld, 1985.

Burke, Gerald L. *The Making of Dutch Towns*. London: Cleaver-Hume Press, 1966.

Carr, E. H. *A History of Soviet Russia*. Vol. 4, *The Interregnum, 1923–24*. Harmondsworth, Middlesex, Eng.: Penguin Books, 1969.

Cattell, David T. *Leningrad: A Case Study of Soviet Urban Government*. New York: Frederick A. Praeger, 1968.

———. "Local Government and the Provision of Consumer Goods and Services." In Everett M. Jacobs, ed., *Soviet Local Politics and Government*, 172–185. London and Boston: George Allen & Unwin, 1983.

Chotiner, Barbara Ann. *Khrushchev's Party Reform: Coalition Building and Institutional Innovation*. Westport, Conn.: Greenwood Press, 1984.

Conquest, Robert. *Power and Policy in the U.S.S.R.* New York: St. Martin's Press, 1967.

Conyngham, William J. *The Modernization of Soviet Industrial Management*. New York: Cambridge University Press, 1982.

Cracraft, James. *The Petrine Revolution in Russian Architecture*. Chicago: University of Chicago Press, 1988.

Dennis, Michael. *Court & Garden: From the French Hôtel to the City of Modern Architecture*. Cambridge: MIT Press, 1986.

Dewitt, N. "Reorganization of Science and Research in the USSR." *Science* 133, no. 3469 (June 23, 1961): 1981–1990.

DiMaio, A. J., Jr. *Soviet Urban Housing: Problems and Policies*. New York: Praeger Publishers, 1974.

Dobson, Richard B. "Soviet Education: Problems and Policies in the Urban Context." In Henry W. Morton and Robert C. Stuart, eds., *The Contemporary Soviet City*, 156–179. Armonk, N.Y.: M. E. Sharpe, 1984.

Dunmore, Timothy. *Soviet Politics, 1945–1953*. New York: St. Martin's Press, 1984.

Eisenstadt, S. N., and A. Shachar. *Society, Culture, and Urbanization*. Beverly Hills, Calif.: Sage Publications, 1987.

Eldredge, H. Wentworth, ed. *World Capitals: Toward Guided Urbanization*. Garden City, N.Y.: Anchor Press/Doubleday, 1975.

Filippov, Boris. *Leningradskii Peterburg v poezii i proze*. Paris: La Presse Lib., 1972.

Fitzpatrick, Sheila, ed. *Cultural Revolution in Russia, 1928–1931*. Bloomington: Indiana University Press, 1978.

French, R. A., and F. E. Ian Hamilton, eds. *The Socialist City: Spatial Structure and Urban Policy*. New York: John Wiley & Sons, 1979.

Friedgut, Theodore H. *Political Participation in the U.S.S.R.* Princeton: Princeton University Press, 1979.

Frolic, B. Michael. "Moscow: The Socialist Alternative." In H. Wentworth Eldredge, ed., *World Capitals: Toward Guided Urbanization*, 295–339. Garden City, N.Y.: Anchor Press/Doubleday, 1975.

Goodman, Ann, and Geoffrey Schleifer. "The Soviet Labor Market in the 1980s." In United States Congress, Joint Economic Committee, *Soviet Economy in* the 1980s: Problems and Prospects, pt. 2: 323–348. Washington: Government Printing Office, 1982.

Goure, Leon. *The Siege of Leningrad: August, 1941–January, 1944.* New York: McGraw-Hill Book Co., 1964.

Grava, Siguard. "Urban Transportation in the Soviet Union." In Henry W. Morton and Robert C. Stuart, eds., *The Contemporary Soviet City*, 180–201. Armonk, N.Y.: M. E. Sharpe, 1984.

Grossman, Gregory, ed., *The Second Economy in the USSR*. Berkeley: University of California Press. Forthcoming.

Gustafson, Thane. *Selling the Russians the Rope? Soviet Technology Policy and US Export Controls.* Santa Monica: RAND Corp., 1981.

Hahn, Jeffrey. *Soviet Grassroots: Citizen Participation in Local Soviet Government.* Princeton: Princeton University Press, 1988.

Hahn, Werner G. *Postwar Soviet Politics.* Ithaca: Cornell University Press, 1982.

Hamilton, George Heard. *The Art and Architecture of Russia.* Baltimore: Penguin Books, 1975.

Hamm, Michael F., ed. *The City in Russian History.* Lexington: University of Kentucky Press, 1976.

Harris, Chauncy. *Cities of the Soviet Union: Studies in Their Functions, Size, Density and Growth.* Chicago: Rand McNally, 1970.

Harvey, David. *Consciousness and the Urban Experience: Studies in the History and Theory of Capitalist Urbanization.* Baltimore: Johns Hopkins University Press, 1985.

———. *The Urbanization of Capital: Studies in the History and the Theory of Capitalist Urbanization.* Baltimore: Johns Hopkins University Press, 1985.

Hewett, Ed A. *Reforming the Soviet Economy: Equality versus Efficiency.* Washington, D.C.: Brookings Institution, 1988.

Hill, Ronald J. "The Development of Soviet Local Government since Stalin's Death." In Everett M. Jacobs, ed., *Soviet Local Politics and Government*, 18–33. London and Boston: George Allen & Unwin, 1983.

———. *Soviet Politics: Political Science and Reform.* White Plains, N.Y.: M. E. Sharpe, 1980.

Hoffman, Erik P., and Robbin F. Laird, eds. *The Soviet Polity in the Modern Era.* New York: Aldine Publishing Co., 1984.

Hollander, Paul. "The Dilemmas of Soviet Sociology." *Problems of Communism* 14, no. 6 (November–December, 1965):34–46.

Hough, Jerry. *The Soviet Prefects: The Local Party Organs in Industrial Decision-Making.* Cambridge: Harvard University Press, 1969.

———. "USSR: The Urban Units." In Donald C. Rowat, ed., *International Handbook on Local Government Reorganization: Contemporary Developments*, 343–353. Westport, Conn.: Greenwood Press, 1980.

Jacobs, Everett M., ed. *Soviet Local Politics and Government.* London and Boston: George Allen & Unwin, 1983.

Jacobs, Jane. *Cities and the Wealth of Nations.* New York: Random House, 1984.

———. *The Death and Life of Great American Cities.* New York: Random House, 1961.

———. *The Question of Separatism.* New York: Random House, 1980.

Johnson, Robert Eugene. "Peasant Migration and the Russian Working Class:

Moscow at the End of the Nineteenth Century." *Slavic Review* 35, no. 4 (1976):652–664.

Jones, Robert E., "Getting the Goods to St. Petersburg: Water Transportation from the Interior, 1703–1811." *Slavic Review* 43, no. 3 (1984):413–433.

Juviler, Peter H. "The Urban Family and the Soviet State: Emerging Contours of a Demographic Policy." In H. W. Morton and R. C. Stuart, eds., *The Contemporary Soviet City*, 84–111. Armonk, N.Y.: M. E. Sharpe, 1984.

Kaplan, Cynthia S. "The Communist Party of the Soviet Union and Local Policy Implementation." *Journal of Politics* 45, no. 1 (1983):2–27.

Katz, Z. "Sociology in the Soviet Union." *Problems of Communism* 20, no. 3 (May–June 1971):22–40.

Kaufman, Herbert. *The Forest Rangers: A Study in Administrative Behavior.* Baltimore: Johns Hopkins University Press, 1960.

Koenker, Diane. *Moscow Workers and the 1917 Revolution.* Princeton: Princeton University Press, 1981.

Kopp, A. *Changer la vie, changer la ville.* Paris: U.G.E., 1975.

———. *Town and Revolution.* New York: Braziller, 1970.

Kornai, Janos. *Economics of Shortage.* Amsterdam and New York: North-Holland, 1980.

———. " 'Hard' and 'Soft' Budget Constraints." *Acta Oeconomica* 25, no. 3–4 (1980):231–246.

Leonhard, W. *The Kremlin since Stalin.* New York: Oxford University Press, 1962.

Lewis, Carol W. "The Economic Functions of Local Soviets." In Everett M. Jacobs, ed., *Soviet Local Politics and Government*, 38–66. London and Boston: George Allen & Unwin, 1983.

Lindblom, Charles E. *Politics and Markets: The World's Political-Economic Systems.* New York: Basic Books, 1977.

Linz, Susan J., ed. *The Impact of World War II on the Soviet Union.* Totowa, NJ: Rowman & Allanheld, 1985.

McAuley, Alastair. *Economic Welfare in the Soviet Union.* Madison: University of Wisconsin Press, 1979.

Maggs, Peter B., Gordon B. Smith, and George Ginsburgs, eds. *Law and Economic Development in the Soviet Union.* Boulder: Westview Press, 1982.

Mandelker, Daniel R. "City Planning in the Soviet Union: Problems of Coordination and Control." *Urban Law and Policy* 2, no. 2 (1979):97–109.

Matthews, Mervyn. *Education in the Soviet Union: Policies and Institutions since Stalin.* Boston: George Allen & Unwin, 1982.

———. *Poverty in the Soviet Union.* New York: Cambridge University Press, 1986.

Mayo, Elton. *The Human Problems of an Industrial Civilization.* Cambridge: Harvard University Graduate School of Business Administration, Division of Research, 1933. Reprint. Salem, N.Y.: Ayer Co., 1977.

———. *The Social Problems of an Industrial Civilization.* Cambridge: Harvard University Graduate School of Business Administration, Division of Research, 1945. Reprint. Salem, N.Y.: Ayer Co., 1977.

Morton, Henry W., and Robert C. Stuart, eds. *The Contemporary Soviet City.* Armonk, N.Y.: M. E. Sharpe, 1984.

Nelson, Daniel, ed. *Communism and the Politics of Inequalities*. Lexington, Mass.: D. C. Heath & Co., 1988.

Nobuaki, Shiokawa. "Labor Turnover in the USSR, 1929–33: A Sectorial Analysis." *Annals of the Institute of Social Science, University of Tokyo*, no. 23 (1982):65–94.

———. "The Collectivization of Agriculture and *Otkhodnichestvo* in the USSR, 1930." *Annals of the Institute of Social Science, University of Tokyo*, no. 24 (1982–1983): 129–158.

Norr, Henry. "Shchekino: Another Look." *Soviet Studies* 38, no. 2 (1986):141–169.

Pallot, Judith, and Denis J. B. Shaw. *Planning in the Soviet Union*. Athens: University of Georgia Press, 1981.

Parkins, M. F. *City Planning in Soviet Russia*. Chicago: University of Chicago Press, 1953.

Peterson, Paul E. *City Limits*. Chicago: University of Chicago Press, 1981.

Raimondo, Henry J., and Robert C. Stuart. "Financing Soviet Cities." In Henry W. Morton and Robert C. Stuart, eds., *The Contemporary Soviet City*, 45–64. Armonk, N.Y.: M. E. Sharpe, 1984.

Reiner, T. A., and R. H. Wilson. "Planning and Decision-Making in the Soviet City: Rent, Land and Urban Form." In R. A. French and F. E. Ian Hamilton, eds., *The Socialist City: Spatial Structure and Urban Policy*, 49–71. New York: John Wiley & Sons, 1979.

Roethlisberger, Fritz J., and William J. Dickson. *Management and the Worker: An Account of a Research Program Conducted by the Western Electric Company, Hawthorne Works, Chicago*. Cambridge: Harvard University Press, 1939.

Rowat, Donald C., ed. *International Handbook on Local Government Reorganization: Contemporary Developments*. Westport, Conn.: Greenwood Press, 1980.

Ruble, Blair A. "Cultural Ethnicity among the Tatars of Leningrad: An Ethnographic Report." *Canadian Review of Studies in Nationalism* 13, no. 2 (1986):275–282.

———. "The Expansion of Soviet Science." *Knowledge: Creation, Diffusion, Utilization* 2, no. 4 (June 1981):529–553.

———. "The Leningrad Affair and the Provincialization of Leningrad." *Russian Review* 42, no. 3 (1983):301–320.

———. "Policy Innovation and the Soviet Political Process: The Case of Socioeconomic Planning in Leningrad." *Canadian Slavonic Papers* 24, no. 2 (June 1982):161–174.

———. *Soviet Trade Unions: Their Development during the 1970s*. New York: Cambridge University Press, 1981.

———(with the assistance of Mark H. Teeter, Rosemary Stuart, Eleanor B. Sutter, and Mary Giles). *Soviet Research Institutes Project*. Vol. 1, *The Policy Sciences*. Washington, D.C.: International Communication Agency, 1980. Vol. 2, *The Social Sciences*, and vol. 3, *The Humanities*. Washington, D.C.: Kennan Institute for Advanced Russian Studies, Woodrow Wilson International Center for Scholars, 1981.

Rutland, Peter. "The Shchekino Method and the Struggle to Raise Labour Productivity in the Soviet Union." *Soviet Studies* 36, no. 3 (1984):345–365.

Salisbury, Harrison E. *The 900 Days: The Siege of Leningrad*. New York: Harper & Row, 1969.

Sayre, Wallace S., and Herbert Kaufman. *Governing New York City: Politics in the Metropolis*. New York: W. W. Norton & Co., 1965.

Sbragia, Alberta. "Not All Roads Lead to Rome: Local Housing Policy in the Unitary Italian State." *British Journal of Political Science* 9, pt. 3 (1979):315–339.

Schlesinger, Rudolph. "The Education Reform." *Soviet Studies* 10, no. 4 (April 1959):432–444.

Schroeder, Gertrude E. "Retail Trade and Personal Services in Soviet Cities." In Henry W. Morton and Robert C. Stuart, eds., *The Contemporary Soviet City*, 202–220. Armonk, N.Y.: M. E. Sharpe, 1984.

Schwartz, Joel J., and William R. Keech. "Group Influence and the Policy Process in the Soviet Union." *American Political Science Review* 62, no. 3 (September 1968):840–851.

Shalin, Dimitry. "The Development of Soviet Sociology, 1956–1976." *American Review of Sociology* 4, no. 4 (1978):171–191.

Sharlet, Robert. *The New Soviet Constitution of 1977: Analysis and Text*. Brunswick, Ohio: King's Court Communication, 1978.

Shaw, Denis J. B. "Planning Leningrad." *Geographical Review* 68, no. 2 (April 1978):183–200.

———. "Problems of Land Use and Development in the USSR." University of Birmingham, Working Paper Series no. 5 (Birmingham, 1980).

———. "The Soviet Urban General Plan and Recent Advances in Soviet Urban Planning." *Urban Studies* 20 (1983):393–403.

Shelley, Louise I. *Lawyers in Soviet Work Life*. New Brunswick, N.J.: Rutgers University Press, 1984.

Simirenko, Alex. "Post Stalinist Social Science." *Transaction Journal* 6, no. 7 (June 1969):37–42.

Skrjabina, Elena. *Siege and Survival: The Odyssey of a Leningrader*. Translated by Norman Luxenburg. Carbondale: Southern Illinois University Press, 1971.

Slider, Darrell. "More Power to the Soviets? Reform and Local Government in the Soviet Union." *British Journal of Political Science* 16, no. 4 (October 1986):495–515.

Smith, S. A. *Red Petrograd: Revolution in the Factories, 1917–18*. Cambridge: Cambridge University Press, 1983.

Starr, S. Frederick. *Melnikov: Solo Architect in a Mass Society*. Princeton: Princeton University Press, 1978.

———. "The Revival and Schism of Urban Planning in Twentieth Century Russia." In Michael F. Hamm, ed., *The City in Russian History*, 222–242. Lexington: University of Kentucky Press, 1976.

———. "Visionary Town Planning during the Cultural Revolution." In Sheila Fitzpatrick, ed., *Cultural Revolution in Russia, 1928–1931*, 207–240. Bloomington: Indiana University Press, 1978.

Stewart, Philip D., Roger Blough, and James N. Warhola. "Soviet Regions and Economic Priorities: A Study in Politburo Perceptions." *Soviet Union/Union Soviétique* 11, pt. 1 (1984):1–30.

Tarkowski, Jacek. "Local Influences in a Centralized System: Resources, Local Leadership and Horizontal Integration in Poland." In Sidney Tarrow, Peter

A. Katzenstein, and Luigi Graziano, eds., *Territorial Politics in Industrial Nations*, 213–244. New York: Praeger Publishers, 1978.

Tarrow, Sidney G. *Between Center and Periphery: Grassroots Politicians in Italy and France*. New Haven: Yale University Press, 1977.

Tarrow, Sidney G., Peter A. Katzenstein, and Luigi Graziano, eds. *Territorial Politics in Industrial Nations*. New York: Praeger Publishers, 1978.

Tatu, Michel. *Power in the Kremlin: From Khrushchev to Kosygin*. Translated by Helen Katel. New York: Viking Press, 1968.

Theen, Rolf H. W. "Party and Bureaucracy." In Erik P. Hoffman and Robbin F. Laird, eds., *The Soviet Polity in the Modern Era*, 131–165. New York: Aldine Publishing Co., 1984.

U.S. Congress. Joint Economic Committee. *Soviet Economy in the 1980s: Problems and Prospects*. Washington: Government Printing Office, 1982.

———. *USSR: Measures of Economic Growth and Development, 1950–1980*. Washington: Government Printing Office, 1982.

Weinberg, E. A. *The Development of Sociology in the Soviet Union*. London: Routledge & Kegan Paul, 1974.

Werth, Alexander. *Leningrad*. London: Hamish Hamilton, 1944.

Ziegler, Charles E. *Environmental Policy in the USSR*. Amherst: University of Massachusetts Press, 1987.

Index

Note: Italicized page numbers indicate illustrations.

Singer building, 68
Slaughterhouses, 39
Slavophilism, 92
Smith, Steven, 57
Smolenskii cemetery, 108
Smol'ninskii District, 75, 108, 131
Social change: and migration, 50, 53–54, 64; and physical planning, 64
Socialism, 1, 4, 136, 164, 174, 179, 181, 184, 187–189; and property relations, 7; and urban planning, 4, 7, 12, 45, 93, 95
Social services, 83, 85, 94, 204; and districts, 168–169, 207; and economic reforms, 158; and municipal government, 82; and socioeconomic planning, 159, 168
Social structure: and bourgeoisie, 38, 41, 93; and education, 144, 150; and industry, 160; and peasants, 7, 39, 41, 54–56; and systems theory, 175; and working class, 38–39, 41, 145. *See* also Population; Social change
Sociology, industrial, 96, 103, 122, 142, 153; and educational institutions, 156–157; interdisciplinary nature of, 157, 173; and labor discipline, 157, 159; and labor productivity, 160–161; and labor shortage, 157; and mathematical modeling, 173; and psychology, 160; rebirth of, 155–156; and scientific institutions, 155–157, 173–174, 185; and social services, 159; and socioeconomic planning, 157, 159–160, 163, 171–176; and systems theory, 173–175; and turnover, 159–160; and worker motivation, 156, 157; and workplace improvement, 159–161
Sokolov, S. I., 89–92
Solov'ev, Iurii, xx, 61, 95, 106, 116, 135–136, 178, 222, 261n8
Sotsialisticheskii trud (periodical), 147
Sovety narodnykh deputatov (periodical), 172
The Soviet Prefects (Hough), 180, 232n3
Soviets (councils), 3, 8, 193–194, 289; and bureaucracy, 15, 206, 209; and center-periphery relations, 206–208; and Communist Party, 12, 14–15, 72, 91, 205, 214–216; and constituent contact, 204–205; and constitution, 196–197; and construction, 70, 197; and consumer goods and services, 82,

197; and culture, 197; deputies of, 198–204, 232n4; and economic relations, 10–11; and educational institutions, 197; and elections, 197–198, 203–205, 207, 280n1, 282–283n32; and enterprises, 8, 10; and environmental protection programs, 197–198; and executive committees, 205–206, 209, 211, 215, 290; and Five-Year Plan, 203; and housing, 82; and labor, 197; and land use, 197; and municipal budget, 209, 211; and municipal government, 11, 15, 70, 72–73, 91, 105–106, 133, 196–206, 214–218, 236n4; and national government, 211; and 1986 general plan, 105–106; and personnel appointment (*nomenklatura*), 213–215; and political relations, 196–197; and regional government, 72–73, 102, 105, 169, 199, 203–204, 282n32; and scientific institutions, 197; and socioeconomic planning, 10–11, 161; and suburban areas, 100, 102; and transportation, 197; and urban planning, 104
Spiridonov, Ivan, 61
Sports. *See* Recreational facilities
Squares, 32, 34, 35, 42, 43, 88–89
Stalinism, 7–8, 15, 40–42, 44–45, 72
Stalin, Joseph, 7–8, 11, 58–59, 110, 118, 141, 145, 155, 176, 193, 243n48
Stalinskii Prospekt, 50
Starye gody (periodical), 40
Stavropol', 170
Stepanenko, Anatolii, 174–175
Stewart, Philip, 194
Streetcars, 66, 69, 94
Streets, 26, 30, 71, 108, 166, 246n86, 255n71
Students, 82; demonstrations by, 92; in professional-technical schools (PTUs), 150–151
Suburban areas, 6, 77, 179; and economic relations, 243n42. and 1966 general plan 74, 78; and population, 70, 78, 83; and satellite cities, 74, 78, 79; and soviets (councils), 100, 102; and urban planning, 100
Subways, 66, 78, 83, 84, 94, 104, 228
Sukhumi, 173
Summer Gardens, 166
Superblocks, 7, 66, 67, 71, 82, 229
Surovtsev, Boris, 91

Designer: Sandy Drooker
Compositor: J. Jarrett Engineering, Inc.
Text: 10/12 Melior
Display: Melior Bold
Printer: Malloy Lithographers Inc.
Binder: Malloy Lithographers Inc.

45.00